Christ in the Gospels of the Liturgical Year

Christ in the Gospels of the Liturgical Year

Raymond E. Brown, S.S. (1928–1998)

Expanded Edition,
with introductory essays by
Ronald D. Witherup, S.S., and John R. Donahue, S.J.

Edited by Ronald D. Witherup, S.S.

LITURGICAL PRESS
Collegeville, Minnesota

www.litpress.org

Nihil Obstat: Rev. Robert C. Harren, J.C.L., *Censor deputatus.*

Imprimatur: ✠ Most Rev. John F. Kinney, J.C.D., D.D., Bishop of St. Cloud, Minnesota.
April 25, 2008.

Cover design by Ann Blattner. Illustration by Mary Jo Pauly.

All Scripture in Raymond E. Brown's texts appears in his own translation unless otherwise noted.

Raymond E. Brown's work previously appeared in the following volumes published by Liturgical Press:

A Coming Christ in Advent © 1988
An Adult Christ at Christmas © 1978
A Crucified Christ in Holy Week © 1986
A Risen Christ in Eastertime © 1991
A Once-and-Coming Spirit at Pentecost © 1994
Christ in the Gospels of the Ordinary Sundays © 1998

Library of Congress Cataloging-in-Publication

Brown, Raymond Edward.
    Christ in the Gospels of the liturgical year / Raymond E. Brown. — Expanded ed. / with introductory essays by Ronald D. Witherup and John R. Donahue ; edited by Ronald D. Witherup.
        p. cm.
    Includes bibliographical references and indexes.
    ISBN 978-0-8146-1860-8 (pbk.)
        1. Bible. N.T. Gospels—Criticism, interpretation, etc.   2. Church year.
I. Witherup, Ronald D., 1950–   II. Donahue, John R.   III. Title.

BS2555.52.B76 2008
226'.06—dc22

                                                                2008012385

Contents

Editor's Preface   ix

PART I
Ronald D. Witherup, S.S., and John R. Donahue, S.J.

Chapter 1:   **The Hermeneutical Approach of Raymond E.
             Brown,** by Ronald D. Witherup, S.S.   3

Chapter 2:   **The Marriage of Biblical Scholarship and
             Liturgical Preaching in Debt to Raymond E.
             Brown,** by John R. Donahue, S.J.   12

Chapter 3:   **Resources for Preaching the Liturgical Year,**
             by John R. Donahue, S.J.   20

PART II
Raymond E. Brown, S.S.

Introduction   25

Chapter 4:   **Understanding How Gospels Were Written
             and Their Use in the Sunday Liturgy**   30

A Coming Christ in Advent:
Essays on the Gospel Narratives Preparing for the Birth of Jesus
Matthew 1 and Luke 1

Chapter 5:   **The Origin and Purpose of the Infancy Narratives**   43

Chapter 6:   **The Genealogy of Jesus Christ** (Matthew 1:1-17)   50

Chapter 7:   The Annunciation to Joseph (Matthew 1:18-25)   59

Chapter 8:   The Annunciation to Zechariah and the
               Birth of the Baptist (Luke 1:5-25, 57-66, 80)   70

Chapter 9:   The Benedictus (Luke 1:67-79)   77

Chapter 10:   The Annunciation to Mary, the Visitation,
               and the Magnificat (Luke 1:26-56)   86

An Adult Christ at Christmas:
Essays on the Three Biblical Christmas Stories
Matthew 2 and Luke 2

Chapter 11:   **On Putting an Adult Christ Back into Christmas**   99

Chapter 12:   **The First Christmas Story (Matthew 2:1-23): The
               Meaning of the Magi; the Significance of the Star**   107

Chapter 13:   **The Second Christmas Story (Luke 2:1-40),
               Part I (2:1-21): The Meaning of the Manger;
               the Significance of the Shepherds**   112

Chapter 14:   **The Second Christmas Story (Luke 2:1-40),
               Part II (2:22-40): The Presentation of Jesus
               in the Temple**   121

Chapter 15:   **The Third Christmas Story (Luke 2:41-52):
               The Finding of the Boy Jesus in the Temple**   131

A Crucified Christ in Holy Week:
Essays on the Four Gospel Passion Narratives

Chapter 16:   **General Observations on the Passion Narratives**   145

Chapter 17:   **The Passion According to Mark**   155

Chapter 18:   **The Passion According to Matthew**   165

Chapter 19: **The Passion According to Luke**   175

Chapter 20: **The Passion According to John**   183

Chapter 21: **Diverse Portrayals of the Crucified Jesus**   192

A Risen Christ in Eastertime:
Essays on the Gospel Narratives of the Resurrection

Chapter 22: **The Resurrection in Mark** (16:1-8; 16:9-20)   197

Chapter 23: **The Resurrection in Matthew** (27:62–28:20)   208

Chapter 24: **The Resurrection in Luke** (24:1-53; Acts 1:1-12)   221

Chapter 25: **The Resurrection in John 20—**
             A Series of Diverse Reactions   242

Chapter 26: **The Resurrection in John 21—**
             Missionary and Pastoral Directives for the Church 255

A Once-and-Coming Spirit at Pentecost:
Essays on the Liturgical Readings between Easter and Pentecost,
Taken from the Acts of the Apostles and from the Gospel According to John

Chapter 27: **Introduction Explaining this Treatment of the**
             Liturgical Season   269

Chapter 28: **The Church Begins in Jerusalem** (Acts 2:14-41)   275

Chapter 29: **The Jerusalem Church of One Mind**
             (Acts 2:42–5:42)   284
             Brief Reflections on John 3 and John 6   297

Chapter 30: **Diversity in the Jerusalem Church;**
             Expansion to Judea and Samaria (Acts 6–9)   303
             Brief Reflections on John 10 and John 12   313

Contents

vii

Chapter 31: **Outreach to the Gentiles; the Church of Antioch**
(Acts 10–14)   316

Brief Reflections on John 13–16   325

Chapter 32: **The Jerusalem Conference Propels the Church
to the Ends of the Earth** (Acts 15–28)   330

Brief Reflections on John 17 and John 21   343

Christ in the Gospels of the Ordinary Sundays:
*Essays on the Gospel Readings of the Ordinary Sundays
in the Three-Year Liturgical Cycle*

Chapter 33: **The Gospel According to Matthew**
(Liturgical Year A)   347

Chapter 34: **The Gospel According to Mark**
(Liturgical Year B)   369

Chapter 35: **The Gospel According to Luke**
(Liturgical Year C)   387

Chapter 36: **The Gospel According to John**
(Latter Part of Lent; Post-Easter Season)   408

Appendix: **Chart on Overview of the Gospels and Acts
in the Sunday and Seasonal Mass Lectionary**   428

Scripture Citations Index   429

Select Topical Index   435

Editor's Preface

Only days after the untimely death of Father Raymond E. Brown, S.S., on August 8, 1998, his final book in the Liturgical Press series on preaching the Scriptures in the liturgical year appeared, *Christ in the Gospels of the Ordinary Sundays*. The arrival of this slim volume brought to completion a project that had begun in the mid-1970s. At that time Father Brown had published in *Worship* several popular essays on the Christmas stories narrated in Matthew and Luke. These essays were a convenient digest of his monumental *The Birth of the Messiah*. The result of this popularization, *An Adult Christ at Christmas*, resonated with many people, especially Catholics who were eager to learn more about the Gospels but who often lacked the inclination or background to plow through the larger, more technical study. Thus began the series of six volumes (published over a span of twenty years, 1978–1998) that are now collected here in one volume to mark the tenth anniversary of Father Brown's death.

This volume began in a conversation with Peter Dwyer of Liturgical Press when I suggested that it might be good to reissue all six volumes in a new and updated format to reach a new audience. As individual volumes, they have continued to attract interest. Yet since more than thirty years have passed since the appearance of the first volume, it seemed opportune to enhance the collection with a few useful additions. First, there are two new essays on preaching the liturgical year and on Father Brown's hermeneutical method, respectively, by John R. Donahue, S.J., and myself. In addition, Father Donahue has provided a bibliography of useful resources for preaching the word of God in the context of the lectionary. There are also useful indexes and a revised chart on the liturgical year. It should also be emphasized that I have used some literary license in merging the six forewords of the original volumes into one introduction that attempts to preserve the tone and content of the originals but in a unified edition. (I trust the author would be indulgent to a Sulpician confrere!)

Also, the order of the volumes has now been adjusted somewhat. The first chapter of the last-published volume on Ordinary Time has been placed at the head of the entire collection because it provides the clearest statement of Brown's intention and method. This essay orients the reader to the whole enterprise. The rest of the essays are arranged to follow the flow of the liturgical year, from Advent through Pentecost and into Ordinary Time. Otherwise, the text and notes have not been revised other than to make changes necessitated by this reorganization. No attempt has been made to update Brown's bibliography in the notes, except in obvious instances of revised works now available.

It is my hope that this commemorative edition will reach a whole new generation of readers and, especially, preachers of the word, for the original essays still contain a lot of wisdom that can inform our understanding of God's word for today. As is well known, Father Brown, a scholar's scholar, had the rare capacity to simplify complex biblical studies in a manner that did not "dumb down" the material but allowed it to be understood by a wide audience devoid of technical expertise in biblical studies. He did this in a fashion that was both inspiring and educational.

I wish to thank sincerely Peter Dwyer and his colleagues at Liturgical Press for supporting this project enthusiastically from the beginning. I am also grateful to John Donahue, S.J., Research Professor in Theology at Loyola College in Maryland, for his willingness to contribute to this volume from his own vast experience of biblical exegesis and preaching the word of God. Father Donahue was the first Raymond E. Brown Distinguished Professor of New Testament Studies at St. Mary's Seminary & University (2001–2004), and his essay on liturgical preaching and his list of annotated bibliographical resources have greatly enhanced the utility of this book.

R.D.W.
Solemnity of Mary, Mother of God, 2008

Christ in the Gospels of the Liturgical Year

Part I

Ronald D. Witherup, S.S.
John R. Donahue, S.J.

Chapter 1

The Hermeneutical Approach of Raymond E. Brown

Ronald D. Witherup, S.S.

All avid readers probably have certain books they return to time and again, so much so that the binding breaks or the pages get dog-eared. For me, the little books by Raymond E. Brown, S.S., on preaching the Gospels in the liturgical year have become such objects of endearment. Produced and used over the span of some thirty years, I have nonetheless gone back to them with relish each time a new lectionary year begins.

But what makes them so appealing? How do they retain their attractiveness year after year? This essay attempts to answer these questions by an analysis of Father Brown's hermeneutical method, that is, his approach to biblical interpretation.

One biographical note may be pertinent to this discussion. As a Sulpician[1] colleague of Father Brown, I became aware over time that he was almost always at work on a smaller publishing project (or multiple ones!) while he was engaged in the strenuous years of research and writing his monumental works. Several volumes in the original Liturgical Press preaching series provide examples, such as *An Adult Christ at Christmas* and *A Crucified Christ in Holy Week*. The reason for this pattern was simple. Brown was a priest and a man of faith who never lost sight of the pastoral dimension of his ministry, even after he

---

[1] For those not familiar with the term, the Sulpicians (i.e., the Society of St. Sulpice, hence the "S.S.") are a group of Catholic priests who specialize in initial and ongoing formation of priests. Founded in France in 1641, the Sulpicians have operated many seminaries around the world. Father Brown began his teaching career at the Sulpician St. Mary's Seminary & University in Baltimore, the oldest Catholic seminary in the U.S. (1791).

had attained the rare extraordinary heights in scholarship that characterized his career.[2] This pastoral sensitivity was particularly focused on teachers, catechists, priests, deacons, seminarians, and all who are charged to preach or teach the word of God.

As a homilist himself, Brown was characteristically *biblical*. One did not go to his services to hear cute illustrative stories or to receive lengthy discourses on erudite topics. One went to hear the word of God. And he seldom disappointed. More importantly, he believed that part of his Sulpician ministry, whether educating teachers, seminarians, priests, or permanent deacons, was to help instruct them to become *biblical* preachers. That was the primary purpose of the small books on preaching the Gospels and Acts. Becoming a biblical preacher is not as easy as it would seem. There are pitfalls. Brown knew that a homily was neither a classroom lecture nor a theological or moral discourse. A homily is meant to elucidate the biblical text(s) of the day and to help people make connections between God's word and their contemporary lives, so that they receive a message that is true to the biblical text yet applicable today.

I believe the success of this preaching series demonstrates that Brown's approach was effective. Furthermore, there are characteristics of his method that may help us see why his approach retains its value, even decades after he began publishing these pastoral guides. Three aspects of his hermeneutical method are worth highlighting: context, faith perspective, and the historical-critical method.

SENSITIVITY TO CONTEXT

Context is a word that has multiple meanings with regard to the task of preaching. The next essay in this volume by Jesuit Father John Donahue treats the "liturgical context" very well and need not be considered here. In his six volumes on preaching the Gospels of the liturgical year, Brown occasionally made mention of the liturgical context, but that was not his focus. Indeed, in favor of concentrating on

---

[2] I have addressed the pastoral dimension of Brown's writings elsewhere. See my article "The Incarnate Word Revealed: The Pastoral Writings of Raymond E. Brown," in *Life in Abundance: Studies of John's Gospel in Tribute to Raymond E. Brown*, ed. John R. Donahue, S.J. (Collegeville, MN: Liturgical Press, 2005), 238–52. A short biography of Brown and a full bibliography of his writings are also available in the same book, 254–89.

Christ in the Gospels of the Liturgical Year

only the four canonical Gospels and the Acts of the Apostles, he admittedly left out the other readings from the Sunday liturgies (i.e., the OT first reading, the Psalm response, and the second reading from the NT letters [except for Acts, which occurs in the Easter season]). But as he also pointed out, other resources addressed *all* the lectionary readings in the liturgical year, and this was not his intention. His focus was on the *biblical context* of the Gospel readings of the liturgical seasons.

One of the great strengths of Brown's approach to preaching from the Gospels is the insistence to be mindful of context. Each Gospel passage chosen for a Sunday or a feast is excerpted from the larger Gospel. In the liturgy it is consequently cut off from its context. The preacher who ignores this reality risks misinterpreting the passage precisely because it is not viewed within its native context. Thus when Brown wrote, for example, *An Adult Christ at Christmas* and *A Coming Christ in Advent*, which were devoted to the infancy narratives of Matthew and Luke—the only Gospels that give this kind of portrayal of the conception and birth of Jesus—he was attempting to highlight why the differences in these accounts reflect the respective theological concerns of each evangelist. Historical questions (such as, what really happened on Christmas night?) took a back seat to theological interests (i.e., why does each evangelist tell his story in a particular fashion?). Only context can help one see how the individual passages of the infancy story fit into the larger picture that each Gospel presents in order to comprehend the meaning of the birth of Jesus of Nazareth.

Brown made explicit his concern about context in the opening essay of the final book in the series, which appeared posthumously and which addressed the Sundays of Ordinary Time (that essay appears as chapter 4, the introductory chapter to part 2, in this book). He explicitly said that homilists or proclaimers of the Gospel should ask the following question: "[H]ow does this Sunday passage lead us into the Gospel [i.e., Matthew, Mark or Luke], and fit its purposes?"[3] The reason for

---

[3] *Christ in the Gospels of the Ordinary Sundays*, 15, below page 349. Although this book was the last to be published in the series, its first chapter is placed first in this collection (chap. 4) because it gives the most explicit statement of Brown's intentions when he was conceiving and writings these books. Anyone wishing to track the development of Brown's thought or presentation in these volumes could examine the order in which they were published: *An Adult Christ at Christmas* (1978),

The Hermeneutical Approach of Raymond E. Brown

this orientation is quite clear. Brown understood that many people in the pew, and perhaps not a few homilists, have a tendency to harmonize the Gospels into one continuous story and thus fail to appreciate the distinctive theological outlook of each individual Gospel. In his approach, Brown attempted to correct this tendency by noting the uniqueness of each Gospel in presenting its story of Jesus. Each Gospel passage proclaimed Sunday after Sunday really makes full sense only in this larger context.

Another illustration of Brown's concern for context is his presentation of both the infancy narratives (Matthew and Luke) and the passion narratives (all four Gospels). Although he is attentive to the specific details of each story as narrated, he also regularly makes observations that connect the story to the larger narrative of the respective Gospel. Thus, when speaking of the magi in Matthew, Brown recalls Matthew's interest in the universalism of the gospel and likelihood that the magi represent the future acceptance of Jesus as the Messiah by the Gentiles. This constitutes a major theme in Matthew. Or regarding the passion narrative, when discussing Luke's particular presentation of Jesus' passion, Brown highlights connections with the portrayal of Jesus as a healer throughout Luke. Even in the midst of his own suffering Jesus heals the high priest's slave's ear that is cut off. Again, the larger context can play a role in understanding how a particular passage is interpreted.

One other example is pertinent here, especially because it illustrates the one time that Brown went beyond his concentration on the Gospels to another part of the NT. In *A Once-and-Coming Spirit*[4] Brown departed from his usual emphasis on the Gospels and shifted to the Acts of the Apostles, which provides the second reading throughout the church's Easter season (from Easter to Pentecost). Yet even here, Brown's attention to context is paramount. Primarily, Brown makes observations about each passage of Acts used in the lectionary in terms of the larger context of the Book of Acts. However, he also rightly makes connections between the Gospel of Luke and the readings from Acts,

---

A Crucified Christ in Holy Week (1986), *A Coming Christ in Advent* (1988), *A Risen Christ at Eastertime* (1990), *A Once-and-Coming Spirit at Pentecost* (1994), and *Christ in the Gospels of the Ordinary Sundays* (1998). I would like to think Brown would have approved the reorganization for purposes of this book.

[4] Liturgical Press, 1994; see below, chapters 27–32.

Christ in the Gospels of the Liturgical Year

even though the Gospel of John is used as the Gospel for liturgies throughout the Easter season.[5] Brown's goal, of course, is to make sure that the homilist understands the connection between Luke and Acts. This is the only two-volume work in the NT, written by the same author and intended to be read and understood together. Thus, many themes in Luke recur in Acts, and there are parallels established between the story of Jesus, as Luke tells it, and the story of the church.

In short, Brown's approach, with its sensitivity to context, aids the homilist especially to be sensitive to the unique perspective of each Gospel and to resist the temptation to blend them all together. By paying attention to context, certain themes or emphases can be a guide to the preacher who wants to be faithful to proclaiming God's word.

FAITH PERSPECTIVE AND SERVICE TO THE CHURCH
A second aspect of Brown's method was the faith perspective he brought to his task. He wrote as a man of faith and as a priest in service to the church. This is apparent in several ways, two of which I highlight here.

First, in his interpretations of the readings chosen for the lectionary cycle Brown was mindful of the *religious* message of each text. He did this in a number of ways. One way was his attentiveness to the OT background of the Gospels and Acts. He sometimes commented privately that he felt privileged to have been trained in OT (with a doctorate in Semitic languages from Johns Hopkins University) and to have had to teach it, because nothing could provide a better background for a NT scholar. Thus his familiarity with the entire biblical canon, and the unified biblical message of salvation, enhanced his interpretational acumen. He regularly points out connections between the Gospels and background OT passages that help understand the evangelist's religious message.

Another way he promoted a faith dimension to his interpretations might be said to have a positive and negative aspect. Positively, Brown made connections with everyday life that resonated with people. This did not come in the form of stories so much as observations about Christian life. For instance, he could reference where certain characters

---

[5] Brown includes in that set of essays some explanatory comments about the sections of John's Gospel used in the Easter season so that there is attention to the church's use of this Gospel along with Acts.

The Hermeneutical Approach of Raymond E. Brown

in the biblical stories could function as "models" of faith (e.g., Mary as a model Christian believer) or the starkness of death that everyone must one day face, seen in John's story of the "resurrection" of Lazarus from the tomb.[6] Yet more importantly, what Brown did *not* do is significant. He avoided the frequent homiletic temptation to moralize every passage of the Gospel. His interpretations often centered on the theological, christological, or ecclesiological dimensions of the text in a way that did not trivialize the message in a "do this" or "don't do that" fashion. All too often homilists turn the biblical message into a moralizing one. Brown emphasized that sometimes the Scriptures are not about *us*, but about the nature of God or the nature of Christ. They provide a window into the divine. They help us keep our eyes focused on the truth, not ourselves. Some homilists, no doubt, find this challenging, but such an approach provides a more authentic religious orientation to the biblical text.

A second religious or faith perspective is found in Brown's practice of placing his interpretational method in the context of official Catholic Church teachings about the Bible and its interpretation. He accepted and understood that the church has the authority to teach authentically about how to approach the Scriptures and how to interpret them. He understood himself to function as an exegete within the context of the church and at her service. He was also well aware of the controversies over biblical interpretation that are a part of our history as a church. He utilized the best instruction from the church concerning the Scriptures so that people would understand that his approach was indeed Catholic. In particular with regard to the Gospels, Brown drew attention to the Pontifical Biblical Commission document on historical questions related to the Gospels. Titled "The Historical Truth of the Gospels" (1964), this document pointed out that the Gospels as we have them in our NT are not eyewitness accounts per se but are based upon oral and written traditions that went through three stages.[7] By

---

[6] See, respectively, *An Adult Christ at Christmas*, 25, below p. 120, and *Christ in the Gospels of the Ordinary Sundays*, 105, below p. 426.

[7] See below, chapter 4, footnotes 1 and 2, for bibliographical information on this document. Brown's book, *Biblical Reflections on Crises Facing the Church* (New York: Paulist Press, 1975), 109–18, contains an appendix with excerpts from official Catholic teachings on biblical interpretation that guided his work, including "The Historical Truth of the Gospels."

Christ in the Gospels of the Liturgical Year

noting this teaching, which itself was adopted by the Second Vatican Council's "Constitution on Divine Revelation"[8] and thereby became a hallmark of the Catholic tradition of Gospel interpretation, Brown was emphasizing the priority of theological concerns apparent in the Gospels as they have come down to us. Each evangelist assembled, edited, and presented the traditions about Jesus Christ that came to him and his community in a way that made each Gospel portrait unique. Brown took all pains to show that this Catholic perspective is not detrimental to the faith and in no way compromises the "truth" of the Gospel.

HISTORICAL-CRITICAL METHOD AND ITS APPLICATION

Everyone who has read Brown's works, whether his monumental ones or the short, pastorally oriented ones, knows that he was an expert in the historical-critical (or scientific) method of biblical interpretation.[9] He acknowledges this several times in his writings but also notes that in his books on preaching the liturgical year, his interest was not primarily in the historical aspects of the biblical readings, though these are not totally ignored, but in the religious meaning of the texts. Yet it is clear that at every step along the way, he remains the historical critic, carefully dissecting every word of the biblical passage and looking more deeply beneath it for the truth that is embedded there. We can actually be more explicit about Brown's method as regards historical criticism. At least with respect to his books on preaching the Gospels and Acts, he showed himself primarily to be a redaction critic.

Redaction criticism came into play in NT biblical scholarship in the 1950s, just at the time when Brown was pursuing his graduate studies. Without going into great detail, redaction criticism of the Gospels is a method whereby the interpreter notices even the most trivial difference in language or structure of the text, in comparison to parallels found in the other Gospels. For the NT this method was primarily applied to the Synoptic Gospels (Matthew, Mark, Luke), which are obviously

---

[8] For a detailed presentation of this constitution and its use of prior church teachings, see Ronald D. Witherup, *Scripture:* Dei Verbum (*Rediscovering Vatican II*; New York: Paulist Press, 2006).

[9] For more information on this method and the controversy surrounding it, see Witherup, *Scripture*, 100–110.

parallel, but it has also been applied to John and other NT works. The method focuses on changes that the final editor (redactor) of the Gospel may have made from his sources and asks why such changes have been made. Responses to this question could range from the possibility of differing oral or written sources available to the evangelist to an interest in other theological themes or emphases that shaped the final text.

Brown was by any estimation a master redaction critic. Many astute observations that appear in his books reproduced here are the result of a keen application of redaction criticism to the biblical text. More remarkably, Brown for the most part avoided a pitfall that can befall redaction critics. Carried to excess, redaction criticism can lead to an endless set of theories about hypothetical sources and traditions that might lie behind the text. To his credit, Brown concentrated on the biblical text as it exists in the canon (or in some cases, as it has been edited to fit into the lectionary). Although Brown could handily make reference to alternative readings in diverse manuscripts of the Gospels (textual criticism), he concentrated his interpretational interest primarily on the final form of the text as we have it in the Bible. I would suggest, in fact, that this is the only just approach that a homilist can take. Preaching the word of God is not about propounding scholarly theories of origin, hypothetical sources or situations, or imaginary editions of the biblical text. It is about preaching the word of God as it is proclaimed in a certain given form from the canon and assembled in the lectionary.

Although scholarly methods have long since evolved in many other directions, redaction criticism has made a lasting contribution to biblical studies. It has enabled us permanently to see the uniqueness of each Gospel and its way of telling the story of Jesus. That is why Brown's preaching series remains so helpful. In my experience, many homilists (let alone congregations) have yet to grasp the richness of the message of the Gospels sounded in four "keys" at once. Each tells the story of the same Jesus of Nazareth, the Christ, yet in such unique ways. Brown's presentation highlights this diversity and still provides a gold mine of preaching perspectives that can be plumbed over time.

I should add that the historical-critical method remains controversial, despite decades of useful experience with it. Some, even in the Catholic Church, have assailed it as a threat to the faith. But I would point out that Pope Benedict XVI, who as Cardinal Prefect of the

Congregation for the Doctrine of the Faith expressed some grave concerns about the excesses of certain applications of the historical-critical method, emphasized in his book on Jesus of Nazareth that this method is "an indispensable tool."[10] One cannot adequately explore Scripture without it. But neither is this method the final word in biblical interpretation.

If Brown was an expert in applying the historical-critical method to Scripture, he was also sensitive to other issues. For instance, he clearly was open to deeper senses to the Scriptures beyond the literal (e.g., the spiritual sense), and he incorporated the insights of early, precritical, patristic, and medieval interpreters where useful. But one would have to admit that Brown's true genius was in the application of the historical-critical method that he had honed through a lifetime of research and writing.

CONCLUSION

With these three topics—context, a faith perspective and service to the church, and the historical-critical method and its application—I make no claim to have analyzed Brown's hermeneutical method in its entirety. But I have tried to explain why reissuing these books in a new format on the tenth anniversary of Raymond Brown's death can still serve the church. For those interested in familiarizing themselves with the Gospels and Acts as they will be read in the context of a new liturgical year, Brown remains a good place to start, whether you are in the congregation or in the pulpit. Brown would also be the first to advise that while his writings can orient you toward a useful and even deeper reading of Scripture, nothing takes the place of encountering the word of God directly. So my advice would echo that given to Saint Augustine long ago: *Tolle, lege!* Take up the word of God and read it! But have Raymond Brown by your side to help you understand it.

---

[10] Joseph Ratzinger (Pope Benedict XVI), *Jesus of Nazareth* (New York: Doubleday, 2007), xvi. The pope also takes pains to emphasize the limitations of this method and to stress the need for supplementary methods, such as incorporation of patristic insights and openness to the spiritual sense of the Scriptures. The Pontifical Biblical Commission also emphasizes that the historical-critical method is "indispensable" for Bible study (*Interpretation of the Bible in the Church* [1993], §I.A). Any reasonable practitioner of this method would acknowledge that it is not the *sole* way to interpret the Bible. Yet those who would banish it altogether are overreacting to the excesses of the method that are relatively scarce today.

The Hermeneutical Approach of Raymond E. Brown

Chapter 2

The Marriage of Biblical Scholarship and Liturgical Preaching in Debt to Raymond E. Brown

John R. Donahue, S.J.

Though it is axiomatic that the Dogmatic Constitution on Divine Revelation (*Dei Verbum*) of Vatican II fostered the flowering of Catholic biblical scholarship that was blossoming since *Divino Afflante Spiritu* (1943), engagement with the Bible was not to be limited to the classroom, but was to accompany the celebration of every sacrament. Scripture was to be the soul of theology. The lectionary was revised to include three annual cycles covering the Synoptic Gospels, with John prominent during the paschal season; the Old Testament, rarely heard in churches prior to the council, was to be read at Sunday liturgies. The responsorial psalm unlocked the beauty of Israel's prayer and praise. Preaching and explaining God's word in Scripture was listed by the council as the prime ministry of priest and bishop.

Well before I became aware of the emerging scholarship of Raymond Brown, my family in Baltimore told me how inspired they were by the homilies Brown offered as a young Sulpician at St. Mary's Parish (Govans) in Baltimore. Throughout his years of teaching, lecturing, and monumental scholarship, Brown in practice and publication reflected on how proclamation of the word is shaped by the liturgical context. The various books combined in this volume are the fruit of Brown's sensitivity to the liturgical context. They offer fine descriptions of the major passages appropriate to the various seasons and, as ever, contain gems for fruitful preaching. Since adapting preaching to the liturgical context is a never-ending challenge, in debt to Brown's legacy, I will propose some reflections on the task along with some practical suggestions.

Christ in the Gospels of the Liturgical Year

12

The practice of Scripture readings at the celebration of the Lord's
Supper is attested as early as Justin Martyr who recounts: "And on the
day called Sunday, all who live in cities or in the country gather together to one place, and the memoirs of the apostles or the writings of
the prophets are read, as long as time permits; then, when the reader
has ceased, the president verbally instructs, and exhorts to the imitation of these good things" (1 *Apol* 67). This practice most likely was
influenced by the Jewish tradition of set readings for different festive
cycles. Throughout history there has been a plethora of lectionary
arrangements but with Lent and Easter the most stable.

In 1570 Pope Pius V promulgated the *Missale Romanum* that governed
the celebration of Mass for the next four centuries. There were two
readings at Mass and, with only three exceptions, the first reading was
from New Testament letters and the second from the Gospels, mainly
Matthew and Luke, with two readings from John (John 6:1-15; 8:46-59).
During Lent the Johannine passion narrative was proclaimed on Good
Friday and sections of the Gospel of John from Easter to the Ascension.
Outside of the festal season (Advent, Lent, Easter) the Gospel readings
were random, with the same readings prescribed year after year.[1] In
commenting on the *General Introduction to the Lectionary for Mass*
(2nd ed., 1992), Ralph Kiefer notes that prior to the reforms following
Vatican II, "there was no embarrassment at all" for the preacher who
ignored the readings. Preaching tended to fall into three categories:
devotional ferverinos, moral exhortations, or doctrinal instruction.[2]

Vatican II's Dogmatic Constitution on Divine Revelation (*Dei Verbum*)
states: "The church has always venerated the divine scriptures as it
has venerated the Body of the Lord, in that it never ceases, above all in
the sacred liturgy, to partake of the bread of life and to offer it to the
faithful from the one table of the word of God and the Body of Christ"
(21), a statement virtually repeated in the Constitution on the Sacred
Liturgy: "The treasures of the bible are to be opened up more lavishly
so that richer fare may be provided for the faithful at the table of

---

[1] Comments here are dependent on the fine study by Normand Bonneau, *The
Sunday Lectionary: Ritual Word, Paschal Shape* (Collegeville, MN: Liturgical Press,
1998), esp. 14–19.

[2] Ralph A. Keifer, *To Hear and Proclaim: Introduction to the Lectionary for Mass*
(Washington, D.C.: Pastoral Press, 1993), 64–65.

The Marriage of Biblical Scholarship and Liturgical Preaching

God's word. In this way the more significant part of the sacred scriptures will be read to the people over a fixed number of years" (51). These powerful statements became the mandate for a renewal of biblical preaching where care for God's word was to be equal to care for the Body of Christ.[3]

Summarizing the teachings of Vatican II, the *Catechism of the Catholic Church* states: "Bishops, with priests as co-workers, have as their first task 'to preach the Gospel of God to all men,' in keeping with the Lord's command" (888). The *Introduction to the Lectionary for the Mass* states the goal of preaching succinctly: "it must always lead the community of the faithful to celebrate the Eucharist wholeheartedly."[4]

The decrees following Vatican II provided a double revolution with the introduction of readings from the OT and of a three-year cycle of these readings and of the Gospels. Most often the Old Testament reading provides a thematic link to the Gospel, while the Pauline reading is simply sequential. John Baldovin, a historian and liturgical theologian notes "the lectionary passages . . . are a means of shaping the consciousness of Christian assemblies as they try to allow the gospel pattern of living to determine their own."[5] Following the council many Christian churches adopted similar lectionary cycles, so most Christians are invited to make their own this same gospel pattern.

Contemporary preaching often suffers not only from lack of attention to the Scripture and the liturgical context but also from using the homily for the wrong purpose, for example, to attempt an explanation of the three Scripture readings, to address contemporary moral and social issues unrelated to the particular readings, to give overly pious or moralistic applications, or to focus on the unrelated experiences of the preacher. All preaching is contextual and the primary context is

---

[3] The selection of readings in the now widely allowed use of the Tridentine Mass is contrary to the central role given Scripture in the documents of Vatican II and in post-conciliar statements, while the omission of readings from the Old Testament is contrary to the document issued by the Pontifical Biblical Commission in 2001, *The Jewish People and Their Sacred Scriptures in the Christian Bible* (with a laudatory preface by Cardinal Joseph Ratzinger).

[4] John F. Baldovin, "The Nature and Function of the Liturgical Homily," *The Way: Supplement* 67 (Spring, 1990): 94, citing *Introduction to the Lectionary for Mass*, 24–25.

[5] John F. Baldovin, "Biblical Preaching in the Liturgy," *Studia Liturgica* 22 (1992): 117.

Christ in the Gospels of the Liturgical Year

the sacramental life of the community. Vatican II mandated the use of Scripture and recommended short reflections on the Scripture readings for all the sacraments. The celebration of the paschal mystery on Sunday is the privileged setting for preaching but is itself varied, first according to the rhythm of the liturgical year, equally by the context of a particular parish and even different celebrations in the parish, all of which can be influenced by events outside the Sunday morning world.

There are really two distinct lectionary cycles. The first, a festal cycle, celebrates events of salvation history from Advent, through the seven weeks of Lent, the celebration of Easter, and the seven weeks of Paschaltide culminating at Pentecost. The festal cycle uses a principle of *lectio selecta* (readings chosen for the particular season or feast).[6] Interspersed between Advent and Lent are readings from Ordinary Time, which then resumes after the feast of Corpus Christi. Both sets of readings are spread over a three-year cycle, with the readings in Ordinary Time, a semi-continuous reading of the three Synoptic Gospels. The Gospel is preeminent in the celebration of the liturgy and determines the selection from the Old Testament, which most often is thematically related, or according to promise and fulfillment.[7] The responsorial psalm that follows often captures well the theme of a given Sunday, and the second reading provides most often a continuous reading of one of the New Testament letters.

PREACHING THE LECTIONARY

Simply stated, the role of the preacher is to preach the *gospel* (that is, the good news of the Christ event) on the basis of a *Gospel* (a particular *Gospel* on a given Sunday), in the context of the *Gospel* (that is, how the Gospel fits into the particular liturgical season). Raymond Brown expressed well the need to preach the Gospel passage from a particular Gospel: "I want to give an overall picture of each Gospel: how it shapes its narrative, its theological emphases, and what it is trying to say to its readers/hearers—a larger picture that supplies the context

---

[6] Bonneau, *The Sunday Lectionary*, 45.

[7] Biblical scholars have reservations about not recognizing the independent value of Old Testament texts and the omission of great Old Testament themes; see, e.g., G. Sloyan, "Some Suggestions for a Biblical Three-Year Lectionary," *Worship* 63, no. 6 (1989): 521–35.

The Marriage of Biblical Scholarship and Liturgical Preaching

for understanding the individual readings."[8] Such preaching demands a number of moments or approaches that need not be sequential.

First, the homilist must, like Ezekiel, "eat th[e] scroll," and let the Scripture become part of his daily bread (Ezek 3:1-3; see Rev 10:9-10).[9] Preparation of a biblical homily is not only part of a homilist's ministry but essential to priestly spirituality. Homily preparation should begin with a prayerful reflection on the Sunday readings and should be spread over a number of days. It often helps to jot down some thoughts during this time and also to write out a paraphrase of the reading.

The next "moments" involve hearing the Gospel in different voices and in different contexts that involve engagement with various resources (see bibliography in chapter 3). Studies of the Gospels over the last forty years have shown that each Gospel has a deliberate literary and theological structure and that each section (pericope) has meaning in the context of the theological themes permeating the whole Gospel.[10] A double movement is involved: first, a study of the theology of the specific Gospel, and second, interpreting a given selection in this context, in effect shedding light on the part from the whole, while the various individual sections contribute to theology of the whole Gospel. For example, Mark recounts a series of mighty works done by Jesus in Jewish territory and then repeats a similar series in Gentile territory, which highlights the missionary dimension of the Gospel (e.g., 6:30-56; 7:24–8:10). Luke very frequently juxtaposes narratives where a male is central to narratives where a woman is central, for example, annunciation to Zechariah and to Mary (1:8-23; 26-28); hymn of praise of Mary (1:46-55) and of Zechariah (1:67-79); twin parables: man with mustard seed and woman with leaven (13:18-21), lost sheep and lost coin (15:4-10), widow and judge (18:1-8), Pharisee and toll collector (18:9-14). Isolation of a given selection of a Gospel from its larger context can impoverish biblical preaching.

[8] See p. 29.

[9] See Eugene Peterson, *Eat This Book: A Conversation in the Art of Spiritual Reading* (Grand Rapids: Eerdmans, 2006). Reflecting Ezekiel and the Book of Revelation, Peterson offers a renewed appreciation of *lectio divina*. Translation is from the New American Bible.

[10] See Mark G. Boyer, "Ten Dangers on Preaching From Pericopes," *Modern Liturgy* 15, no. 8 (1988): 12–25.

Christ in the Gospels of the Liturgical Year

When preaching from the lectionary it is very helpful to review the readings for a number of Sundays to note the sequence of the readings over a longer period, even to the extent of planning a number of homilies in advance. Yet problems arise from the often poor selection of lectionary readings, or truncating of unified passages. The reading for the Easter Sunday Gospel is weakened by listing only John 20:1-9, omitting both 20:10 and, more important, the appearance to Mary Magdalene (20:11-18). Since Mary is among the first to receive the proclamation of the resurrection in the other Gospels, John elaborates this appearance into a major theological statement on the meaning of the resurrection. On Holy Thursday the Pauline selection is often limited to 1 Corinthians 11:23-26, "the institution narrative," so that the larger context of Paul's citing this is forgotten. Paul cites the example of Jesus here as a model of service to a community that had distorted the celebration of the Lord's Supper (11:17-22) by shaming the "have nots," for which Paul "does not praise them." Attention to this context provides a fine link to the Gospel for the feast, the foot-washing (John 13:1-15), where Jesus offers a model of humble service.[11] Women scholars have called attention to the omission from both the Sunday and daily lectionaries of passages that portray notable women of the Bible.

Equally important to the moment of hearing the word is "hearing the hearers of the Word." This presents definite challenges to an often beleaguered homilist since parishes differ considerably, as do particular liturgies—one size does not fit all. Vatican II summoned the church in proclaiming the Gospel to "the responsibility of reading the signs of the times and of interpreting them in the light of the Gospel, if it is to carry out its task. In language intelligible to every generation, it should be able to answer the ever recurring questions which people ask about the meaning of this present life and of the life to come, and how one is related to the other."[12]

Ask yourself how the text speaks to the faith life of the people today. Visualize yourself as the audience and ask how you will hear it, how it speaks to your faith. Never give a homily that does not first move you or to which you are not committed. Be aware that different

---

[11] Baldovin, "Biblical Preaching," 116.
[12] Pastoral Constitution on the Church in the Modern World (*Gaudium et Spes*), 4.

The Marriage of Biblical Scholarship and Liturgical Preaching

audiences relate to the same biblical text in different ways. For example, a well-off suburban parish might be challenged by the feeding of the 5,000 to be more aware of world hunger and of their own obligation to imitate Jesus in feeding the hungry. A community of migrant workers might relate to a Jesus who is present in a deserted place. They might need to hear of a God who is with them and cares about them in their own times of hunger and being away from their homes. Church leaders might remember the disciples who become aware of the needs of the crowds and assist Jesus.

Despite the variety of congregations and settings, preaching should show how the good news of Christ touches the deepest longings and sufferings of contemporary life and gives hope in troubled times. The excellent guide to preaching, *Fulfilled in Your Hearing*, published by the U.S. bishops in 1982, urges the homilist to make "connections between the real lives of people who believe in Jesus Christ but are not always sure what difference faith can make in their lives, and the God who calls us into ever deeper communication with himself and with one another."[13] What Karl Rahner wrote over four decades ago is true today:

> It is not a few isolated beliefs of faith from a host of other convictions which are in danger today, but faith itself: the ability to believe, the capacity for developing an unequivocal comprehensive and challenging belief and making it powerfully effective in our lives and throughout our lives.[14]

Also, as John Baldovin has noted, "much of contemporary liturgical celebration suffers from forgetting that the liturgy is God's service to us before it is our service to God."[15] Preaching is ultimately in the context of *eucharistia*, an act of thanksgiving to a loving God, and should lead people to a deep experience of this love.

At last comes the moment of composition and presentation of the homily. I would like to propose a few concrete reflections on this stage:

- From the moment of explaining the text and from hearing the hearers you might have a number of ideas of what you feel would

---

[13] *Fulfilled in Your Hearing: The Homily in the Sunday Assembly* (Washington, D.C.: Bishops' Committee on Priestly Life and Ministry, 1982), 8.

[14] *Belief Today* (New York: Sheed and Ward, 1967), 68.

[15] "The Nature and Function of the Liturgical Homily," 94.

Christ in the Gospels of the Liturgical Year

make a good sermon. Try to focus on one or two major points and organize the sermon around them. Think carefully about what you want to accomplish in the sermon. Don't try to preach on all three Sunday readings or even two of them. Make one of them your central focus and use the other two for support or illustration. The most important parts are the beginning and the end. Avoid "false endings."

• Think concretely about the homily. Try to think of stories, comparisons, or illustrations that capture people's attention. Often it is good to begin with a story or with a real-life situation that you feel illustrates the Gospel. When using personal examples, be careful of making them too private or not related to the experiences of the people to whom you are preaching. Stories in which the homilist is the central character can be banal.

• Remember that preaching is the communication of "the good news." People's lives need to be touched by God's love; their faith should be nurtured; their hope sustained. Don't moralize, that is, don't always turn the good news into good advice. In the Gospels themselves a gift from Jesus always precedes the demand. Even when touching on evil or injustice be very careful to avoid being overly critical or harsh in a sermon. In the Gospels Jesus attacked injustice and hypocrisy, but he never talked harshly to a sinner who came to him.

Finally, every homilist can rejoice in St. Paul's vision of the mission of those who are servants of God's word:

> But how can they call on him in whom they have not believed? And how can they believe in him of whom they have not heard? And how can they hear without someone to preach? And how can people preach unless they are sent? As it is written, "How beautiful are the feet of those who bring [the] good news!" (Rom 10:14-15, quoting Isa 52:7)

The Marriage of Biblical Scholarship and Liturgical Preaching

Chapter 3

Resources for Preaching the Liturgical Year

John R. Donahue, S.J.

The bibliography and web resources for preaching the liturgical year are virtually endless. Listed below are select items that people have found helpful. These are in addition to those listed in the notes to my chapter above. Least helpful are canned homilies, and even reflections on specific readings are best consulted *after* the homilist grapples personally with the text.

On Preparing Homilies:

Burghardt, Walter J. *Preaching: The Art and the Craft*. New York/Mahwah: Paulist, 1987. A wealth of insight and information for students who are learning to preach and for ministers who have been preaching for years. Contains excellent annotated bibliography. Burghardt has published with Paulist Press over 10 collections of eloquent homilies that contain insights that individual homilists can develop.

Maloney, Robert P. "Echoing the Lord's Voice: Seven keys to successful preaching." *America Magazine*, 181, no. 12, (1999): 16–20.

Skudlarek, William. *The Word in Worship: Preaching in a Liturgical Context*. Abingdon Preacher's Library. Nashville: Abingdon, 1981. Skudlarek is one of the premier guides to good preaching and was influential in the composition of *Fulfilled in Your Hearing*.

Waznak, Robert. *An Introduction to the Homily*. Collegeville, MN: Liturgical Press, 1998.

Study Bibles: Very helpful for general essays, introductions of biblical books, and notes on individual passages.

The Catholic Study Bible. 2nd ed. New York: Oxford University Press, 2006. (New American Bible)

The College Study Bible. Winona, MN: St. Mary's Press, 2006. A work containing helpful learning tools. (New American Bible)

Christ in the Gospels of the Liturgical Year

The New Interpreter's Study Bible. Nashville: Abingdon, 2003. Based on The New Revised Standard Version of the Bible.

The New Oxford Annotated Bible with the Apocrypha. Augmented Third Edition, College Edition. The New Revised Standard Version (Paperback). Oxford University Press, 2007.

One-Volume Commentaries on Scripture

Barton, John, and John Muddiman, eds. *Oxford Bible Commentary*. Oxford: Oxford University Press, 2007.

Bergant, Dianne, and Robert J. Karris, eds. *The Collegeville Bible Commentary*. Collegeville, MN: Liturgical Press, 1989. Published originally as a collection of individual volumes, now gathered into one volume. Very helpful and readable. Totally new commentaries of the New Testament by new authors have appeared as separate small volumes in the *New Collegeville Bible Commentary* series, and the Old Testament volumes are forthcoming.

Brown, Raymond E., Joseph A. Fitzmyer, and Roland E. Murphy, eds. *New Jerome Biblical Commentary*. Englewood Cliffs, NJ: Prentice Hall, 1990. Excellent resource for all aspects of biblical study.

Dunn, James D. G., ed. *Eerdmans Commentary on the Bible*. Grand Rapids: Eerdmans, 2003. Very useful basic commentary.

Farmer, William R., ed. *The International Bible Commentary: A Catholic and Ecumenical Commentary for the Twenty-first Century*. Collegeville, MN: Liturgical Press, 1998. Very helpful and readable with an international group of authors.

Mays, James L., ed. *The HarperCollins Bible Commentary*. Rev. ed. San Francisco: HarperSanFrancisco, 1988.

Newsom, Carol A., and Sharon H. Ringe, eds. *Women's Bible Commentary*. Louisville: Westminster John Knox, 1998.

Commentaries on the Lectionary

Bergant, Dianne, with Richard Fragomeni. *Preaching the New Lectionary*. Collegeville, MN: Liturgical Press, 1999–2001. Covers the three-year cycle.

Days of the Lord. Collegeville, MN: Liturgical Press, 1991–1994. A seven-volume series covering the whole year that contains great insights into the readings in their liturgical settings.

Fuller, Reginald H., and Daniel Westburg. *Preaching the Lectionary: The Word of God in the Church Today*. 3rd ed. Collegeville, MN: Liturgical Press, 2006. Reissue of a work that Walter Burghardt called perhaps the most useful resource for preaching biblical homilies.

Gregory, Andrew, ed. *New Proclamation Commentary on the Gospels*. Minneapolis: Fortress, 2006.

Irwin, Kevin W. *A Guide to the Eucharist and Hours*. Collegeville, MN: Liturgical Press, 1990. A three-volume set covering Advent and Christmas, Lent, and Easter.

Lott, David, ed. *New Proclamation Commentaries on Feasts, Holy Days, and Other Celebrations*. Minneapolis: Fortress, 2007. The proclamation series has been a fine resource since the early 1970s, frequently updated with new volumes and contributors.

Nocent, Adrian. *The Liturgical Year*. 4 vols. Collegeville, MN: Liturgical Press, 1977. Very helpful in showing how the scriptural readings fit into the liturgical cycle.

Sloyan, Gerard. *Preaching from the Lectionary: An Exegetical Commentary*. Minneapolis: Fortress/Northam: Roundhouse, 2003. An often-used and well-respected work accompanied by a CD ROM.

Homily Services: A vast but varied number of services are available both in printed form and on the web. Only a few, widely used and recommended, are listed. Many diocesan web sites contain good resources, and the daily readings are listed by the U.S. Bishops' Conference: www.usccb.org.

Celebration: A Comprehensive Worship Resource. Published monthly by the *National Catholic Reporter*; contact Celebration, 115 E. Armour Blvd., Kansas City, MO, 64111-1203, or www.celebrationpubs.org. Contains helpful reflections on both Sunday and weekday readings.

Homily Helps. St. Anthony Messenger Press; contact St. Anthony Messenger Press, 28 W. Liberty Street, Cincinnati, OH, 45202-6498.

Catholic Resources: http://Catholic-Resources.org. An excellent web site maintained by New Testament scholar Felix Just; contains excellent resources on the lectionary.

Dominican Preaching: http://www.domcentral.org/preach/. Very helpful suggestions and "first impressions" by Rev. Jude Siciliano, former professor of homiletics.

Liturgy Preparation: http://www.smnz.org.nz/liturgy/. A fine site from New Zealand that contains multiple links to many other helpful resources.

The Text This Week, www.textweek.com. This is an excellent site with multiple resources and commentaries on the Sunday readings ranging from Patristic and classical theologians to numerous contemporary sites.

Part II

Raymond E. Brown, S.S.

Introduction

In the six small volumes collected here Liturgical Press presents my reflections on the liturgical New Testament readings for Advent, Christmas, Holy Week, Easter, the season leading up to Pentecost, and the lengthy liturgical season designated (not too imaginatively) as "Ordinary Time." After an explanation of my general approach (chap. 4), each set of chapters reproduced here will address the diverse liturgical seasons in their logical order, beginning with Advent.

The chapters on Advent (chaps. 5–10) completed my reflections (begun in *An Adult Christ at Christmas*, the first volume published in the series) on the infancy narratives by discussing in a similar way chapter 1 of Matthew and chapter 1 of Luke—what happened by way of *preparation* for the birth of Jesus. Logically the Advent season is the time when the church treats this material in her liturgy, preparing the way for the coming of Christ at Christmas. This liturgical preparation relives in a microcosmic way the long historical preparation for the coming of Christ in the history of Israel (seen through the eyes of Christian faith). It is no accident that in the first chapter of the Gospel both Matthew (explicitly) and Luke (implicitly) turn to that history and begin their narratives with the story of Abraham and Sarah conceiving Isaac. For the evangelists that was already the beginning of the story of Jesus Christ. As narrated in the Law and the Prophets, the God who acted in Israel, often with surprising graciousness in the lives of the patriarchs, the judges, and the kings, is the same God who is acting again with surprising graciousness in the lives of Joseph and Mary as He reveals what He is going to accomplish. Thus the Advent liturgy in retelling the first chapter of Matthew and the first chapter of Luke is also retelling the story of Israel which lies beneath it. One might think of a double exposure where the older picture is seen through the more visible picture that emerges on top.

The Messiah did not come without the preparatory period of Israel's history or without the preparatory responses of fidelity by Joseph and

Mary. The liturgy offers a third time of preparation that affects our lives, for Christ will not come in his fullness to us unless we too are prepared. These essays attempt to use Matthew 1 and Luke 1 as they are read in the last days of Advent to inform that preparation, so that our answer to God's invitation may be as affirmative as those of our ancestors in Israel and in the New Testament period.

The next section (chaps. 11–15), focusing on the Christmas season, grew out of my full-scale commentary on the infancy narratives in Matthew and Luke, entitled *The Birth of the Messiah*, which was published by Doubleday in 1977 and then in an updated and expanded edition in 1993. Almost a decade of my life and work went into that commentary, and as it was nearing completion I was eager to share with readers some of the insights I had gained. For two reasons, a series of short essays seemed reasonable.

First, *The Birth of the Messiah* is a long work (750 pages); and even though it is written so that large parts of it can be useful to any educated reader, it has scholarly aspects which many would find formidable. A set of shorter essays could also serve as a text in Bible study groups where the leader would have worked through *The Birth of the Messiah*. Second, even many of those who have read the long commentary may not see immediately how to present its contents in a simpler way to others. I think particularly of preachers who wish to incorporate the contents of *The Birth of the Messiah* into their sermons. The essays in this section may help them as examples of how to pick out what is more important. There is material for fifty sermons in the long commentary; but the topics I have chosen in these essays touch on sections most appropriate for Christmas, and that in itself may be a help to interested clergy and teachers.

Next comes a section (chaps. 16–21) devoted to the passion narratives of the Gospels, which have been a research interest for many years, leading me to publish a full-scale commentary that would be a companion to my commentary on the infancy narratives. Entitled *The Death of the Messiah*, it appeared in 1994 (Doubleday) in two volumes and ran over 1,600 pages. I faced the same problem of length and time when I was working on the infancy narratives and *The Birth of the Messiah*. Thus I have used the same format to publish this set of essays as a simplified and digestible introduction to the comprehensive commentary. Inevitably the format means that some major questions of historicity, sources, and non-canonical passion material must be left to the comprehensive commentary; but I hope that these brief essays will enrich Holy Week for a wider number of preachers, hearers, and readers.

The following section (chaps. 22–26) turns our attention to the Easter season. Elsewhere I have written on the resurrection from the view-point of historical criticism.[1] There I commented on the earliest preaching references to the raising of Jesus (e.g., Acts 5:30) and to his appearances (1 Cor 15:5-8); I investigated whether a bodily resurrection and an empty tomb were presumed from the beginning, even if narratives of the empty tomb were late; and I endeavored to reconcile the sharp divergences in those narratives. With none of that am I concerned in these essays, for now my interest is to see how the treatment of the resurrection in an individual Gospel fits the theology and plan of that Gospel.

Modern biblical scholarship insists that each Gospel has its own integrity and distinct outlook; and overall the liturgical lectionary has been guided by this principle since it reads consistently through one Gospel on the Ordinary Sundays of the Year (Matthew in Year A, Mark in Year B, Luke in Year C), rather than indiscriminately mixing passages from different Gospels as in times past. In Eastertime itself, however, the lectionary departs from the consecutive Gospel approach.

On Holy Saturday and Easter Sunday various Gospels supply the pericopes; on the Second Sunday of Easter in all three years the passages are from John; and on the weekdays of the Easter octave pericopes from the different Gospels are gone through with the interest that every tomb or appearance account in the New Testament be read.

While one can understand the joyous desire to hear as much as possible about the resurrection of Jesus, the deeper understanding of the Gospel narratives, which is related to the individual evangelist's overall view of Jesus, suffers. By concentrating on that aspect in these essays, perhaps I can enhance the appreciation of the resurrection on the part of those who reflect on the lectionary, since in a given year an individual Gospel will have been read on Sundays, and the respective resurrection passage from that Gospel will evoke memories of those readings.

---

[1] *The Virginal Conception and Bodily Resurrection* (New York: Paulist, 1973). More concisely, see my article in *The New Jerome Biblical Commentary* (Englewood Cliffs: Prentice Hall, 1990), 81:118–34.

In this part of the book, then, I shall cover all the Gospel passages dealing with the resurrection, i.e., accounts both of the visits to the empty tomb and of the appearances of Jesus. In each chapter I shall explain any peculiarities about what I have included, e.g., the addition to Mark constituted by 16:9-20, or the complement to the Gospel of Luke offered by Acts 1:1-12. Only in John does the resurrection account cover two chapters, and I shall devote an essay to each.

Even though each Gospel has its own emphasis in narrating the raising of Jesus, when readers move from one Gospel to the other, a fascinating picture emerges. There is in the accounts a whole spectrum of reactions, ranging from hostility through puzzlement to spontaneous faith, so that the resurrection functions as a final test of response to Jesus. In commenting on the passion I became convinced that the Gospel narratives were meant to pose to the readers the question: "What stance would you have taken were you there when this happened?" As I wrote these essays, I became aware of a similar goal of the evangelists: "In the days surrounding the first Easter which of the reactions recounted would have been yours?" The fact that those who feature in the stories often doubted or misunderstood is a warning that the answer to the question requires meditation. These essays are intended to foster such meditation.

The next section (chaps. 27–32) is devoted to the post-Easter season leading up to Pentecost. During this season at the eucharistic liturgy the church reads from the Acts of the Apostles, recounting the external life of the early Christian community once the Spirit had come at Pentecost, and reads from John's Gospel words of Jesus portraying the internal life of the Christian disciple and promising a coming Paraclete to be sent by the Father. No better guidance can be found for our own quest to be Christians living externally in a church responsive to the vagaries of history and internally as branches attached to Jesus the vine.

The final section (chaps. 33–36) addresses the large expanse of Ordinary Time. Many liturgists look on Ordinary Time as the time of the church when we turn from reflecting on the mystery of Christ in itself to considering directly how that mystery affects the lives of those who believe in him. Here in a triennial cycle, the lectionary of the A Year takes its consecutive readings from Matthew, the B Year from Mark, and the C Year from Luke. Passages from John are read every year during the last part of Lent and the post-Easter season till Pentecost.

Christ in the Gospels of the Liturgical Year

(Actually the arrangement is more complicated, and so at the end of the book I shall supply a table illustrating in more detail the use of the Gospels and Acts in the Sunday and seasonal lectionary.) A chapter will be devoted to each of the four Gospels and its unique perspective on Jesus.

Clergy frequently ask about homily guides for each Sunday. That is not what I intend to supply here, for there are many other resources available that can meet this need. (See the resources recommended in part 1, chap. 3.) Rather, I want to give an overall picture of each Gospel: how it shapes its narrative—its theological emphases, and what it is trying to say to readers/hearers—a larger picture that supplies a context for understanding the individual readings.

I believe strongly that every time we start the Ordinary Sundays of a new year (and every Lent or post-Easter season in the case of John) preachers need to familiarize themselves with the type of material presented in this section *and to share such material with their Sunday audiences* so that all grasp how unique is the Gospel, the pages of which are now being opened in church. Obviously the same thing may be said for Bible study groups who are beginning to reflect on the Gospel of the year.

Each section of this book is comparable in scope and format. My goal has always remained the same: to make the rich insights of modern biblical exegesis conveniently available for reflection during the great feasts of the liturgical year.

Chapter 4

Understanding How Gospels Were Written and Their Use in the Sunday Liturgy

Many people probably think of the Gospels as biographies of Jesus. In any modern sense they are not. Some of the most basic biographical information about Jesus (when and where born, name of one parent) is absent from Mark and from John. Even more people would be unaware of how much one Gospel differs from another. The sharp differences not only raise further difficulties for the biographical approach (and perhaps create fears about the historical truth of the Gospels) but also lead into the question of the origin and goal of the Gospels.

CHURCH TEACHING ON THE THREE STAGES OF GOSPEL FORMATION

Fortunately the church has given us a very helpful guide for dealing with these issues—a guide that wins the approval of most centrist scholars. I refer to the Instruction on the Historical Truth of the Gospels issued by the Roman Pontifical Biblical Commission in 1964 (the substance of which was incorporated into Vatican II's Dogmatic Constitution on Divine Revelation in 1965).

When some Catholics are told that the Gospels are not necessarily literal accounts of the ministry of Jesus, they become suspicious of the "orthodoxy" of the person who makes such a claim. It may be important, therefore, to stress that this Instruction, which offers that evaluation, constitutes binding teaching of the Catholic Church on all its members. Let me use the Instruction as a springboard to explain the Gospels by elaborating on its implications.[1] No better guidance can be

---

[1] An English translation of the actual text appears in the Appendix to my small book *Reading the Gospels with the Church* (Cincinnati: St. Anthony Messenger Press, 1996). With the kind agreement of that press, I am adapting material from chapter 2 of that book for the present chapter.

offered in preaching about the Gospels at the beginning of each liturgical year, in Bible discussion groups, and in catechetical teaching.

The Instruction orients its treatment of the reliability of the Gospels by insisting that diligent attention should be paid to THE THREE STAGES OF TRADITION by which the life and teaching of Jesus have come down to us. Those three stages, which follow chronologically one upon the other, are the Ministry of Jesus, the Preaching of the Apostles, and the Writing by the Evangelists. We would not be far from common scholarly opinion if we assigned one-third of the first century A.D. to each, since Jesus died *ca.* 30–33, the main preaching apostles were dead by the mid-60s, and the evangelists probably wrote in the period 65–100.

STAGE ONE: THE PUBLIC MINISTRY OR ACTIVITY OF JESUS OF NAZARETH

We may date this to the first third of the first century A.D. The Instruction does not concern itself with Jesus' birth and infancy.[2] Rather, it focuses on the words and deeds of Jesus from the time of his calling the first disciples. Jesus did noteworthy things (which the first three Gospels label "deeds of power" and we refer to as miracles) as he orally proclaimed his message. At the same time, he chose companions who traveled with him and saw and heard what he said and did. Their memories of his words and deeds supplied the raw Jesus material or Jesus tradition that would be preached in Stage Two (below). These memories were already selective, since they concentrated on what pertained to Jesus' proclamation of God, not the many details of ordinary existence, some of which would have been included if a biography were intended.

On a practical level it is important for modern readers to keep reminding themselves that these were memories of what was said and done by a Jew who lived in Galilee, Jerusalem, and environs in the 20s.[3]

---

[2] Several years after the Instruction was issued, the Roman Pontifical Commission did meet to discuss the historicity of the infancy narratives, presumably with the hope of issuing a similar instruction pertinent to them—a project never completed. I have treated these narratives in chapters 5–15 below.

[3] Such a reference to Jesus will often raise the immediate objection "Was he not Son of God?" One must remember, however, that Christian dogma describes him equally as true God and *true man*.

Jesus' manner of speaking, the problems he faced, his vocabulary and outlook, were those of that specific time, place, and circumstance. Often he had new ways of looking at things, but his newness did not remove him from his time and place. Many failures to understand Jesus and misapplications of his thought stem from the fact that people who read the Gospels remove him from space and time and imagine that Jesus was dealing with issues he never encountered.

Both liberal and conservative Christians make that mistake. For instance, liberal pacifist Christians may ask whether Jesus would serve as a soldier in a modern war (in Vietnam or in the Gulf). The exact, even if somewhat brutal, answer to such a question is that a Galilean Jew would not have known of the existence of Vietnam or of mechanized war. A better-phrased question would be: In fidelity to what Jesus taught and to his example, what is a *Christian's* duty in relation to a modern war? Conservative Christians often want to settle questions of church structure and practice by appealing to Jesus. Once after a series of lectures on the origin of the church a well-intentioned member of the audience asked me: "Why didn't Jesus prevent all future confusion by saying, 'I came to found the Roman Catholic Church, the Bishop of Rome or the Pope will be the leader of the church, and everyone must obey him'?" The difficulty is that Jesus is recorded only twice in all the Gospels as having spoken of "church" (Matt 16:18; 18:17, in the second of which he is clearly talking about a local community). Thus there is little recorded proof that he spent much time thinking about the structure of a future church. Rather, he was concerned with proclaiming God's kingdom or rule to those whom he encountered in his lifetime. Moreover, a Galilean Jew would scarcely have thought of an institution in Rome where the emperor was, or of categories like "pope" and "bishop." A better phrasing of the issue is whether the community called "church" that emerged from the preaching of his followers, and the centralizing of that church in Rome where Peter died as a martyr, are valid developments from what he proclaimed, and in that sense may be said to be founded by him. Catholics answer yes, for they trace *a line of development* from what Jesus said and did to what the apostles said and did, and to later growth. In Christian faith the Jesus tradition truly has decisive ramifications for problems and issues that did not appear in his lifetime, but *the Holy Spirit* clarifies these ramifications by helping to translate from Jesus' time to subsequent periods.

Christ in the Gospels of the Liturgical Year

Church life and teaching are the usual context of such translation. That is why, when we meet together to worship on Sunday, the Gospels are not simply read but also preached on so as to bring out their implications for our time. When church documents speak about the actions of "Christ" or "Jesus Christ," they are not simply talking about the Jesus as he was in his public ministry but about the Jesus portrayed in apostolic preaching and reflected on in subsequent tradition and development.

STAGE TWO:
THE (APOSTOLIC) PREACHING ABOUT JESUS

We may date this to the second third of the first century A.D. The Biblical Commission Instruction contains this clause: "After Jesus rose from the dead and his divinity was clearly perceived." This is a recognition by the Catholic Church that during the ministry of Jesus, although his disciples followed him they did not fully perceive who he was. Thus in this stage a whole new perception colors the Jesus tradition.

Those who had seen and heard Jesus during his public ministry had their following of him confirmed through appearances of the risen Jesus (1 Cor 15:5-7) and came to full faith in him as the one through whom God had brought salvation to Israel and eventually the whole world. They vocalized this faith through the titles under which we find Jesus confessed (Messiah/Christ, Lord, Savior, Son of God, etc.), all of which were gradually transformed by the perception of his divinity. Such post-resurrectional faith illumined the memories of what the disciples had seen and heard during the pre-resurrectional period, and so they proclaimed his words and deeds with enriched significance. This was not a distortion of the Jesus tradition from Stage One; rather it involved a perception of what was already there but had not previously been recognized. (Modern readers, accustomed to a media goal of uninvolved, factual reporting, need to understand that this was not at all the atmosphere of early Christian preaching, which was committed and interpretative.)

We speak of these preachers as "apostolic" because they understood themselves as sent forth (Greek: *apostellein*) by the risen Jesus; their preaching is often described as kerygmatic proclamation (*kerygma*) intended to bring others to faith. Eventually the circle of missionary preachers was enlarged beyond the original companions of Jesus, and

Understanding How Gospels Were Written

the faith experiences of all the preachers enriched what they had received and were now proclaiming.

Another factor operative in this stage of development was the necessary adaptation of the preaching to a new audience. If Jesus was a Galilean Jew of the first third of the first century, by mid-century the Gospel was being preached in cities to urban Jews and Gentiles in Greek, a language that Jesus did not normally speak (if he spoke it at all or knew more than a few phrases). This change of language involved translation in the broadest sense of that term, that is, a rephrasing of the message in vocabulary and patterns ("literary forms," in the terminology of the Instruction) that would make it intelligible and alive for new audiences.

In terms of vocabulary, sometimes the rephrasing affected incidentals, for instance, Luke 5:19 substitutes a tile roof familiar to a Greek audience for the Palestinian village-style roof of pressed clay and branches through which a hole was opened, as envisioned in Mark 2:4. But other choices had theological repercussions. For instance, Jesus spoke in Aramaic at the Last Supper of his "flesh and blood." While the more literal Greek translation, *sarx*, "flesh," is attested in John 6:51, the first three Gospels and 1 Corinthians 11:24 chose an idiomatic Greek translation, *soma*, "body," for the eucharistic component. That choice may have facilitated the figurative use of "body" in the theology of the body of Christ of which Christians are members (1 Cor 12:12-27). Thus developments in this preaching period of the Jesus tradition served the growth of Christian theology.

Another type of development came from encountering new issues that Jesus never dealt with. The first three Gospels and Paul agree that Jesus took a severe stance against divorce and remarriage: If a man divorces his wife and marries another, he commits adultery. But Jesus was dealing with Jews—how was his demand to be applied once Christianity began to be preached among Gentiles? Jewish women could not divorce Jewish men, but in many Gentile areas women *could* divorce men. Mark 10:12 (and Mark alone) has a second demand: If a woman divorces her husband and marries another, she commits adultery. Jesus probably never said that, but it was the obvious corollary of his teaching as the preachers encountered this new possibility. Similarly Matthew 5:32; 19:9 (and Matthew alone) adds an exceptive phrase: If a man divorces his wife, except for *porneia*, and marries another, he commits adultery. On the basis of other NT uses (1 Cor 5:1;

Acts 15:20) it seems likely that by *porneia* Matthew means unions within the forbidden degrees of kindred—"forbidden" and deemed impure by the Mosaic Law and therefore not encountered among Jews but encountered among Gentiles by the preachers. Matthew is teaching that a man not only can but should divorce a wife who is close kinfolk because that is no marriage at all.

We may find it odd that such expansions (or "explications," to use the language of the Instruction) are included *within* the words of Jesus. If we were writing the account, we would have Jesus' words in the body of the text and add explanatory footnotes in order to apply his teaching to situations unforeseen by him. But one cannot preach with footnotes, and both original word and explication became part of the preached Jesus tradition.[4]

I hope these examples help to show how remarkably formative was this Stage Two of Gospel development. While staying substantially faithful to "what was really said and done by Jesus" and in that sense remaining historical, it moved away from exact literal retention and reproduction and thus kept the Jesus tradition alive, meaningful, and salvific, even as it was in Stage One when it originated.

STAGE THREE: THE WRITTEN GOSPELS

We may date this to the last third of the first century A.D. Although in the middle of the previous period as the Jesus tradition was being preached, some early written collections (now lost) would have appeared, and although preaching based on *oral* preservation and development of the Jesus tradition continued well into the second century, the era from 65 to 100 was probably when all four canonical Gospels were written.

According to titles ("The Gospel according to . . .") attached in the middle or late second century, two Gospels were attributed to the

---

[4] Paul, when writing letters, could be more precise. In 1 Corinthians 7:10-11 he presents as a word of the Lord that a man should not divorce his wife and that any woman separated from her husband cannot remarry. But then a few verses later (7:12-15) by a word of his own he deals with a situation that Jesus never dealt with—a word that he stresses is *not* a word of the Lord. In the case of a believing Christian married to a nonbeliever, if they cannot live together in peace and the unbelieving partner desires to separate, let it be so. If Paul were writing a Gospel, such an exception might very well have found its way into the text describing Jesus' attitude toward marriage!

Understanding How Gospels Were Written

eyewitness apostles Matthew and John and two to "apostolic men" who themselves were not eyewitnesses, Mark, the companion of Peter, and Luke, the companion of Paul. Relatively few modern scholars, however, think that any evangelist was an eyewitness of the ministry of Jesus. This surely represents a change of view. Yet the shift may not be so sharp as first seems, for the early traditions about authorship may not always have been referring to the writer in our sense of the one who put the Gospel on papyrus. Ancient attribution may have been more concerned with the one responsible for the tradition enshrined in a particular Gospel, the *authority* behind the Gospel, or the one who wrote one of the main sources of the Gospel. The section of the Instruction of the Biblical Commission that treats Stage Three does not deal with this question directly but takes care to speak of "apostles" in Stage Two and of "sacred authors/writers" in Stage Three, allowing the interpretation that two different sets of people were involved.[5]

The wide recognition that the evangelists were *not* eyewitnesses of Jesus' ministry is important for understanding the differences among the Gospels. In the older approach wherein eyewitness testimony was directly posited, it was very difficult to explain differences among the Gospels. How could eyewitness John report the cleansing of the Temple at the beginning of the ministry in his chapter 2 and eyewitness Matthew report the cleansing of the Temple at the end of the ministry in his chapter 21? To reconcile them it was maintained that the cleansing of the Temple happened twice and that each evangelist chose to report only one of the two instances. Many other examples of improbable reconciliations stemming from the theory of direct eyewitness accuracy can be offered. Since Matthew has a Sermon on the Mount and Luke has a similar Sermon on the Plain (Matt 5:1; Luke 6:17), there must have been a plain on the side of the mountain! Since Matthew has the Lord's Prayer taught in that sermon and Luke has it later on the road to Jerusalem (Matt 6:9-13; Luke 11:2-4), the disciples must

---

[5] Although in the early 1900s the Pontifical Biblical Commission taught that substantially the apostle Matthew stood behind Matthew and the apostle John wrote John, "full freedom" about those decrees was acknowledged in 1956 by the Secretary of the Commission. As a result there are no longer binding Catholic Church positions about the date or authorship of the Gospels but only on issues where the decrees affected faith and morals.

Christ in the Gospels of the Liturgical Year

have forgotten it, so that Jesus repeated it! Mark 10:46 places the healing of the blind man after Jesus left Jericho; Luke 18:35; 19:1 places it before Jesus entered Jericho; perhaps Jesus was leaving the site of OT Jericho and entering the site of NT Jericho!

On the other hand, if direct eyewitness writing was not involved, these harmonizing improbabilities can be avoided. Each evangelist was the recipient of preached Jesus tradition, but there was little in those reports of what Jesus said and did that would clarify the respective where and when. Yet the evangelists, who themselves were not eyewitnesses, had a task that the preachers of Stage Two never had, namely, to shape a sequential narrative from Jesus' baptism to his resurrection. If we suppose that the first and fourth evangelists had received a form of the story of the cleansing of the Temple from an intermediate source, and neither evangelist knew when it occurred during the public ministry, then each placed it where it seemed best in the sequence he was fashioning.

This leads to the insight that the Gospels have been arranged in *logical* order, not necessarily in *chronological* order. Each evangelist has ordered the material according to his understanding of Jesus and his desire to portray Jesus in a way that would meet the spiritual needs of the community to which he was addressing the Gospel. Thus the evangelists emerge as full authors of the Gospels, shaping, developing, and pruning the transmitted Jesus tradition, and as full theologians, orienting that tradition to a particular goal. The Biblical Commission Instruction teaches, "From the many things handed down, they selected some things, reduced others to a synthesis, (still) others they explicated as they kept in mind the situation of the churches."

This means that Stage Three of Gospel formation moved the end-product Gospels still another step further from being literal records of the ministry of Jesus (Stage One). Not only did decades of developing and adapting the Jesus tradition through preaching intervene in Stage Two, but the evangelists themselves reshaped what they received.

We are children of our time, and so we are curious about Stage One. However, judgments about details of Jesus' life in the first third of the first century require painstaking scholarship; and when properly phrased, those judgments use the language of "possibly" or "probably"—rarely "certainly." Indeed, a wise caution is to be extremely skeptical when we read that some scholars are claiming that now they know exactly how much (or how little!) is literally historical

Understanding How Gospels Were Written

in the Gospels—most of the time they are proposing what they want to be historical to fit their own theology.

How can today's preachers, then, know what to preach, and today's hearers know what to believe? It is ridiculous to maintain that Christian proclamation and faith should be changed by every new vagary of scholarship. Rather, preaching and reception are to be based on Stage Three, not on uncertain theories about Stage One. In the wisdom of God we were not given eyewitness notes from Stage One but written Gospels from Stage Three, and those Gospels actually exist, while scholarly reconstructions remain theoretical. *The Gospels are what was inspired by the Holy Spirit*, and Christians believe that the Holy Spirit guided the process of Gospel formation, guaranteeing that the end-product Gospels reflect the truth that God sent Jesus to proclaim.

Stage Three, if properly understood, also has consequences for more conservative Christians. In the history of biblical interpretation much time has been spent in harmonizing Gospel differences, not only in minor matters but also on a large scale. For instance, "Lives of Christ" try to make one sequential narrative out of the very different Matthean and Lucan infancy narratives, or out of Luke's account of appearances of the risen Jesus in Jerusalem and Matthew's account of an appearance on a mountain in Galilee. Besides asking whether this is possible, we need to ask whether such harmonization is not a distortion. In an outlook of faith, divine providence gave us four different Gospels, not a harmonized version; and it is to the individual Gospels, each with its own viewpoint, that we should look. Harmonization, instead of enriching, impoverishes.

The "bottom line" of this discussion based on the Roman Instruction is that modern scholarship creates no embarrassment about the church's traditional insistence that the Gospels are historical accounts of the ministry of Jesus, provided that, as the church also insists, "historical" not be understood in any crassly literal sense. Indeed, a 1993 Pontifical Biblical Commission statement about different methods of interpretation is harsher than the 1964 Instruction in criticizing undue stress on historical inerrancy and the historicizing of material that was not historical from the start.

To some Christians any thesis that does not present the Gospels as literal history implies that they are not true accounts of Jesus. Truth, however, must be evaluated in terms of the intended purpose. The Gospels might be judged untrue if the goal was strict reporting or exact biography. If the goal, however, was to bring readers/hearers to a faith in Jesus that leads them to accept God's rule or kingdom, then adaptations that made the Gospels less than literal by adding the dimension of faith and by adjusting to new audiences facilitated that goal and thus enhanced the truth of the Gospels. The Instruction is lucidly clear: "The doctrine and life of Jesus were not simply reported for the sole purpose of being remembered, but were 'preached' so as to offer the church a basis of faith and morals."

THE USE OF THE GOSPELS IN THE LITURGY

How does this discussion affect the liturgical use of the Gospels? In particular I am concerned with how each Gospel is used in the Sunday liturgy, the context in which the doctrine and life of Jesus are most often preached. Clearly an understanding of Stage Three inculcates respect for the individuality of each Gospel, and accordingly in the last half of the twentieth century the Roman Catholic Church felt the need to replace the one-year lectionary that paid no attention to Gospel individuality. In it, without any discernible theological pattern, the reading was taken one Sunday from Matthew, another Sunday from Luke; and Mark was practically never used (on the thesis that everything in Mark was found in Matthew or Luke). A liturgical reformation introduced a triennial Sunday lectionary, where in the first or A Year the Gospel readings are primarily taken from Matthew, in the second or B Year from Mark, and in the third or C Year from Luke.[6] This change of lectionary recognizes that selections should be read sequentially from the same Gospel if one is to do justice to the theological orientation given to those passages by the individual evangelist. For example, a parable that appears in all three Synoptic Gospels can have different meanings depending on the sequence in which each evangelist has placed it. Other churches have followed the Catholic lead in setting up a triennial lectionary, producing the admirable situation that Christians of diverse background are hearing the same Scripture on Sundays—an important ecumenical step toward unity!

---

[6] In chapters 33–35 below I am chiefly concerned with Sunday Gospel readings, but the distinctiveness of the individual Gospels is also acknowledged in the weekday lectionary, where (with allowance for festal exceptions) in the course of each year the three Gospels are read sequentially in the order Mark, Matthew, Luke.

Understanding How Gospels Were Written

(It would be helpful for readers to see the preliminary statement and note at the beginning of chapter 33, which address the sequential reading of the Synoptic Gospels in the three-year lectionary cycle.)

A Coming Christ in Advent

Essays on the Gospel Narratives Preparing for the Birth of Jesus

Matthew 1 and Luke 1

Chapters 5–10

Chapter 5

The Origin and Purpose of the Infancy Narratives

The heart of this section of the book (chaps. 5–10) will be a discussion of the biblical text of Matthew 1 and Luke 1 as an Advent preparation for the coming of Christ. But readers unfamiliar with the peculiar character of the infancy narratives may well find useful a general introduction explaining why and how these stories were written. This chapter will attempt to do that simply and concisely.

WHY ARE THERE GOSPEL STORIES OF JESUS' INFANCY?

Surprisingly in the whole NT only two authors pay attention to Jesus' birth and childhood—only Matthew and Luke give us "infancy narratives."

Most scholars think that Mark was the first Gospel to be written, but it begins with the baptism of Jesus by John. It tells us nothing of Jesus' earlier family existence, never even mentioning Joseph, his legal father. In this approach Mark is far from alone in early Christianity, for the other twenty-four books of the NT (outside Matthew and Luke) are like Mark in failing to show interest in Jesus' family origins before he began the ministry. Even John who starts his Gospel, not with the baptism but with the divine Word before creation, ignores the family circumstances in which the Word became flesh.

What then caused Matthew and Luke to begin with a story of Jesus' conception and birth? One probable factor was curiosity about the origins of this Jesus who was hailed as God's Son. Were his beginnings marked with the divine power that characterized his ministry? Mere curiosity, however, would not explain the judgment that Jesus' infancy should be made part of a written Gospel. Neither Matthew nor Luke was composing simply a life of Jesus; and for information about his birth to be part of their "good news" it had to have religious value—a value that is the key to understanding the infancy narratives. Indeed, as we shall see, despite the fact that the two evangelists fashioned very different birth stories, they agreed remarkably in a common religious message about the conception of Jesus.

If it comes as a shock to many Christians to find that Matthew and Luke are our only sources for knowledge about Jesus' infancy, it may be an even greater shock to realize that the two Gospels differ so much. Our Christmas crib or crèche scenes combine them; but if you pick up the NT without previous assumptions and read separately Matthew 1–2 and Luke 1–2, the enormous difference is obvious.

Matthew gives a picture wherein Mary and Joseph live at Bethlehem and have a house there. The coming of the magi, guided by the star, causes Herod to slay children at Bethlehem and the Holy Family to flee to Egypt. The fact that Herod's son Archelaus rules in Judea after him makes Joseph afraid to return to Bethlehem, and so he takes the child and his mother to Galilee to the town of Nazareth—obviously for the first time.

Luke, on the other hand, tells us that Mary and Joseph lived at Nazareth and went to Bethlehem only temporarily because they had to register there during a Roman census. The statement that Mary gave birth to her child and laid him in a manger because there was no place for them in "the inn" implies that they had no house of their own in Bethlehem. And Luke's account of the peaceful return of the Holy Family from Bethlehem through Jerusalem to Nazareth leaves no room for the coming of the magi or a struggle with Herod.

Some scholars have tried very hard to reconcile the differences between Matthew and Luke but with little convincing success. A greater fidelity to Scripture as we have received it would recognize that the Holy Spirit was content to give us two different accounts and that the way to interpret them faithfully is to treat them separately. Sometimes the drive to harmonize them arises from the false idea that, since Scripture is inspired, each infancy account must be completely historical. For some fifty years since Pope Pius XII, the Catholic Church has taught firmly and clearly that the Bible is a library handed down to us by Israel and the early church. In that collection of inspired books there are many different types of literature, including poetry, drama, history, and fiction. Indeed, between history and fiction there is a whole range of possibilities covering imaginative retellings that have a core of fact.

Christ in the Gospels of the Liturgical Year

The birth stories differ from the NT accounts of Jesus' ministry and death where *known eyewitnesses*, the apostles, are presented as the sources of the traditional preaching embodied in the Gospels and the Book of Acts. Some may object that Matthew and Luke surely got their information about Jesus' birth from his parents. Yet that is never claimed in the NT, nor in the earliest church writings; and the great difference between the two Gospels' birth stories causes difficulty for that solution. Nor does the rest of the NT offer any confirming echo of what is told us in the infancy narratives. Hard to reconcile are a great commotion at Jesus' birth and a public revelation as to who he was with the fact that, later when he comes to be baptized, he is an unknown and no one at Nazareth expects him to be a religious figure. We must content ourselves that there is no way to know precisely how historical the infancy narratives are, or to know where Matthew and Luke got them. Thus we avoid both a naive fundamentalism that would take every word of these accounts as literal history and a destructive skepticism that would reduce them to sheer mythology. (As will be seen below, the items on which the two accounts agree militate against the purely fictional approach and must be taken seriously.)

Does this limitation of our knowledge take away value from them? Not at all. Too much worry about historicity and sources of information distracts from the inspired meaning of the biblical text, which is centered on what the two evangelists were trying to teach us—the religious message on which they both agree. There are two major points in that message: first, the identity of Jesus; second, his role as the dramatic embodiment of the whole of Israel's history.

THE IDENTITY OF JESUS

Matthew and Luke agree that Jesus' descent is to be traced genealogically through Joseph who was of the house of David. According to Jewish law, Joseph's acknowledgment of Jesus would make him the legal father of the child (a status not dependent on physical fatherhood), and so Jesus was truly a Son of David. Matthew and Luke agree that Mary conceived Jesus not through sexual relations with Joseph but by the creative power of the Holy Spirit. Thus Jesus was truly the Son of God. This dual identity, Son of David and Son of God, was a very important component in the NT conception of gospel or "good news."

The Origin and Purpose of the Infancy Narratives

When Paul was writing to the Roman Christians about the year A.D. 58 and assuring this community whom he had not converted that he preached the same gospel that they knew, he phrased his description of Jesus thus: "Born of the seed of David according to the flesh; designated Son of God in power according to the Holy Spirit as of resurrection from the dead" (Rom 1:3-4). This is the same twofold identity found in the two infancy narratives, but in Paul (who wrote earlier than Matthew and Luke) sonship through the Holy Spirit is attached to the resurrection. Elsewhere an affirmation of both divine and Davidic sonship is attached to the baptism of Jesus. For instance, in Luke's account of the baptism (3:21ff.), God declares to Jesus, "You are my beloved Son" while the Holy Spirit descends on Jesus; and Luke then gives a genealogy tracing Jesus' descent from David and the patriarchs. In other words, as Christians reflected on Jesus' life, the great "moments" of that life (the resurrection, the baptism, and eventually the conception) were used to clarify who he was: the Messiah or anointed King of the house of David and the unique Son of God through the Holy Spirit. When and because birth stories became the vehicle of that message, they could appropriately be included in the written Gospels.

Many other essential aspects of the gospel message about the identity of Jesus are taught us by the infancy narratives. In both Matthew and Luke this identity is proclaimed by an angel as God's messenger. Similarly, Paul insists that he did not receive his gospel from human sources, but God "was pleased to reveal His Son" (Gal 1:12, 16). And in Matthew 16:16-17, Peter's confession of Jesus as Messiah, the Son of God, is hailed by Jesus as "not revealed by flesh and blood but by my Father in heaven." In the baptismal accounts of Mark, Matthew, and Luke, God's voice speaks from heaven about His Son. Thus there was a fundamental understanding that the identity of Jesus was a divine revelation, not a human deduction.

Another common feature in the two Gospels is the insistence that the identity of Jesus was quickly shared with others. In Matthew the revelation given to Joseph is in God's plan made known to the Gentile magi. In Luke the revelation given to Mary is in God's plan made known to the Jewish shepherds. Although the cast of characters differs sharply, the evangelists are each in his own way teaching us that Christ's identity is never received to be kept a private possession. And in God's providence, there are others eager to receive it, even if those others are not the ones we might have expected.

Christ in the Gospels of the Liturgical Year

There is a negative side also to the agreement of the two evangelists: a warning that not all will accept the gospel, especially some who should have been eager. If the magi come without hesitation to worship Jesus, guided by the star and, even more specifically, by the prophetic words of Scripture (Matt 2:2-6), the king and the chief priests and the scribes who possess the Jewish heritage and can read the Scriptures easily are quite hostile to Jesus. If Luke describes the rejoicing of the shepherds and of Simeon and Anna over the birth of "a Savior who is Christ the Lord" (2:11), there is nevertheless a solemn warning that this child is set for the fall as well as the rise of many in Israel, a sign to be contradicted who will cause the hostile thoughts of many to be revealed (2:34-35). In other words, the Christmas crib lies under the shadow of the cross; the gospel is always a factor that produces judgment; and the joy of the "good news" has also an element of sadness because not all will believe.

In a very real way, then, the infancy narratives of Matthew and Luke are whole gospels. They contain the basic revelation of the full identity of Jesus and the way in which this revelation was quickly shared with others, evangelizing some, but causing rejection and hatred among others.

THE EMBODIMENT OF ISRAEL'S HISTORY

There is a second religious message on which Matthew and Luke agree that goes beyond the identity of Jesus, and this second message may be even more necessary to proclaim today since so few Christians appreciate it. When Matthew and Luke wrote, the Scriptures of the Christian community consisted of what would later be called the OT—there was not yet a NT. Those Scriptures were known to Jews as "the Law, the Prophets and the other books." Both Matthew and Luke used their first two chapters, the infancy narratives, as a transition from these Jewish Scriptures to the story of Jesus' ministry. The evangelists made a summary of OT stories and motifs because they felt it impossible to appreciate Jesus without such preparation.

This OT context is often very foreign to Christians today, especially to Catholic audiences; and, alas, they hear little preaching about it. Working with the infancy narratives, priests and catechists might well use the Advent period to proclaim the Jewish Scriptures as a setting with which the church begins her liturgical year. (Concentration on the Bible is often far more effective when people see how it fits in with the church's liturgy in which they worship God.) The chapters that

The Origin and Purpose of the Infancy Narratives

follow in this section of the book will explain in detail how Matthew and Luke incorporate OT background in their infancy narratives, but let me give a brief overview here.

Matthew begins "the story of the origin of Jesus Christ" (1:1) with Abraham begetting Isaac. His genealogical list of names resumes in capsule form the story of the patriarchs and the rise and fall of the monarchy from David to the Babylonian Exile. We learn a lesson from the names that separate Zerubbabel from Joseph at the end of the list: these were people too insignificant to be mentioned in Israel's history, but they were significant to God as He prepared for the Messiah. Then in a double-exposure technique Matthew's story of the conception and birth of Jesus reenacts the story of Israel's deliverance from Egypt. Joseph the father of Jesus is deliberately reminiscent of the OT Joseph, as he receives revelation in dreams and goes to Egypt, thus saving the family. The wicked king Herod is a carbon copy of the wicked Pharaoh who killed the Hebrew male children, only to have God protect the life of the one who would save his people (Moses = Jesus). In the story of Moses, the Magus Balaam came from the East and saw the star of the Davidic king rise from Israel (Num 22–24); so too after Jesus' birth magi come from the East, having seen the star of the King of the Jews. Matthew fortifies these reminiscences from the saga of Moses recounted in OT Books of the Law (Pentateuch) with five pertinent quotations from the Prophets, so that the fulfillment of the Law and the Prophets may be seen as an introduction to what God will do through Jesus when the Gospel proper begins with the baptism at the Jordan.

Luke uses a similar double exposure to tell the story of Israel and of Jesus' infancy at the same time, but his technique is more subtle than Matthew's. Zechariah and Elizabeth, the parents of John the Baptist, are portrayed as similar to Abraham and Sarah in Genesis, the first Book of the Law. The messenger of revelation is Gabriel, the angel of the endtime who appears in Daniel, the last book of the Hebrew Scriptures to be composed—thus Luke covers the range of the OT. The annunciations of the conception of the Baptist and of Jesus echo OT birth annunciations. The four canticles that enhance the Lucan infancy narrative (Magnificat, Benedictus, Gloria in Excelsis, Nunc Dimittis) are a mosaic of OT recollections, with almost every line parallel to a verse from the Prophets and the Psalms. Mary's presentation of Jesus in the Temple echoes Hannah's presentation of Samuel at the shrine in 1 Samuel 1:24-28. In the story of Jesus' youth from his circumcision to his rearing at Nazareth a constant refrain is that everything was done according to the Law of the Lord. For Luke the infancy chapters bridge the Jewish Scriptures and the Gospel of Jesus—a bridge on which OT characters like Zechariah, Elizabeth, Simeon, and Anna meet with Gospel figures like the Baptist, Mary, and Jesus.

*   *   *

As we turn now to a consideration of scenes from chapter 1 of Matthew and chapter 1 of Luke, we should keep in mind the twofold religious message just described. The one whose coming we anticipate in Advent is Son of David and Son of God. As Son of David he is heir to all the history of Israel so allusively described beneath the surface of the birth stories. As Son of God he embodies that divine grace which always goes beyond expectation. The OT past illustrates God's gracious mercy even to the unworthy: He has always lifted up the lowly. He has always heard the prayers of the faithful and obedient. Now His Son will share revelation and grace even more widely for the glory of Israel and a light to the Gentiles.

Chapter 6

The Genealogy of Jesus Christ
(Matthew 1:1-17)

¹The story of the origin of Jesus Christ, son of David, son of Abraham:

²Abraham was the father of Isaac;
Isaac was the father of Jacob;
Jacob was the father of Judah and his brothers;
³Judah was the father of Perez and Zerah by *Tamar*;
Perez was the father of Hezron;
Hezron was the father of Aram;
⁴Aram was the father of Amminadab;
Amminadab was the father of Nahshon;
Nahshon was the father of Salmon;
⁵Salmon was the father of Boaz by *Rahab*;
Boaz was the father of Obed by *Ruth*;
Obed was the father of Jesse;
⁶Jesse was the father of David the king.

David was the father of Solomon by *Uriah's wife*;
⁷Solomon was the father of Rehoboam;
Rehoboam was the father of Abijah;
Abijah was the father of Asaph;
⁸Asaph was the father of Jehoshaphat;
Jehoshaphat was the father of Joram;
Joram was the father of Uzziah;
⁹Uzziah was the father of Jotham;
Jotham was the father of Ahaz;
Ahaz was the father of Hezekiah;
¹⁰Hezekiah was the father of Manasseh;
Manasseh was the father of Amos;
Amos was the father of Josiah;
¹¹Josiah was the father of Jechoniah and his brothers
at the time of the Babylonian Exile.
¹²After the Babylonian Exile,

Jechoniah was the father of Shealtiel;
   Shealtiel was the father of Zerubbabel;
¹³ Zerubbabel was the father of Abiud;
   Abiud was the father of Eliakim;
   Eliakim was the father of Azor;
¹⁴ Azor was the father of Zadok;
   Zadok was the father of Achim;
   Achim was the father of Eliud;
¹⁵ Eliud was the father of Eleazar;
   Eleazar was the father of Matthan;
   Matthan was the father of Jacob;
¹⁶ Jacob was the father of Joseph, the husband of *Mary*;
   of her was begotten Jesus, called the Christ.

¹⁷ Thus the total generations from Abraham to David were fourteen generations; and from David to the Babylonian Exile fourteen more generations; and finally from the Babylonian Exile to the Christ fourteen more generations.

* * *

This genealogy that opens Matthew's Gospel has one principal occurrence in liturgy, namely, on the Advent weekday December 17 which begins the pre-Christmas octave of infancy gospel readings.[1] It was read more frequently in the pre–Vatican II liturgy, but often with disastrous results as the priest-celebrant stumbled over names and sometimes skipped large sections, under the pretense that the reading was a boring and meaningless exercise. To the contrary I have been conducting a somewhat solitary campaign to make this Matthean genealogy a major Advent topic, even to the extent that, if I am invited to give a special pre-Christmas sermon, especially on an Advent Sunday, I go out of my way to make Matthew 1:1-17 the subject of the homily. The stunned look on the faces of the parish audience when I launch into the solemn list of begettings is proof that one of the pre-requisites for effective preaching has been accomplished—attention has been caught, even if the initial impression may be that the selection of the Gospel pericope is slightly daft.

   As a preliminary to comment on the genealogy, let me make a series of remarks to highlight its importance. If a Christian today were asked

---

[1] It is also assigned to the afternoon Mass on December 24—a Mass that seems not to be frequently celebrated in the U.S.A.

The Genealogy of Jesus Christ

to tell someone who knows nothing about Christianity the basic story of Jesus Christ, where would he or she be likely to begin? I am willing to wager that not one in ten thousand would begin where the author of the Gospel that the church puts first begins—where the first line of the first page of the NT begins—with the majestic assurance: This is "the story of the beginning/the origin/the genesis of Jesus Christ." Indeed, we might approximate: "the story of the advent of Jesus Christ."[2] For Matthew the origin of Jesus Christ starts with Abraham begetting Isaac! In other words the story of the Hebrew patriarchs, of the kings of Judah, and of other Israelites is the opening stage of the story of Jesus Christ. That such an OT component to the Jesus story would not occur to most Christians today is a sad commentary on how far we have moved from our ancestors' understanding of the good news. Matthew's list of people who are an integral part of the origin of Jesus Christ contains some of the most significant names in the biblical account of God's dealing with His people Israel, and I for one wish strongly that at least once a year their names were allowed to resound in the Christian church on a Sunday when all the worshiping NT people of God were there to hear.

The Matthean sense of the genesis or origin or advent of Jesus Christ, however, goes beyond recalling the OT; and that is why I would insist it must be *preached*. I am not at all the first to claim this. In thinking about the initiators of the Protestant Reformation most Roman Catholics would recall Martin Luther and John Calvin; but there was a third famous Reformer, perhaps the most radical, Ulrich Zwingli, who was based in Switzerland. While he was still a functioning Catholic priest, he became pastor of the Cathedral of Zurich. Already imbued with the growing stress on the supreme importance of Scripture, he conceived the idea of preaching on the whole NT—yes, from the first verse of Matthew to the last verse of Revelation—an idea that in a sense found ultimate acceptance in the Catholic Church after Vatican II with the three-year lectionary of readings that cover most of the NT and invite even daily homilies. Accordingly, in January 1519 Zwingli began his project by preaching on the Matthean genealogy, a homiletic challenge that would have caused most preachers then and there to retreat in

---

[2] The Greek is literally: "The book of the genesis of Jesus Christ"; that expression probably plays on the literal meaning plus the Septuagintal rendering of the Hebrew term for "genealogical record."

Christ in the Gospels of the Liturgical Year

despair. But Zwingli maintained that if one understood it correctly, this genealogy contained the essential theology of the Reformation. I would be even bolder: it contains the essential theology of the Old and the New Testaments that the whole Church, Orthodox, Roman Catholic, and Protestant, should proclaim. Let me illustrate this by comments on the three sections of the genealogy.

THE PATRIARCHS

"The story of the origin of Jesus Christ" begins with the patriarchal period when Abraham begets Isaac. With even a catechism knowledge of Bible stories the hearer might remember with a little puzzlement that Abraham had two sons of whom Ishmael was the older and wonder why the story of the origin of Jesus Christ does not involve the begetting of Ishmael who with his mother Hagar was the more abused figure. (Indeed their story constitutes one of those tales of terror of which Phyllis Trible writes.[3]) The puzzlement should increase when "the story of the origin of Jesus Christ" goes on with Isaac begetting Jacob. Here too there was another, older brother Esau—a bit of a clod, it is true, but in his rustic way more honest than the calculating, deceptive Jacob who, *salva reverentia* to Augustine, was more a liar than a mystery when he stole the birthright. (It is to the credit of OT Israel that it recognized that its own seizure of the land of Canaan had elements of usurpation from other peoples who had a prior claim, a usurpation hinted at by what it attributed to its eponymous ancestor Jacob/Israel.)

The puzzling "story of the origin of Jesus Christ" goes on with Jacob begetting Judah and his brothers. Why is Judah singled out, and why ultimately is the Messiah from his tribe? Was not Joseph clearly the best of the brothers? Favored by God with visionary dreams that aroused the hatred of the others, Joseph forgave their selling him into captivity in Egypt and saved them when they would have perished from starvation in the famine. Surely he is the embodiment of Jesus' story, not Judah who sold his brother and sought out prostitutes.

Matthew's choice of Isaac over Ishmael, of Jacob over Esau, of Judah over Joseph is faithful to the OT insight that God frequently does not choose the best or the noble or the saintly. In other words, Matthew is

---

[3] *Texts of Terror* (Philadelphia: Fortress, 1984), 8–35.

The Genealogy of Jesus Christ

faithful to an insight about a God who is not controlled by human merit but manifests His own unpredictable graciousness. No wonder Zwingli saw here the theology of the Reformation (which in this case is simply the theology of both Testaments), a theology of salvation by grace. Truly this theology, at work in the choices among the patriarchs, is "the beginning story of Jesus Christ," since he will preach salvation to tax collectors and sinners, proclaim that they need a physician and not those who are already religious, and who will ultimately die for us "while we were still sinners" (Rom 5:8). Matthew's genealogy is telling us that the story of Jesus Christ contains as many sinners as saints and is written with the crooked lines of liars and betrayers and the immoral, and not only with straight lines.

THE KINGS

But perhaps one may object that in concentrating on the patriarchal beginnings of the story, I am giving undue emphasis to the rude and the primitive. Does not the first section of Matthew's genealogy build up from Abraham to the high point of "David the king"? And does not the second section of the genealogy consist of the gloriously reigning Judean kings of the house of David? The answer to both those questions invokes the basic biblical issue of God's values versus human appearances—"My thoughts are not your thoughts," says the Lord (Isa 55:8). Seemingly the first part of the genealogy does build up from an Abraham who had no land but received a promise to a David who rules as king in possession of this Promised Land. But the second part of the genealogy calls into question whether that really was a progressive buildup, for it shows that the monarchy went downhill from David the king to "the deportation to Babylon." In other words, it goes from possessing the land to losing it. As for gloriously reigning monarchs of the house of David, of the fourteen Judean kings that Matthew lists between David and the deportation only two (Hezekiah and Josiah) could be considered as faithful to God's standards in the law code of Deuteronomy, which were applied to the monarchs by the author of the Books of Kings. The rest were an odd assortment of idolaters, murderers, incompetents, power-seekers, and harem-wastrels.

David himself was a stunning combination of saint and sinner. There was, of course, the arranged murder of Bathsheba's husband so that David might possess the wife legally. Even more indicative of

David's shrewd piety was his personal innocence combined with mafia-like politics whereby his relatives murdered opponents for him. He seized Jerusalem, a city that henceforth belonged to him and no tribe, and moved the Ark of the Covenant there to give the blessing of religion to his consolidation of power. Indeed, he succeeded in writing a codicil to God's covenant with His people. Now the covenant no longer simply stated: "You will be my people and I will be your God, if you keep my commandments"; it had an added condition: "and if you have a king of the house of David reigning over you" (see 2 Sam 7:24-26). All of this was combined with the sanctity of the sweet singer of psalms and originator of prayers so beautiful and profound that they have been the heart of divine praise, Jewish and monastic Christian, ever since.

This curious story of a Davidic monarchical institution that had divine origins but was frequently corrupt, venal, and uninspiring, was also part of "the story of the origin of Jesus Christ." Yes, that story involved not only individuals with their strengths and weaknesses like the patriarchs, but an institution, an organization, a structure, indeed a hierarchy (literally, in Greek, a sacred order) embodied in absolute rulers. I am not sure whether Zwingli would have been happy with that part of the story, but those of us who must be loyal both to the spontaneous grace of God and to a church with authority may get encouragement from this phase of Matthew's theology reflected in the incipient story of Jesus Christ.

THE UNKNOWN AND THE UNEXPECTED

If the "progress" from Abraham to the monarchy proved a mirage in the light of God's values, the last part of the genealogy from the deportation to Babylon to the divinely sent Christ or anointed king is more genuinely upbeat. It leads to the messianic savior of God's people. But what a curious cast of characters this more genuine progress involves. Except for the first two (Shealtiel and Zerubbabel) and the last two (Joseph and Mary), they are a collection of unknown people whose names never made it into sacred history for having done something significant. In other words, while powerful rulers in the monarchy brought God's people to a low point in recorded history (deportation), unknown people, presumably also proportionately divided among saints and sinners, were the vehicles of restoration. Still another indicator of the unpredictability of God's grace is that

The Genealogy of Jesus Christ

He accomplishes His purpose through those whom others regard as unimportant and forgettable.

Perhaps this is the moment to comment on the theological import of Matthew's including five women in the genealogy of Jesus Christ. In the light of OT genealogies this is an unexpected item. Matthew's consistent "A was the father of B" pattern is not as male chauvinistic as it might seem if we remember that in the evangelist's view God was active in each begetting, so that biology is never the primary issue. It is refreshing, nevertheless, that Matthew took care to remind us explicitly that women as well as men were human components in Jesus' origins—a fitting reminder in a list that is described as "a story of the *genesis* of Jesus Christ," evoking memories of an earlier Genesis story. The choice of the women who are mentioned is as surprising as the choice of many of the men. We hear nothing of the saintly patriarchal wives, Sarah, Rebekah, Rachel. Matthew begins rather with Tamar, a Canaanite outsider left childless by the death of her first and second husbands, both of them Judah's sons. When Judah failed to do his duty in providing her with a third son as husband, she disguised herself as a prostitute and seduced him. Only later when he found his widowed daughter-in-law in a pregnant situation that he regarded as disgraceful did she reveal that he was the father, causing Judah to recognize that she was more just and loyal to God's law then he was.[4] The next in the list is another outsider, the Canaanite Rahab—this time a real prostitute, but one whose kindness in protecting the Israelite spies made the conquest of Jericho possible (Josh 2). Odd figures to be part of the beginning story of Jesus Christ, unless we remember his gracious dealings with sinners and prostitutes which were part of the story of his ministry. Ruth was another foreigner, a Moabite. Yet it was from her and not from her Israelite relatives that the impulse came to be faithful to the Law in raising up a child to her dead husband as she literally threw herself at the feet of Boaz. That child was to be the grandfather of David the king. The last OT woman in the list is named by Matthew only through her pious husband Uriah, a Hittite, whom David had slain; she is Bathsheba, the victim of David's lust. The scandal of the affair and the loss of their love child did not discourage

---

[4] Although not included by Trible, this story borders on being a text of terror (footnote 3 above).

her from making certain that a second son, Solomon, succeeded David in the monarchy. All these women had a marital history that contained elements of human scandal or scorn; they were enterprising instruments, however, of God's spirit in continuing the sacred line of the Messiah. They fittingly introduce the fifth woman, Mary,[5] whose marital situation is also peculiar, since she is pregnant even though she has not had relations with her betrothed husband. Joseph is just or holy in his decision to divorce her, but divine revelation makes it clear that the last woman mentioned in the genealogy is more holy than he, for she is the instrument par excellence of the Holy Spirit who has begotten Jesus Christ in her womb.

Looking back at the analysis of Matthew's genealogy that I have just given, we see how extraordinarily comprehensive is its theology of the roots of Jesus' story in the OT. The genealogy is more than retrospective and instructive, however. We must recognize that in acting in Jesus Christ God is consistent with His action in Abraham and David, in the patriarchs, in the kings, and in the unknown. But that is only one aspect of the story of Jesus Christ, a story that has a sequence as well as a beginning; and the ongoing aspects are what make the genealogy "good news" for Matthew's audience and for us. If the beginning of the story involved as many sinners as saints, so has the sequence. This means not simply a Peter who denied Jesus or a Paul who persecuted him, but sinners and saints among those who would bear his name throughout the ages. If we realize that human beings have been empowered to preserve, proclaim, and convey the salvation brought by Jesus Christ throughout ongoing history, the genealogy of the sequence of Jesus contains as peculiar an assortment of people as did the genealogy of the beginnings. The God who wrote the beginnings with crooked lines also writes the sequence with crooked lines, and some of those lines are our own lives and witness. A God who did not hesitate to use the scheming as well as the noble, the impure as well as the pure, men to whom the world hearkened and women upon whom the world frowned—this God continues to work through the same mélange. If it was a challenge to recognize in the last part of Matthew's genealogy that totally unknown people were part of the

---

[5] The fact that the OT women were foreigners does not prepare the way for Mary but prepares for Matthew's audience, which contained Gentile Christians along with Jewish ones (cf. Matt 10:5-6; 28:19).

story of Jesus Christ, it may be a greater challenge to recognize that the unknown characters of today are an essential part of the sequence. A sense of being unimportant and too insignificant to contribute to the continuation of the story of Jesus Christ in the world is belied by the genealogy, and the proclamation of that genealogy in the Advent liturgy is designed to give us hope about our destiny and our importance. The message of the genealogy is an enabling invitation.

The genealogy has also taught us that God did not hesitate to entrust to a monarchical institution an essential role in the story of His Son's origins—an authoritative institution (at times authoritarian) which He guaranteed with promises lest it fail but which was frequently led by corrupt, venal, stupid, and ineffective leaders, as well as sometimes by saints. He has not hesitated to entrust the sequence of the story to a hierarchically structured church, guaranteed with promises, but not free from its own share of the corrupt, the venal, the stupid, and the ineffective. Those "Christians" who proclaim that they believe in and love Jesus but cannot accept the church or the institution because it is far from perfect and sometimes a scandal have not understood the beginning of the story and consequently are not willing to face the challenge of the sequence.

At the end of these comments let us return to the reference to Zwingli's approach mentioned at the beginning. By stressing the all-powerful grace of God, the genealogy presents its greatest challenge to those who will accept only an idealized Jesus Christ whose story they would write only with straight lines and whose portrait they would paint only in pastel colors. If we look at the whole story and the total picture, the genealogy teaches us that the beginning was not thus; the Gospels teach us that his ministry was not thus; the history of the church teaches us the sequence was not thus. That lesson is not a discouragement but an encouragement as we look forward to the liturgical coming of Christ. God's grace can work even with people like us. A meditation on "The story of the origin of Jesus Christ—Abraham fathered Isaac . . . Jesse fathered David the king . . . Achim fathered Eliud"—should convince reader and hearer that the authentic "story of the sequence of Jesus Christ" is that Jesus called Peter and Paul . . . Paul called Timothy . . . someone called you . . . and you must call someone else.

Chapter 7

The Annunciation to Joseph
(Matthew 1:18-25)

For most Christians "annunciation" automatically means the scene in
Luke 1:26-38 where the Angel Gabriel appears to Mary at Nazareth to
announce that she will conceive and bear a son to be called Jesus. Yet
that is not the only annunciation of Jesus' birth. In Matthew's infancy
narrative there is no annunciation to Mary; she remains a background
figure. Rather there is an annunciation by an "angel of the Lord" to
Joseph in a dream, telling him not to divorce Mary as he has planned,
but to take her to his house, for her pregnancy is of the Holy Spirit.
Matthew's annunciation may not have the poetic beauty of Luke's
annunciation; one rarely if ever sees it portrayed in art. Yet it has its
own dramatic force and theological insight, making it well worthy of
proclamation as it occurs in the liturgy of the last week of Advent.

THE SETTING

In the genealogy that we have just discussed, i.e., the list of begettings
that constitute the genesis or origin of Jesus Christ, Son of David, Son
of Abraham (1:1), there is a set pattern (A was the father of B; B was
the father of C) through three sets of fourteen generations. Yet when it
comes to "the bottom line," to the generation that is the whole point of
the genealogy, the format changes: not "Jacob was the father of Joseph,
and Joseph was the father of Jesus who is called the Christ," but
"Jacob was the father of Joseph, the husband of Mary, of whom was
begotten Jesus, called the Christ." Subconsciously at least, the attentive
reader of Matthew is bound to wonder about the peculiar phrasing.
Matthew is going to explain that through his annunciation story, as he
indicates in its opening line (1:18): "Now, as for Jesus Christ, his
genesis [birth] took place in this way."[1] Christ or Messiah means

---

[1] The double use of *genesis* in reference to Jesus Christ in 1:1 and 1:18 has a
parallel in the double use of genesis in reference to Noah in Genesis 5:1; 6:9.
Matthew is following OT parallels very closely here.

"anointed one," and in particular the anointed king of the house of David. The genealogy has stressed the role of David the king, mentioning him more than anyone else (five times, 1:1, 6, 17); the annunciation will continue that theme since it is addressed to "Joseph, son of David." Although Matthew does not specifically localize the annunciation, in chapter 2 which follows the annunciation, we are told that Bethlehem was where Joseph and Mary had a home (2:11). It is fitting that Joseph, son of David, father of Jesus, Son of David, should live in Bethlehem, the place where David was born.

Nevertheless, the annunciation to Joseph not only looks back to and continues the themes of the genealogy; it looks forward to the rest of the Gospel. In that Gospel Matthew refers to Jesus as Son of David more often than do the other three Gospels taken together. Yet Matthew 22:41-46 makes it clear that Jesus is more than Son of David. He is decisively, by divine revelation, the Son of God (see 3:17; 16:16-17; 17:5). Accordingly, if the genealogy begins in 1:1 with the genesis of Jesus, Son of David, the annunciation will draw to an end in 1:23 describing the genesis of Emmanuel, "God with us."

Mary's strange pregnancy, which explains how Jesus is God with us, namely through the Holy Spirit, is another echo of the genealogy. As we saw in chapter 6, anomalously for genealogies, among Matthew's forty-two fathers (his count) were listed four OT women, all of them with a history before marriage or childbirth that made their situation either strange or scandalous. In particular, Tamar, the widow of Judah's son, was found to be pregnant indecently long after her husband's death; Judah denounced her till he was made to realize that he was the father. Bathsheba, the wife of Uriah, became pregnant not by her husband but by David. Yet in all these instances the woman was God's instrument in preserving Israel and/or the lineage of the Messiah. So also, the fifth woman of the genealogy, Mary, is in a seemingly scandalous pregnancy. She and Joseph have been married,[2] but they are now in the customary interim period separating the marriage contract from the bride's living with the groom. Marriage, agreed upon by

---

[2] The verb in 1:18 is not the regular Greek verb "to marry"; evidently it was difficult to describe Jewish marriage customs in that language, even as it is in English. Nevertheless, translations such as "engage, betroth" do not do justice to the fact that the formal contract had been exchanged before witnesses and that Joseph is Mary's "husband" (1:16, 19).

parents, usually came almost immediately after the age of puberty; but the girl continued to live with her parents for a time after the wedding until the husband was able to support her in his home or that of his parents. Marital intercourse was not permissible during that period;[3] yet Mary was now with child. What was Joseph to do?

THE DILEMMA OF A JUST MAN

A crucial verse in understanding the impact of the annunciation is Matthew 1:18-19: "Before they came together, Mary was found to be with child of the Holy Spirit; and Joseph her husband, being a just man and unwilling to shame her, decided to divorce her quietly." The logic of this description is not easy to discern. A popular view, especially among Roman Catholics, has interpreted the first clause literally, so that the discovery of Mary's pregnancy brought knowledge that it was through the efficacy of the Holy Spirit. Joseph's decision to divorce her stemmed from his awe or reverence for this divine intervention, of which he already knew when the angel appeared to him. This knowledge gave him a sense of unworthiness in relation to Mary and an unwillingness to enter an ordinary marriage relationship with such an instrument of God. This interpretation is linguistically possible; it spares Joseph from ever having thought that Mary could behave shamefully.

For most scholars, however, this interpretation runs against the obvious flow of the narrative. Storywise, is it really plausible that the discovery that Mary was with child brought with it the knowledge that the pregnancy was of the Holy Spirit? Some interpreters argue that Matthew presupposed the Lucan annunciation where Mary learned of the overshadowing of the Holy Spirit and presumed that she had shared this knowledge along with the news of her pregnancy. But there is not an iota of evidence that Matthew or his readers knew of Luke's account. Similarly unrealistic is the thesis that Mary was so transparently holy that a knowledge of her pregnancy would bring the assumption that this was of God—we have no evidence that a virginal conception of the Messiah was expected in Judaism. Rather, as indicated above, the four OT women mentioned in the genealogy

---

[3] It is highly dubious whether reputed differences on this point between Galilee and Judea, suggested by later rabbinic references, were applicable at this time.

The Annunciation to Joseph

prepare us for a seeming scandal in the fifth woman named in the Messiah's lineage. Matthew's statement that Mary "was found to be with child of the Holy Spirit" does not describe a knowledge that the finders had but a knowledge that the readers need, lest for a moment they think that the origin of Jesus Christ, in whom they believe, could have been scandalous.

That the dramatis personae in the story did *not* have a knowledge of the divine origin of Mary's child is the whole point of the angelic revelation to Joseph. The decision to divorce stems from Joseph's ignorance of the paternity; he is not the father, and he can only think that another is. When the angel says to him, "Do not fear to take Mary your wife to your home, for the child conceived in her is of the Holy Spirit," the angel is not telling Joseph something he already knows but something he needs to know. Patterned on angelic revelations to biblical fathers-to-be (see Abraham in Gen 17:15-22, and Zechariah in Luke 1:8-23), this is a communication of a divine plan for both the conception and the future of the infant.

Thinking Mary's pregnancy to be of human origin would not detract from Joseph's saintliness, unless one imposes on him a standard that would not be appropriate for a Jew of his time. Indeed, Matthew insists that Joseph was "just" (or "upright" or "righteous"), a designation that implies conformity to the Law of God, the supreme Jewish standard of holiness. (Compare the same adjective applied to Zechariah and Elizabeth in Luke 1:6: "They were both righteous before God, walking blamelessly in all the commandments and ordinances of the Lord.") Mary should have come to Joseph a virgin, and now she was with child. His decision to divorce her showed a sensitivity to Israel's understanding of the sanctity of marriage required by God's Law, since her loss of virginity might have been considered adultery (Deut 22:20-21).[4] But Joseph was also sensitive to the protective character of the Law, which indicated two ways in which a woman might become pregnant before joining her husband: she might willingly have relations with another and commit adultery (Deut 22:20-24), or she might be forced against her will and thus remain innocent (Deut 22:25-27).

---

[4] A second-century Christian interpretation of the scene is found in the *Protevangelium of James* 14:1: "If I hide her sin, I am fighting the Law of the Lord." Justin Martyr, Augustine, and Chrysostom all understood that Joseph was being obedient to the Law.

Christ in the Gospels of the Liturgical Year

To determine Mary's complicity or innocence and the treatment to which she might be subject, Joseph could have demanded a trial (and presumably have escaped returning the dowry if she were guilty). Joseph, however, did not manifest his righteousness at Mary's expense: "He was unwilling to expose her to public disgrace" or "to make a public spectacle of her" (two precise translations of the Greek verb involved in 1:19). Accordingly, Joseph was going to divorce her "quietly"—not in the sense that no one would know of it, but in the sense that there would be no formal inquiry into Mary's behavior.

In my judgment, this understanding of the justice of Joseph, rather than the "awe" or "reverence" explanation mentioned above, is essential to Matthew's picture of Christianity. In the next chapter Matthew will describe Gentile magi coming to worship the King of the Jews guided by divine revelation through the star, while Jewish leaders who have more precise revelation available in the Scriptures (Herod, the chief priests, and the scribes) seek to kill him—note the plural in 2:20: "Those who sought the child's life." One might falsely assume that in Matthew's dualistic view there are only good Gentiles and bad Jews. Rather, the hero of Matthew's infancy story is Joseph, a very sensitive Jewish observer of the Law, who is brought through God's revelation to accept Jesus, saving him from destruction. For Matthew it was perfectly possible to be simultaneously a Law-observant Jew and a Christian, since Jesus proclaimed that every jot and tittle of the Law would be preserved (5:18), praised those who kept even the least commandments (5:19), and appreciated scribes who could treasure what is new along with what is old (13:52). Such Law-observant, believing Jews preserved the memory of Jesus and through their proclamation made disciples of the Gentiles (28:19). Thus, in Joseph, the evangelist was portraying what he thought a Jew should be and probably what he himself was.

In the proclamation of the annunciation scene, this point is worth developing. There is a poignancy in Matthew's Joseph, righteously concerned for the Law of God, but seeking also to prevent Mary's public disgrace. Obviously, Matthew's story may imply Joseph's love for his bride, but we should not contrast too simply obedience to the Law and love as the opposing motives in his behavior. Rather, Joseph understands that the Law in all its complexity allows behavior that is sensitive, neither assuming the worst nor seeking the maximum punishment. That is why Matthew can reconcile a profound obedience to the Law with an acceptance of Jesus. His objection to the legalists is not that they keep God's Law exactly, but that they do not understand the depth of God's purpose in the Law. In 12:1-8 he will describe Jesus as the Lord of the Sabbath, accused of condoning violations of the Law, but truly perceptive as to how God has acted in past applications of the Law. In the church of our own times where a mention of law may evoke legalism (either because of past memories or because of unimaginative enforcement by those who should be interpreting), Matthew's sensitive description of a Law-obedient or righteous Joseph may give new import to the invocation "St. Joseph."

THE "HOW" OF JESUS' IDENTITY

That Joseph should not divorce Mary was crucial in God's plan, not primarily for the sake of Mary's reputation, but for Jesus' identity. The child must be the son of Joseph, the son of David, thus fulfilling God's promise to David, "I will raise up your son after you. . . . I will make his royal throne firm forever" (2 Sam 7:12-13). The angel points to this essential element by addressing Joseph as "Son of David." Yet the most frequent question asked by modern readers is: "How can Jesus be Joseph's son if Joseph did not beget him?" Evidently, this issue disturbed Gentiles in antiquity as well, for soon it was being claimed that Mary was of the house of David, presumably in an attempt to trace Jesus' Davidic line through her. But for Judaism, as the genealogy indicates, the royal lineage of the Messiah had to be traced through a series of fathers to David. Matthew gives the answer to the modern question when Joseph is told, "She is to bear a son, and *you* are to name him Jesus." Judaism wrestled with the fact that it is easy to tell who a child's mother is, but difficult to tell who is a child's father. To establish paternity, it is not sufficient to ask the wife because she might lie about the father in order to avoid being accused of adultery. Rather the husband should give testimony since most men are reluctant to acknowledge a child unless it is their own. The Mishna *Baba Bathra* (8:6), written some 200 years after Jesus' birth, is lucidly clear: "If a man says, 'This is my son,' he is to be believed." Joseph gives such an acknowledgment by naming the child; thus he becomes the legal father of Jesus. (This is a more correct description than adoptive father or foster father.) The identity of Jesus as Son of David is in God's plan, but Joseph must give to that plan a cooperative obedience that befits a righteous man.

Christ in the Gospels of the Liturgical Year

The name that Joseph is to give the child is Jesus "because he will save his people from their sins." The sequence in chapter 2 of Matthew will show how this NT Joseph, who receives revelation in dreams and goes to Egypt to save the infant, is reliving the great epic of the OT figure named Joseph who interpreted dreams and went to Egypt, thereby saving Israel/Jacob (Gen 45:5; 50:20). That Genesis epic is continued in Exodus by the story of Moses: he escaped as an infant from the wicked pharaoh who killed male children and then returned after those who sought his life were dead (Exod 2:1-10; 4:19). Similarly, with Joseph's help, the infant Jesus escapes the wicked Herod who killed male children and is brought back to Palestine after those who sought his life are dead.[5] The name Jesus fits into this parallelism between the Matthew story of Joseph and the OT story of Joseph and Moses, for Moses' successor who completed his work by bringing Israel back to the Promised Land was also named Jesus (Joshua). In reference to the latter, the Jewish philosopher Philo, who lived in NT times, explains: "Jesus is interpreted 'salvation of the Lord'—a name for the best possible state." But Matthew's explanation of the name goes beyond this basic idea of salvation: "You shall call his name Jesus, for he will save *his people* from their sins." The latter clause is also an echo of the Moses story; for the first-century A.D. Jewish historian Josephus in his *Antiquities* (2.9.3; #216) relates that in a dream God told Moses' father that the child about to be born would ultimately "deliver the Hebrew race from their bondage in Egypt." Both Moses and Jesus are saviors of their people, but in Matthew's understanding the people of Jesus would be not only the Jewish descendants of Moses' Hebrews but all the nations (28:19). The bondage is no longer that of Egypt but of sin.

Matthew has now told us that the child in Mary's womb will through Joseph's naming be Son of David and the savior of his people. Yet there is a greater identity which Joseph must accept, but to which he cannot contribute: the child will be Emmanuel, "God with us," because Mary has conceived him through the Holy Spirit. Matthew has nothing of Luke's elaboration of this element in the annunciation to Mary (Luke 1:35): "The Holy Spirit will come upon you; the power of the Most High will overshadow you; therefore the one to be born will be called holy, Son of God." Yet the fact that the two different accounts

---

[5] Matthew 2:20 is a literal echo of Exodus 4:19.

mention conception through the Holy Spirit rather than through male generation[6] suggests that this is a most ancient phrasing, antedating both evangelists and coming from Christian tradition. The NT indicates clearly that the awesome, creative, life-giving power of the Spirit was associated with the resurrection of Jesus—God's Son who was enabled to conquer death dispenses the Spirit enabling believers to become God's children. In the Gospels the Spirit is primarily associated with the baptism of Jesus as he begins his public life of proclaiming the kingdom. But in the two infancy narratives it is related to the very beginning of Jesus' life: he is so much God's Son that God is his only Father, not through sexual intervention but through the same power of the Spirit that brought life into the world at the creation. If the genealogy of Matthew takes the story of Jesus back to Abraham, implicitly the virginal conception finds an analogy further back with Adam, the other human being whose life did not come from human generation.

In order to explain to his readers the full import of this generation by the Spirit announced in 1:20-21 ("It is by the Holy Spirit she has conceived this child; she will bear a son"), Matthew in the subsequent verses turns to the prophet Isaiah (7:14): "Behold the virgin will be with child and will give birth to a son, and they will call his name Emmanuel." Thus, there is a second name for the child beyond that of Jesus Son of David, the savior of his people; he is Emmanuel, "God with us." If this name comes through begetting by the Holy Spirit, we are not surprised in finding the name related to the post-resurrectional setting in which that Spirit functions. The risen Jesus' last words in Matthew (28:20) are, "I am *with you* always to the end of the world." The enduring presence of God's Spirit in the risen Jesus was already a reality at the conception of Jesus; what was made known by angelic revelation to Joseph, the just Jew, would be made known to all the nations until the end of the world by the apostolic preaching and teaching.

Matthew clearly rejoices to find that what God speaks through the angel fulfills what He had already spoken through the prophet. We have emphasized Matthew's sense of continuity with Israel: the names in the genealogy show continuity with the Law and the Former

---

[6] While both evangelists think that Jesus was conceived without a human father, neither concentrates on the biological aspect; the christological revelation of Jesus' identity is their concern.

Prophets (that is, those Books of the OT that we call the Pentateuch and Historical Books, extending from Genesis to the end of Kings). But the corpus of the Latter Prophets (that is, the works of the Writing Prophets) bears preeminent witness to God's plan. In chapter 2 Matthew will quote these Latter Prophets four times (Micah, Hosea, Jeremiah, and presumably Isaiah) as having referred to the places where the Messiah would accomplish his task. In this chapter, Matthew begins with a quote from Isaiah 7:14 about the Messiah's origin. He does not necessarily mean that the prophets themselves foresaw Jesus,[7] but through their words Matthew sees the divine plan. In these various quotations, Matthew's wording tends to be closer to the Greek translation of the Jewish Scriptures, known to us as the Septuagint, than to the wording of the Hebrew text—not illogically since he is writing for Greek speakers. Yet often, as here, Matthew agrees verbatim with neither Hebrew nor Greek. (In his rendering of Isaiah 7:14, the "virgin" and the future tenses agree with the Greek; the "be with child" is closer to the Hebrew; the "they will call" agrees with neither.) The evangelist's ability to move back and forth among the variants of the Scriptures has caused some to think of a Matthean school; at least such technical ability may be the mark of a scribe trained for the kingdom of heaven (13:52). To the modern mind, Matthew seems almost dishonest in picking wording that best suits his application, even to the point of adjusting the scriptural wording for a better fit.[8] But that attitude mistakenly assumes that Matthew is interpreting the Scriptures to explain Jesus, even as the Dead Sea Essenes strove to throw light on their present situation by writing commentaries on the OT Books line-by-line, word-by-word. The fact that no such commentary exists in the NT suggests that the process was the other way around: Christians interpreted Jesus who cast light on the Scriptures. The technical hermeneutical procedures were often the same whether used by Jews

[7] Some moderns are far more literalist in their hermeneutics than were the Jews of Jesus' time. The Dead Sea Essenes stated explicitly that the full meaning of their words lay beyond the comprehension of the prophets.

[8] Besides the observations made above, it should be noted that at this time, while there were sacred writings or books, there was not yet in regard to many books one fixed form of the text that was regarded as sacred. Evidently the Dead Sea group was not bothered to have the members using copies of Isaiah, for example, that had very different readings and spellings.

The Annunciation to Joseph

or by Jewish believers in Jesus, but for the latter the hermeneutical focus was different. For them the revelation in Jesus was the supreme authority even over the Scriptures.

Scholars point out that Isaiah 7:14 was addressed by the prophet to King Ahaz of Judah about an event soon to occur in Isaiah's time, over seven hundred years before Christ. But they sometimes miss the exact words of Isaiah's address which would have influenced Matthew's approach. In 7:13, the prophet speaks to the king not by personal name but as "House of David." Thus the second identity of Jesus as Emmanuel, "God with us," made evident in Isaiah, is not unrelated to the first identity as "Son of David." The prophet's words are appropriately placed by Matthew after a genealogy that led from David the King through the descendants of his house to Joseph son of David, "husband of Mary of whom was begotten Jesus, called the Christ." Matthew's insistence that "*they* will call his name Emmanuel," rather than the "she will call" of Isaiah's Hebrew or the "you will call" of the Greek rendition of Isaiah, opens the reader's vision to a wider audience, namely, the "his people" whom he saves from sin—not only those who accepted the Davidic lineage in Judea, but the nations of the world. In the chapter immediately following, those nations of the world will begin to make their appearance through their representatives, the magi from the East.

Matthew ends the annunciation with an emphasis on Joseph's compliance, illustrating the extent to which he is truly just or righteous. Joseph completed the second stage of his marriage to Mary by taking his wife to his home; and he named the child Jesus, thus acknowledging his son—the two specific commands of the angel. But Joseph went beyond the angel's command in order to fulfill the prophet's word. The angel had told Joseph that the child in Mary's womb was of the Holy Spirit, thus matching the first clause of Isaiah: "The virgin shall conceive." The prophet continued by affirming that the virgin would "bear a son"; and so we are told explicitly by Matthew that Joseph did not know Mary until she bore a son. This is Matthew's affirmation that Mary not only conceived as a virgin but remained a virgin until she gave birth. Unfortunately, some modern polemics have obscured the import of what Matthew was telling us by assuming that he was giving information implicitly about what happened after birth. Whether or not he had such information, he was not indicating it even implicitly here; his concern was with the fulfillment of the prophetic past rather

Christ in the Gospels of the Liturgical Year

than Christian disputes of subsequent centuries. Matthew's concern was with a Joseph who fulfilled every jot and tittle of the Law and the Prophets, worthily serving as a father to a son who would insist on the fulfillment of the Law and the Prophets. Concentration on that image of Joseph should be the real concern of Christians who claim to be loyal to the Scriptures.

The Annunciation to Joseph

Chapter 8

The Annunciation to Zechariah and the
Birth of the Baptist (Luke 1:5-25, 57-66, 80)

Thus far we have reflected on the two scenes that constitute chapter 1 of Matthew—scenes with which the church's liturgy begins the last week of the Advent season (December 17–23). We now turn to Luke's much longer chapter 1 with which the liturgy continues the rest of the days of that week. This chapter tells us a very different story from Matthew's chapter, alike in only a few (but very important) details, namely, that an angel announced that Mary, who was married to Joseph of the house of David, would give birth to a child conceived through the Holy Spirit and that child, the Son of God, should be named Jesus. Even in these similarities there is a major difference: the angel in Luke announces to Mary, not to Joseph as in Matthew. The rest of Luke's narrative and Luke's cast of characters is very different from Matthew's. Luke tells us of the annunciation to Zechariah informing him that his wife Elizabeth would give birth to John the Baptist, of the visitation of Mary to Elizabeth which occasions the Magnificat, and of the birth of the Baptist which occasions the Benedictus.

Yet in basic motifs and theology Matthew and Luke are quite similar despite the different stories they tell. Matthew's genealogy, which has "the origin of Jesus Christ" begin with Abraham fathering Isaac, has shown us that the story of God's action in Israel may be seen as part of the story of Jesus. Matthew's annunciation to Joseph combines clear echoes of OT patriarchal stories with NT "good news" that Jesus is not only the Messiah of the house of David but the presence of God among us. The believing acceptance of this by Joseph, the just man, illustrates how faith was combined with observance of the Law by the believing Jews who were the first to hear the good news. All these motifs will reappear, even if in a different guise, in Luke 1. Each of the two evangelists in his own way has preserved for us from very early Christian tradition insights about God's preparation for His Messiah and Son, insights that are still an essential part of the church's Advent preparation.

LUCAN STRUCTURE AND THE FUNCTION OF CHAPTER 1

To appreciate how Luke uses the annunciation of the Baptist's birth to prepare for Jesus' birth, one must first appreciate the role of the infancy narrative in the overall structure of Lucan theology; for Luke is a writer who uses structure artistically to convey his thought. No Gospel begins the story of Jesus' public ministry without telling the reader of John the Baptist. Evidently the Baptist's preceding Jesus was fixed in Christian tradition, indeed so irradicably fixed that in two of the three Gospels that begin their story before the public ministry with Jesus' first appearance on earth, the Baptist is brought back to precede that appearance as well. In John's Prologue before the light comes into the world we hear that "There was sent by God a man named John." In Luke not only does the annunciation of the Baptist's conception precede that of Jesus but the Baptist's birth (hailed by Zechariah's canticle) precedes Jesus' birth (hailed by Simeon's canticle). This carefully crafted parallelism has often been compared to a diptych painting with its two facing panels.

Luke's activity, however, goes beyond the Baptist-Jesus parallelism. His architectonic perception of God's plan divides all history into three parts: the time of the Law and the Prophets, the time of Jesus, and the time of the church—a triptych this time. Jesus is the centerpiece; beforehand the Law and the Prophets bear witness to him (Acts 13:14); afterwards the Spirit and those whom Jesus has chosen bear witness to him (Acts 1:9). The time of the Law and the Prophets is the period that Christians associate with the OT. The time of Jesus runs from the baptism to the ascension (Acts 1:21-22) and is the subject of the Gospel proper. The two are connected by the infancy narratives in Luke 1–2, the bridge chapters that open the Gospel. The time of the church's bearing witness to Jesus runs from after the coming of the Spirit at Pentecost until the message reaches the ends of the earth (Acts 1:8). The time of Jesus and the time of the church are connected by the reappearance of Jesus (who ascended on Easter Sunday night in Luke 24:51) to instruct those whom he has chosen; this is described in Acts 1–2, the bridge chapters that open Luke's second book. Both the "bridge" sections (Luke 1–2; Acts 1–2) have similar features: they begin

The Annunciation to Zechariah and the Birth of the Baptist

in Jerusalem; revelation comes from heaven in extraordinary ways; the earthly participants break forth in eloquent prophecy, as God dramatizes the coming of the Son and the coming of the Spirit. In both, characters from the material that precedes encounter characters from the material that is to follow, i.e., in Luke 1–2 characters and motifs from the Law and the Prophets encounter characters from the Gospel account of the ministry (John the Baptist and Mary); in Acts 1–2 the Jesus of the Gospel encounters the Twelve, including Peter, who are to proclaim him to the ends of the earth.

Drawing from this structure and confining ourselves to the Lucan infancy chapters, we can see that Luke's technique, while different from Matthew's, accomplishes much the same purpose. Matthew opens his first chapter with "Abraham was the father of Isaac"; as we shall see, Luke opens his first chapter with a description of Zechariah, the father of the Baptist as an Abraham-like figure. Both rehearse the story of Israel even though they choose different moments in that story to emphasize. And both anticipate the essential gospel message.

THE ANNUNCIATION AND THE BIRTH

Luke begins the annunciation of the Baptist's coming by introducing the principal human agents in the conception, Zechariah and Elizabeth, impeccably upright or just figures, even as Matthew's annunciation (1:19) described Joseph as upright or just. No other NT author even mentions the Baptist's parents or suggests that he was the son of a priest, or related to Jesus. While for some of these details Luke may be drawing on historical tradition, he is primarily interested in the symbolism of what he narrates. Several OT parents were barren but made capable of childbearing by divine intervention, even as Elizabeth is; but in only one OT instance were both parents also incapacitated by age, as Zechariah and Elizabeth are, namely, Abraham and Sarah, so prominent in Genesis, the first book of the Law. That Luke intends a parallelism between the two sets of parents is made clear by Zechariah's response to the angel after hearing the news of the conception: "How am I to know this?" (Luke 1:18), a verbatim quotation from Abraham's response to divine revelation in Genesis 15:8. Also Elizabeth's rejoicing with her neighbors who hear the good news (1:58) echoes Sarah's rejoicing with all who hear her good news (Gen 21:6).

Luke's artistry goes further, however. Zechariah and Elizabeth are portrayed as similar to another pair of OT parents whose yearning for a child was answered by God, namely, Elkanah and Hannah, the parents of Samuel. Indeed the opening of the Lucan story in 1:5, "There was a certain priest named Zechariah . . . he had a wife . . . and her name was Elizabeth," reminds us strongly of the opening of 1 Samuel 1:1-2: "There was a certain man . . . whose name was Elkanah . . . and he had two wives; the name of one was Hannah." The revelation to Hannah that she would give birth to Samuel came through the priest Eli during the annual visit to the sanctuary to offer sacrifice (1 Sam 1:3, 17), even as the forthcoming birth is revealed to the priest Zechariah in the sanctuary of the Jerusalem Temple. In both stories the child to be born would drink neither wine nor strong drink (Luke 1:15; 1 Sam 1:9-15) and thus be a Nazirite dedicated to the Lord (Num 6:1-21). The Magnificat of Luke 1:46-55 is strongly evocative of Hannah's canticle of 1 Samuel 2:1-10.[1] If the story of Abraham and Sarah belongs to the Law, the story of Samuel belongs to the Prophets.[2] Reminiscences of the Law (Leviticus) are again found in the setting of the annunciation of the Baptist's conception, namely, the priestly offering of incense; and the prophetic theme is continued when Zechariah speaks prophetically in Luke 1:67, and implicitly in the description of the future Baptist as Elijah in 1:17, which echoes Malachi 3:1, 23-24 (RSV 3:1; 4:5-6), the last of the prophetic writings.

The Lucan technique of echoing the Scriptures of Israel is continued even more dramatically in the appearance of the angel who identifies himself as Gabriel. After the Law and the Prophets in the collection of canonical Scriptures come the Writings, one of which was the Book of Daniel.[3] Only in that OT book does Gabriel make an appearance. In both Luke (1:22) and Daniel (six times in chapters 9–10) the appearance is called a vision. In both (Luke 1:10-11, Dan 9:20-21) Gabriel comes at the time of liturgical prayer to a figure who has been praying in distress (Luke 1:13; Dan 9:20). In both the visionary becomes afraid, is told not to fear, and eventually is struck mute (Luke 1:12-13, 20, 22;

---

[1] The parallelism to the Samuel story is continued in Luke 2 as Jesus is presented in the Temple and in the greeting given him by a figure named Hannah/Anna.

[2] Most of the "Historical Books" of the Christian Bible were considered "Former Prophets" in Jewish terminology.

[3] In the Hebrew Scriptures, unlike the Christian OT, Daniel is not classified as a Book of Prophecy. Luke 24:44 shows consciousness of further writings beyond the Law and the Prophets.

The Annunciation to Zechariah and the Birth of the Baptist

Dan 10:8, 12, 15). There can be little doubt, then, that Luke intends us to see a parallelism between Gabriel's appearance to Daniel and his appearance to Zechariah. We have seen Zechariah described in language reminiscent of Abraham, the first of the patriarchs, who is described in the first book of the Hebrew Scriptures. Now he encounters Gabriel, the angel of the endtime, who interprets the seventy weeks of years—that panoramic description of God's final plan in the last part of which "everlasting justice will be introduced, vision and prophecy will be ratified, and a Holy of Holies will be anointed." (Luke probably understood the Greek of this last phrase in Daniel 9:24 in terms of a *christos*, an anointed one or messiah.) Gabriel is described in a book that belongs to the last portion of the Hebrew Scriptures and indeed, perhaps, was the last book of the collection to be written. Matthew may be more methodical in his genealogy by proceeding from Abraham to the time of the Messiah, but in his allusive way Luke has covered the same span in this encounter between Zechariah/Abraham and Gabriel, the final messenger who brings the years of history to a close. Both authors have covered the span of God's dealing with Israel down to the last times.

The child to be born is an appropriate figure in this eschatological context: John the Baptist who "will go before the Lord in the spirit and power of Elijah to turn the hearts of the fathers to the children . . . to make ready for the Lord a prepared people." Luke (16:16) expresses his view of the Baptist in a famous saying of Jesus: "The Law and the Prophets were until John; since then the kingdom of God is preached." We have seen that these infancy chapters of Luke are a bridge between the time of the Law and the Prophets and the time of Jesus' proclamation of the kingdom. As part of that bridge the Baptist's parents, parallel to Abraham and Sarah and to the parents of Samuel, belong to the Law and the Prophets, observing all the commandments and ordinances of the Law (1:6) and prophesying themselves (1:41, 67). But the Baptist belongs to the time of Jesus. Consequently, the child is described in language anticipatory of the descriptions of him found in the Gospel accounts of Jesus' public ministry. Indeed the communication about his conception is described as proclaiming the good news or gospel in 1:19. If Luke 1:15a promises that the Baptist "will be great," this anticipates Jesus' description of him in Luke 7:28, "Among those born of women, none is greater than John." That the child will be "before the Lord" (1:15b) anticipates 7:27, "Behold, I send my messenger before your face who will prepare your way ahead of you" (even if the Greek vocabulary differs slightly). The prediction in 1:15b that the Baptist "will drink no wine or strong drink" is an adaptation of the tradition in 7:33: "John the Baptist has come eating no bread and drinking no wine." The promise that the child "will be filled with the Holy Spirit even from his mother's womb" is the initial step of what will culminate in 3:2: "The word of God came to John, the son of Zechariah, in the desert." (To appreciate the full force of the two descriptions one should compare the alternation of spirit and word in biblical vocations, e.g., Isa 61:1 and 2:1; Joel 3:1 [RSV 2:28] and 1:1.)[4] In short, Luke knows of the Baptist from the traditions of Jesus' ministry, and he has anticipated this information in the annunciation of the conception of the Baptist. This illustrates my contention that in the Lucan infancy narratives there are OT figures (Zechariah and Elizabeth) and Gospel figures (the Baptist) encountering each other in order to bridge the two periods of God's salvific action.

The immediate aftermath of the annunciation draws out further the symbolism of that scene. We are told that, struck mute (like Daniel), Zechariah went to his home and afterwards Elizabeth conceived, a description that echoes the behavior of the parents of Samuel: "Then they went to their home . . . and in due time Hannah conceived" (1 Sam 1:19-20). Elizabeth's reaction (Luke 1:25), "The Lord has dealt with me in this way," is reminiscent of 1 Samuel's description of Hannah: "The Lord remembered her." The taking away of Elizabeth's "disgrace" reminds us of Rachel's reaction to conception in Genesis 30:23, "God has taken away my disgrace." (The visitation of Mary to Elizabeth and Elizabeth's praise of Mary really belong more to the annunciation of the conception of Jesus and will be discussed in relation to that scene.) The actual birth of the Baptist is described by Luke with surprising brevity in 1:57-58. The rejoicing of the neighbors when they hear echoes the rejoicing of all who hear of Sarah's giving birth (Gen 21:6).

More attention is concentrated on the naming of the Baptist. Zechariah had been struck mute following the angel's annunciation because

---

[4] The promise that the Baptist will "turn the hearts of the fathers to the children" quotes the description of Elijah in Malachi 3:24 (RSV 4:6), but it may have been influenced by Gospel sayings pertinent to the Baptist which speak of father and/or children (Luke 3:8; 7:31-33).

The Annunciation to Zechariah and the Birth of the Baptist

he had not believed (1:20); now his obedience in wanting the child to be named John as the angel commissioned shows that indeed he has believed; consequently, his muteness is relieved. The marvelous coincidence that Elizabeth also chooses the name John, even though there is no one in the family with that name, is a further sign that the hand of the Lord was with the child (1:66). The miracle, like the miracles of Jesus in the ministry, provokes awe and wonder. The statement that "as the child grew up, he became strong in spirit" (1:80) and "the hand of the Lord was with him" (1:66) are final reminiscences of the Abraham-Sarah and the parents-of-Samuel stories. After the birth and circumcision of Isaac, the child born to Abraham and Sarah, we are told, "The child grew up" (Gen 21:8), and of Samuel we hear, "The child grew strong before the Lord" (1 Sam 2:21).[5] The last sentence of this chapter (Luke 1:80), "He stayed in the desert until the day of his public appearance to Israel," is Luke's final artistic touch in developing the bridge aspect of the story—it connects to 3:2, "The word of God came to John, the son of Zechariah, in the desert."

Thus far there has been nothing said about Zechariah's canticle, the Benedictus. I shall devote the next essay to that magnificent poem and to the Lucan canticles in general.

---

[5] See also the Samson story in Judges 13:24-25 (Greek): "The child became mature and the Lord blessed him, and the Spirit of the Lord began to go with him."

Christ in the Gospels of the Liturgical Year

Chapter 9

The Benedictus (Luke 1:67-79)

In the Lucan infancy narrative there are four canticles (hymns or psalms): in chapter 1, the Benedictus and the Magnificat, which are read in the Gospels of the last week of Advent; in chapter 2 the Gloria in Excelsis and the Nunc Dimittis, which are read in the Gospels of the Christmas season. Of course, the church's liturgical use of these canticles is far wider since three of them are prominent in the daily Divine Office, and an expanded form of the Gloria is part of the Mass. For that reason let me comment in general on all four before I turn to the Benedictus. While I shall treat them together, the Gloria is so brief that only by analogy can we guess that its origin may be the same as that of the others. Let me note, however, the fact that the Gloria is spoken by angels while the others are spoken by human beings is not an important difference. The Gloria may have been structured antiphonally, with one set of lines now assigned to the angels:

> "Glory in the highest heavens to God,
> and on earth peace to those favored (by Him),"

while the other set of lines was assigned to the disciples as Jesus enters Jerusalem in Luke 19:38:

> "Peace in heaven,
> and glory in the highest heavens."

THE ORIGIN OF THE LUCAN CANTICLES

Although in the infancy narrative Luke has various characters speak these canticles, modern scholarship has moved away from thinking that they were respectively the historical compositions of Mary, Zechariah, or Simeon (or, a fortiori, of angels). They have an overall common style and a poetic polish that militate against such individual, on-the-spot composition. Indeed, in several of the canticles there are individual lines that do not fit the situation of the putative spokesperson. For example, how has Mary's conception "scattered the proud in the imagination of their hearts," "filled the hungry with good things," and "sent the rich away empty" (lines from the Magnificat)? How does the birth of the Baptist constitute "salvation from our enemies and from the hand of all those who hate us" (Benedictus)? Accordingly most scholars think that the canticles had a common origin and were adapted and inserted into the infancy narrative.

Some think that the evangelist himself composed them, but then one might have expected a greater uniformity among the canticles and a smoother fit into their present context. (If the Magnificat, Benedictus, and Nunc Dimittis [and the line that leads into each] were omitted from their present context, no one would even suspect that there was anything missing.[1]) More scholars, therefore, think that substantially the canticles came from a pre-Lucan source and were taken over by the evangelist and inserted into their present places. I say "substantially" because there are Lucan additions to make them fit their context. For instance, Luke may have added 1:48 to the Magnificat,

> "Because He has regarded the low estate of His handmaid—for behold, henceforth all generations will call me fortunate."

That verse echoes language that Luke has already used of Mary in 1:38, 42, and thus helps to make the canticle appropriate on her lips. Similarly in the Benedictus verses 76-77 may well be a Lucan addition to make the canticle appropriate to the birth of John the Baptist (cf. Luke 1:17; 3:4; 7:27):

> "But you, child, will be prophet of the Most High,
> for you will go before the Lord to make ready His ways,
> to grant His people knowledge of salvation
> in the forgiveness of their sins."

What was the source from which Luke drew these canticles if he did not compose them himself? There is no doubt whatever that they represent Jewish hymnic style and thought of the general period from 200 B.C. to A.D. 100, as illustrated in 1 Maccabees, Judith, 2 *Baruch*, 4 *Ezra*, and the Dead Sea (Qumran) *War Scroll* and *Thanksgiving Psalms*. The dominant stylistic pattern is that of a cento or mosaic pattern

---

[1] For instance, 1:56 reads very smoothly following 1:45; 1:80 smoothly following 1:66. Greater effort was made by the evangelist in incorporating the canticles of chapter 2 in the flow of the narrative.

where almost every phrase and line is taken from the earlier poetry of Israel, i.e., the Psalms, the Prophets, and hymns in the Pentateuch and the Historical Books. In my *Birth of the Messiah* (2d ed.; Garden City: Doubleday, 1993) I supplied whole pages of OT poetic background for each line of the Magnificat (355–65), the Benedictus (377–92), and the Nunc Dimittis (456–60). Let me give one illustration here from the opening of the Benedictus (Luke 1:68-69):

> "Blessed be the Lord, the God of Israel,
> because He has visited
> and accomplished the redemption of His people,
> and has raised up for us a horn of salvation
> in the house of David His servant."

In Psalm 41:14(13) and in other psalm passages we find: "Blessed be the Lord, the God of Israel." Psalm 111:9 says that God "sent redemption to His people," while Judges 3:9 states, "The Lord raised up a Saviour for Israel." Psalm 132:17 has God saying, "I shall make a horn to sprout for David," a statement similar to the motif in Ezekiel 29:21: "On that day I shall make a horn sprout for all the house of Israel." In a Jewish prayer contemporary with the Lucan Benedictus (the Fifteenth Benediction of the *Shemoneh Esreh*) we find a similar mosaic, "Let the shoot of David (Your servant) speedily spring up and raise his horn in Your salvation. . . . May you be blessed, O Lord, who lets the horn of salvation flourish."

So Jewish are the Lucan canticles that some scholars have thought that the evangelist took them over from a collection that had nothing to do with Jesus Christ. There is, however, a particular tone of divine salvation *accomplished* and (in the Benedictus) an emphasis on the house of David that would not be readily explicable from the non-Christian Jewish history of this period. The non-Christian Jewish hymns that offer the best parallels to the Benedictus and the Magnificat are prayers yearning for salvation. True, the Maccabean victories of the second century b.c. might have prompted songs of deliverance, but that deliverance would not be described as Davidic, for the Maccabee leaders were levitical priests. Thus the probability is that we are dealing with Jewish Christian hymns celebrating the salvific action of God in Jesus, the Messiah.

Indeed, the tendency has been to speak of the hymns of a Jewish-Christian *community*; for, despite the overall similar style, there are enough differences among the canticles to make us posit different

The Benedictus

authors with the same background. The "we" of the Benedictus and the latter part of the Magnificat ("our fathers") reflect the spokespersons of a collectivity. More particularly attempts have been made to derive the canticles from a group within Israel of Christian "Poor Ones" (*Anawim*): those who, in part, were physically poor but more widely would not trust their own strength and had to rely totally on God for deliverance—the lowly, the sick, the downtrodden. Their praises are sung in Psalm 149:4: "The Lord takes pleasure in His people; He adorns the Poor Ones with victory." Certainly the Dead Sea *Thanksgiving Hymns* have this ambiance, "You, O Lord, have assisted the soul of the Poor Ones and the needy against one who is strong. You have redeemed my soul from the hand of the mighty." The Magnificat, in particular, would fit such a background, with its lines, "He has exalted those of low degree; He has filled the hungry with good things."

This proposed background has been made even more specific by those scholars who think of a community of Jewish Christian Poor Ones *at Jerusalem*. In Acts 2:43-47; 4:32-37, Luke pays particular attention to the first Jewish believers in Jesus in that city, describing them as people who sold their possessions and gave their wealth to be distributed to the needy. His description of these Poor Ones borders on nostalgia and may well be idealized, but Paul's collection of money for the Jerusalem church, often mentioned in his letters (see also Gal 2:10), shows there was a historical basis for the picture Luke describes. Acts also stresses the Temple piety of the Jerusalem Jewish Christians: "They went to the Temple together every day" (2:46; 3:1). Certainly such a context is that of Simeon to whom the Nunc Dimittis is attributed and also that of Zechariah, the priestly spokesman of the Benedictus.[2]

To be exact, however, such specificities (Poor Ones, at Jerusalem, with Temple piety) are shrewd speculations about the origins of the canticles, and they cannot be proved. Sometimes they are tied in with another, even more unprovable, thesis that the canticles were translated into Greek from Hebrew or Aramaic, presumably the language of the first Christians. For our purposes it is better to be content with the simple probability that the canticles are (from a collection of?) the

---

[2] Although Acts' description does not say that the Jerusalem Christians sang hymns, 2:47 speaks of their praising God, and technically the canticles of the infancy narrative are to be categorized as hymns of praise.

hymns of an early Jewish Christian group[3] without being more specific. Thus the church's frequent and sometimes daily use of them in the liturgy recovers their origin in the sense that we are reciting the words that our most ancient ancestors in the faith used as community praise of God.

Has Luke done violence if, as we theorize, he has taken over these canticles and placed them on the lips of infancy narrative figures like Mary, Zechariah, and Simeon? To the contrary, his insight is most appropriate: If these were the hymns of early Jewish Christians, they now appear in the Gospel on the lips of the first Jewish believers in the good news about John the Baptist and Jesus.[4] Going beyond this general connaturality, Luke has skillfully made his canticles match the spokespersons, often following leads in the narrative. In 1:40 we are told that Mary greeted Elizabeth, but no words are reported; the insertion of the Magnificat (1:46-55) supplies her with words that (as we shall see) are most appropriate. In the narrative (1:64) we read that Zechariah began to speak in praise of God, but again no words are recorded; the insertion of the Benedictus in 1:68-79 supplies that praise of God. That the spokespersons are different is also respected. The beginning of the Magnificat echoes the opening of Hannah's hymn in 1 Samuel 2:1-2 (Greek: "My heart is strengthened in the Lord; my horn is exalted in my God . . . I delight in Your salvation"). The appropriateness goes beyond the same gender of the speakers; Hannah's canticle is in the context of having given birth to her firstborn son, while Mary has just conceived her firstborn. As we shall see, although the Magnificat is a mosaic of OT words and themes, some of the lines also anticipate Jesus' Beatitudes in Luke's account of the ministry. Such a reaching forward is appropriate on Mary's lips because she is a Gospel-ministry figure who has been brought back to Luke's "bridge" chapters of the infancy narrative. She encounters OT figures like Zechariah and Simeon whose canticles do not have such clear anticipations of Gospel wording.

---

[3] "Early," not only because they are pre-Lucan, but also because their christology is phrased entirely in OT language, unlike the developed hymns we find in post-50 Christian writing.

[4] As I pointed out, the appropriateness is enhanced if the Jewish Christian authors were "Poor Ones" with lives of Temple piety: Mary is a Poor One, and Zechariah and Simeon are exemplary of Temple piety.

The Benedictus

After these general remarks on the origin and the placing of the canticles in Luke 1–2, let me turn more specifically to the canticle that greets the conception and birth of John the Baptist and thus constitutes the sequence to the preceding essay.

THE BENEDICTUS AND EARLY JEWISH CHRISTIAN CHRISTOLOGY

To accompany this discussion I have supplied a translation,[5] incorporating the analysis and division I deem most plausible. (Other scholars favor a slightly different division, but the differences would not really affect our discussion here.) In the classification of hymns that was developed for analyzing the OT psalms, the Benedictus would most closely resemble a hymn of praise; and it does begin with the praise of the God of Israel. Clearly, the Jewish Christians who composed this canticle thought of themselves as continuing to belong to Israel. This same blessing of the God of Israel occurs at the end of three sections or "books" of the psalter, a work attributed to David (Pss 41:14 [13]; 72:18; 106:48), but also in 1 Kings 1:48 on the lips of David after Solomon's enthronization. That is appropriate, for the Jewish Christian authors of the canticle are praising what God has done in the last anointed king of David's lineage.

The original messianic reference of the canticle is retained even after Luke has placed it in the context of the Baptist's birth. Although Zechariah is praising God for his child, the lines that Luke has inserted in reference to that child (1:76-77: the Lucan adaptation of the canticle) will make clear that the salvific action for Israel comes not from the Baptist but from the Lord before whom the Baptist only prepares the way.[6] The subordination of the Baptist to the implicit main subject of the canticle, i.e., the messianic agent of God, is further indicated by where Luke places the inserted verses 76-77 pertinent to the Baptist. They do not stand at the end lest they appear to be the culmination of the praise; they stand before a final poetic description (78-79) of the

---

[5] Taken from my *Birth of the Messiah*, 2d ed., 367–68.

[6] Probably Luke's use of "the Lord" is deliberately ambiguous: in his own lifetime the Baptist thought he was preparing for the direct intervention of the Lord God of Israel, but the one who came after the Baptist was Jesus, child of Mary, whom Elizabeth lauded in 1:43 as "the mother of my Lord."

Christ in the Gospels of the Liturgical Year

THE BENEDICTUS

(Luke 1:68-79)

Introductory Praise
[68a] "Blessed be the Lord, the God of Israel:

First Strophe
[68b] Because He has visited
[68c] and accomplished the redemption of His people,
[69a] and has raised up for us a horn of salvation
[69b] in the house of David His servant,
[70] as He spoke by the mouth of His holy prophets from of old:
[71a] salvation from our enemies
[71b] and from the hand of all those who hate us,

Second Strophe
[72a] Showing mercy to our fathers
[72b] and remembering His holy covenant,
[73] the oath which He swore to our father Abraham,
to grant us [74]that, without fear,
delivered from the hands of our enemies,
we might serve Him [75]in holiness and justice,
before Him all the days of our lives.

Lucan Insertion
[76a] *But you, child, will be called prophet of the Most High;*
[76b] *for you will go before the Lord to make ready His ways,*
[77a] *to grant to His people knowledge of salvation*
[77b] *in the forgiveness of their sins.*

Conclusion
[78a] Through the heartfelt mercy of our God
[78b] by which there has visited us a rising light from on high,
[79a] appearing to those who sat in darkness and the shadow of death,
[79b] guiding our feet into the way of peace."

"rising light from on high"[7] who embodies "the heartfelt mercy of our God." Always the proper sequence must be kept: the Baptist did not constitute an end in himself, for as John 1:8 will insist: "He was not the light, but came to bear witness to the light." The Baptist is mentioned before Jesus, but Jesus is the one who guides out from darkness and death (Luke 1:79)—the work of the Messiah in the salvific action of God.

This salvific action, which supplies the motive for the praise of the God of Israel in the canticle, is described in the two strophes that constitute its body. These strophes are of approximately the same length and have similar structure. Each begins with what God has done by way of mercy and redemption for His people, "our fathers"; and each then proceeds to describe how this has been done for "us," filling promises respectively to David and to Abraham. We recall that the Matthean genealogy spoke of "Jesus Christ, Son of David, Son of Abraham." Matthew himself may have put together the elements of that genealogy, but he derived from Christian tradition the importance of those two ancestors who symbolized not only the special Jewish descent (David) of Jesus but also his wider reach (Paul uses Abraham to make the Gentiles sharers in the promises of God fulfilled in Jesus). Thus the Benedictus and the genealogy express in different ways an important common theme in the preparation for the coming of Jesus.

The first strophe indicates that the messianic inheritance from David was anticipated by the prophets (2 Samuel [chapter 7] was a prophetic book), while the second strophe connects Abraham with the covenant. The fulfillment of the Prophets and the Law is a motif that we have already seen in the Lucan infancy narrative. Notice that the salvific action is described in the two strophes in past (aorist) tenses,[8] even though in the flow of the narrative Christ, the Lord, has not yet been born at Bethlehem. That is intelligible, for Jewish Christians composed

---

[7] This is the Greek word *anatolē* which is used in Zechariah 3:8; 6:12 to translate the Hebrew references to the Davidic "branch" or "shoot." It is the same word used in Matthew 2:2 in the description of "His star at its *rising*," the star that signals the birth of the King of the Jews.

[8] The manuscripts do not agree whether to read an aorist or a future form in the key verb of the conclusion, thus "visited" or "will visit" in 1:78. I prefer the aorist, thinking that the scribes have conformed this description of Jesus to the future tenses that precede in the inserted description of the Baptist (1:76-77).

Christ in the Gospels of the Liturgical Year

the canticle after the resurrection when all this had already happened and the Messiah had come. In the infancy narrative context Zechariah is described as uttering a prophecy (1:67), and the past tenses show the surety of that prophetic view of what the Messiah would accomplish.

One may call the Benedictus a christological hymn since it concerns the Messiah, the "horn of salvation" (1:69; cf. Hannah's canticle in 1 Sam 2:10: "the horn of His anointed" [= Messiah, Christ]). Yet it is very different from the christological hymns we find in the Pauline and Johannine traditions, which spell out the human career of Jesus. For instance a hymn that Paul quotes in Philippians 2:6-11 speaks of Jesus' origins, his humble life as a servant, his obedient death on the cross, and his exaltation. The Johannine Prologue hymn (John 1:1-18) speaks of his coming into the world, being rejected by his own, and manifesting his glory. The Benedictus, however, describes the messianic salvation entirely in OT terms without appealing to any event in Jesus' life. One cannot explain that phenomenon simply from the fact that in the narrative context in which Luke has placed the canticle none of the events of Jesus' life had yet taken place, for Luke did not hesitate to insert references to what the Baptist would do. Rather, in the Benedictus and in the other Lucan canticles (for the same phenomenon is true of them), we are hearing very early Christian christology that did not require and perhaps had not yet acquired a peculiarly Christian vocabulary—*perhaps the oldest preserved Christian prayers of praise* wherein Jewish believers expressed themselves entirely in the language of their ancestors. I have sometimes asked Jews of today who believe in the coming of a personal messiah whether, if someone whom they considered as worthy of that title were to come, they could recite the Benedictus (without the inserted Lucan verses 76-77). None of them found it alien language. Such an insight shows how appropriate is the use of the Benedictus as an Advent Gospel reading. This is the season where we relive the story of Israel and its expectations; we who believe that this story is encapsulated in Jesus and those expectations are fulfilled in him praise God in the language of Israel when we recite the Benedictus.

The Benedictus

Chapter 10

The Annunciation to Mary, the Visitation, and the Magnificat (Luke 1:26-56)

Of all the scenes that the church uses in the Advent liturgy, these Lucan episodes would be best known to Christians. And certainly this is the annunciation par excellence, far more famous than the annunciations to Joseph and to Zechariah. This is the annunciation that has been taken up so frequently in theology, spirituality, art, and literature. Seeking necessarily to be selective amidst the wealth of material offered by these scenes, I have chosen as best fitting the Advent motif of this section the Lucan presentation of Mary as a model disciple in receiving and reacting to the Gospel message. In this emphasis, however, a caution is necessary. Some scholars, mostly Catholic, have wished to rename this scene the calling of Mary as if its primary message was about her. I reject that firmly: The primary message is centered on the conception of Jesus as Messiah and God's Son and what he will accomplish by way of salvation for those who depend on God. Nevertheless, exhibiting true Christian instinct that the gospel is not good *news* unless there is someone to hear it, Luke presents Mary as the first to hear and accept it and then to proclaim it. Thus he holds her up as the first and model disciple.[1] The vocation of the disciple is not the primary message of the scene, but a necessary corollary and one that well serves our Advent motif.

In discussing Mary's discipleship we should be aware that we know very little about the psychology and personal feelings of the historical Mary;[2] yet here Luke gives us our strongest NT evidence for the mas-

---

[1] It is worth noting that this is not a peculiarly Catholic view. It was clearly advocated by the Finnish Lutheran scholar, H. Räisänen; and it has been accepted from him by the ecumenical study *Mary in the New Testament*, ed. R. E. Brown, et al. (New York: Paulist, 1978).

[2] See above in chapter 5 for some general remarks on historical problems.

sively important fact that she was a disciple of Jesus. How important that is can be appreciated when we realize that one could not derive it from Mark. That Gospel clearly distinguishes between Mary (accompanied by Jesus' brothers or male relatives) on the one hand and his disciples on the other hand, with only the latter placed in the context of doing the will of God (Mark 3:31-35). Mark has a deprecatory attitude toward Jesus' family who think he is beside himself and do not honor him (3:21; 6:4). Even Matthew, who knows that Mary conceived Jesus through the Holy Spirit and so excises the deprecatory statements of Mark about the family, never clarifies that Mary became a disciple. Only John exhibits the same positive view as Luke on this question of specifically bringing Jesus' mother into the family of disciples; for he describes Jesus as constituting her to be the mother of the disciple whom he loves (the model disciple) and thus gives her a shared preeminence in discipleship. Reflecting on the role of Mary as a preeminent disciple was probably a second-stage development in NT thought. After Christians had reflected on the mystery of Jesus, they turned to reflect on how he impinged on those who were close to him physically and then included that reflection in the "good news."[3]

THE ANNUNCIATION

Following the same format he used to introduce the annunciation to Zechariah, Luke introduces this scene with notes on time, place, and the primary characters. The time (the sixth month, i.e., of Elizabeth's pregnancy) helps to call the reader's attention to the relationship between the two annunciations. For the previous annunciation, the place was Jerusalem and the heritage was priestly—circumstances befitting OT characters like Zechariah and Elizabeth. In this annunciation the place is Nazareth in Galilee and the heritage is Davidic—circumstances befitting Gospel characters like Mary and Joseph intimately involved with Jesus, whose public ministry will be in Galilee and who is the Messiah of the house of David.[4]

---

[3] Written earlier than Luke or John, Mark is very christologically focused and does not include in its scope this wider understanding of the gospel.

[4] Interestingly, despite their very different annunciations of Jesus' birth, Matthew and Luke agree on the status and situation of the parents: Joseph is of the house of David; Mary is a virgin; yet they are married—both use the less customary verb *mnēsteuein* to describe this marriage where the principals do not yet live together

The Annunciation to Mary, the Visitation, and the Magnificat

A close comparison of the introductions to the two Lucan annunciations reveals an even more significant difference between them. Zechariah and Elizabeth in their piety have been yearning for a child, so that the conception of the Baptist was in part God's answer to Zechariah's prayers (Luke 1:13); but Mary is a virgin who has not yet been intimate with her husband, so that what happens is not a response to her yearning but a surprise initiative by God that neither Mary nor Joseph could have anticipated. The Baptist's conception, while a gift of God, involved an act of human intercourse. Mary's conception involves a divine creative action without human intercourse; it is the work of the overshadowing Spirit, that same Spirit that hovered at the creation of the world when all was void (Gen 1:2; see p. 66 above). When one compares the Gabriel-Zechariah and Gabriel-Mary dialogues, there is a similarity of format, flowing from the set pattern of annunciations of birth that one can find in the OT accounts of the births of Ishmael, Isaac, and Samson,[5] and that also appears in Matthew's annunciation of Jesus' birth. Nevertheless, despite similarities, throughout Luke underlines the uniqueness of Jesus who, even in conception and birth, is greater than the Baptist (Luke 3:16).

Worthy of note is Gabriel's addressing Mary in 1:28 as "Favored One." This has the connotation of being especially graced, whence the Latin translation that gave rise to the "full of grace." The favor or grace that Mary "has found with God" (1:30) is explained in 1:31 in future terms: She will conceive and give birth to Jesus. The address "Favored One" anticipates that future favor with certitude, but it also corresponds to a status that Mary has already enjoyed. The one whom God has chosen for the conception of His Son is one who has already enjoyed

---

(note 2, p. 60). Luke pays less attention than Matthew, however, to how Jesus would have David lineage when Joseph did not beget him; see pp. 64–65.

[5] Genesis 16:7-12; chapters 17–18; Judges 13:3-20. In the pattern the appearance of (an angel of) the Lord leads the visionary to fear or prostration. Then the heavenly messenger addresses the visionary, usually by name, sometimes with an added phrase pertinent to the visionary's role, and urges, "Do not fear." The message is that the future mother is or will be with child to whom she will give birth—a child who is to be named X (sometimes with an explanatory etymology) and whose accomplishments will be Y. The visionary poses an objection as to how this can be, sometimes asking for a sign. Some of these features, plus others pertinent to Luke's annunciation, are found in angelic annunciations of vocation, e.g., of Moses in Exodus 3:2-12; of Gideon in Judges 6:12-23.

His grace by the way she has lived. Her discipleship, as we shall see, comes into being when she says yes to God's will about Jesus; but such readiness is possible for her because by God's grace she has said yes to Him before. Thus Mary's discipleship does not exhibit conversion but consistency. The same may be true for many of us at those unique moments when we are conscious of being invited to say yes to God's will in something important.

The heart of the annunciation to Mary concerns the twofold identity of Jesus, the child to be conceived—an identity that was also central in Matthew's annunciation to Joseph. The identity of the Messiah as the Son of David goes back in Jewish thought to 2 Samuel 7 where Nathan promises David that he will have an enduring line of descendants who will rule over Israel forever. Luke makes this explicit in 1:32-33 by having Gabriel quote that promise from 2 Samuel in a slightly rephrased manner (evidently customary at this time as we can see in the Dead Sea Scrolls). The following comparison of the wording shows this:

> Luke 1:
> [32a] "He will be great and will be called Son of the Most High.
> [32b] And the Lord God will give him the throne of his father David;
> [33a] and he will be king over the house of Jacob forever,
> [33b] and there will be no end to his kingdom."
>
> 2 Samuel 7:
> [9] "I shall make for you a *great* name . . .
> [13] I shall establish *the throne of his kingdom forever*.
> [14] I shall be his father, and he will be *my son* . . .
> [16] And your *house* and your *kingdom* will be made sure *forever*."

Mary's questioning response (stereotypic of such annunciations), "How can this be?" and her insistence that she has not had relations with a man allow Gabriel to explain God's role and thus highlight the other half of Jesus' identity. He is not only Son of David, he is Son of God (1:35):

> "The Holy Spirit will come upon you and power from the Most High will overshadow you. Therefore, the child to be born will be called holy—Son of God."

This is not the language of OT prophecy but of NT preaching. In chapter 5 of this book I noted how set elements of a description of Jesus as Son of God were reused in various parts of the NT in reference to

The Annunciation to Mary, the Visitation, and the Magnificat

different aspects of Jesus' career (his parousia, resurrection, baptism, and now his conception) as part of the essential task of proclaiming who he was. The Pauline phraseology in Romans 1:3-4, which Paul knew from earlier preaching, is particularly close to Luke's presentation of Jesus' twofold identity in the annunciation:

> "Born of the seed of David according to the flesh; designated Son of God in power according to the Holy Spirit."

Thus, in revealing to Mary the identity of Jesus, Gabriel is speaking both the language of the OT prophets about the Son of David and the language of the NT preachers about the Son of God—language that Paul in Romans specifically calls "gospel." Thus it is no exaggeration to say that for Luke Mary has heard the gospel of Jesus Christ, and indeed is the first one to have done so.

In all of this Luke has anticipated a christological terminology that is appropriate to Jesus' ministry and beyond. He continues that anticipation in describing Mary's basic response to the gospel she has heard. In the common tradition of Jesus' ministry shared by the first three Gospels, Mary appears in only one scene (Mark 3:31-35; Matthew 12:46-50; Luke 8:19-21). That scene interprets the relationship of Jesus' natural family to his disciples by having Jesus define family, not in terms of physical descent, but in terms of accepting his gospel about God: "Whoever does the will of God is my brother, and sister, and mother" (Mark 3:35) or, more pertinently, in the Lucan form, "My mother and my brothers are those who hear the word of God and do it" (Luke 8:21). When in the annunciation Luke reports Mary's answer, "Let it be done to me according to your word," he is describing not only one who is consenting to be the physical mother of Jesus but also and very importantly one who meets Jesus' criterion for his family of disciples—indeed the first one.

Read in Advent, Luke's message in this annunciation is as pertinent as when he first wrote it. We Christians must be very clear as to what we believe about the identity of the one to be born at Christmas. He is not just the Prince of Peace, the title that even noncommittal media commentators are willing to give him. He is the Messiah of the house of David, embodying in himself all that rich OT background that these Advent passages have evoked again and again. Beyond that he is the unique Son of God, the very presence of God with us. Anything less is not the gospel, and assent to anything less will not make us disciples.

Christ in the Gospels of the Liturgical Year

And assent to that double identity is not just an intellectual assent; it involves being willing to hear Jesus' proclamation of God's will and doing it.

As part of the annunciation, Gabriel tells Mary (1:36-37), "Your relative Elizabeth, despite her old age, has also conceived a son; indeed, this is the sixth month for a woman who was deemed barren. Nothing said by God can be impossible."[6] That verse prepares for the visitation of Mary to Elizabeth, which brings together the mothers affected by the two annunciations. Accordingly, when Luke tells us (1:39) that, after the angel departed, Mary arose and went hastily into the hill country of Judea to the house of Zechariah, he is not describing simply her eagerness to see her relative. Precisely because the angel spoke of Elizabeth's pregnancy as part of the plan of God, Mary's haste reflects her obedience to that plan.

Elizabeth's prophetic greeting is of interest in Luke's portrait of Mary's discipleship. During the public ministry a woman in the crowd will shout out a blessing (macarism) in praise of Jesus: "Fortunate is the womb that bore you and the breasts you sucked" (11:27—a scene peculiar to Luke). This is a very Jewish blessing echoing the sentiment of Deuteronomy 28:1, 4 where a benediction was promised to Israel if it would be obedient to the voice of God: "Blessed be the fruit of your womb." In saying to Mary, "Blessed are you among women[7] and blessed is the fruit of your womb," Elizabeth, like the woman in the crowd, is appreciating not only the joy of Mary's being the mother of a son, but the enormous honor of being the physical mother of the Messiah. In the ministry, however, Jesus reacted to that praise with the same instinct that he showed in the scene concerning the relationship of discipleship to natural family (discussed above). He corrected the woman in the crowd, "Fortunate rather are those who hear the word of God and keep it" (Luke 11:28). Elizabeth is the mother of a prophet; and being filled with the Holy Spirit (1:41), she can supply her own modification. After blessing Mary's physical motherhood, she goes on

---

[6] This last sentence is still another echo of the Abraham-Sarah story which is so prominent in Luke's portrait of Zechariah-Elizabeth (Gen 18:14).

[7] "This line of the blessing echoes a praise of distinguished women of Israel: Jael (Judg 5:24) and Judith (Jdt 13:18).

The Annunciation to Mary, the Visitation, and the Magnificat

to say climactically, "Fortunate is she who believed that the Lord's word to her would be fulfilled." This reiterates the supreme importance of hearing the word of God and doing it, and anticipates Jesus' own encomium of his mother (Luke 8:21). Mary is doubly blessed; she is the physical mother of the Messiah and one who meets the criterion for Jesus' family of disciples. The fact that the mother of the Baptist utters this blessing with the babe literally jumping with joy in her womb (1:44) is an anticipation of the Baptist's own witness to the one to come after him.

Thus far in the interchange between the two women during the visitation, Elizabeth has twice blessed Mary. Noblesse oblige would almost require that Mary in turn bless Elizabeth. But in Luke's vision of the scene this is the appropriate moment to insert the Magnificat with the clear effect that if Elizabeth blesses Mary, "the mother of my Lord" (1:43), Mary now blesses the Lord himself. The preceding chapter discussed how the Lucan infancy canticles exhibit the style of the Jewish psalmody of this era in being mosaics of OT passages. That is true of the Magnificat in particular.

On page 81 above, we noted that the opening of the Magnificat is a deliberate parallel to the opening of Hannah's canticle after the birth of her child in 1 Samuel 2:1-2. The Hannah parallelism continues throughout the Magnificat, e.g., Luke 1:48, "Because He has regarded the low estate of His handmaid," echoes the prayer in 1 Samuel 1:11, "O Lord of Hosts, if you will look on the low estate of your handmaid." This handmaid motif was anticipated by Luke in 1:38 where "Behold the handmaid of the Lord" was part of Mary's final response to Gabriel. The term employed is literally the feminine form of "slave"; and besides the religious context of servants of the Lord (see Acts 2:18), it may reflect the sociological situation of many early Christians. When the Roman governor Pliny in the early second century went looking for Christians to find out what this strange group was, he turned to slavewomen because among such lowly creatures he was likely to find Christians. That Mary designates herself a handmaid is poetically beautiful in our hearing, but to outsiders in early times it would be another confirmation that Christianity was bizarre: a group consisting of many slaves, worshiping a crucified criminal. Whether or not the Magnificat came from an early Christian group of "Poor Ones" (see preceding chapter), it clearly shares their mentality. Mary has become the spokeswoman of their ideals.

Christ in the Gospels of the Liturgical Year

That same mentality dominates the body of the Magnificat describing the salvific action of God (1:51-53):

> "He has shown His strength with His arm;
> He has scattered the proud in the imagination of their hearts.
> He has put down the mighty from their thrones and has exalted those of
> low degree.
> He has filled the hungry with good things, and the rich He has sent
> away empty."

This section continues the parallelism with Hannah's hymn (1 Sam 2:7-8):

> "The Lord makes poor and makes rich;
> He reduces to lowliness and
> He lifts up.
> He lifts the needy from the earth;
> and from the dung heap He raises up the poor
> to seat them with the mighty,
> making them inherit a throne of glory."

Yet in the conciseness of its antitheses the Magnificat does more than echo Hannah and the OT; it anticipates the gospel message, especially the Beatitudes and Woes spoken by Jesus in Luke 6:20-26. I know that most readers are familiar with Matthew's eight Beatitudes and the hallowed phrasing of "poor in spirit" and "hunger and thirst after justice." But Luke has only four Beatitudes, and like sharp hammer blows they have no mollifying, spiritualizing clauses like "in spirit" or "after justice":

> "Blessed are you who are poor, for yours is the kingdom of God.
> Blessed are you who are hungry now, for you shall be satisfied.
> Blessed are you who weep now, for you shall laugh.
> Blessed are you when all hate you . . . your reward is great in heaven."

And so that the reader will not miss that Jesus is talking about concrete poor, hungry, and suffering people, Luke follows this with four antithetical Woes uttered by Jesus:

> "Woe to you who are rich, for you have received your consolation.
> Woe to you who are full now, for you shall hunger.
> Woe to you who laugh now, for you shall mourn and weep.
> Woe to you when all speak well of you, for so their fathers did to the
> false prophets."

The Annunciation to Mary, the Visitation, and the Magnificat

93

The Magnificat, historically composed after Jesus had proclaimed such a gospel, reuses Jesus' antithetical style to celebrate what God has done, exalting the low and the hungry, putting down the proud, the mighty, and the rich.

By placing this canticle on Mary's lips, however, Luke has made a statement about discipleship and gospel. We have seen that in the annunciation Mary becomes the first disciple, indeed, the first Christian, by hearing the word, i.e., the good news of Jesus' identity as Messiah and God's Son, and by accepting it. In the visitation she hastens to share this gospel word with others, and now in the Magnificat we have her interpretation of that word, resembling the interpretation that her son had given it in the ministry. This sequence gives us an important insight on christology and its interpretation. At the beginning of the public ministry in Luke's Gospel (as in the other Gospels) God's voice identifies Jesus as His Beloved Son (3:22)—the good news from the start is christological. But when Jesus speaks the gospel to people, he does not reiterate his own identity to people, saying, "I am God's Son." Rather he interprets what the sending of the Son means, so that the Beatitudes and the Woes show both its salvific and judgmental results. In the infancy narrative Mary has heard from Gabriel the christological identity of Jesus; but when she gives voice interpreting what she has heard, she does not proclaim the greatness of the saving God because He has sent the Messiah, His Son. Rather, her praise of Him interprets the sending: He has shown strength, exalting the lowly, filling the hungry. In short (Luke 1:54-55):

> "He has helped His servant Israel
> in remembrance of His mercy,
> as He spoke unto our fathers, to
> Abraham and his posterity forever."

The first Christian disciple exemplifies the essential task of discipleship. After hearing the word of God and accepting it, we must share it with others, not by simply repeating it but by interpreting so that they can see it truly as *good* news. As we look forward in Advent to the coming of Christ, let us ask ourselves how this year we are going to interpret for others what we believe happens at Christmas, so that they will be able to appreciate what the angel announced at the first Christmas (Luke 2:10-11). "I announce to you good news of a great joy which will be for the whole people: To you this day there is born in the city of David a savior who is Messiah and Lord."

Christ in the Gospels of the Liturgical Year

*   *   *

Let me close this chapter with the remarks of perhaps the most theologically perceptive and nuanced deceased pope of the last century,
Paul VI, as contained in the last significant document he wrote on Mary
(*Marialis Cultus*, February 1974). I cannot phrase better what the Bible
tells us about Mary in the infancy narratives and elsewhere:

> The Virgin Mary has always been proposed to the faithful by the church
> as an example to be imitated, not precisely in the type of life she led and
> much less for the sociocultural background in which she lived and
> which scarcely today exists anywhere. Rather she is held up as an
> example to the faithful for the way in which in her own particular life
> she fully and responsibly accepted the will of God, because she heard
> the word of God and acted on it, and because charity and the spirit of
> service were the driving force of her actions. She is worthy of imitation
> because she was the first and most perfect of Christ's disciples.

The Annunciation to Mary, the Visitation, and the Magnificat

An Adult Christ at Christmas

Essays on the Three Biblical Christmas Stories

Matthew 2 and Luke 2

Chapters 11–15

Chapter 11

On Putting an Adult Christ Back into Christmas

The Gospels of Matthew and Luke begin with stories of Jesus' conception and birth (henceforth called infancy narratives). In this they differ notably from the other two Gospels which tell us nothing of Jesus' family origins; indeed, Mark does not even mention Joseph, while John never gives the name of the mother of Jesus. The Matthean and Lucan infancy narratives, which are not at all alike, have supplied the raw material for the Christmas feast so dear to Christians. How are we to evaluate them?

The Roman Catholic Church, often thought to be painfully conservative in its official positions, has issued a rather liberal pronouncement on the general historicity of the Gospels. Through its official organ for biblical teaching,[1] Rome has insisted that one should speak of the Gospels as historical in the sense that the four accounts of the ministry of Jesus took their origin in words that Jesus spoke and deeds that he performed. Nevertheless, the pronouncement made clear that those words and deeds underwent considerable adaptation from the time of Jesus' ministry until the time when they were written down in the Gospels.[2] For instance, there was a period of oral transmission

---

[1] I refer to the Pontifical Biblical Commission which issued its Instruction on *The Historical Truth of the Gospels* in 1964. A full English translation and commentary was given by J. A. Fitzmyer, *TS* 25 (1964): 386–408. The most important sections of the Instruction appear in an appendix of my book *Biblical Reflections on Crises Facing the Church* (New York: Paulist 1975).

[2] The Instruction distinguishes "three stages of tradition by which the doctrine and life of Jesus have come down to us." Stage one, the ministry of Jesus, certainly belongs to the first third of the first century A.D. (*ca.* 28–30). Stage two, the period of apostolic preaching, can plausibly be dated to the second third of the century (*ca.* 30–65) since the best-known apostles were dead by the mid-60s. Stage three, the period of Gospel writing, can reasonably be dated to the last third of the century (probably Mark in the late 60s; Matthew and Luke in the 70s or 80s; John in the late 80s or 90s).

wherein the apostles preached what Jesus had said and done; but they infused their accounts of Jesus with a post-resurrectional insight into his divinity—an insight they had not had when he was alive.[3] Then, in the commission to writing by the evangelists[4] there was a further selection, synthesis, and explication of the accounts that had come down from apostolic preaching with the result that the final Gospel narratives of the ministry are not necessarily literal accounts of what Jesus did and said. As the Roman document affirmed, "The truth of the story is not at all affected by the fact that the Evangelists relate the words and deeds of the Lord in a different order and express his sayings not literally but differently, while preserving their sense."

Unfortunately most Roman Catholics, including many clergy and religion teachers, do not know this official position about the Gospels taken by their church, so that there is still uneasiness if someone argues that a particular section dealing with Jesus' ministry is not literal history. Consequently, before any Catholic turns to a serious study of the infancy narratives, he or she should become familiar with the Roman Biblical Commission's approach to the Gospels in general. One will never understand the infancy narratives without first being convinced that, in the course of transmission from Jesus to the evangelists, all Gospel material has been colored by the faith and experience of the church of the first century.

The next step in approaching the infancy narratives is the recognition that the Instruction of the Biblical Commission about the Gospels does *not* cover the birth stories,[5] for it concerns only what Jesus said

---

[3] The Instruction (VIII) speaks of Jesus' divinity being perceived after he rose from the dead.

[4] The Instruction distinguishes between the apostles who preached and the sacred authors who composed their Gospels from what had been handed down in this preaching. This corresponds to the general scholarly position today that no one of the Gospels was written by an eyewitness to the ministry of Jesus. An earlier position, reflected in Biblical Commission decrees at the beginning of the twentieth century, that Matthew and John were written by members of the Twelve (something never claimed by the Gospels themselves) has been almost universally abandoned, as tacitly acknowledged in 1955 by the Secretary of the Commission who gave Catholics "complete freedom" with regard to such previous decrees.

[5] The Commission was aware of this, for after 1964 there was a movement to issue a second statement pertaining to the infancy narratives. This attempt was abandoned after the consulters were asked for their advice—probably because the

and did *during his ministry*—words and deeds witnessed by apostles who subsequently passed them on. (No one has ever suggested that such apostolic witnesses as Peter and John were around for the events at Bethlehem.) If one wishes to discuss the infancy material, one must extend even further the liberal attitude of the Commission about historicity. That is why I claim that for many people the narratives of Jesus' birth and infancy constitute "the last frontier" to be crossed in gaining an appreciation of the implications of a modern scientific (critical) approach to the NT. In this collection of essays I would like to see if I can make this frontier seem less a barrier.

One way to assist readers in crossing the frontier is by acquainting them with previous attempts in this direction, for in a certain sense readers must work through in their own minds the kinds of questions that have been asked in the history of scholarship about the infancy narratives. They are basic questions and there is no way to avoid them.

At the risk of oversimplification, I would say that scholarship on the infancy narratives has passed through two stages and is entering a third. The first stage was one of recognizing the importance of the distinction mentioned above, namely, that the birth material had a different origin from the material concerning Jesus' ministry. Our knowledge of the substance of the ministry came from apostolic testimony; but we simply do not know whose testimony, if anyone's, supported a story like that of the magi and the star. There was a tendency to posit family testimony (of Joseph and Mary) underlying the infancy stories, but that was simply a guess.

And that guess became more and more difficult to sustain as scholarship moved into the second stage, involving biblical criticism of the infancy stories taken separately from the rest of the Gospel. There was the overall striking fact that Matthew and Luke tell two very different stories of Jesus' birth and infancy—stories that agree in very few details[6] and almost contradict one another in other details.[7] A complicating

---

cardinals who composed the Commission thus came face-to-face with the enormous difficulties to be encountered in pronouncing on the historicity of the infancy narratives.

[6] Albeit very important details, such as the birth at Bethlehem and the virginal conception.

[7] The most notorious discrepancy is between Matthew's account of a flight to Egypt in face of Herod's persecution and Luke's account of a peaceful return to

On Putting an Adult Christ Back into Christmas

factor was the impossibility of substantiating some of the startling events which should have attracted public notice—for example, a star that moved through the heavens in a totally irregular way but left no astronomical record.[8] The resulting doubts about historicity were aggravated when it was recognized that the infancy stories echo OT stories to an extent unparalleled in the rest of the Gospels. They were sometimes conceived to have arisen through meditation on OT motifs, a process to which the name *midrash* was frequently applied (and not always with a real understanding of *midrash*). Were the essays in this booklet written during that second stage of scholarship, they might have been entitled: "Were There Magi? Was There a Star? Was There a Census? Did Angels Appear to Shepherds?"

But we are now entering a third and much more positive stage of investigation. Without neglecting the historical problems uncovered in the previous stage, scholars have turned their attention to the theology of the infancy narratives. Whatever their origin or historicity,[9] why were these stories included by Matthew and Luke in their Gospels? How does each infancy narrative accord with the respective evangelist's theology? How do the infancy narratives convey the good news of salvation, so that they are truly and literally "gospel"? Such questions

Nazareth through Jerusalem without the slightest involvement of Herod. A perceptive reading shows that Matthew thinks that the home of Mary and Joseph was in Bethlehem (2:11), so that he has to explain why, when they came back from Egypt, they went to Nazareth instead of to Bethlehem (2:22-23); for Luke, they came from Nazareth in the first place.

[8] There are unverifiable (and even unlikely) historical statements as well, such as the Herodian slaughter of the children at Bethlehem, and the universal census of the Roman Empire under Augustus (involving Herod's kingdom!). There have been many ingenious attempts to "prove" these as facts—unsuccessful in my judgment. For instance, there was a remarkable conjunction of planets in 7–6 B.C., and Halley's comet appeared in 12–11 B.C. But Matthew describes a star—in fact, a star that came to rest over the place where Jesus was. If one wishes to invoke astronomy to explain Matthew 2, one should recognize the probable direction of the ancient thought pattern. *After* people came to believe in the risen Jesus as the Son of God, in retrospect they would begin to look for an astronomical phenomenon to associate with the birth of such a figure—and the result may have been a combination of vague memories of astronomical phenomena in the period 12–6 B.C. with the OT imagery of the Davidic star (see below).

[9] In *The Birth of the Messiah* I devote the necessary attention to questions of historicity, but I deliberately place such questions last lest they get out of focus.

Christ in the Gospels of the Liturgical Year

are my real interest in these essays, as I have tried to indicate in two of the titles by speaking of meaning and significance. The answer to them can play a role in proclamation to the Christian community.

Let me turn here to the first of the above questions: Why were these stories deemed appropriate by Matthew and Luke to be included in their Gospels? In the period before the application of biblical criticism this question would not have been asked: the Gospels were looked on as biographies of Jesus, and so it would have been only common sense to include material about the birth of Jesus. But now we have come to recognize that the Gospels are not primarily biographical in their origins; rather they stem from an apostolic preaching where salvific import determined what was preserved about Jesus.

The oldest preaching concerned the salvific action par excellence— that is, the death and resurrection of Jesus; and so the passion narrative was the oldest part of the gospel tradition. To the passion narrative (and thus in a process that worked chronologically backwards) were eventually joined collections of sayings and healings, precisely because in the light of the resurrection the true salvific import of such memories of the ministry of Jesus became clear. It is noteworthy that the most ancient evangelist, Mark, called the baptism of Jesus "The beginning of the gospel of Jesus Christ": the beginning of the gospel was equated with the beginning of the preaching of the kingdom. Clearly Mark's interests were not biographical; indeed, he tells us nothing of Jesus' origins.[10]

Having discarded biographical completeness as the primary motive, we then have to ask why Matthew and Luke moved the beginning of the gospel of Jesus Christ from the baptism back to the conception. The answer lies in the christological significance that they saw in the conception and birth. For them, not the baptism but the conception and birth constituted the moment when God revealed who Jesus was. Let me sketch briefly the chronologically backwards growth in the first-century Christian understanding of this "christological moment."

[10] Mark does not show favor to Jesus' natural family; it is firmly replaced by a true family consisting of disciples (3:31-35, especially when read in sequence to 3:19-21, where "his own" think Jesus is frenzied). Thus, the suggestion of M. Miguens that Mark does not mention Joseph because he wants his readers to know that Jesus was virginally conceived is implausible; see note 4, p. 133 below.

On Putting an Adult Christ Back into Christmas

In the ancient preaching the moment of God's revealing the christological identity of Jesus was the resurrection-exaltation:[11] "This Jesus
God raised up. . . . God made him both Lord and Messiah, this Jesus
whom you crucified" (Acts 2:32, 36; also 5:31). We hear in Acts 13:33
that by raising Jesus from the dead, God fulfilled his words in Psalm
2:7: "You are my son; today I have begotten you." As the Christian
creedal statement quoted by Paul in Romans 1:4 phrases it: by resurrection from the dead Jesus was designated Son of God in power
according to the Spirit of holiness (the Holy Spirit). Such a concentration on the resurrection as the christological moment was consonant
with the earliest stage in gospel formation, which, as I mentioned
above, centered on the death and resurrection of Jesus.

As more attention was focused on Jesus' ministry and on his Galilean proclamation of the kingdom through words and mighty deeds,
the emphasis on the resurrection as the moment when Jesus was
"made Lord" and "begotten" or "designated" as God's Son was seen
as inadequate. It did not do justice to the continuity between the Jesus
of the ministry and the risen Lord. Christian penetration of the mystery
of Jesus illuminated the fact that he was already Lord and Messiah
during his lifetime, so that the resurrection was the unveiling of a
divine sonship that was already there. Thus, for the oldest written
Gospel, Mark, the christological moment has moved from the resurrection to the baptism, where Jesus is designated by divine revelation
as God's Son. The Holy Spirit, which in early Christian experience was
associated with the risen Jesus, now descends on him at the baptism
and remains with him during his ministry.[12]

But this development in Christian understanding[13] still left unsolved
the question of whether the baptism was the moment when Jesus

[11] A still earlier christology, leaving only faint traces in the NT, may have made
the parousia the christological moment: Jesus would be the Messiah, the Son of
Man, when he would return again—a *possible* interpretation of Acts 3:20-21.

[12] The themes present in a creedal statement like Romans 1:4 appear in narrative
form in Mark 1:10-11 and Luke 3:22; 4:14 (designation as Son; Holy Spirit; power).
The Western text of Luke 3:22 ("You are my son; today I have begotten you")
applies to the baptism the same psalm passage that Acts 13:33 applies to the resurrection.

[13] Let me stress that I am speaking of a development in the understanding of a
reality that was already there. This approach is quite different from the liberal
thesis that Christians created *ex nihilo* a christology by making Jesus the Son of

Christ in the Gospels of the Liturgical Year

became God's Son. Was the heavenly voice adopting Jesus? Such a misunderstanding is ruled out by the prefixing of infancy narratives in Matthew and Luke, narratives which make clear that Jesus was God's Son during his whole earthly life, from the moment of his conception through the Holy Spirit. The divine declaration of sonship, once attached to the resurrection and then to the baptism, is now attached by an "angel of the Lord"[14] to the conception of Jesus in the womb of the Virgin Mary.[15] This declaration makes it clear that the child is the Messiah, "the king of the Jews" (Matt 2:2), "a Savior who is the Messiah and Lord" (Luke 2:11). And so the story of Jesus' conception is no longer just an item of popular biography; it is the vehicle of the good news of salvation; in short, it is gospel. Reflection on how this came about will explain to readers why I have entitled this chapter 11: "On Putting an Adult Christ *Back* into Christmas." The process was literally an interpretative one of reading back later insights into the birth stories, and those later insights involved an adult Christ who had died and risen.

Both in Matthew and in Luke the *first* chapter of the Gospel narrates the story of the conception of Jesus with the accompanying revelation of who he is. The essays that follow concern the *second* chapter of each Gospel—the Christmas story of the birth at Bethlehem of the child who has been conceived in Mary's womb. Why is this also gospel? The answer to this question lies in the historical aftermath of the revelation of the good news of salvation—a revelation that, as we have seen, was once attached to the resurrection. After the resurrection of Jesus the apostles went forth and *proclaimed* that good news, first to Jews and then to Gentiles. This proclamation was met by a twofold *response*: some believed and came to worship the exalted Lord Jesus; others rejected both the message and the preachers. When the evangelists looked back into the life of Jesus with post-resurrectional

---

God. See the survey of modern scholarship on Gospel christology that constitutes chapter 2 of my *Biblical Reflections on Crises Facing the Church* (note 1 above).

[14] The classic OT image for the revealing God.

[15] In the light of Romans 1:4 (and note 12 above), notice the phraseology of the divine revelation in Luke 1:35: "The *Holy Spirit* will come upon you, and the *power* of the Most High will overshadow you; therefore the child to be born *will be called* holy, the *Son of God.*"

On Putting an Adult Christ Back into Christmas

hindsight, they could see the same sequence after the baptism of Jesus (which had become an earlier moment of the revelation of who he was). Jesus *proclaimed* the good news of the kingdom throughout Galilee and this led to a twofold *response*: some drew close to him and became his disciples; others rejected him and came to hate him. And so when the evangelists told stories of the conception of Jesus, attaching the revelation of Jesus' identity to that moment of his life, they tended to follow the sequence once more. In the second chapter of each infancy narrative we hear how the good news was *proclaimed* to others and how that proclamation met a twofold *response*. Let us turn now to the way in which the sequence is narrated in each Gospel, with the hope that in our own lives the recognition that there is an adult message about Christ in Christmas will lead us to proclaim that revelation to others that they too may respond in faith.

Chapter 12

The First Christmas Story (Matthew 2:1-23)

The Meaning of the Magi; the Significance of the Star

The evangelist tells the story of the magi and the star after he has already given the genealogy of Jesus and told how an angel announced to Joseph in a dream the forthcoming birth of the child who would be the Davidic Messiah (see 1:1, 16, 18), a child conceived through the Holy Spirit and therefore the Son of God (see also 2:15).

For brevity's sake, let me simply list scholarly observations about the parts of the Matthean infancy narrative that supply a *framework* for the story of the magi and the star:

1. In the annunciation to Joseph, Matthew follows the pattern of the typical annunciation of birth in the OT—for example, of the births of Isaac (Gen 17:15-21) and Samson (Judg 13).[1]

2. Matthew's portrayal of Joseph who receives revelation in dreams (1:20; 2:13, 19) and who goes down to Egypt (2:14) resembles the portrait of Joseph in the OT, the patriarch who was "the dreamer" par excellence (Gen 37:19—literally, "the master of dreams") and who went down to Egypt, escaping an attempt on his life (Gen 37:28).

3. Matthew's account of Jesus' escape from Herod is remarkably like the Jewish story of Moses' escape from the Pharaoh—the Moses who, like Jesus, came back from the Egypt to which Joseph had gone. The biblical narrative of Moses' birth had undergone considerable

---

[1] The annunciation pattern for the birth of Jesus is found also in Luke and was presumably developed in popular circles anterior to both written Gospels, each of which uses the pattern in its own way.

popular expansion by the first century A.D., as we can see in writers of that period like Philo and Josephus. In the expanded narrative Pharaoh was forewarned through his scribes (see Matt 2:4) that a child was about to be born who would prove a threat to his crown, and so he and his advisers decided to kill all the Hebrew male children. At the same time, through a dream there was divine revelation to Moses' father that his wife, already pregnant, would bear the child who would save Israel, a child who would escape Pharaoh's massacre. Forewarned, the parents acted to preserve the life of Moses when he was born. Later in life, Moses fled into Sinai and returned only when he heard from the Lord: "All those who were seeking your life are dead" (Exod 4:19; cf. Matt 2:20).

The story of the magi and the star also echoes the Pentateuchal account of Moses but combines this with the imagery of a Messiah descended from David—an imagery for which Matthew has prepared us by beginning the infancy narrative with "the genealogy of Jesus Christ, the son of David." The Pentateuchal passage is Numbers 22–24, the episode involving Balaam. When Moses was leading Israel through the Transjordanian region on the way to the Promised Land, he encountered another wicked king who, like the Pharaoh of Egypt, tried to destroy him. This was Balak, king of Moab, who summoned *from the East* (Num 23:7)[2] a famous seer named Balaam who was to use his arts against Moses and Israel. Balaam was a non-Israelite, an occult visionary, a practicer of enchantment—in short, what would have been called in Jesus' time a *magus*.[3] He and his two servants (Num 22:22) came; but instead of cursing Moses and Israel, he had a favorable vision of the future: "There shall come a man out of Israel's seed, and he shall rule many nations. . . . I see him, but not now; I behold him, but not close: *a star shall rise* from Jacob, and a man [scepter] shall come forth from Israel" (Num 24:7, 17—partially the Greek Septuagint: LXX).

---

[2] The Matthean story seems to echo the Greek Septuagint [LXX] version more closely than it echoes the Hebrew, since some of the items in Numbers 22–24 to which I call attention are found only in the Greek.

[3] In NT times "magi" covered a wide range of those engaged in occult arts: astronomers, fortune-tellers, priestly augurers, and magicians of varying degrees of plausibility. Matthew probably thinks of astronomers.

Christ in the Gospels of the Liturgical Year

Almost certainly this passage refers to the emergence of the Davidic monarchy:[4] it was understood that David was the star that Balaam had foreseen, the man who would be given the scepter over the United Kingdom of Judah and Israel. In later Judaism the passage was taken as a reference to the Messiah, the anointed king of Davidic descent. The passage played a role in the second century A.D. when Rabbi Aqiba hailed as Messiah the revolutionary Simon ben Kosibah, nicknamed "Bar Cochba," which by popular etymology became the "son of the star."

The Herod of Matthew's story has the features not only of the Pharaoh who tried to destroy the baby Moses by killing the male children of the Hebrews, but also of King Balak who sought to destroy Moses by means of a magus from the East. Just as Balaam saw the star of David rise, the NT magi saw the star of the King of the Jews at its rising.[5]

The realization that such OT imagery lies behind the Matthean story of the magi and the star[6] was one of the positive results of the second stage of scholarship I described in chapter 11. But now I wish to concentrate on how Matthew used this story in chapter two of his Gospel to describe the aftermath of the revelation of who Jesus is—the good news which Matthew has attached to the annunciation of the conception of Jesus in chapter one. I have said above that this aftermath or sequence normally consisted of the *proclamation* of the good news to Jews and Gentiles, with the consequent twofold *response* of acceptance and rejection. The story of the magi and the star becomes for Matthew the anticipation of the fate of the good news of salvation, a fate that he knew in the aftermath of the resurrection.

First, the christological good news draws believers, and those believers, the magi, are Gentiles.[7] Yet the evangelist is Jewish enough

[4] The Book of Numbers was composed after the emergence of the Davidic dynasty, and so it is difficult to be sure how much is *post factum* in the oracle of Balaam.

[5] In the translation of Matthew 2:2, "at its rising" is preferable to "in the East."

[6] In a more technical discussion I would spell out the arguments for the thesis that some of what is in Matthew 1–2 came to the evangelist already shaped into stories which he combined and modified.

[7] Matthew writes his Gospel from a vantage point in time when his church has become predominantly Gentile. He knows that Jesus confined himself to Israel

The First Christmas Story

to continue the tradition that, deprived of the Scriptures, the Gentiles never had so explicit a revelation as was given to the Jews. It was through nature that God revealed himself to the Gentiles (see Rom 1:19-20; 2:14-15), and so Matthew shows the magi receiving a revelation through astrology: the birth star associated with the King of the Jews brings them the good news of salvation. This is an imperfect revelation; for while it tells them of the birth, it does not tell them where they can find the King of the Jews. The ultimate secret of his whereabouts is locked in the special revelation of God to Israel, in the Scriptures (Matt 2:2-6). The Gentiles come to worship, but they must learn from the Jews the history of salvation. Then Matthew highlights the paradox: those who have the Scriptures and can see plainly what the prophets have said are not willing to worship the newborn king. To the contrary, the king and the chief priests and the scribes conspire against the Messiah,[8] and the wicked king decrees his death. But God spares Jesus and ultimately brings back his Son from another land (2:15).

In other words, stories reflecting OT reminiscences of Joseph, Moses, and Balaam have now been worked into a unified anticipation of the passion and resurrection narrative. The same cast of characters is present: the secular ruler, the chief priests and the scribes are all aligned against Jesus, who has only God on his side. But God makes Jesus victorious by bringing him back. And in this process, those who have the Scriptures reject Jesus, while Gentiles come and, with the help of the Scriptures, find and adore him.

The Matthean infancy story is not only gospel (the good news of salvation)—it is the essential gospel story in miniature. And so, when we look back at the history of Christianity, perhaps we can understand better now why this infancy narrative has been one of the most popular sections of the whole Jesus story, one of the best known and of worldwide appeal. This was due not only to the appreciation of a good story that was satisfying to emotion and sentiment; it also reflected a Christian instinct recognizing therein the essence of the good news—that is, that God has made himself present to us (Emmanuel)

(10:5-6; 15:24), but he expands the parable of the wicked tenants to allow for a transfer of attention to the Gentiles (21:43; no parallel in Mark and Luke).

[8]Although Matthew 2:4-6 describes the chief priests and scribes as consulting the Scriptures, the plural in Matthew 2:20 would seem to join them with Herod in the plot against the newborn king.

Christ in the Gospels of the Liturgical Year

in the life of one who walked on this earth, indeed, so truly present that this one, Jesus, was his Son. This revelation was an offense and contradiction to some, but salvation to those who had eyes to see.

Of the latter the magi are truly the forerunners, the anticipation of all those who would come to worship the risen Jesus proclaimed by the apostles. The Book of Numbers presented Balaam as one from the East who could say, "I see him, but not now," since the star would not rise from Jacob until David's time. So also the Matthean magi, in seeing the star of the King of the Jews at its rising,[9] see (but not now) the one whose kingship would not be visible historically until he had hung on the cross beneath the title *The King of the Jews* and would not be communicable until he had been elevated to God's right hand through the resurrection.

[9] See note 5 above.

The First Christmas Story

Chapter 13

The Second Christmas Story (Luke 2:1-40)

Part I (2:1-21): The Meaning of the Manger; the Significance of the Shepherds

Let me emphasize that here again I am confining myself to a portion of the *second* chapter of the Gospel, the portion that narrates with remarkable brevity the birth of Jesus at Bethlehem and the events that surrounded it. It is possible to concentrate on the second chapter thus because nothing in Luke 2:1-40 (or in Matt 2:1-21) presupposes anything that happened in chapter 1. The reader can test this by reading 2:1-40 and seeing how self-understandable the narrative is, even to the point of reintroducing and identifying Joseph and Mary as if nothing had been said of them previously. This has led many to argue that the material in Luke 2 was originally independent of the material in Luke 1, even as the Matthean story of the magi was probably once independent of the Matthean story of the dream visions of Joseph.

But if one leaves aside the question of origins and concentrates on the existing structure, the parallel patterns in Luke and Matthew are striking despite the very different story lines. In both Gospels chapter 1 tells of an annunciation to one parent (to Joseph in Matthew; to Mary in Luke): an annunciation in which an angel of the Lord reveals the forthcoming birth of the child who will be the Messiah. Then in chapter 2, after a brief reference to the birth of that child at Bethlehem, the story focuses in each Gospel upon the divine proclamation of the messianic birth to an audience. In Matthew the proclamation is to Gentile magi; in Luke it is to Jewish shepherds. Each group is guided by the revelation to come to Bethlehem, and there they find the child with the parent(s). The magi pay him homage and bring gifts; the shepherds praise God for all they have seen and heard. Then they both return to whence they came.

This similar structural pattern in two very different stories is quite intelligible if one recognizes that the same "backwards" christological development described in chapter 11 underlies both. In both Matthew and Luke the christological insight of Jesus' identity as God's Son has been moved back from the resurrection to the conception and birth. Moreover, the aftermath of that christological revelation has also been retroverted. Historically, when the good news was revealed through the resurrection, there was a sequence: it was proclaimed by preachers, and some of those who heard the proclamation believed and worshiped. So also in the second chapters of Matthew and Luke there is a proclamation of the christology revealed in chapter 1. It is a proclamation by a star to the magi and by an angel to the shepherds; and both shepherds and magi believe and worship.[1] Even the departure of the shepherds and the magi is dictated by the logic of christological revelation. The two evangelists know that, when the public ministry of Jesus began, there was no surrounding chorus of adoring believers, treasuring the memories of the marvels that surrounded the birth at Bethlehem. And so these forerunners of the later Christian believers have to be removed from the scene. The magi "went away to their own country," and the shepherds "returned" to their fields.

If the birth narratives of Matthew and Luke share the same christology, they also share the tendency to dramatize that christology against a background of the OT, mixed in with an anticipation of Jesus' ministry. Let me show how Luke does this in 2:1-20.

The center of the narrative is the proclamation to the shepherds and their reaction, and Luke introduces this in two steps. In verses 1-5 he tells us of a census which brings Joseph and Mary to Bethlehem; and in verses 6-7 he tells us that while they were there, Mary gave birth to Jesus, swaddled him, and laid him in a manger.

Luke needs the story of the census because he believes that Mary and Joseph lived in Nazareth ("their own city," according to 2:39), and so he has to explain what they were doing in Bethlehem. (Matthew's

---

[1] In Christian history there is also a negative reaction to the proclamation, i.e., of those who refuse to believe and then seek to destroy. In Matthew's infancy narrative these are represented by Herod, the chief priests, and the scribes; in Luke's infancy narrative it is prophesied that the child is set for the *fall* and rise of many in Israel and for a sign to be contradicted (2:34).

The Second Christmas Story—Part I

problem was just the opposite: he pictured Mary and Joseph living in a house in Bethlehem [2:22-23].) There are formidable historical difficulties about every facet of Luke's description and dating of the Quirinius census, and most critical scholars acknowledge a confusion and misdating on Luke's part.[2] Such a confusion would offer no difficulty to Catholics, since Vatican II made it clear that what the Scriptures teach without error is the truth intended by God for the sake of our salvation,[3] and that scarcely includes the exact date of a Roman census. But, faithful to the purpose of this chapter, let us concentrate on the theological wealth that can be drawn from Luke's description of the census.

Luke speaks of an edict that went out from Augustus Caesar when Quirinius was governor of Syria. He thus gives the birth of Jesus a solemn setting, comparable to that which he would give the baptism of Jesus by John—under Tiberius Caesar when Pontius Pilate was prefect of Judea (3:1). In the instance of the baptism Luke was hinting that the ripples sent forth by the immersion of Jesus in the Jordan would ultimately begin to change the course of the Tiber. He is hinting at cosmic significance for the birth of Jesus as well. The name of Augustus would evoke memories and ideals for Luke's readers. In 29 B.C., one hundred years before Luke wrote this Gospel, Augustus had brought an end to almost a century of civil war that had ravaged the Roman realms; and at last the doors of the shrine of Janus in the Forum, thrown open in times of war, were able to be closed. The Age of Augustus was propagandized as the glorious age of pastoral rule over a world made peaceful by virtue—the fulfillment of Virgil's dreams in the *Fourth Eclogue*. In 13–9 B.C. there was erected a great altar to the peace brought about by Augustus, and this *Ara Pacis Augustae* still stands in Rome as a monument to Augustan ideals.

---

[2] Minor difficulties are that there was no single census of the whole Roman Empire under Augustus, and that there is no evidence that Roman censuses required one to go to one's place of ancestry (unless one had property there). More serious is Luke's connection between the reign of Herod the Great (1:5) and the census under Quirinius. Herod died in 4 B.C.; Quirinius became governor in Syria and conducted the first Roman census of Judea in A.D. 6–7—and notice it was a census of Judea, not of Galilee as Luke assumes. In Acts 5:37 Luke mistakenly mentions the revolt of Judas the Galilean (provoked by the census of Quirinius) after the revolt of Theudas which occurred in A.D. 44–46. See my commentary, *The Birth of The Messiah*, for detail.

[3] Dogmatic Constitution *Dei Verbum* on Divine Revelation, III, 11.

Christ in the Gospels of the Liturgical Year

The Greek cities of Asia Minor adopted September 23rd, the birthday of Augustus, as the first day of the New Year. He was hailed at Halicarnassus as the "savior of the whole world"; and the Priene inscription grandiosely proclaimed: "The birthday of the god marked the beginning of the good news for the world." Luke contradicts this propaganda by showing that paradoxically the edict of Augustus served to provide a setting for the birth of Jesus. Men built an altar to the *pax Augustae*, but a heavenly chorus proclaimed the *pax Christi*: "On earth peace to those favored by God" (2:14). The birthday that marked the true beginning of a new time took place not in Rome but in Bethlehem, and a counterclaim to man-made inscriptions was the heraldic cry of the angel of the Lord: "I announce to you the good news of a great joy which will be for the whole people: To you this day there is born in the city of David a Savior who is Messiah and Lord" (2:10-11).

Luke's mention of the census would also have a meaning for readers who knew Jewish history. Past censuses had been causes of catastrophe. King David ordered a census for Israel and Judah (2 Sam 24) and incurred the wrath of God in the form of a pestilence. Most recently the census of Quirinius in Judea in A.D. 6–7 had provoked the rebellion of Judas the Galilean which was the beginning of the Zealot movement. It was this ultranationalistic movement which culminated in the Jewish revolt against Rome and the disastrous destruction of Jerusalem in A.D. 70. Those evangelists who wrote after 70 were aware that Jewish revolutionary movements had "bad press" in the Roman Empire; and so Luke went out of his way in the passion account to insist that Pilate three times acknowledged Jesus' innocence of the political and revolutionary charges against him (23:4, 14, 22). Luke's picture of the census at Jesus' birth may have had the same goal. If Judas the Galilean revolted because of the Roman census under Quirinius, the parents of Jesus were obedient to it; thus even from birth Jesus was never a party to a rebellion against Rome. Instead of being a disaster for Roman-Jewish relations, the census of Quirinius, if one understood it correctly, provided the setting for the birth of a peaceful Savior who would be a revelation to the Gentiles and a glory for the people of Israel (2:32). Indeed, this was the census foretold in Psalm 87:6 where God says:[4] "In the census of the peoples, this one will be born there."

[4] The Hebrew of the psalm refers to the registering of people from various nations in Jerusalem which now becomes their spiritual home; the Septuagint refers to princes being born there; the (late) Aramaic targum speaks of a king being brought

The fulfillment of the OT becomes a stronger motif when Luke moves on from the census to the actual birth, or rather to what Mary does after the birth (2:6-7). Like Matthew, Luke is laconic about the birth itself: simply, "She gave birth to a son, her first-born." What is of importance is the description which follows: "She swaddled him in strips of cloth and laid him down in a manger, since there was no place for them in the lodgings."[5] Luke will keep coming back to this description, for the angels will tell the shepherds: "This will be your sign: You will find a baby swaddled in strips of cloth and lying in a manger" (2:12). The shepherds will know that they have come to their goal when they have found "Mary and Joseph, with the baby lying in the manger" (2:16). Speculations as to why there was no room in the lodgings erroneously distract from Luke's purpose, as do homilies about the supposed heartlessness of the unmentioned innkeeper or the hardship for the impoverished parents—equally unmentioned. Luke is interested in the symbolism of the manger, and the lack of room in the lodgings may be no more than a vague surmise in order to explain the mention of a manger. This manger is not a sign of poverty but is probably meant to evoke God's complaint against Israel in Isaiah 1:3: "The ox knows its owner and the donkey knows *the manger of its lord*; but Israel has not known me, and my people have not understood me." Luke is proclaiming that the Isaian dictum has been repealed. Now, when the good news of the birth of their Lord is proclaimed to the shepherds, they go to find the baby in the manger and begin to praise God. In other words, God's people have begun to know the manger of their Lord.[6]

---

up there. I have cited the psalm according to Origen's *Quinta* or fifth Greek column, which we now suspect was an early recension of the Greek, somewhat parallel to the *kaige* revision of the Septuagint known to us through Dead Sea discoveries (see *The New Jerome Biblical Commentary*, article 68, nos. 67, 70–74). D. Barthélemy, *Les dévanciers d'Aquila* (Leiden: Brill, 1963), 148, argues that Luke may have known the *Quinta* Greek version.

[5] It is probable that *phatnē* is better translated by "manger" than by "stall"; it is quite unclear whether *katalyma* means "the home," "the room," or "the inn."

[6] This suggestion is well defended by C. H. Giblin, *CBQ* 29 (1967): 87–101. He suggests that Luke's reference to the lodgings echoes Jeremiah 14:8, addressed to the Lord and Savior of Israel, "Why are You like an alien in the land, like a traveler who stays in lodgings?" For Luke this dictum too is repealed, for the Lord and Savior of Israel no longer stays in lodgings.

Christ in the Gospels of the Liturgical Year

To modern romantics the shepherds described by Luke take on the gentleness of their flock and have even become Christmas symbols for the common man.[7] But such interests are again foreign to Luke's purpose. The basic OT background seems to be the memory that David was a shepherd in the area of Bethlehem—the city Luke refers to as "the city of David." The mention of the shepherds' flock (2:8) may betray more complicated biblical reflections. The primary passage used to relate the Messiah's birth to Bethlehem is Micah 5:1(2): "And you, O Bethlehem Ephrathah, small to be among the clans of Judah, from you there will come forth for me one who is to be a ruler in Israel." In the immediate context Micah mentions Migdal Eder, the "Tower of the Flock," which he identifies with Jerusalem/Zion: "O Tower of the Flock, hill of the Daughter of Zion, to you will come back the former dominion, the kingdom of the Daughter of Zion" (4:8). Now, it is noteworthy that Luke has shifted over to Bethlehem a terminology formerly applied to Jerusalem/Zion. In 2:4 he tells us, "Joseph went up from Galilee . . . into Judea to the city of David which is called Bethlehem." Not only is the verb "go up" a standard OT expression for ascent to Jerusalem, but Jerusalem is "the city of David," never Bethlehem. Has Luke also shifted over the designation "Tower of the Flock" (Migdal Eder) from Jerusalem to Bethlehem, so that Micah's promised restoration of the former kingdom and dominion has now been fulfilled in Bethlehem? This would explain the emphasis in the proclamation given to the shepherds who are pasturing their flock near Bethlehem: "To you this day there is born *in the city of David* a Savior who is Messiah and Lord" (2:11)—a proclamation to which they respond, "Let us go over *to Bethlehem* and see the event that has taken place" (2:15).

Other evidence supports this suggestion that the Lucan mention of the shepherds and their flock may be associated with reflection upon Bethlehem as the Tower of the Flock. The only other biblical reference to Migdal Eder, the "Tower of the Flock," besides Micah 4–5, is Genesis 35:19-21, where after Rachel has died on the way to Ephrath, that is, Bethlehem, Jacob journeys on to Migdal Eder. In his infancy narrative Matthew used both Micah 5 and Genesis 35:19 by way of

---

[7] Later rabbinic writings often considered shepherds as dishonest, for they grazed their flocks on other people's lands (Babylonian Talmud, *Sanhedrin* 25b).

reflection on the birthplace of Jesus,[8] so it is not impossible that these two passages which mention both Bethlehem and Migdal Eder were part of an earlier reflection on the Messiah—perhaps an earlier Christian reflection antedating both Matthew and Luke, or perhaps a pre-Christian Jewish reflection. In a passage that can scarcely have been borrowed from Christians, the Targum Pseudo-Jonathan[9] offers as an Aramaic translation of Genesis 35:21: "The Tower of the Flock, the place from which it will happen that the King Messiah will be revealed at the end of days."

The Lucan story has a twofold proclamation of the Messiah by angels. The first and most important is: "I announce to you good news of a great joy which will be for the whole people: To you this day there is born in the city of David a Savior who is Messiah and Lord" (2:10-11). We have seen that this proclamation echoes in its style the imperial propaganda of Augustus, but Luke has borrowed the precise titles from his accounts of early Christian preaching. In Acts 2:32, 36 Peter says that God raised Jesus and "made him both Lord and Messiah"; in Acts 5:31 he says that God exalted Jesus as "Savior." Now that the christological understanding has been moved back from the resurrection to the conception/birth, the same titles are applicable to the newborn child.

The second angelic proclamation is of a different nature; it is the canticle Gloria in Excelsis (2:13-14):

> "Glory in the highest heavens to God, and on earth peace to those favored by Him."

This is one of the four poetic canticles in the Lucan infancy narrative; like the other three (Magnificat, Benedictus, Nunc Dimittis) its structural connection with its immediate context is very loose.[10] A good case can be made for the thesis that Luke added these canticles after he wrote the main body of the infancy narrative, and that they came to

---

[8] Matthew 2:5-6 directly cites Micah 5:1(2); and Matthew 2:17-18 presupposes Genesis 35:19 where Rachel dies on the road to Bethlehem.

[9] The dating of this targum is uncertain, and in its present form it may be as late as the third century A.D.

[10] One can omit the canticles in 1:46-55; 1:67-79; and 2:28-33 and never miss them. This is also true of 2:13-14 if one reads "angel" rather than "angels" in 2:15, as do some Old Latin witnesses.

him already composed from a collection of hymns sung by Jewish Christians in praise of what God had done in the death and resurrection of Jesus.[11] A very close parallel to the Gloria is found in the praise sung by the disciples as Jesus enters Jerusalem to begin his passion (Luke 19:38):

"Peace in heaven and glory in the highest heavens."

These may even be antiphonally recited lines of the same hymn, with the heavenly host imagined as proclaiming peace on earth, while the disciples proclaim peace in heaven. Jewish scholars have recognized a similarity between the Gloria sung in honor of Jesus and the Sanctus sung by the seraphim to the Lord of Hosts in the Jerusalem Temple (Isa 6:3), especially when we realize that in Jewish prayer tradition each of three "Holies" ("holy, holy, holy") was expanded: "Holy in the highest heavens; . . . holy on earth, etc."[12] If the Gloria resembles the Sanctus, Luke is again shifting the focus from Jerusalem to Bethlehem: the hosts of angels have moved from the Temple to praise the new presence of the Lord in Bethlehem.

The Lucan birth scene closes with the reactions of three different participants (2:15-20). First, there are the shepherds, the main characters of the birth scene, who come and find the angelic sign verified: the infant Messiah lies in the manger. As I have explained above, they symbolize an Israel who at last recognizes its Lord; and they glorify and praise God for all they have seen and heard (2:17, 20).[13] Second, Luke introduces unexpectedly a group of hearers who are astonished at all the shepherds report (2:18). Astonishment is a standard reaction in the Gospel (see also 1:21, 63; 2:33), and it does not necessarily lead to faith. These hearers in the infancy narrative are like those in the parable of the seed who "hear the word, receive it with joy, but have no root" (Luke 8:13).

---

[11] In this thesis Luke would have added a few lines to the canticles, such as 1:48 and 1:76-77 (lines remarkably Lucan in style), in order to adapt them to their present setting.

[12] See D. Flusser, "Sanktus und Gloria," in *Abraham unser Vater*, ed. O. Betz, et al. (Festschrift O. Michel; Leiden: Brill, 1963), 129–52.

[13] Bystanders glorify and praise God for what they have seen and heard both in the Gospel (Luke 7:16; 13:13; 17:15; 18:45; 19:37) and in Acts (2:47; 3:8-9; 4:21; 11; 18; 21:20).

The Second Christmas Story—Part I

But there is one exception among the astonished hearers, and she constitutes the third participant in the scene, namely, Mary who "kept with concern all these events, interpreting them in her heart" (2:19). She is not above being astonished (2:33), but her hearing is more perceptive. In the same parable of the seed she exemplifies "Those who, hearing the word, hold it fast in an honest and good heart" (8:15).[14] Luke's description of Mary keeping with concern all these events has often been misused for the implausible thesis that she narrated the infancy narrative to Luke.[15] The idea of "keeping events with concern" appears in Genesis 37:11, Daniel 4:28 (LXX), and *Testament of Levi* 6:2, not with any suggestion of eyewitness tradition, but for attempts to discover the hidden meaning behind marvelous happenings. The Lucan Mary is making a similar attempt, and Luke mentions this because Mary is the only adult in his infancy narrative who will last into the public ministry and even into the church. In the Gospel (8:21) she will appear with the "brothers" of Jesus among those who hear the word of God and do it, and in Acts (1:14) she will again appear with the "brothers" of Jesus as part of the believing community awaiting Pentecost. Thus Luke knows that Mary must have sought to interpret these events surrounding the birth of Jesus and ultimately have succeeded, for she became a model Christian believer.

---

[14] Mary makes her only appearance in the Lucan Gospel account of the public ministry immediately after these words (8:19-21) and is praised for hearing the word of God and doing it.

[15] The implausibility is most visible when we consider Lucan inaccuracies about the census and the customs of presentation and purification.

Christ in the Gospels of the Liturgical Year

Chapter 14

The Second Christmas Story (Luke 2:1-40)

Part II (2:22-40):
The Presentation of Jesus in the Temple

Besides constituting the gospel reading on the feast of the Presentation (February 2), this Lucan narrative serves as the gospel for the Sunday in the octave of Christmas. The liturgical instinct is correct: the presentation scene is an intrinsic part and, indeed, the climax of the Lucan infancy narrative.

Although the Lucan story line is very different from that of the Matthean nativity scene, thematically the two stories are remarkably similar. In both Gospels the christological "good news" that Jesus is the Son of God has been attached to the conception and birth of Jesus; this good news is proclaimed by celestial intervention to a group who were not present (by a star to magi, or by an angel to shepherds); they come to Bethlehem to believe and worship; at the end they are removed from the scene, and they go back to whence they came.

Does the thematic parallel between Matthew and Luke stop with the departure of the magi and of the shepherds, or does it continue into the next scene (the second part of chapter 2 in each Gospel), that is, into the aftermath of the magi and shepherd scenes? For Matthew this aftermath involves the attempt of the wicked King Herod to kill the child Jesus, his slaughter of the male infants, the flight to Egypt, and the return after the king's death—a story clearly patterned on the attempt of the wicked Pharaoh to kill the baby Moses, and on the return of Israel from Egypt under Moses. Luke's account of the peaceful presentation of Jesus in the Jerusalem Temple where he is greeted by Simeon and Anna is obviously a very different story in content and tone,[1] and is modeled on Hannah's (Anna's) presentation of the boy Samuel in the shrine at Shiloh where he was accepted by the priest Eli (1 Sam 1–2). Yet, if one understands that the Matthean story is a passion narrative shifted to the infancy, with the king, the chief priests and the scribes aligned against Jesus (Matt 2:4; 26:27), seeking to kill him, it is noteworthy that Luke too introduces into the presentation a theme of opposition to Jesus and of persecution. Simeon identifies Jesus as a sign to be contradicted, set for the fall of many in Israel, and as the occasion for a sword passing through the soul (Luke 2:34-35). Thus again, despite the different story lines, each evangelist uses the aftermath of the birth to introduce the same passion and suffering motif. Neither is satisfied to terminate the nativity on a totally positive note with the acceptance of Jesus by magi and shepherds. Opposition must also be depicted or predicted; for that is the history of the good news as the two evangelists know it, writing some fifty years after the death of Jesus. By some the good news has been accepted, and they have come and worshiped; but by others it has been rejected and vigorously opposed, and their rejection has produced a division in Israel.

Having compared Luke to Matthew, let us turn now to reflect upon the particular message of Luke's account of the presentation (2:22-40). In discussing the nativity itself (2:1-20), I pointed out that, in order to get Joseph and Mary from Nazareth to Bethlehem, Luke had introduced the motif of the census, and that his information about the census posed severe historical problems. Similarly here, in order to get the family from Bethlehem to Jerusalem, Luke introduces the motifs of the purification and presentation, and once again this introduction presents historical difficulties. Luke seems to be confused about two different religious customs.[2] The first custom was that of the purification of the mother at the sanctuary (Temple) after the birth of a child, a purification at which she offered two young pigeons or doves (Lev 12:1-8). The second custom was that of the presentation of the first male child to the Lord, and the paying at the sanctuary of the sum of five shekels

---

[1] From the viewpoint of history, the two infancy narratives are quite irreconcilable at this point without an extraordinary use of imagination.

[2] It is worth repeating that Vatican Council II (Dogmatic Constitution *Dei Verbum* on Divine Revelation, III, 11) states that the Scriptures teach without error the truth intended by God for the sake of our salvation. Exactitude about Jewish customs would scarcely come under this category of inerrancy.

Christ in the Gospels of the Liturgical Year

to buy him back. Imprecisely Luke seems to think that both parents needed to be purified ("their purification" in 2:22), that the child needed to be brought to Jerusalem to be presented to the Lord (2:22b-23), and that the offering of two young pigeons was related to the presentation (2:24 in sequence to 2:22b). For our purposes here let us leave aside these minor confusions[3] in order to concentrate on Luke's theological outlook.

It is clearly the presentation that captures Luke's interest since he never mentions the purification after the initial verse of the scene (2:22a). He stresses that this action in the Jerusalem Temple was according to the Law of the Lord which he mentions five times (2:22, 23, 24, 27, 39). Previously (2:21) Luke told us that Jesus was circumcised on the eighth day; now at another temporal interval ("when the time came") the parents obey the laws of purification and presentation. In his narrative of the census of Quirinius Luke portrayed Jesus' parents as obedient to a Roman edict which caused many Jews to revolt;[4] here he shows them obedient to the demands of Jewish religious custom. In his origins Jesus was an offense neither to Rome nor to Israel. By the time that Luke writes his Gospel the Jewish leaders have rejected Jesus; but Luke insists that Jesus did not reject Judaism.

As Jesus is presented in the Temple in fulfillment of the Law, he is met by Simeon and Anna, two characters who could have stepped out of the pages of the OT. Luke identifies Anna as a prophetess (2:36), and he has Simeon moved by the Spirit[5] to utter a prophecy about Jesus' future (2:34-35). Thus, added to the Law is the element of prophecy; "the Law and the prophets," as Luke describes the heritage of Israel,[6] come together to establish a context for the beginning of Jesus' career. And this takes place in the court of the Temple during the observance

---

[3] Their presence, however, militates against the supposition that Luke got the birth story from Mary. Mary would have known the customs; Luke, a Gentile convert (and perhaps a proselyte to Judaism), would have only a book knowledge of them.

[4] The Quirinius census provoked the rebellion of Judas the Galilean which was the beginning of the Zealot movement against Roman rule in Judea, as we saw in the previous chapter.

[5] Even as Luke mentions "the Law" three times in the consecutive verses 22, 23, 24, so he mentions the Spirit three times in the consecutive verses 25, 26, 27. It is the same prophetic Spirit which moved Zechariah (1:67).

[6] Luke 16:16; 24:27; Acts 13:15; 24:14; 26:22; 28:23.

of a cultic duty, so that the Temple cult joins the context established by the Law and the prophets.

At an earlier level of composition it is likely that the Lucan infancy narrative came to an end with this scene in the Jerusalem Temple[7] and so was a narrative with an almost perfect inclusion or correspondence between beginning and end. The narrative had begun with the description of an upright and pious man and woman, Zechariah and Elizabeth (1:5-7) and with the proclamation in the Temple of the good news about John the Baptist. In the original plan the narrative came to a close in the courts of the same Temple with another pious pair, Simeon and Anna, proclaiming the good news about Jesus (2:38). Just as Zechariah was filled with the Holy Spirit to utter the Benedictus in honor of John the Baptist, the prophet of the Most High (1:67, 76), so Simeon is filled with the Holy Spirit (2:25, 26, 27) to utter the Nunc Dimittis in praise of Jesus, the Son of the Most High (1:32). The woman Elizabeth reacted to the good news about John the Baptist by thanking God that he had dealt with her thus (1:24-25); and when she gave birth to the child, the good news reached her neighbors (1:57-58). Similarly the woman Anna "gave thanks to God and spoke about the child [Jesus] to all those waiting for the redemption of Jerusalem" (2:38).

The key to this remarkable parallelism between Zechariah/Elizabeth and Simeon/Anna is the fact that both pairs have their biblical foreshadowing in the dramatis personae of the story of the birth of Samuel. Zechariah and Elizabeth were patterned by Luke on the model of Samuel's parents, Elkanah and Hannah (Anna), who yearned for a child and had their prayer granted while praying in the sanctuary. Ultimately they presented that child Samuel to the Lord (1 Sam 1:25),

---

[7] There are good reasons for supposing two stages of composition, in the second of which Luke would have added the canticles and the story of Jesus at age twelve—all of which are quite detachable. I shall show in the next chapter how that story, which is of another literary genre (similar to the hidden-life stories we find in the apocrypha), is quite independent of what has gone before and implies that the parents had no previous indication of Jesus' true identity (2:48-50). The original ending of the infancy narrative was 2:39-40; when Luke added the story of the boy Jesus, he had to repeat the information in that ending by supplying a second ending in 2:51-52—the idea of growth or progress at Nazareth was needed to serve as a transition to the ministry.

Christ in the Gospels of the Liturgical Year

and there at the sanctuary was the aged high priest Eli,[8] as well as women who served at the entrance.[9] Eli blessed the parents of Samuel for having presented their son to the Lord (1 Sam 2:20), even as Simeon blessed Jesus' parents. Afterwards the parents of Samuel returned to their home (1 Sam 2:20), even as Luke 2:39 tells us that the parents of Jesus, "when they had finished all their duties according to the Law of the Lord, returned to Galilee." We are assured twice that Samuel grew in stature and favor with God and men (1 Sam 2:21, 26), even as Luke tells us that Jesus grew and became strong, filled with wisdom and favored by God (2:40).[10] And so Luke, who began his infancy narrative by portraying the birth of John the Baptist in the light of a Samuel background, closes the infancy narrative by portraying the birth of Jesus against the same background.

In order to pursue further the Lucan theology of the scene, we need to concentrate upon the words uttered by Simeon as he embraces the child Jesus in the Temple court. To him are attributed two poetic oracles: first, the Nunc Dimittis in verses 29-32; second, the oracle concerning the sign to be contradicted in verses 34-35. In introducing each oracle Luke mentions a blessing by Simeon (28, 34). A critical study of the history of composition suggests that, like the other three canticles in the infancy narrative (Magnificat, Benedictus, Gloria in Excelsis),[11] the Nunc Dimittis was added by Luke to an already extant narrative about Simeon—if it were to be omitted, that narrative would make

---

[8] Eli, Zechariah, and Simeon were all old men; Eli and Zechariah were high priest and priest respectively; but the *Protevangelium of James* (8:3; 24:3-4) made a high priest of Zechariah and made Simeon his successor to make the parallelism perfect for second-century Christians.

[9] The picture of these women in 1 Samuel 2:22 is not favorable, but in the Septuagint and in the Aramaic Targums of Exodus 38:8 (the only other reference to them) we are told that they fasted and prayed at the sanctuary. This may account for Luke's description of Anna who in the Temple courts "day and night worshiped God, fasting and praying" (2:37).

[10] Also 2:52. The fact that there are two growth statements in reference to Jesus (note 7 above) has an antecedent in the two Samuel growth statements.

[11] A collection of Jewish Christian hymns may be posited as Luke's source for the four canticles—a collection which may have had its distant origin in the early post-pentecostal Jerusalem community which (like Simeon and Anna) was remembered as "day by day attending the Temple" and "praising God" (Acts 2:46-47).

perfect sense with verse 27 leading directly into verse 34. Be that as it may, our interest is in the final form of the scene where the oracle of the Nunc Dimittis is Simeon's blessing of God, while the second oracle is a blessing upon the parents and especially upon Mary.

The first oracle, the Nunc Dimittis, is spoken by one who has been "waiting for the consolation of Israel" (2:25).[12] This picture of one in Jerusalem waiting for consolation echoes the language of the second and third parts of Isaiah. In the Septuagint, Deutero-Isaiah (40:1) opens with the words: "Console, console my people, says your God; speak, priests, to the heart of Jerusalem, for her time of humiliation has been filled out." In Isaiah 66:12-13, a Septuagint passage which speaks of the glory of the Gentiles, we hear: "As one whom a mother consoles, so also shall I console you; and you will be consoled in Jerusalem." If the Lucan presentation of Simeon has Isaian background, it is not surprising that Simeon's Nunc Dimittis echoes the same background. Let us recall its message:

> "Mighty Master, now you may let your servant depart
> in peace, since you kept your word.
> For my eyes have seen this salvation
> that you made ready in the sight of all peoples:
> a light to be a revelation to the Gentiles
> and to be a glory for your people Israel."

The themes of seeing salvation, the sight of all the peoples, a light to the Gentiles, and glory for Israel constitute almost a pastiche[13] from passages like Isaiah 40:3; 42:6; 46:13; 49:6; 52:9-10.

Theologically it is striking that the universalism of Deutero-Isaiah has been brought over into the infancy narrative. In the previous scene Luke's view was narrower, for it was proclaimed to the shepherds that the good news of the birth of the Messiah was meant for the whole people of Israel (2:10-11). But now we hear of a salvation made ready "in the sight of all peoples"—a salvation that is "to the Gentiles" as well as "for your people Israel." Simeon can depart in peace because

---

[12] Notice the parallel expression for Anna's audience: "Those waiting for the redemption of Jerusalem" (2:38).

[13] The cento or pastiche technique of composition is a mark of the other three Lucan canticles and is characteristic of the hymnology of early Judaism, as visible in the Dead Sea Scrolls *Hodayoth* (hymns of praise).

the consolation of Israel which he awaited has come, and this consolation of Israel has proved to be a revelation to the Gentiles as well. In introducing the Gentiles into the presentation scene, Luke once more agrees with Matthew whose interest in the Gentiles was evident in the story of the magi from the East. Luke speaks of "a light to be a revelation to the Gentiles"; Matthew (2:2) spoke of a star which the magi saw at its rising. True, Matthew showed that Jesus meant salvation for the obedient in Israel, since the angel promised Joseph that the child would "save his people from their sins" (Matt 1:21). But in the dramatis personae, with the important exception of Joseph, Matthew's infancy narrative concentrated on Jews who were hostile to Jesus. On the other hand, Luke has hitherto been concentrating on obedient Jews, like Zechariah, Elizabeth, the shepherds, and Simeon. Now, having mentioned Gentiles, he turns in the words of Simeon's second oracle to the many in Israel who will be disobedient.

This *second oracle*, the sign to be contradicted, is much less general than the Nunc Dimittis, which like the other canticles could refer to the work of Jesus at any time in his career. (Indeed, the reference to an accomplished salvation may once have been directed to the cross and resurrection before Luke adapted the canticles and added them here.) But the second oracle of Simeon, which was probably originally composed as part of the infancy narrative is strongly futuristic and quite appropriate to a child whose work had not yet begun:

> "Behold, he is set for the fall and rise of many in Israel
> and for a sign to be contradicted—
> indeed, a sword will pass through your own soul—
> so that the inmost thoughts of many may be revealed."

The language is poetic and symbolic but also deliberate. Luke wrote "the fall and rise"; and the emphasis belongs on "fall," as we see from the second line with its reference to "a sign to be contradicted," and from the fourth line, for in the NT "inmost thoughts" (*dialogismoi*) are always pejorative. At the end of his life Simeon holds in his arms a child who is just beginning life. Simeon's eyes have peered into the distance and seen the salvation that the child will offer to the Gentiles and Israel alike; but, true prophet that he is, he has also seen rejection and catastrophe. Alas, the majority of Israel will reject Jesus. Of course, from Luke's viewpoint this rejection is no longer future; he knows what has happened in the course of apostolic preaching. Luke ends

The Second Christmas Story—Part II

his story of Jesus and of the church when Paul comes to Rome, the capital of the Gentile empire. There he accepts the truth of Isaiah's prediction that this people (the Jews) would never understand. Paul's last words emphasize "that the salvation of God has been sent to the Gentiles; they will listen" (Acts 28:28).

The really obscure line in Simeon's second oracle is addressed to Mary: "A sword will pass through your own soul." Patristic interpretations of the sword run the gamut from doubt through calumnious rejection to violent death—interpretations invalidated by the fact that Luke gives us no evidence of Mary's doubting or of her being calumniated as an unfaithful wife (contrast Matt 1:18-19) or of her dying violently. But if we smile at the lack of method in such ancient suggestions, we should recognize that a similar defect is present in the most frequent current Catholic interpretation of the line, namely, that the sword of sorrow passed through Mary's soul when she stood at the foot of the cross and saw her son die. This suggestion violates an elementary canon of interpretation: the self-intelligibility of a writing. In the Lucan description of the crucifixion Mary is never mentioned as present, and the women who had followed Jesus from Galilee are portrayed as standing at a distance (23:49). The scene in which the mother of Jesus stands at the foot of the cross is found only in John (19:25-27); it involves "the disciple whom Jesus loved," a figure who appears in no other Gospel;[14] and so there is not the slightest reason to suspect that Luke's audience would have known of the scene. The key to "A sword will pass through your own soul" should lie in Luke's own Gospel, not in John's Gospel.

The language of the statement has its closest OT parallel in Ezekiel 14:17 where we are told that by way of judgment the Lord may say, "Let a sword pass through the land so that I may cut off man and beast." Evidently this was a well-remembered oracle, for it is quoted in the *Sibylline Oracles* (III, 316) to describe the invasion of Egypt by Antiochus Epiphanes (*ca.* 170 B.C.): "For a sword will pass through the midst of you." The image is of a selective sword of judgment, destroying some and sparing others, a sword of discrimination and not merely of punishment. This OT background is perfectly in harmony

---

[14] Compare, for instance, John 20:2-10 (which has the Beloved Disciple accompany Peter to the tomb) and Luke 24:12 (where only Peter is mentioned).

with the rest of Simeon's second oracle in Luke where the child is set for the fall and rise of many in Israel. Simeon proclaims that a discriminating judgment will come upon Israel and that it will touch Mary too, as an individual Israelite.

Is there a scene in Luke's Gospel that can show how? Yes—the one scene in the Synoptic tradition where she appears in the public ministry.[15] It is the scene where the mother and brothers come seeking Jesus, only to have him reply that his eschatological family, established by the proclamation of the kingdom, consists not in physical relationship but in a relationship of obedience to the will of the Father. Clearly it is a discriminatory scene putting the demands of God above the privilege of human relationship. (It is Jesus' application to his own situation of the truth that he proclaimed for all: "Do you think that I have come to bring peace on the earth? No, I tell you, *rather division*; for henceforth in the one house they will be divided . . . father against son and son against father, mother against daughter and daughter against mother."[16]) In the Marcan form of the discriminatory scene (Mark 3:31-35), Mary fares poorly; for she and the brothers, standing outside, are sharply contrasted with the family of disciples surrounding Jesus inside.[17] But in Luke's form (8:19-21) Mary emerges as part of the eschatological family of Jesus: "My mother and my brothers are those who hear the word of God and do it" (see Acts 1:14). Mary has had to meet the same discriminatory demand as all others. If in Luke's view she has emerged successfully as part of the family of disciples, it was not because of a physical claim upon Jesus.

[15] Mark 3:31-35; Matthew 12:46-50; Luke 8:19-21.

[16] Luke 12:51-53—it is interesting that in the Matthean form of that saying, which may represent better the "Q" original, Jesus says: "I have not come to bring peace *but a sword*" (Matt 10:34-36). Was this the origin of the sword imagery in Simeon's oracle? Yet the Greek word for "sword" in Matthew 10:34 differs from the word in Luke 2:35.

[17] In the Marcan context the scene is preceded by the notice that "his own" had set out to seize Jesus because they thought he was beside himself (3:21). Evidently Mark associated Mary and the brothers with "his own" and judged that they did not understand Jesus; indeed in 6:4 he describes Jesus as a prophet who is not honored "*among his own relatives* and in his own house." Luke omits all these negative references to Mary. For further information, see R. E. Brown et al., *Mary in the New Testament* (New York: Paulist, 1978), 51–61, 164–70.

The Second Christmas Story—Part II

The interest that Luke shows in Mary's fate in Simeon's second oracle is consonant with the interest in Mary that he showed in 2:19. In the previous chapter where I discussed that verse, I pointed out that the idea that Mary "kept with concern all these events, interpreting them in her heart" had no implication that she was the eyewitness source for Luke's infancy narrative. Rather, since Mary was the only adult in the infancy narrative who would last into the public ministry and even into the church (Acts 1:14), Luke was hinting that later on she would discover the real meaning of all the marvelous happenings associated with Bethlehem. Through Simeon's oracle Luke tells us that part of this discovery will be that she too has to face the judgment implied in Jesus' proclamation. However, since Luke has already shown Mary as doing the will of God at the time of the annunciation (1:38), he suggests here that she will be a positive exception to the generally negative reaction in Israel which is the subject of Simeon's prophecy. For her Jesus will not be a sign to be contradicted but a sign to be affirmed.

If I were to draw a practical conclusion for Mariology from this interpretation of the sword of decision that passes through Mary's soul, it would be that Mary's greatness stems from the way she made that decision to become a disciple by hearing God's word and doing it. Her decision enabled God to make her "blessed among women" (1:42). A popular piety has suggested prayer to Mary on the grounds that surely Jesus listens to his mother. This stress on physical motherhood is a misunderstanding both of the Gospel and of her greatness. The physical fact of motherhood gave her no special status according to the values Jesus preached. If she is remembered as a mother in the Christian community, it is not only because her womb bore Jesus and her breasts nourished him (11:27); rather it is because she believed the Lord's word in a way that gave her a preeminent membership in his true family of disciples (1:41; 8:21).

Chapter 15

The Third Christmas Story (Luke 2:41-52)

The Finding of the Boy Jesus in the Temple

Some readers may be surprised to have the finding of Jesus in the Temple designated a "Christmas story." Since Jesus is already age twelve, this is no birth narrative as were the other Christmas stories. But if the theme of the Christmas feast involves the first revelation to others of the presence of God's Son in the world, then I maintain that the finding-in-the-Temple story had exactly that purpose.

In the present sequence of the Lucan infancy narrative, the conception of God's Son was revealed to Mary by Gabriel (Luke 1:35); and the birth of Jesus the Savior, Messiah, and Lord was revealed to the shepherds by an angel (2:11). Consequently, when the boy Jesus calls God his Father (2:49—the core of the finding-in-the-Temple story), this is scarcely the first revelation in the Lucan Gospel of the presence of God's Son in the world. However, careful scholarly investigation of the pre-Gospel history of the Lucan infancy material shows that the present sequence may not be original. Indeed, at one time the finding-in-the-Temple story may have been a narrative quite independent of the infancy sequence that now precedes it.[1]

Let me list some of the reasons for positing the original independence of this story: (a) The finding-in-the-Temple story is of a different literary genre from the Matthean and Lucan stories of the conception and birth of Jesus. In content and tone, as we shall see, it is a canonical example of those stories of the "hidden life" of Jesus (that is, his life

---

[1] The most important study in English is that of B. Van Iersel in *Novum Testamentum* 4 (1960): 161–73. I give a complete bibliography in my commentary, *The Birth of the Messiah*.

with his family before the ministry) which appear in apocryphal gospels dealing with Jesus' youth. The best example of these is the second-century *Infancy Gospel of Thomas*.[2] Despite the title, this apocryphal gospel does not treat Jesus' infancy but his youth. Stories are told therein of what Jesus did at ages five, six, eight, and twelve—the last mentioned being a retelling of Luke 2:41-52. (b) The story of the finding in the Temple does not fit into the Lucan diptych arrangement of the infancy narrative, namely, one diptych containing matching annunciation scenes (Gabriel's annunciation of the conception of John the Baptist carefully parallel to Gabriel's annunciation of the conception of Jesus), and a second diptych containing matching scenes of birth, circumcision, and naming (again, the one pertaining to John the Baptist parallel to the one pertaining to Jesus). This double diptych arrangement stretches from Luke 1:5 to 2:40. It begins with the description of the aged Zechariah and Elizabeth, involving Zechariah's vision in the Temple; it ends with the description of the aged Simeon and Anna, involving Simeon's vision in the Temple. The final verse (2:40) is an ideal transition to the Gospel proper and the story of the ministry: "And the child grew up and became strong, filled with wisdom and favored by God." The finding-in-the-Temple story, coming after that conclusion in 2:40, has the air of an awkward appendage and spoils the symmetry of the diptychs. (c) In terms of intelligibility, the finding-in-the-Temple story can be read without having a knowledge of what now precedes it in the Lucan sequence. In fact, the story is read more easily as an independent unit. A reader of the present sequence, who already knows that Jesus was not conceived by Joseph, will find it curious that in the finding story Joseph is included among the "parents" of Jesus (2:41, 43) and specifically called the father of Jesus (2:48). Even more curious, in the present sequence, is the failure of Mary and Joseph to understand Jesus when he refers to God as his Father (2:49-50), since they already knew that he was God's Son from angelic revelation. If the finding in the Temple was once totally independent of such previous infancy narratives, all these curiosities are explained. (d) Finally, there are at least slight indications that the Greek of the finding story

---

[2] The attribution to Thomas is not easy to explain unless the tradition was already in circulation that Thomas, "the Twin," was the twin brother of Jesus, a tradition not mentioned in this particular Gospel, however.

Christ in the Gospels of the Liturgical Year

is less marked by Semitisms than is the Greek of the preceding infancy narrative.

It seems probable, then, that Luke appended to his infancy narrative (which originally ended in 2:40) a once-independent story of the finding of Jesus as a youth in the Temple. Our understanding of NT christology may be deepened by reflecting on this story of Jesus' boyhood. In chapter 11 I explained the "backwards development" of NT christology, tracing the revelation of who Jesus was (the Son of God) back from the resurrection to the baptism to the conception. The first two Christmas stories were written against the background of "conception christology"—in relation to the conception of Jesus an angel revealed either to Joseph (Matthew) or to Mary (Luke) who the child-to-be-born was.

But such "conception christology" was not the only possible way of moving the perception of divine sonship back from the baptism to an earlier period. One could have gone further back to before conception, or one need not have gone so far back as conception and could have fastened on Jesus' youth as the moment of revelation. Preexistence christology (thus, implicitly, before conception) appears in the Pauline letters.[3] But among the Gospels it is only John who follows this route and centers his pre-ministry christology on the *preexistence* of the Word before creation (John 1:1), thus jumping over the conception and birth of Jesus which he never mentions.[4] I would suggest that the *"hidden*

---

[3] In 1 Corinthians 8:6 there is a *hint* of creational activity by Jesus Christ, but this theme is much clearer in Colossians 1:15-17. The language of Philippians 2:6-7 (being "in the form of God"—emptying and "taking the form of a servant") was once thought to be clearly incarnational; but recent writing by Protestants and Catholics alike (Talbert, Bartsch, Grelot, Murphy-O'Connor) questions a reference to preexistence. This means that the attitude of the indisputably Pauline letters (Corinthians, Philippians) is uncertain; but in the late-Pauline (60s) or in the post-Pauline period (80s—date of Colossians?) the theme of preexistence becomes clearer. This period from the 60s to the 90s would also cover the span of Johannine composition (final Gospel in the 90s), although the Johannine theme of preexistence represents an "advance" over the Pauline theme in two ways: [a] The Johannine Word is not a creature—compare Colossians 1:16; [b] Preexistence is historicized in a Gospel about the earthly Jesus (John 17:5), rather than simply appearing in poetic hymns of wisdom derivation.

[4] The preexistence christology of John and the conception christology of Matthew/Luke are two *different* Christian answers to the question of pre-ministry christology. There is not a word in John about the virginal conception of Jesus; and

life" stories follow the second route of pre-ministry christology. They have not concerned themselves with something so remote as Jesus' conception and birth but are centered on the first moments of his rational life when he himself could express a self-evaluation. In the conception stories the revelation of Jesus as God's Son had to be placed on the lips of an "angel of the Lord"; in the hidden life stories Jesus can speak and make his own revelation.

In discussing boyhood stories as a vehicle of christology, let us consider more carefully the literary genre. Anyone who studies the birth narratives in Matthew 2:1-23 and Luke 2:1-40 must be aware of the literary genre of the birth narratives of other biblical figures, for example, of Moses, of Samson, and of Samuel, which influenced the shaping of the birth story of Jesus. Similarly, when we study a narrative of Jesus' boyhood, we find analogies in the boyhood stories of other figures. In world literature there are stories about great men who already at an age between ten and fourteen showed astounding knowledge, for example, legends about the Buddha in India, Osiris in Egypt, Cyrus the Great in Persia, Alexander the Great in Greece, and Augustus in Rome. Within the Jewish background, Josephus (*Life* 2 [#9]) reports this of himself: "While still a boy about fourteen years old, I won universal applause for my love of letters, with the result that the chief priests and leading men of the city used to come to me constantly for precise information on some particulars in our ordinances." At a later age Eliezer ben Hyrcanus ran away from home; and when he was found by his father, he was studying the Law. The Jewish legends of Moses which are contemporary with the NT attribute to him extraordinary knowledge as a boy; they comment on how God gave him understanding and stature and beauty of appearance. (Incidentally, the reflections on Moses as a boy are placed by Philo between the birth story of Moses and the well-known ministry story—this is the same procedure I am positing for Luke who inserted a boyhood story

---

there is not a word in Matthew or Luke about preexistence or about incarnation (which logically presupposes preexistence). The attempt of Manuel Miguens, *The Virgin Birth* (Westminster, MD: Christian Classics, 1975) to find references to the virginal conception outside the Matthean and Lucan infancy narratives is a total failure, as recognized by reviewers in *CBQ* 28 (1976): 576–77 ("the exegesis is faulty and the polemic wide of the mark") and in *TS* 38 (1977): 160–62 ("an uncautious book which is bound to mislead many naive readers").

between an infancy story which he had already composed and an account of the ministry which he had borrowed from Mark and reshaped.) In treating Samuel, Josephus (*Antiquities* V, x, 4 [#348]) tells us that the boy began to act as a prophet at the completion of his twelfth year, thus supplying a date for the call of Samuel by God in the Temple (1 Sam 3:1-18). In the Septuagint Greek story of Susanna (v. 45), Daniel as a youth ("of twelve," according to the Syro-Hexaplar version) receives a spirit of "understanding" that makes him wiser than the elders (see also v. 63). I am not suggesting that the Lucan story of Jesus' boyhood was borrowed directly from any of these examples, but simply that there was a clear pattern of boyhood stories of famous figures at about age twelve which explains why and how a boyhood story about Jesus would have been fashioned. And the Moses and Samuel examples explain why a story of Jesus' boyhood could have been attached to an infancy narrative as a preparation for his ministry.

We must also compare the Lucan story to the apocryphal accounts of Jesus' boyhood in the *Infancy Gospel of Thomas*. Too often those accounts are facilely dismissed as fantastic without a real analysis of their function and origin. By concentrating on the magical element in a story of the five-year-old Jesus making birds out of clay, one may neglect the real point of the story, namely, that in so doing the child Jesus provoked the charge of violating the Sabbath (*Thomas* 2:3). Thus, there is anticipated in Jesus' youth the drama of Sabbath violation and of Jesus' sovereignty over against the Law. Again, if one finds repulsive a story in which the boy Jesus caused the son of Annas the scribe to wither up like a tree and bear no fruit (*Thomas* 3:2), one may wrongly overlook the parallel to hostility during the ministry between Jesus and the scribes, and between Jesus and Annas the priest, and the further parallel to the cursing of the fig tree. The villagers of Jesus' youth react to his childhood displays by asking, "From where does this child come, since his every word is an accomplished deed?" (*Thomas* 4:1)—a reaction that anticipates the amazement of the citizens of Nazareth about the adult Jesus' teaching and his mighty works. In other words, in the *Infancy Gospel of Thomas* the unknown period of Jesus' boyhood has been filled in by an imaginative use of what was known about him from the accounts of the ministry. The underlying justifying principle is that the child must already have been what the man was known to be, that is, God's Son speaking and acting with divine

The Third Christmas Story

power. I contend that the same christological instinct has been at work in the Lucan story of the finding of Jesus in the Temple.[5]

In this story Jesus has already begun his activity in the Temple, an activity that will mark the culmination of his public ministry (Luke 19:45-48). As a boy Jesus already places priority on the demands of God over the demands of family, as he will do again during the ministry (Luke 8:21). And his first words are to proclaim that God is his Father, anticipating the heavenly voice at the baptism (Luke 3:22).

In the general pattern of boyhood stories there is customarily stress on at least three features anticipated from what is known of the subject's later career: his piety, his wisdom, and some distinctive aspect of his life work. If we examine in detail the Lucan story of the finding of the boy Jesus in the Temple, we shall find those three features present in an ascending order of importance. To facilitate this discussion let me suggest the following outline for Luke 2:40-52:[6]

> *Framework Statement* about Jesus' growth, his wisdom and favor (40)
>> *Geographical Introduction*: Jesus and his parents had gone up to Jerusalem (41-42)
>> *Setting*: The parents lost Jesus and searched for him (43-45)
>> *Core of the Story*: The parents found the child and were amazed; Jesus answered them by stressing his Father's claim (45-50)
>> *Geographical Conclusion*: Jesus went down with his parents to Nazareth (51)
> *Framework Statement* about Jesus' progress in wisdom, maturity, and favor (52)

Luke *first* calls attention to the piety of Jesus and his family. This is harmonious with the picture he has painted throughout the birth narrative; for he described the parents going to Bethlehem in obedience to

---

[5] The author of the *Infancy Gospel of Thomas* recognized kindred material in the Lucan story of the finding in the Temple, for he chose an adaptation of it to end his sequence of hidden-life stories (19:1-5).

[6] Verse 40 of chapter 2 was, in my theory, the original ending of the Lucan infancy narrative providing a transition to the ministry. When Luke added the finding-in-the-Temple story, he supplied another ending-verse transitional to the ministry (v. 52). The presence of these two statements about Jesus' growth is another indication that the finding story is an appendage.

Christ in the Gospels of the Liturgical Year

the edict of Caesar Augustus (2:1, 4), naming the child Jesus in obedience to the angel (2:21), and going to the Jerusalem Temple in obedience to the Law of Moses about purification and presentation (2:22-24).

In the finding story the parents are again obedient to the Law by going up to Jerusalem for the Feast of Passover (2:41).[7] But Luke adds here implicitly a new note, for Jesus is also respectful of duty and is pious in accompanying his parents on the Temple visit to Jerusalem.[8] We are in the same context of "Temple piety" that marks the Lucan description of the first Christians in the Book of Acts (2:46; 3:1; 5:12). Thus, at the beginning of both his books, the Gospel and Acts, Luke makes it clear that the Law and the cult provided a benevolent context for Jesus. If, later on, antipathy developed between his followers and the Jewish authorities precisely over the Law and the Temple, there was no conflict between Jesus himself and the best in Judaism.

Second, Luke calls attention to the wisdom of Jesus. As it now stands, the story of the finding of Jesus in the Temple is framed by two references to Jesus' growth, one terminating the birth narrative which precedes the finding, the other leading into the ministry narrative which will follow:

> 2:40 "And the child grew up and became strong, filled with wisdom and favored by God."
>
> 2:52: "And Jesus made progress in wisdom, maturity [or stature: *hēlikia*], and favor before God and men."[9]

These statements are virtually a Lucan modification of the two growth descriptions in 1 Samuel:[10]

> 2:21: "And the child [Samuel] waxed mighty before the Lord.
>
> 2:26 "The child advanced and was good in the company of God and men."

---

[7] Passover had now been joined to the Feast of the Unleavened Bread, and the combined feast was a "pilgrimage" feast when Jews were obliged to appear "before the Lord" in the Jerusalem Temple to worship and make an offering (Exod 23:17; 34:23; Deut 16:16).

[8] This has nothing to do with the much later custom of Bar Mitzvah. We do not know that at age twelve Jesus would have been *obliged* to go to Jerusalem; the general talmudic principle is that a child reaches manhood at his thirteenth birthday.

[9] Compare the description of the boy Moses in Josephus, *Antiquities* II, ix, 6 [#230]: "His growth in understanding was not proportionate to his growth in stature [*hēlikia*] but far outran the measure of his years."

[10] In my previous essay on the presentation I showed how closely the Lucan account of the infancy of Jesus follows the OT account of the infancy of Samuel.

The Third Christmas Story

The reason why Luke mentions wisdom in both the growth statements which supply a framework for the narrative becomes apparent as we move into the core of the story. Jesus is found in the Temple listening to the teachers and asking them questions; and we are told: "All who heard him were astounded at his understanding and his answers." Clearly here we have anticipated on the boyhood level the kind of amazement at the teaching of Jesus that will mark his ministry. This scenario is presented by an evangelist who already knew the later scene at Nazareth when, after Jesus spoke in the synagogue, all "wondered at the gracious words that proceeded out of his mouth" (Luke 4:22), and the scene in another synagogue when people were amazed at Jesus' authoritative words (4:36), and finally the scene in the Temple near the end of his life where Jesus taught before the chief priests and the scribes (19:47).[11] The boy Jesus is already showing the wisdom in sacred teaching which will mark his career as a man, and the people are reacting in the same way they will react during the ministry.

The *third* Lucan motif, besides piety and wisdom, is a boyhood anticipation of a basic attitude of Jesus' life. I have already noted that, while the apocryphal boyhood stories anticipate the themes of Jesus' ministry, they allow an admixture of the marvelous to dominate their presentations. If the finding-in-the-Temple story were preserved only in an apocryphal gospel, we can be sure that the amazement over Jesus' teaching would be greatly enlarged.[12] But Luke wisely makes the theme of Jesus' wisdom subordinate to a dialogue between Jesus and his parents (2:48-49). The question asked by Jesus' mother ("Child, why have you done this to us? Behold your father and I have been so worried looking for you") has a slight tone of reproach, a tone better

---

[11] In the ministry scene the chief priests and scribes are hostile to the teaching of Jesus, but in the boyhood story Luke does not surround Jesus with any hostility on the part of the teachers in the Temple—perhaps that is why Luke prefers here to call them "teachers" rather than "scribes," a term that might evoke hostility in the minds of his readers.

[12] In the apocryphal version of the finding story in the *Infancy Gospel of Thomas* we hear: "All paid attention to him and were astounded how he, a child, put to silence the elders and teachers of the people, expounding sections of the Law and the sayings of the prophets" (19:2); and the scribes ask Mary in wonder: "Are you the mother of this child? . . . Never have we seen or heard such glory and such excellence and wisdom" (19:2, 4).

Christ in the Gospels of the Liturgical Year

understood if one posits that this was once an independent story without a preceding narrative of angelic visions to Mary. The atmosphere is not unlike that of the first scene involving Jesus and his mother in Mark. According to Mark 3:21, when "his own" heard about his all-consuming ministerial activity, "they set out to seize him." This is preparatory for 3:31: "And his mother and his brothers came; and standing outside, they sent to him and called him." Similarly, too, in the first conversation between Jesus and his mother reported in the Fourth Gospel (John 2:3), the mother lays upon Jesus a type of family claim in reporting that her friends (or, perhaps, relatives) are out of wine. In all these scenes where a demand is placed on Jesus in the name of family obligations, his response shows that his priorities are with God rather than with earthly family. And so in Luke 2:49 he responds to his parents, "Why were you looking for me? Did you not know that I must be in my Father's house?" In Mark 3:33-34, to the demand of his mother and brothers, Jesus says: "Who are my mother and my brothers? . . . Whoever does the will of God is my brother and sister and mother." In John 2:4 Jesus replies to his mother's request, "Woman, what has this concern of yours to do with me? My hour has not yet come"—priority is given to the "hour" of Jesus determined by his relation to the heavenly Father (13:1). The three Gospels have different wording but the same import.

Thus the dialogue between Jesus and his parents brings a real gospel motif into the story of the finding in the Temple. Moreover, in stressing the priority of God's claim, Jesus refers to God as his Father: "Did you not know that I must be in my Father's house?"[13] This reference makes the finding story a vehicle of self-revelation: Jesus is acknowledging that he is God's Son. The christological revelation, which we discussed above, has been moved back to the first moment of Jesus' adulthood.

[13] The Greek of Luke 2:49 is ambiguous; literally the key phrase is "in the . . . of my Father," with the plural of the definite article used in place of a noun. The suggestion that Luke means "in the dwelling-place (house) of my Father" is slightly more probable than the suggestion that he means "in or about the things (business, affairs) of my Father." However, since the word "house" is not used but at most implied, there is no stress on the identity of the Temple as the house of God, a stress falsely placed by some commentators.

The Third Christmas Story

Let me pause here to make a parenthetical remark about the implications of modern biblical criticism for this scene: the scene teaches us *nothing* about the historical development of Jesus' self-knowledge. Conservative interpreters have argued on the basis of 2:49 that already as a boy Jesus knew that he was the Son of God; liberal interpreters have argued from 2:52 ("Jesus made progress in wisdom") that as a boy Jesus did not know all things. Neither argument respects the nature of this story. The statement that we hear in 2:49 on the lips of Jesus represents the God-given insight of the post-resurrectional Christian community that Jesus is the Son of God. The statement about Jesus' progress in 2:52 is a stereotyped imitation of similar OT growth statements, for example, those referring to Samuel. What one can legitimately infer from the respective verses is that *Luke's appreciation* of Jesus did not cause him any difficulty in stating that Jesus grew in wisdom and God's favor, and that *Lucan christology* did not hesitate to affirm that Jesus was God's Son even before the baptism in the Jordan.[14]

Returning to the Lucan story, we find that Jesus' reference to his Father is not understood by his parents (2:50). In the pre-Lucan form of the story their lack of understanding offered no problem because this was probably the first revelation of Jesus' identity. In the present

[14] Although I have already written on the issue in *Jesus God and Man* (Macmillan paperback edition, 1972), 79–102, may I be allowed to repeat that the question "When did Jesus find out that he was God?" makes little sense (even as the liberal affirmation "Jesus did not know that he was God" makes less sense). This question is usually asked by a Christian who is presupposing a trinitarian conception of God, phrased in the categories of Greek philosophy of the fourth century, to test the human knowledge of a Galilean Jew of the first century in whose language "God" would mean the Father in heaven. If the question is phrased more intelligently, "When did Jesus come to understand his unique relationship to God?"—a uniqueness that *we* have rightly come to phrase in terms of divinity—then the question is not answerable biblically. Moreover, it is probably no more answerable psychologically than the question of when we come to understand that we are human. To a certain extent people understand who they are from the first moment they can think, even though it may take a lifetime to phrase that inchoative understanding adequately. By psychological analogy, if Jesus was God's Son (as we believe), he should have had some human awareness of his uniqueness from the first moment he could think, even though he never had the Greek philosophical language of the fourth century to phrase his self-understanding. But then is psychological analogy valid in the instance of Jesus?

Christ in the Gospels of the Liturgical Year

Lucan sequence where the parents already know that Jesus is God's Son,[15] the lack of understanding centers not on his identity but on the priority that he gives to the claims of his vocation over the claims of his parents. Particular Lucan attention is given to Mary, the one adult from these infancy and youth stories who will continue into the account of the ministry. Only later will she come to understand the true nature of Jesus' family. In Luke 8:19-21, when Mary and the brothers come asking for Jesus, Jesus will finally make clear that their importance is based not on physical relationship but on obedience to God: "My mother and my brothers are those who hear the word of God and do it." But Mary cannot understand that before the ministry, and so here Luke tells us: "His mother kept with concern all these events in her heart."[16] She is like the good disciple in the parable of the sower and the seed, where the seed that falls on good soil stands for "those who, hearing the word of God, hold it fast in an honest and good heart, and bring forth fruit with patience" (Luke 8:15).

At the end of the finding story (2:51) Luke wrestles with a problem that faces all pre-ministry tales. If the revelation of Jesus' identity is already given long before the baptism (whether at birth or in boyhood), why is it that people do not know who he is when he begins his ministry? In the birth stories Matthew and Luke handle this difficulty by specifying that those who received the revelation (the magi or the shepherds) left the scene and returned to whence they came (compare Matt 2:12 and Luke 2:20). But in this boyhood story the problem is complicated by the fact that Jesus himself has made the revelation and has begun to show his wisdom. If Jesus should continue behaving in this way, how will Luke plausibly describe a situation where the people at Nazareth will have no suspicion that Jesus is God's Son and think that he is merely Joseph's son (Luke 4:22)? To avoid such a conflict Luke insists on the uniqueness of this moment of self-assertion by

---

[15] Note the climactic arrangement pertinent to Jesus' identity in the existing Lucan narrative: in chapter 1 an angel proclaims that Jesus is God's Son; in chapter 2 Jesus proclaims it; in chapter 3 God the Father will proclaim it at the baptism.

[16] I have been suggesting that functionally the revelation by the boy Jesus in the finding story is the same as the revelation by an angel in the earlier Lucan infancy account. It is not surprising, then, that Luke's description of Mary's reaction here echoes his earlier description of Mary's reaction to the revelation following Jesus' birth: "Mary kept with concern all these events, interpreting them in her heart" (2:19).

The Third Christmas Story

Jesus. His normal pattern at Nazareth was to be obedient to his parents: "He went back down with them to Nazareth and was obedient to them" (2:51). And so Jesus gave the people at Nazareth no reason to suspect that God was his Father. In Mark's Gospel Jesus is the Son of God during the ministry, but his followers do not know it because he hides his power from them. Luke has moved the Marcan Secret back to the boyhood of Jesus. The poignancy that God's Son should willingly subject himself to obedience anticipates a fundamental tension of the ministry. Here Luke is remarkably close to Hebrews 5:8: "Although he was a Son, he learned obedience." The last of the Christmas stories proclaims the good news that God's Son is already in the world, but it also foreshadows the cross by insisting that Jesus preserved his identity in the role of a servant.

A Crucified Christ in Holy Week

Essays on the Four Gospel Passion Narratives

Chapters 16–21

Chapter 16

General Observations on the Passion Narratives

Every year during Holy Week the liturgy of the church exposes us to a bit of biblical criticism by appointing two different passion narratives to be read within a short period. On Palm or Passion Sunday we hear the Passion according to Matthew (Year A) or Mark (Year B) or Luke (Year C), while on Good Friday every year we hear the Passion according to John. "Those who have ears to hear" should notice that the two narratives which are read in a given year do not offer the same picture of the crucifixion of Jesus in either content or outlook. Let us consider the importance of that observation.

It has been argued that the gospel tradition was formed "backwards," starting from Jesus' resurrection and working toward his birth. Certainly early Christian preaching paid primary attention to the crucifixion and resurrection. For example, the Acts of the Apostles repeats: You killed Jesus by hanging or crucifying him, but God raised him up (2:32, 36; 5:30-31; 10:39-40). Then, as Christians reflected on the earlier career of the crucified one, accounts of Jesus' public ministry emerged, and eventually (in Matthew and Luke) accounts of his birth. Thus, a basic account of the crucifixion may have been shaped relatively soon in gospel formation.[1]

The shaping of such an account would have been facilitated by the necessary order of the events. Arrest had to precede trial, which, in turn, had to precede sentence and execution. The result in our canonical Gospels is a true narrative with a developing plot, tracing the actions and reactions not only of Jesus, but also of a cast of surrounding

---

[1] The majority of scholars hold this view, but a substantial minority think Mark put together the first consecutive passion account. This is often part of the thesis that exaggerates Mark's inventiveness in "creating" the Gospel format, a thesis that neglects the influence of OT prophetic "lives," such as the life of Jeremiah, which combines public actions, speeches, and a passion. Mark's passion account, however, need not depend directly on an earlier written passion narrative.

characters, such as Peter, Judas, and Pilate. The impact of Jesus' fate on various people is vividly illustrated, and the drama of the tragedy is heightened by contrasting figures. Alongside the innocent Jesus who is condemned is the revolutionary Barabbas who is freed, even though guilty of a political charge similar to that levied against Jesus. Alongside the scoffing Jewish authorities who make fun of Jesus as Messiah or Son of God is a Roman soldier who recognizes him as Son of God. No wonder that the liturgy encourages our acting out the passion narratives with assigned roles read aloud! Each passion narrative constitutes a simple dramatic play.

Indeed, John's account of the trial of Jesus before Pilate comes close to supplying stage directions, with the chief priests and "the Jews" carefully localized outside the praetorium and Jesus alone within. The shuttling of Pilate back and forth between the two sides dramatizes a man who seeks to take a middle position, reconciling what he regards as extremes and not deciding for either. Yet the tables are turned; and Pilate, not Jesus, is the one who is really on trial, caught between light and darkness, truth and falsehood. Jesus challenges him to hear the truth (John 19:37); but his cynical response, "What is truth?" is in reality a decision for falsehood. John is warning the reader that no one can avoid judgment when he or she stands before Jesus.

A. AUDIENCE PARTICIPATION INVITED

Personification of different character types in the passion drama serves a religious goal. We readers or hearers are meant to participate by asking ourselves how we would have stood in relation to the trial and crucifixion of Jesus. With which character in the narrative would I identify myself? The distribution of palms in church may too quickly assure me that I would have been among the crowd that hailed Jesus appreciatively. Is it not more likely that I might have been among the disciples who fled from danger, abandoning him? Or at moments in my life have I not played the role of Peter, denying Jesus, or even of Judas, betraying him? Have I not found myself like the Johannine Pilate, trying to avoid a decision between good and evil? Or like the Matthean Pilate, have I made a bad decision and then washed my hands so that the record could show that I was blameless?

Or, most likely of all, might I not have stood among the religious leaders who condemned Jesus? If this possibility seems remote, it is because many have understood too simply the motives of Jesus' opponents. True, Mark's account of the trial of Jesus conducted by the chief priests and the Jewish Sanhedrin portrays dishonest judges with minds already made up, even to the point of seeking *false* witness against Jesus. But we must recognize that apologetic motives colored the Gospels. Remember our official Catholic teaching (Pontifical Biblical Commission in 1964) that, in the course of apostolic preaching and of Gospel writing, the memory of what happened in Jesus' lifetime was affected by the life-situations of local Christian communities.

One coloring factor was the need to give a balanced portrayal of Jesus in a world governed by Roman law. Tacitus, the Roman historian, remembers Jesus with disdain as a criminal put to death by Pontius Pilate, the procurator of Judea. Christians could offset such a negative attitude by using Pilate as a spokesman for the innocence of Jesus. If one moves consecutively through the Gospel accounts of Mark, Matthew, Luke, and John, Pilate is portrayed ever more insistently as a fair judge who recognized the guiltlessness of Jesus in regard to political issues. Roman hearers of the Gospels had Pilate's assurance that Jesus was not a criminal.

Another coloring factor was the bitter relationship between early church and synagogue. The attitudes attributed to "all" the Jewish religious authorities (Matt 27:1) may have been those of only some. In the group of Jewish leaders who dealt with Jesus it would be astounding if there were not some venal "ecclesiastical" politicians who were getting rid of a possible danger to their own position. (The Annas high-priestly family of which Caiaphas was a member gets low marks in Jewish memory.) It would be equally amazing if the majority did not consist of sincerely religious men who thought they were serving God in ridding Israel of a troublemaker like Jesus (see John 16:2). In their view Jesus may have been a false prophet misleading people by his permissive attitudes toward the Sabbath and sinners. The Jewish mockery of Jesus after the Sanhedrin trial makes his status as a prophet the issue (Mark 14:65), and according to the law of Deuteronomy 13:1-5 the false prophet had to be put to death lest he seduce Israel from the true God.

I suggested above that in assigning ourselves a role in the passion story some of us might have been among the opponents of Jesus. That is because Gospel readers are often sincerely religious people who have a deep attachment to their tradition. Jesus was a challenge to religious traditionalists since he pointed to a human element in their holy traditions—an element too often identified with God's will (see Matt 15:6). If Jesus was treated harshly by the literal-minded religious people of

General Observations on the Passion Narratives

his time who were Jews, it is quite likely that he would be treated harshly by similar religious people of our time, including Christians. Not Jewish background but religious mentality is the basic component in the reaction to Jesus.

B. FACTORS IN THE DEATH OF JESUS

The exact public involvement of Jewish authorities in the death of Jesus is a complicated issue. Early Jewish tradition freely admits responsibility for "hanging" Jesus on the eve of Passover because "he seduced Israel, leading her astray" (Babylonian Talmud, *Sanhedrin* 43a). Yet modern Jewish writers have rejected in whole or in part Jewish involvement in the crucifixion. A frequent argument is that the Sanhedrin legal procedures described in the Gospels do not agree with Jewish Law expounded in the Mishnah and so cannot be factual. The Mishnah, completed about A.D. 200, is the written codification of the *Pharisee* oral law; but in Jesus' time Sadducee priests, not Pharisees, dominated the Sanhedrin, and they rejected oral law, claiming to rely only on the written law of the OT. The trial of Jesus as narrated in the Gospels does not violate the letter of the written law; therefore, the accounts of Jewish involvement cannot be so easily dismissed on technical grounds.[2] We are reminded by this point, however, that, although during his ministry Jesus may have argued with the Pharisees, those Jews who had the most direct involvement in his death were the priests, perhaps angered by his prophetic castigation of Temple practice.

Let us probe further, asking in what way and to what extent the priests and the Sanhedrin were involved. A distinguished Jewish commentator on the trial of Jesus, Paul Winter, would give priority to Luke's account of the procedure against Jesus, for, unlike Mark and

[2] Other explanations exonerating Jewish religious leadership posit two Sanhedrins, e.g., one political which worked with the Romans (and which found Jesus guilty at their bidding) and the other religious (which did not deal with Jesus or was not opposed to him). The evidence for the existence of such diverse bodies is slim; and those who shaped early Christian tradition (among whom some were certainly familiar with the Palestinian scene) make no such distinction. The oldest preserved Christian writing (*ca.* A.D. 50), 1 Thessalonians, speaks baldly about "the Jews who killed the Lord Jesus" (2:14-15—a text that is probably authentically Pauline despite attempts to classify it as a later scribal edition). Such a sentiment may be overgeneralized, but it is scarcely without some foundation in fact.

Matthew, Luke reports no calling of witnesses and no Jewish death sentence on Jesus. Yet the failure to mention a death sentence probably does not mean that in Luke's mind the Jewish leaders were free from responsibility for the death of Jesus, since elsewhere he stresses an active Jewish role (Acts 2:36; 4:10; 5:30; 7:52; 10:39; 13:27-29). Nevertheless, unlike the formal Sanhedrin trial at night recounted in Mark and Matthew (with the latter specifying the high priest to have been Caiaphas), in Luke there is a less formal Sanhedrin questioning of Jesus in the morning. John recounts no Sanhedrin session after the arrest of Jesus but only a police interrogation conducted by the high priest Annas (18:19-24). Further confusion: John 18:3, 12 indicates that the party which arrested Jesus involved not only Jewish police supplied by the high priest but also Roman soldiers with their tribune. Roman soldiers would not have taken part without the prefect's permission or orders; and so, if the Johannine information is historical, Pilate had to have known beforehand about the arrest of Jesus and perhaps had even commanded it.

It is not impossible that, having heard rumors of Jesus as the Messiah (the anointed king of the house of David whom many Jews were awaiting), Pilate wanted the Jewish authorities of the Sanhedrin to investigate him and so assisted in his arrest. Some of those authorities would have had their own religious worries about Jesus and antipathies toward him (for example, as a false prophet). Yet they could have told themselves that they were only carrying out orders in handing Jesus over to the Romans for further action, on the grounds that under interrogation he had not denied that he was the Messiah. (Notice, I say "not denied," for the response of Jesus to the question of being the Messiah differs in the various Gospel accounts of the trial: "I am" in Mark; "That is what you say, but. . . ." in Matthew; "If I tell you, you will not believe" in Luke; see John 10:24-25.) Religious people of all times have accomplished what they wanted through the secular authority acting for its own purposes.

Attention must be paid to such complications lest the liturgical reading of the passion narratives leads to simplistic accusations about guilt for the death of Jesus. As I shall point out when I discuss the individual passion accounts, both Matthew ("all the people" in 27:25) and John ("the Jews" throughout) generalize hostilely, so that participation in the execution of Jesus is extended beyond even the Jewish leadership. Reflective of this, some famous Christian theologians

General Observations on the Passion Narratives

(Augustine, John Chrysostom, Thomas Aquinas, Martin Luther) have made statements about the Christian duty to hate or punish the Jews because they killed the Lord. Thus, modern apprehensions about the anti-Jewish impact of the passion narratives are not groundless. One solution that has been proposed is to remove the "anti-Semitic" passages from the liturgical readings of the passion during Holy Week, a type of "Speak no evil; see no evil; hear no evil" response. But removing offensive passages is a dangerous procedure which enables hearers of bowdlerized versions to accept unthinkingly everything in the Bible. Accounts "improved" by excision perpetuate the fallacy that what one hears in the Bible is always to be imitated because it is "revealed" by God, and the fallacy that every position taken by an author of Scripture is inerrant.[3] In my opinion, a truer response is to continue to read unabridged passion accounts in Holy Week, not subjecting them to excisions that seem wise to us—but once having read them, to preach forcefully that such hostility between Christian and Jew cannot be continued today and is against our fundamental understanding of Christianity. Sooner or later Christian believers must wrestle with the limitations imposed on the Scriptures by the circumstances in which they were written. They must be brought to see that some attitudes found in the Scriptures, however explicable in the times in which they originated, may be wrong attitudes if repeated today. They must reckon with the implications inherent in the fact that God has revealed *in human words*. Congregations who listen to the passion proclamations in Holy Week will not recognize this, however, unless it is clearly pointed out. To include the passages that have an anti-Jewish import and not to comment on them is irresponsible proclamation that will detract from a mature understanding of our Lord's death.

C. HOW DID JESUS HIMSELF VIEW HIS DEATH?
Besides reflecting on what the passion of Jesus should mean for us, we may ask what did it mean for Jesus? We are told in Romans 4:25 that Jesus died for our sins, but would Jesus himself have used such language? Did he foresee the exact manner of his death and victory? In

---

[3] How much more cautious is Vatican II (Dogmatic Constitution *Dei Verbum* on Divine Revelation, #11) in confining inerrancy: "The books of Scripture must be acknowledged as teaching firmly, faithfully, and without error that truth which God wanted put into the sacred writings for the sake of our salvation."

Christ in the Gospels of the Liturgical Year

Mark (8:31; 9:31; 10:33-34, with parallels in Matthew and Luke) there are three predictions of the fate of the Son of Man, one more detailed than the other. Yet, once we recall the Catholic Church's official teaching that sayings uttered by Jesus have been expanded and interpreted by the apostolic preachers and the evangelists before they were put in the Gospels, we have the right and duty to ask whether these predictions have not become more exact by hindsight. Have they not been filled out with details by those who knew what happened to Jesus? John has three statements (3:14; 8:28; 12:32, 34) about the "lifting up" of the Son of Man—a much less precise reference to crucifixion and ascension! Jesus may have originally expressed general premonitions about his suffering and death (a hostile fate discoverable from the example of the prophets), plus a firm trust that God would make him victorious (without knowing exactly how).

Hebrews 5:7-8 reports, "In the days when he was in the flesh, he offered prayers and supplications with cries and tears to God who was able to save him from death, and he was heard because of his reverence. Son though he was, he learned obedience from what he suffered." Jesus had preached that God's kingdom would be realized most readily when human beings acknowledged their dependence on God. The model for this kingdom was not power over others but the helplessness of the little child. We humans come most clearly to terms with our helplessness when we face death. Did Jesus, the proclaimer of the kingdom, himself have to experience the vulnerability of dying before the kingdom could be achieved in and through him? Jesus' reference at the Last Supper (Luke 21:16, 18) to the imminence of the kingdom confirms the possibility that he used "kingdom" language to phrase his own understanding of his death. The coming of the kingdom would involve the ultimate destruction of the power of evil, and Jesus' confrontation with Satan in the great period of trial is echoed in various passion narrative passages (Mark 14:38; Luke 22:53; John 14:30). The thought of such a confrontation may explain Jesus' anguish before his fate; and his trust in God's power to defeat Satan may have been his way of expressing the truth caught by NT writers when they said that he died to remove sin.

D. EARLY CHRISTIAN VIEWS OF JESUS' DEATH

Finally, we should reflect on what Jesus' passion meant to Christians of the NT period, using the Gospels as a guide. It is noteworthy that many features depicted by later artists and writers have no place in the Gospel accounts, for instance, elements of pathos and emotion, and a concentration on pain and suffering. On Calvary, the evangelists report laconically, "They crucified him," without reference to the manner. Strikingly, however, they pay attention to the division of his garments and to the exact placement of the criminals crucified with him. Such details were important to the early Christians because they found them anticipated in OT psalms and prophets. Not biography but theology dominated the choice of events to be narrated, and the OT was the theological sourcebook of the time. (This approach is far more likely than the skeptical contention that Christians created the details of the passion in order to fulfill the OT.) The evangelists were emphasizing that through the Scriptures of Israel God had taught about His Son. Their emphasis also had an apologetic touch against Jews who rejected the crucified Jesus precisely because they did not think he fulfilled scriptural expectations.

Moving beyond the shared Christian theology of the passion, we come now to the distinctive insight in the passion account of each canonical Gospel. The subsequent chapters of this section will be devoted consecutively to each of the four accounts, and in a conclusion I shall make a brief overall comparison. As I stated above, my goal is to enrich Holy Week preaching and reflection on the passion accounts; but let me note two ways in which scholarly practicality forces me to deviate slightly from the lectionary passion narratives read on Palm/Passion Sunday and on Good Friday. (1) The liturgical readings extend from the Last Supper to the burial.[4] In point of fact, scholars debate about where the passion narrative begins and ends (either as a separate entity originating before the written Gospels or as intended by the individual evangelists). Does it begin with the Last Supper and does it include the women's visit to the empty tomb? In 1 Corinthians Paul speaks of a tradition of eucharistic words and actions "on the night when Jesus was handed over" (11:23) and of a tradition that Christ died and was buried, was raised and appeared (15:3). Perhaps, then, there was already a pre-Pauline sequence from the eucharist to the

---

[4] This is the range of the "long form." There are short forms (which throughout the Missal are an abomination to be avoided at all costs), but these eliminate parts of the story that must be considered essential in any comprehensible understanding of the passion.

Christ in the Gospels of the Liturgical Year

tomb. Certainly Luke thought of the Last Supper, the arrest, the passion and death, the burial, and the visit to the tomb as a unit. (He situates the prediction of Peter's denials at the supper, tying the supper into what follows; similarly, after the burial he has the women prepare the spices that they bring to the tomb on Sunday morning.) Mark, however, may have joined separate traditions of the supper, the passion (beginning with the scene in Gethsemane), and the empty tomb. A scholar might wish to subdivide a commentary on Matthew so that the passion section begins with 26:1, or with 26:30, or with 26:36! Be that as it may, in reflecting on the passion in Holy Week we must be practical. Sections of the Gospels dealing with the Last Supper (containing the eucharistic institution) and with the resurrection are extremely complicated from a scholarly viewpoint. Even the long, comprehensive commentary that I produced could not treat those sections within the confines of one volume. Moreover, in our ordinary understanding of liturgical topics, the Last Supper belongs to Holy Thursday preaching, and the resurrection belongs to Easter Sunday and afterwards. One would not normally make those the subject of passion preaching and reflection associated with Palm/Passion Sunday and Good Friday. Thus, a manageable and intelligible definition of the passion narrative as extending *from Gethsemane to the grave* will be operative in this section (as in my *The Death of the Messiah*). In each case, however, I shall try to situate the passion so-defined into the larger context of the individual Gospel so that the evangelist's intent and flow of thought are not neglected.

(2) Within the pattern of A, B, and C years, the liturgy of Palm/ Passion Sunday presents the Synoptic passion narratives in the order Matthew, Mark, and Luke, so that the Matthean narrative is read first, a year before the Marcan narrative. Although a few scholars (who are persistent and vocal) would have Mark dependent upon Matthew and Luke, the majority opinion by far is that both Matthew and Luke drew on Mark. In the passion narrative in particular, Matthew is so close to Mark that there is no need to posit another additional source. Apparently the author of Matthew edited and adapted what he drew from Mark, adding a few items from popular tradition and early Christian apologetics, for example, about the death of Judas, about Pilate (washing his hands) and Mrs. Pilate (dreaming about Jesus' innocence), and about guards placed at the tomb. The interdependence of the canonical passion accounts is not a matter of great importance for the essays in

General Observations on the Passion Narratives

this volume, for I am deliberately concentrating on the distinctive outlook offered by each evangelist and not on where the evangelist got
his ideas. Nevertheless, a sequence in which Mark is placed first will
give a clearer understanding of the passion to someone who reads the
four Gospel essays consecutively. It seems then that nothing will be
lost and something may be gained if I use the order Mark, Matthew,
Luke, and John.

Chapter 17

The Passion According to Mark

The Marcan passion narrative is read on Palm/Passion Sunday in the same liturgical year (B) in which the Gospel of Mark has supplied the readings on the Sundays of the Ordinary Time. In connecting these two Marcan contributions, the church is recognizing that the evangelist does not present his story of Jesus' death without having prepared for it in the narrative of the public ministry. At the very beginning of Mark (1:14) John the Baptist was "handed over" to Herod, who eventually yielded to pressure by others and killed this prophet (6:26). Facing the question of who Jesus might be, Herod evoked the violent death of John: "John whom I beheaded has been raised" (6:16). When Jesus' ministry in Galilee had just begun, Mark (3:6) tells us that Pharisees and Herodians plotted to destroy him. Three times Jesus had predicted his own violent death (8:31; 9:31; 10:33-34); yet his disciples never understood. All of this came to a head when Jesus arrived at Jerusalem and purified the Temple, declaring that it must be a house of prayer for all the nations—that led the priests and the scribes in Jerusalem to plot to destroy him (11:17-18). In this threatening situation, a woman who admired Jesus prepared him for death by anointing his body for burial (14:3-9), but one of his intimates among the Twelve conspired to hand him over to the priests who were his enemies (14:1-2, 10-11). Knowing of this treason (14:21), Jesus at the Last Supper was willing to pour out his blood for all as a sign of the covenant that God was making anew with His people (14:24).

A. GETHSEMANE: PRAYER AND ARREST (14:26-52)
Thus, the Jesus who left the supper room to go with his disciples to the Mount of Olives[1] was one who had come to terms with the necessity that he must suffer and die before the kingdom of God could come. In the Marcan view, however, the disciples had not accepted

---

[1] The symbolism of this place will be treated in relation to Matthew's account which develops the Davidic connections of the site.

that reality. Accordingly, Jesus' words to them institute a tragic message: all will be scattered (14:27). Peter denies this, only to be told that he will be particularly unfaithful, denying Jesus three times. The Marcan passion begins on this gloomy note, and the darkness will intensify until Jesus breathes his last the next day. In all that time no support will come from those who have been his followers, and he will die alone. The tragedy seems almost too much for Jesus himself. Having separated from the larger body of the disciples and then further separated from Peter, James, and John, Jesus confesses plaintively, "My soul is very sorrowful, even to death" (14:34). Previously Jesus had affirmed, "Whoever would save his life will lose it"; but now, more insistently than in the other Gospels, he prays that this hour or this cup might pass from him. Even though he has predicted Peter's denials, he is upset that Peter could not watch one hour with him. Although there is no direct response from God to Jesus' prayer for deliverance, ultimately Jesus rises resolved to encounter the betrayer, leaving us to assume that he has understood God's answer to be that he must drink the cup and face the hour that is at hand.

For Mark (and here he differs from the other three evangelists) Jesus' resignation to his fate may be seen in his failure to respond to the Judas who kisses him or to the bystander who draws the sword and strikes the slave of the high priest on the ear. If the hour and cup could not pass, as Jesus had prayed earlier, let be what God wills. And so when Jesus is arrested, his last words are, "Let the Scriptures be fulfilled." Seeing such resignation, the disciples all forsake him and flee.

Once again differing from the other evangelists, Mark underlines almost brutally the totality of the abandonment. He tells the story of a young man who does seek to follow; but, when seized as Jesus had been, this would-be disciple leaves in the hands of his captors the linen garment that had clothed him, and runs away naked. Some scholars have sought to relate this figure to the young man who after the resurrection will sit at the empty tomb clothed in a white robe. Among the symbolisms suggested is that of the Christian who descends naked into the baptismal water to die with Jesus and then comes forth to be clothed in a white robe. Probably such symbolism lies beyond Mark's intention. Rather, the disciple fleeing naked is symbolic simply of the total abandonment of Jesus by his disciples. The first disciples to be called left nets and family (1:18, 20), indeed everything (10:28), to follow him; but this last disciple, who at first sought to follow Jesus, ultimately leaves everything to get away from him.

Christ in the Gospels of the Liturgical Year

The stark Marcan portrayal of Jesus at Gethsemane has been recognized as difficult both by believers and nonbelievers. Well-meaning preachers and writers have argued that Jesus' sorrow was not in the face of death and that he did not ask to be delivered from suffering; rather, foreseeing all the sin in the world, he shrank at the thought of so much evil. More perceptively, anti-Christian critics have recognized that Mark was indeed describing a reaction to death; but they queried how a Jesus who so feared to die could be divine, or how one so devoted to God could ask to avoid the cross that he proclaimed as necessary for others. Even in recent times the picture of a Jesus distressed and greatly troubled, asking to be delivered, has been contrasted with a Socrates calmly accepting death as a deliverance from this world of shadowy realities and as an entree to a better world. All of this fails to consider the basic outlook on death inherited from the OT. In the theology of Genesis, human beings were created to enjoy God's presence in this life and not to die. Death was an evil imposed on Adam and Eve, and ultimately in Israelite thought it came to be seen as a realm of alienation from God. The NT, even after Christ's victory, speaks of death as the last enemy to be overcome (1 Cor 15:26). For Jesus, the struggle with death is part of the great trial or temptation of the last times; and he is faithful to Judaism when he tells his disciples to pray not to enter into this temptation (Mark 14:38). Their great danger is that the trial comes at a moment when they do not expect and are not watching (13:34-37), and so Jesus warns them to watch. It is not surprising that either ancients or moderns imbued with platonic ideals would find Jesus' attitude toward death disgraceful. The Christian answer lies not in underplaying the apprehension of Jesus, but in stressing the importance of life in this world so that death is seen as a distortion and not as a welcome deliverance—an enemy that, because of Jesus' victory, cannot conquer but an enemy nonetheless. The obedience that Jesus showed to God's will and the trust that this demanded of him are all the more impressive when it is realized how satanic an enemy he was encountering.

B. SANHEDRIN TRIAL; PETER'S DENIAL (14:53-72)
Mark establishes a transition from Gethsemane by two sentences, each giving the scenario for an episode to take place this night. The first sentence (14:53) has Jesus led before the assembly of chief priests, elders, and scribes—the Jewish Sanhedrin, which even under Roman occupation, had certain governmental and judicial functions. The

second sentence (14:54) has Peter follow Jesus into the courtyard of the high priest, where he sits with guards, warming himself at the fire. Jesus will be questioned before the Sanhedrin and Peter will be questioned in the courtyard; the behavior of the two men will form a sharp contrast.

The first of these two night episodes is the trial of Jesus which ends with a judicial sentence leading to his death. The trial begins with false witnesses whose testimony, Mark stresses, does not agree. Indeed, deliberately or indeliberately, Mark has left their testimony about the destruction of the Temple incoherent for his readers; for he never explains what is false in the words they attribute to Jesus: "I will destroy this Temple that is made with hands, and in three days I will build another not made with hands." Did Jesus never say anything like this about the Temple? Or did he say something similar but not with the tone given by the witnesses? Did he prophesy destruction and restoration but not make himself the agent of the destruction (cf. John 2:19)? Or is the development of the tradition still more complicated, namely, that although the witnesses gave a false implication to Jesus' words, Mark is offering a clue for interpreting them correctly by the clarifying clauses "made with hands" and "not made with hands." This elegant pair of positive and negative Greek adjectives (found only in Mark) is very difficult to retrovert into Semitic; the adjectives, then, more likely represent a later Christian explanation that the Temple would be replaced by the church.

In any case, the high priest is annoyed by both the ineptitude of the witnesses and the silence of Jesus—the silence which Christians found foretold in the Isaian picture of the Suffering Servant of the Lord (53:7). Seeking to force an answer, the high priest demands, "Are you the Messiah, the son of the Blessed?" God had proclaimed Jesus as His Son both at the baptism (Mark 1:11) and at the transfiguration (9:7); Peter had proclaimed Jesus as Messiah (8:29); and so it is not surprising that Jesus answers with an affirmative. But he then goes on to explain that he is not only the anointed Davidic prince expected to establish a kingdom: he is the Son of Man who at the endtime will come from God's presence to judge the world. His warning to the high priest, "You will see the Son of Man coming with the clouds of heaven," shows Jesus' conviction that even his enemies will be forced to recognize his triumph. The warning is rejected; the high priest sees only blasphemy in the claim that as Son of Man Jesus will sit at the right hand of the Power, and so he coerces *all* the judges to condemn Jesus as deserving death. Not a voice is raised in his defense. The malice of the procedure is further underlined when some of the Sanhedrin members spit on Jesus. Covering his face, they strike him, challenging him to prophesy. Once more, Christian readers would hear an echo of Isaiah's description of the Suffering Servant of the Lord (50:6): "I hid not my face from shame and spitting."

This trial has combined the themes of destroying the Temple and of acknowledging Jesus as Messiah/Son of God. These themes, which were already evident in the Marcan account of the public ministry, will recur twice more before the passion is over; and by the end Jesus' role as a prophet, mocked by the Sanhedrin, will be vindicated.

If Jesus has not yielded under questioning by the high priest, Peter's behavior under questioning by the retinue of the high priest is quite different. The Lord confesses; the disciple denies. Peter's first denial, directed to a maidservant, is a pretense not to understand, followed by an attempt to get away from the courtyard and from public attention. But the persistent maidservant pursues him, and so Peter is forced to deny his status as a disciple—he is not one of those associated with Jesus. A third denial intensifies the shame, for now Peter swears an oath that he does not even know Jesus. As Peter says this, he curses. If Mark means (as many scholars think) that he is cursing Jesus, truly Peter has reached the depths of degradation in his discipleship—many a later Christian reader of Mark would face martyrdom rather than deny or curse Jesus. But at this moment Peter remembers Jesus' prophetic words about a triple denial, and he is moved to weep. Thus Mark does not finish the portrait of Peter without a redeeming touch; after all, the same Jesus who had prophesied Peter's denials had included him in the promise: "After I am raised up, I will go before you to Galilee" (14:28). If one thinks again of future martyrs, the story of Peter could offer hope to those who had failed and denied Jesus. The reader in concluding this section should not miss the irony that at the very moment when Jesus is being mocked by the Sanhedrin challenge to prophesy, his prophecies are coming true.

C. ROMAN TRIAL (15:1-20)

Mark effects the transition from the Jewish trial to the Roman trial by a reference to a morning consultation of the whole Sanhedrin (15:1). It is not clear whether he intends to describe a second session of this body or is resumptively concluding the night session after the interruption effected by the account of Peter's denials. Nor does Mark make it clear why, when the Sanhedrin had condemned Jesus as deserving death, they do not execute the sentence but decide to bind him and deliver him to Pilate. (This logical difficulty is addressed only by John [18:31] among the evangelists.) It is almost as if Mark is telling a tale well known and is not bothering to supply connectives; for when Pilate confronts Jesus, he has no need to be informed as to what has gone on or about the issues that were the subject of the Jewish trial. Nothing about the Temple or about the Messiah/Son of God is repeated. The issue is immediately shifted from the religious to the political: "Are you the King of the Jews?" (15:3)—a question about a title hitherto never used for Jesus by friend or foe, and therefore presumably reflecting the interests or fears of the Romans.

Jesus' ambiguous affirmation, "You have said so," is deemed no answer by Pilate (Mark 15:4), so that the motif of Jesus' silence before his captors, already echoed in the Jewish trial (14:61), reappears in the Roman trial. As the nations wondered at the Suffering Servant of the Lord who received no glory from others (Isa 52:15 Septuagint), so Pilate wonders at Jesus (Mark 15:5). In Mark's portrayal, the chief priests, having failed to move Pilate to condemn Jesus, are more successful with a crowd that has come to ask for the release of a prisoner on the feast. Knowing that the priests acted out of envious zeal, Pilate offers Jesus, the accused "King of the Jews," to this crowd; but the priests persuade them to ask instead for Barabbas, an imprisoned murderous rebel,[2] and to demand the crucifixion of Jesus. Pilate's last quoted words, "Why, what evil has he done?" serves to underline how outrageously Jesus is treated by those who might have been expected to be enthusiastic for their "King." The only thing that will satisfy them is the decision to flog and crucify Jesus.

Inevitably, there is an anti-Jewish tone in having the priests and, through them, the crowd so hostile to Jesus. Nevertheless, the Marcan portrayal of Pilate is less developed and less sympathetic than that of the other Gospels, and so the contrast with the Jewish leaders is less stark. In Mark, Pilate makes no intensive effort on Jesus' behalf, and

[2] Certain manuscripts of Matthew will offer a peculiar insight into Barabbas; see p. 170 below.

yields rather easily to the crowd in order to avoid unpopularity. The impression, then, is not one of the favorable Roman and the hostile Jew—rather it is of a Jesus who had no support on any side. That impression is reinforced by the gratuitous brutality of the Roman soldiers who interrupt the crucifixion process of flogging the criminal and leading him to the cross to vent their scorn on the "King of the Jews," striking him and spitting on him. Both trials end with mockery: the Jewish trial with the mocking of a prophet, the Roman trial with the mocking of a king. For neither Jew nor Roman was it enough that Jesus die; his claims had to be derided. In a sequence where Judas hands over Jesus to the chief priests (14:10-11), and the chief priests hand Jesus over to Pilate (15:1), and Pilate hands Jesus over to be crucified (15:15), it becomes clear that disciple, Jewish leader, and Roman leader all have a share of guilt.

D. CRUCIFIXION, DEATH, AND BURIAL (15:21-47)
Although among the four Gospels Mark provides the shortest account of the crucifixion, he makes every detail count. On the way to the cross, Mark pauses to identify Simon of Cyrene through the two sons Alexander and Rufus, perhaps because these men were known to the community for which Mark wrote. In his extremely laconic description of the act of crucifixion, Mark highlights the curious details of the offering of wine mixed with myrrh and the division of the garments— a sign of the influence of the Psalm passages 69:22; 22:19 that the later evangelists will make explicit.[3]

Mark's artistry is most apparent in his resort to an organizing pattern of threes (already used so effectively in Jesus' threefold prayer at Gethsemane and in Peter's three denials). Mark spells out a chronological pattern of the third, sixth, and ninth hours (9 A.M., noon, 3 P.M.). Between the third and the sixth hours, three groups mock the crucified. First, the reference to destroying and rebuilding the Temple is taken from the Jewish trial and hurled as a blasphemy at the crucified Jesus by chance passersby who wag their heads and challenge him to save himself. Here Mark is echoing Psalm 22:8-9, a citation that Matthew will strengthen. Second, in a mounting crescendo the chief priests and the scribes take up another motif from the Jewish trial, mocking the

---

[3] See below pp. 172 and 188.

The Passion According to Mark

pretension that Jesus is "the Messiah, the King of Israel." Third, even the criminals crucified with Jesus revile him.

If no human being shows Jesus sympathy in this first three-hour period, nature itself is plunged into a darkness that covers the whole land during the second, from the sixth to the ninth hour. Here Mark may be recalling the warning of Amos 8:9 that the sun would go down at noon and the light would be darkened on the earth by day.

Finally, at the ninth hour, Jesus cries out with a loud voice the only words that Mark reports. In response to three hours of mockery by all who spoke to him, and to three hours of nature's gloom, Jesus repeats the opening words of Psalm 22, asking, "My God, my God, why have you forsaken me?" This cry should not be softened,[4] any more than Jesus' plea to his Father in Gethsemane should be softened. It is paradoxical that the cry is quoted in Aramaic which carries the tone of the intimacy of Jesus' family language, and yet now for the first time Jesus speaks to Yahweh as "God," instead of as "Father." Mark is brutally realistic in showing that, while this desperate plea causes some to offer Jesus wine, it leads to skeptical mockery by others whose cynicism about Elijah's help constitutes the last human words that Jesus will hear—and no Elijah comes to deliver him. John the Baptist had come in the Elijah role not to deliver Jesus, but to die a martyr's death and point to the type of violent death that awaits Jesus (9:12-13). In the Marcan account of the ministry, the demons had cried out with a loud voice as they encountered the presence of God's Son. In this hour of darkness, as Jesus struggles with Satan, it is God's Son who cries out a second time with a loud voice as he expires. The apocalyptic scene evokes the words of Joel 2:10-11; 4:16: "The sun and moon shall be darkened . . . and the Lord shall give His voice before His host. . . . The Lord will give His voice from Jerusalem and the heavens and the earth will be shaken, but the Lord will spare His people."

The Lord God's response to His Son's cry is described with stunning abruptness by Mark. The moment Jesus expires the curtain of the Temple is torn in two from top to bottom. Scholars debate whether the veil was the one that separated the outer court from the sanctuary or the inner veil that led to the Holy of Holies—a debate often centered

---

[4] Under the Matthean form of this cry I shall discuss the implicit christology involved.

on the symbolic signs attached to each veil. There is nothing, however, to suggest that Mark's readers (or even Mark himself) would have had the specialized knowledge to understand the difference or the symbolism. More important is the debate whether the tearing of the Temple veil is meant to signify the displeasure of God abandoning the Temple or an opening of a once-closed sacred place to a wider audience, especially to the Gentiles. While the latter allows a more benevolent interpretation of Mark's attitude toward Judaism, the former is more probable, even if more unpleasant. The language of "schism" from top to bottom indicates a violent rending, similar to the high priest's tearing his garments in judgment at the trial of Jesus.

Indeed, that trial supplies two motifs that recur here immediately after Jesus' death—motifs repeated already once in the mockery at the foot of the cross. The rending of the Temple veil is the incipient fulfillment of the saying attributed to Jesus at the trial: "I will destroy this Temple that is made with hands." With the veil torn, this Temple is being destroyed, not being opened to outsiders; for the Temple to which the outsiders will come is one not built with hands. And the first of the outsiders comes immediately. Seeing how Jesus expired, a Roman centurion confesses, "Truly this man was Son of God." He thus evokes the second motif from the Jewish trial where Jesus was adjured to state whether he was "the Messiah, the Son of the Blessed One." Jesus' answers at the trial caused him to be mocked as a false prophet, but now the prophet is verified. Not only is the Temple being destroyed but also for the first time in the Gospel a human being has recognized Jesus' identity as God's Son.

Abandoned by his disciples, betrayed by Judas, denied by Peter, accused of blasphemy by the priests, rejected in favor of a murderer by the crowd, mocked by the Sanhedrin and by Roman troops and by all who came to the cross, surrounded by darkness, and seemingly forsaken by his God, in this one dramatic moment Jesus is fully vindicated. God has answered Jesus' cry by replacing the Temple as the locus of worship and by offering in its place His own Son who will be confessed by Gentile and Jew alike. Only after the centurion's confession are we told that some of Jesus' followers, women who had ministered to him and others from Galilee, were at Golgotha; and we are led to assume that they too would have shared the centurion's confession. Mark is specific about the reaction of one Jewish figure, Joseph of Arimathea, "a respected member of the Sanhedrin." He had been "looking for the Kingdom of God," but Jesus' death brought him forward to ask for the body of the crucified. Only Mark stresses that this was an act of courage— understandably, since Mark has told us that *all* the members of the Sanhedrin had found Jesus deserving of death.

The Roman centurion and Joseph of Arimathea dramatize Mark's theological outlook on the importance of the passion. People can believe and become true disciples only through the suffering symbolized by a cross which strips away human supports and makes one totally dependent on God. Jesus had been taunted to come down from the cross and save himself, whereas salvation comes only through the acceptance of the cross. If the crucifixion of Jesus is described by Mark with greater severity and starkness than is found in the other Gospels, perhaps the Marcan message had to encourage a community that had endured a particularly severe testing. (The ancient tradition that Mark was addressed to Roman Christians would make sense if they had seen "a vast multitude" brutally martyred under Nero.) The gospel or "Good News" for them was that this trial and suffering was not a defeat but a salvific example of taking up the cross and following Jesus.

At the close of the passion narrative, only Mark among the Synoptics tells us that Pilate checked whether Jesus was dead. This emphasis may be a sign that already Christian apologists were wrestling with the claim that Jesus, not really dead, had been revived by the chill of the tomb, a charge that would be given new emphasis by eighteenth- and nineteenth-century rationalists! Mark's double stress on the presence of Mary Magdalene and the other women (15:40, 47) who "saw where Jesus was laid" is meant to prepare for their Sunday morning visit to a tomb that would be found empty. For Mark, the story of Jesus' death does not close with his burial, but with his resurrection.

Chapter 18

The Passion According to Matthew

The same liturgical year (A) that offers the Matthean passion account on Palm/Passion Sunday draws from the rest of Matthew on the Sundays of the Ordinary Time. Once again this reminds us to set the passion in the context of the whole Gospel story. For instance Matthew opens with Herod the king, the chief priests, and the scribes seeking the death of the child Jesus;[1] as Matthew comes to an end Pilate the governor, the chief priests, and the scribes are instrumental in putting Jesus to death. The two scenes contain Matthew's only references to Jesus as "the King of the Jews." In the infancy narrative there is a fivefold pattern of scenes alternating between those friendly to Jesus (Mary, Joseph, magi) and those hostile to him (Herod, chief priests, scribes). In the burial narrative there is a similar fivefold pattern of alternating friends (Joseph of Arimathea, Mary Magdalene, women, disciples) and enemies (chief priests, Pharisees, guards).[2] Deeper meaning is found in some of those who appear in the passion if we remember their role in the ministry. The Matthean disciples (unlike the Marcan disciples) have clearly professed that Jesus is the Son of God (14:33), and so their failure and flight from Gethsemane is all the more shocking. The Matthean Peter, rescued by Jesus from sinking in the sea (14:30-31), has spoken for all in confessing Jesus as "the Messiah, the Son of the living God"; this makes truly poignant his repeated denial, "I do not know the man" (27:72, 74). In Matthew (23:1-36) Jesus' critique of the Pharisees is particularly severe. Yet, while Matthew (27:62) mentions the Pharisees among the adversaries of Jesus during the passion, he does so only once (elsewhere only John 18:3) and so supports the general Gospel contention that the (Sadducee) chief priests were the principal Jewish agents in Jesus'

---

[1] Matthew 2:5, 16, 20 ("those who have sought the child's life").
[2] Compare 1:18–2:23 to 27:57–28:20.

death. If the Gentile magi are set over against Jewish figures hostile to the child Jesus at the beginning of Matthew's Gospel, the Gentile wife of Pilate is a similar contrasting figure in the trial of Jesus; and both function in a uniquely Matthean context of revelation given in dreams. The dire self-condemnatory "His blood on us and on our children" (27:25) has an antecedent in the self-condemnation of the chief priests and the elders in 21:41 who interpret the parable of the vineyard to mean: "He [God] will put those wretches to a miserable death and let out the vineyard to other tenants." It has a sequence in that by the end of the Gospel (28:15) "the Jews" are an alien group to the followers of Jesus.

But let us move on from the overall context of the Gospel to the individual scenes of the Matthean passion account. Because of the closeness of Matthew to Mark in the passion (p. 153 above), I shall not repeat elements in the previous chapter that are also applicable to Matthew.

A. GETHSEMANE: PRAYER AND ARREST (26:30-56)

The echoes of the Last Supper die out with the hymn the disciples sing as they go to the Mount of Olives, perhaps a hymn of the Passover liturgy. This Mount is mentioned twice in the OT. In Zechariah 14:4ff. it is the site to which God will come from heaven to judge the world— a reference that explains why Luke specifies the Mount of Olives as the place of Jesus' ascension and ultimate return (Acts 1:9-12). More important for our purposes, in 2 Samuel 15:30-31 David in peril of his life has to flee Jerusalem from Absalom's revolt; he goes to the Mount of Olives and weeps there, discovering that he has been betrayed by Ahitophel, his trusted advisor. Small wonder that in Matthew this Mount is the site where Jesus predicts desertion by his disciples, denial by Peter, and where he is arrested through the treason of Judas. The story of the Davidic Messiah echoes the story of David; and yet the attachment of the arrest to Gethsemane, "oil press," an otherwise unknown locale on the Mount, suggests a basis in historical tradition, rather than pure symbolism.

Before Judas arrives at Gethsemane, the relation between Jesus and his disciples comes to a dramatic finale. Leaving behind the group of the disciples and then the three chosen ones, Jesus goes on alone to pray, falling on his face to the earth, with his soul sorrowful like that of the psalmist (Ps 42:6—another instance of the all-pervasive OT coloring of the passion narrative).[3] The touching prayer he pours forth in this moment of distress has often been the subject of historical skepticism. The disciples were at a distance and asleep; how could anyone know what Jesus said to God? It may be observed, however, that the words Matthew attributes to Jesus in Gethsemane echo the Lord's Prayer: "My Father"; "Pray that you may not enter into temptation"; "Your will be done." We know of a tradition that Jesus prayed when he faced death, for in Hebrews 5:7 we read, "Christ offered prayers and supplications with cries and tears to God who was able to save him from death." It is not implausible that Christian reflection filled in this prayer with words patterned on Jesus' prayer during his ministry. This would have been a way of affirming that Jesus' relationship to his Father remained consistent through life and death.

The three times Jesus withdraws to pray and the three times he returns to find the disciples sleeping exemplify the well-attested literary pattern of "the three," namely, that stories are effective and balanced if three characters or three incidents are included. The repetition underlines the continued obtuseness of the disciples and makes their inability to keep awake a perceptive comment on Jesus' prayer that the cup pass from him. It will not pass, and in his moment of trial he will not be assisted by his disciples. Yet Jesus' prayer is not without effect: it begins with him sorrowful, troubled, and prostrate; it ends with him on his feet resolutely facing the hour that has approached: "Rise, let us be going; see, my betrayer is at hand."

The betrayer is "Judas, one of the Twelve." The identification of Judas at this point, as if he had never been mentioned before, is often hailed as a sign that the passion narrative was once an independent unit that needed to introduce the dramatis personae. But "one of the Twelve," as it now stands in Matthew 26, a chapter that has already twice mentioned Judas, helps to catch the heinousness of a betrayal by one who had been an intimate. This intimacy is further stressed when Jesus addresses him as "Friend" or "Companion," a touch peculiar to Matthew here (and previously used as a disappointed address to one who should have been grateful in 20:13). Also Matthean is Jesus' rebuke of armed resistance: "Put your sword back in place, for all who

---

[3] For the christological tension between the situation in Gethsemane and Jesus' prophetic confidence during the ministry, see my discussion of the Marcan account above.

take up the sword will perish by it." There are traces in the Gospels of Christian puzzlement that, when Jesus was arrested, a sword was raised. This puzzlement surely increased when the identification of the assailant moved from Mark's vague "bystander" to "one of the followers of Jesus" (Matthew) to "Simon Peter" (John); and so the later Gospels must clarify that such action was not directed by Jesus. On the other hand, the helplessness of Jesus against those who arrested him was also a problem since the tradition reported previous occasions when he had frustrated attempts to seize him. Matthew has Jesus giving an assurance: "Do you think that I cannot appeal to my Father, and he will at once send me more than twelve legions of angels?" The ultimate explanation is that Jesus is allowing such indignities so that "the prophetic Scriptures might be fulfilled."

B. SANHEDRIN TRIAL; PETER'S DENIAL AND JUDAS' DESPERATION (26:57–27:10)

Matthew is alone among the Synoptics in identifying as "Caiaphas" the high priest before whom Jesus was brought for trial after being arrested. No part of the passion narrative has been more disputed historically than the trial of Jesus before the Jewish Sanhedrin. A session in the middle of the night on a major Jewish feast where the high priest encourages false witness and then intervenes to tell the judges that the prisoner is guilty, and where the judges themselves spit on the prisoner and slap him—all of that violates jurisprudence in general and rabbinic jurisprudence in particular. Moreover, it is never made clear why, having sentenced the prisoner as liable to death, the Sanhedrin then handed him over to the Roman governor for a new trial. (The explanation that the Sanhedrin did not have the right of capital punishment comes from John and does not help us with Matthew.) There are, of course, possible explanations, but these should not distract us from the impression Matthew wants to give. His evangelical concern is to convince his readers that Jesus was totally innocent, for the blasphemy charged against him had distorted his words and intent. Yet there is also irony. Despite the falsehood in the anti-Temple words attributed to Jesus, Matthew's readers in the 80s know that the Temple really was destroyed; and they are invited to see this as a sign of retribution. Despite the malice of the high priest, they also know that Jesus' answer to the definitive question was true: he is the Son of God and is seated at the right hand of the power. If the portrait of the

Sanhedrin is unrelievedly hostile, we must remember that Matthew is writing to Christians who themselves have suffered from confrontations with synagogue leaders. We cannot impose our different religious sensibilities on the first century (see p. 150 above).

The president and the members of the Sanhedrin are not the only ones set over against Jesus in this drama. At the very moment Jesus is being interrogated by the Jewish court, Peter is being interrogated in the courtyard below by maids and bystanders—again the effective pattern of three times. Jesus shows himself resolute, remaining silent before false witnesses and nuancing his answer to the high priest; but Peter tries to avoid the issue ("I do not know what you mean"); then he lies ("I do not know the man"); and finally he abjures Jesus with an oath.[4] The best proof that Jesus' words before the Sanhedrin will ultimately come true is offered by the fact that, even as he utters them, his previous prediction about Peter is being verified: "Before the cock crows, you will deny me three times."

Indeed, still another prophecy of Jesus is verified as he is taken to be delivered to Pilate. Among the evangelists, only Matthew stops at this moment to dramatize a threatening word that Jesus had spoken to another of his followers earlier in the night: "Woe to that man by whom the Son of Man is betrayed; it would be better for him if he had never been born" (26:24). Logically Matthew's reintroduction of Judas here is awkward. The chief priests and elders are said to lead Jesus to Pilate (27:1); yet simultaneously they are portrayed in the Temple wrestling with the issue of the blood money that Judas has thrown back. They decide to buy with the money a burial field for Judas who has hanged himself (even as did Ahitophel who, as we saw, betrayed David: 2 Sam 17:23). This detail increases the awkwardness of the Matthean narrative if one thinks of Acts 1:18-19 where Judas himself buys the field and dies from a type of internal combustion (even as did the anti-God figure Antiochus Epiphanes in 2 Macc 9:7-10). We must assume that, unexpectedly, Judas died soon after the crucifixion and that early Christians connected the "Field of Blood" where he was buried with his betrayal or his death, a death described according to patterns supplied by the demises of OT unworthies. However, the

---

[4] No less than in Mark (above), Matthew's account of Peter's denials, followed implicitly by a rehabilitation so that he became a rock of Christian faith, could have served to encourage those who failed when first tested by persecution.

The Passion According to Matthew

main goal of Matthew's narrative about Judas is in a different direction. Judas' violent death matches Jesus' prophecy, and the use of his ill-gotten thirty pieces of silver matches prophecies of Jeremiah and Zechariah. A divinely sketched triptych has provided not only Jesus on trial in the center panel, but also Peter's denial on one side panel and Judas' desperation on the other. The mystery of the different fate of these two prominent disciples, both of whom failed Jesus, is penetratingly captured by Matthew's laconic description of the last action taken by each in the passion narrative: Peter "went out and wept bitterly"; Judas "went away and hanged himself."

C. ROMAN TRIAL (27:11-31)

Deserted by disciples, surrounded by enemies, Jesus now confronts the governor who can decree his death. Self-possessed, Jesus remains silent—a silence that puts the governor on the defensive. Matthew joins the other evangelists in describing the custom of releasing a prisoner at the feast, a custom that provides a possible solution for Pilate. Yet, despite the fourfold reference of the Gospels to Barabbas, this episode has been the subject of much scholarly controversy, for such an amnesty custom is not attested among either the Romans or the Jews. (The parallels offered by ingenious defenders of historicity leave much to be desired when examined carefully.) Matthew's account is the most problematical because it is interrupted by the dream of Pilate's wife. As a dramatic touch, however, this peculiarly Matthean insert is highly effective: a Gentile woman through dream-revelation recognizes Jesus' innocence and seeks his release, while the Jewish leaders work through the crowd to have the notorious Barabbas released and Jesus crucified. Some important manuscripts of Matthew's Gospel counterpose Barabbas and Jesus in a unique way, for they phrase Pilate's question in 26:17 thus: "Whom do you want me to release to you—Jesus Barabbas or Jesus called Christ?" Since "Barabbas" probably means "Son of the Father," it is a fascinating irony to think that Pilate may have faced two men charged with a crime, both named Jesus, one "Son of the Father," the other "Son of God." But Matthew calls no attention to the meaning of the patronymic; he is satisfied with the irony of the guilty man being acclaimed and the innocent being thrust toward death.

The governor is overwhelmed by the demand of all for the crucifixion of Jesus; and so, in a dramatic gesture peculiar to Matthew's

Christ in the Gospels of the Liturgical Year

account, he publicly washes his hands to signify, "I am innocent of this [just] man's blood." Like his wife, the Gentile recognizes innocence; but "all the people" answer: "His blood on us and on our children." No line in the passion narratives has done more to embitter Jewish and Christian relations than this. It echoes OT language describing those who must be considered responsible for death (2 Sam 3:28-29; Josh 2:19; Jer 26:15), even as washing one's hands is an OT action signifying innocence in reference to murder (Deut 21:6-9). One can benevolently reflect that the Matthean statement was not applicable to the whole Jewish people of Jesus' time, for relatively few stood before Pilate, and also that it was an affirmation of present willingness to accept responsibility, not an invocation of future punishment or vengeance. (Yet rabbinic law exemplified in Mishnah *Sanhedrin* 4:5 holds perjurers accountable for the blood of an innocent man until the end of time.) On the whole Matthew's attitude is generalizing and hostile, and we can not disguise it.[5] He thinks of the Pharisees and Sadducees as a "brood of vipers" who kill and crucify saintly prophets, wise men, and scribes, so that on them comes "all the righteous blood shed on earth, beginning with the blood of the innocent Abel" (23:33-35). Judas acknowledged that he had sinned in betraying Jesus' innocent blood; Pilate dramatized his own innocence of this just man's blood; but "all the people" agree that, if Jesus is innocent, his blood will be on them and their children. Any amelioration of this self-judgment in Matthew must be sought in the words that Jesus spoke at the supper, referring to his blood "as poured out for many [all] for the forgiveness of sins" (26:27).

The obduracy of the leaders and the people leads Pilate to have Jesus flogged and crucified. Ultimately, then, the Roman governor passes on Jesus the same sentence that the Jewish high priest passed; and at the end of the Roman trial Jesus is mocked and spat upon and struck even as he was at the end of the Jewish trial. Matthew has shown Pilate and his wife as favorable to Jesus, but the Galilean is a challenge to Gentiles as well as to Jews and is rejected by many from both sides.

---

[5] For the obligation to deal pastorally with such passages lest they produce anti-Semitism, see p. 150 above.

The Passion According to Matthew

D. CRUCIFIXION, DEATH, AND BURIAL (27:32-66)

The journey to Golgotha, which introduces Simon of Cyrene, is narrated with almost disconcerting brevity, as Matthew hews close to Mark in the finale of the story. Incidents at the place of execution are merely listed with little comment and no pathos. If there is a dominating motif behind the selection, it is correspondence to the OT. For instance, only Matthew has Jesus offered wine mixed with gall—an echo of Psalm 69:22: "For my food you gave me gall, and for my thirst sour wine to drink."

As in Mark, three groups parade by the cross in derision of Jesus. (Once more the pattern of "the three.") The most general group of passersby begins by blaspheming against Jesus' claim to destroy the Temple, echoing the false witnesses of the trial. Also choosing a motif from the trial, the chief priests with the scribes and elders mock Jesus' claim to be Son of God. Without specification the robbers are said to revile in a similar manner. Peculiarly Matthean is the phrasing of the mockery so as to strengthen the reference to Psalm 22:8-9: "All who see me scoff at me; they deride me. . . . 'He trusted in the Lord; let Him deliver him.'"

Darkness covers the land at the sixth hour (noon) until the ninth hour (3 P.M.) when Jesus finally breaks his silence with a loud cry, making his only and final statement: "*Eli, Eli, lema sabachthani*; my God, my God, why have you forsaken me?" Matthew's Semitic form of the first verse of Psalm 22 is more Hebraized than Mark's "*Eloi, Eloi, lama sabachthani*" and makes more intelligible the misunderstanding by the bystanders that Jesus is calling for Elijah. Those who exalt the divinity of Jesus to the point where they cannot allow him to be truly human interpret away this verse to fit their christology. They insist that Psalm 22 ends with God delivering the suffering figure. That may well be, but the verse that Jesus is portrayed as quoting is not the verse of deliverance but the verse of abandonment—a verse by a suffering psalmist who is puzzled because up to now God has always supported and heard him. It is an exaggeration to speak of Jesus' despair, for he still speaks to "*my* God." Yet Matthew, following Mark, does not hesitate to show Jesus in the utter agony of feeling forsaken as he faces a terrible death. We are not far here from the christology of Hebrews which portrays Jesus as experiencing the whole human condition, like us in everything except sin. Only if we take these words seriously can we see the logic of the Matthean Jesus' anguished prayer that this cup might pass from him.

Christ in the Gospels of the Liturgical Year

In Matthew's view God has not forsaken Jesus, and that becomes obvious immediately after his death. All three Synoptics know of the tearing of the Temple curtain, but only Matthew reports an earthquake where rocks are split and tombs are opened and the dead rise. Some of these phenomena resemble wondrous events that the Jewish historian Josephus associates with the destruction of Jerusalem and the Temple by the Romans under Titus. Certainly, too, there are echoes of OT apocalyptic passages (Joel 2:10; Ezek 37:12; Isa 26:19; Nahum 1:5-6; Dan 12:2). Matthew did not hesitate to have the moment of Jesus' birth marked by a star in the sky; the moment of his death is even more climactic, marked by signs in the heavens, on the earth, and under the earth. It is a moment of judgment on a Judaism represented by the Temple; a moment of new life for the saintly dead of Israel; and a moment of opportunity for the Gentiles, represented by the Roman guards who confess, "Truly this man was the Son of God."

What follows is anticlimactic. Matthew, like Mark, mentions the women followers of Jesus but does nothing to relate their "looking on from a distance" to the stupendous phenomena they should have seen. The tradition of Joseph of Arimathea, common to all four Gospels, is embellished in Matthew. Joseph is "a rich man," probably a deduction from his owning a tomb, but also a sign that for Matthew's community the model of a rich saint is not repugnant. He is also a disciple of Jesus, and the tomb in which Jesus is buried is *his*. These details, missing from Mark, complicate the scene. If a disciple buried Jesus, why can Jesus' women followers only look on without participating? Does Matthew's tradition represent a simplified remembrance about a pious Jew who buried Jesus in loyalty to Deuteronomy 21:22-23, which stipulates that the body of a criminal should not hang overnight? Did this Jew subsequently become a believer in Jesus, whence the tradition that he was a disciple?

Entirely peculiar to Matthew is the aftermath of the burial where the chief priests and Pharisees get permission from Pilate to post a guard at the tomb. These soldiers were meant to frustrate any machinations based on Jesus' prediction that he would rise on the third day; but, as Matthew sees it, their presence helped to confirm the resurrection since it excluded obvious natural explanations as to why the tomb was empty. For good reasons most scholars are skeptical about the historicity of this scene in Matthew. Elsewhere the followers of Jesus are portrayed as showing no expectation that Jesus would rise, and so

The Passion According to Matthew

it is unlikely that the chief priests and Pharisees would anticipate this. Moreover, no other evangelist shows any awareness that the women coming to the tomb on Easter morning would face an armed guard. Matthew's story fits into his apologetics as we see from its conclusion. In the last words they speak in this Gospel the chief priests tell the soldiers to lie, and that lie "has been spread among the Jews to this day" (28:15). By the time this Gospel is written, the synagogue and the church are accusing each other of deceit about the principal Christian claim. More theologically, the guard at the tomb helps Matthew to illustrate the awesome power of God associated with Jesus. Men do all they can to make certain that Jesus is finished and his memory is buried; they even seal and guard his tomb. Yet the God who shook the earth when Jesus died will shake it again on Sunday morning; the guards will grovel in fear (28:2-4); and the tomb will be opened to stand as an eloquent witness that God has verified the last promise made by His Son: Jesus sits at the right hand of the Power (26:64).

Chapter 19

The Passion According to Luke

In the C or third year of the liturgical cycle, the Lucan passion narrative is read on Palm/Passion Sunday, even as its Synoptic "brethren," Matthew and Mark, have been read in A and B years, and before the Johannine passion is read on Good Friday. This "in-between" setting is appropriate, for in many aspects of the passion Luke stands between Mark/Matthew and John. Nowhere else, when there is common material, does Luke so differ from Mark—a fact that has prompted a debate whether Luke drew on a consecutive passion narrative other than Mark. In many of the differences from Mark, both factual and theological, Luke approaches John. Yet once again neither technical inter-Gospel comparisons nor corresponding historical issues are a major concern in this short book which concentrates on material for Holy Week reflection.

The Lucan passion narrative is read in the same liturgical year in which the Gospel of Luke has supplied the readings on the Sundays of the Ordinary Time; it will be followed immediately in the Easter Season by readings from the Acts of the Apostles, the other half of the Lucan two-volume work. This total setting is necessary to understand the passion message, for the original author (conventionally but very uncertainly identified as Luke, the companion of Paul) is a consistent thinker and writer. The Jesus who is accused before Pilate by the chief priests and scribes of "perverting our nation" (Luke 23:2) is one whose infancy and upbringing was totally in fidelity to the Law of Moses (2:22, 27, 39, 42). Similarly, the Jesus who is accused of "forbidding us to give tribute to Caesar" is a Jesus who had only recently (20:25) declared concerning the tribute: "Render to Caesar the things that are Caesar's." All of this casts light on the affirmation made by various dramatis personae in the passion that Jesus is innocent (23:4, 14, 22, 41, 47). The Jesus who calmly faces death is one who had already set his face deliberately to go to Jerusalem (9:51), affirming that no prophet should perish away from Jerusalem (13:33). In the Lucan account of the ministry Jesus showed tenderness to the stranger (the widow of Nain) and praised the mercy shown to the Prodigal Son and to the man beset by thieves on the road to Jericho; it is not surprising then that in his passion Jesus shows forgiveness to those who crucified him. When one has been forewarned that the devil departed from Jesus after the temptations "until the opportune time" (4:13), one is not surprised to find the devil returning in this hour of the passion which belongs to "the power of darkness" (22:53) and entering into Judas the betrayer (22:3), while demanding to sift Simon Peter the denier (22:31).

Luke, who has described the disciples/apostles with extraordinary delicacy during the ministry (unlike Mark who dwells on their failures and weaknesses), continues a merciful portrayal of them during the passion, never mentioning that they fled. Indeed, he places male acquaintances of Jesus at Calvary (23:49). This fits with Luke's unique post-resurrectional picture where all the appearances of Jesus are in the Jerusalem area (as if the disciples had never fled back to Galilee), and where apostles like Peter and John will become chief actors in the Book of Acts. The Jesus of the passion, accused by chief priests before the Roman governor and the Herodian king, prepares the way for a Paul brought before the same cast of adversaries (Acts 21:27–25:27). The innocent Jesus who dies asking forgiveness for his enemies and commending his soul to God the Father prepares the way for the first Christian martyr, Stephen, who will perish uttering similar sentiments (Acts 7:59-60). Consistency from the Law and the Prophets to Jesus and ultimately to the church is a Lucan theme in which the passion is a major component.

A. MOUNT OF OLIVES: PRAYER AND ARREST (22:39-53)

The Lucan form of this scene[1] is less suspenseful and dramatic in relation to the disciples than is the comparable account in Mark/Matthew.

---

[1] Even though, for reasons of manageability and intelligibility, under the rubric "passion" I continue to confine the discussion to the sequence of events from *Gethsemane to the grave*, this procedure may be least justifiable in the case of Luke; for the whole of chapter 22, including the Last Supper, is clearly united with the passion in the author's design (see pp. 153–54 above).

Christ in the Gospels of the Liturgical Year

Jesus goes to a *customary place*, the Mount of Olives,[2] so that Judas has no problem in finding him. No words of rebuke are spoken to the disciples who follow Jesus. After all, at the Last Supper (in Luke alone) Jesus has praised them by anticipation, "You are those who have continued with me in my trials"; and he has assured them that they will have a kingdom, as well as a place at the eschatological table, and thrones of judgment (22:28, 29)—how can they then seriously fall away? Accordingly, Jesus does not separate himself from the body of the disciples and then from the three chosen ones, as he does in Mark/Matthew. He simply withdraws a stone's throw urging them to pray. If they sleep, it is "for sorrow" (22:45); and they are found sleeping only once, not three times.

All the drama in the scene is centered in Luke's unique portrayal of Jesus. He is not one whose soul is sorrowful unto death or who lies prostrate in the dust. He has prayed often during the ministry; so now on his knees he utters a prayer to his Father, prefaced and concluded by a subordination of his will to God's wish. The Son's prayer does not remain unanswered; rather God sends an angel to strengthen him.[3] This divine assistance brings Jesus to *agonia* (whence the "agony" in the garden), a Greek term which does not refer to agony in the ordinary sense but describes the supreme tension of the athlete covered with sweat at the start of the contest. In that spirit Jesus rises from his prayer ready to enter the trial, even as he mercifully tells his disciples to pray that they be spared from that trial (22:46).

It is a mark of exquisite Lucan sensitivity that when the arresting party comes, led by Judas, the perverse kiss is forestalled. Jesus addresses his betrayer by name (the only time in all the Gospels) and shows a foreknowledge of the planned strategy (22:48). Sensitively, too, Luke adds a motif to the traditional cutting off the ear of the high priest's slave, namely, that Jesus who has so often healed in the ministry heals this opponent, even in the midst of his own peril. The figures who come to arrest Jesus on the Mount of Olives are not simply emissaries of the Jewish authorities as in the other Gospels;

[2] Luke, writing for Gentiles, avoids what to them might be unintelligible Semitisms, like Gethsemane and Golgotha.

[3] The Lucan passion narrative has key verses that are textually dubious, 22:43-44; 23:34. I agree with the increasing number of scholars who regard these as genuine Lucan texts, omitted by later scribes for theological reasons.

The Passion According to Luke

rather, the high priests, the Temple officers, and the elders themselves come out against him. The scene of the arrest terminates with Jesus' dramatic announcement that it is their hour; with them the power of darkness has come (22:53).

B. PETER'S DENIAL; SANHEDRIN INTERROGATION (22:54-71)

As Jesus is arrested, he is taken to the high priest's house; but seemingly no judicial procedure occurs until day comes (22:66). The night activity is centered on the courtyard. There, after three denials, what causes Peter to weep bitterly is not simply the remembrance of Jesus' prediction; it is the look given to him by Jesus who seemingly is present all the time that Peter is denying him! This dramatic look, peculiar to Luke, is an aspect of Jesus' continuing care for Peter promised at the Last Supper (22:32). The courtyard is also the scene of the abuse of Jesus as a prophet, an action which ironically confirms his foreknowledge that he would die in Jerusalem as a prophet (13:33).

After the denials and the mockery of the night, when day has come, Jesus is led away to the Sanhedrin by the elders, the scribes, and the chief priests (presumably the priests Annas and Caiaphas mentioned so prominently by Luke at the beginning of the public ministry in 3:2). This collective leadership, and not a single high priest as in the other Gospels, poses to Jesus a series of separate questions about his identity as the Messiah and as the Son of God. Jesus answers these questions ambiguously (even as he does during the ministry in John 10:22-39); he will die a martyr's death, but he does not foolishly force the hands of his captors. There are no witnesses and no condemnation at this Sanhedrin session, so that one gets the impression of an interrogation preparatory to the one and only trial conducted by the Roman governor—an impression quite unlike that given by Mark/Matthew. One must not assume, however, that Luke does not hold the Jewish authorities responsible for the execution of Jesus, for numerous passages in Acts affirm such responsibility (see p. 149 above). The self-composure of Jesus throughout the sequence of Peter's denials, the mockery, and the questions is striking. It is not the majestic supremacy of the Johannine Jesus, but the God-given tranquility of one to whom the Father has delivered all things (Luke 10:22) and the human tranquility of one who is totally innocent.

Christ in the Gospels of the Liturgical Year

C. THE TRIAL BEFORE PILATE AND HEROD (23:1-25)

Luke's staging of the Roman trial, almost as elaborate as John's, goes considerably beyond the picture in Mark/Matthew. Although some of the same basic material is included (the issue of the "King of the Jews" and the alternative offered by Barabbas), the overall development is uniquely shaped by parallelism with the Roman trials of Paul in Acts 16:19-24; 17:6-9; 18:12-17; 23:23-30. There are clear similarities in such features as detailed charges involving violations of Roman law and of Caesar's majesty, an indifference by Roman officials to the religious issues that are really involved, and the desire to let the prisoner go, or at most chastise him with a whipping.

The unique and fascinating Lucan contribution to the Pilate scene is the interspersed trial before Herod, the tetrarch or "king" of Galilee, who is present in Jerusalem for the feast, and to whom Pilate sends Jesus upon learning that he is a Galilean. Christian memory has preserved a series of Herodian adversary images: a Herod (the Great) who with the chief priests and scribes conspired to kill the child Jesus (Matt 2); a Herod (Antipas) who killed John the Baptist (Mark 6:17-29; Matt 14:3-12), reputedly sought to kill Jesus (Luke 13:31), and would be remembered as aligned with Pilate against Jesus (Acts 4:27); a Herod (Agrippa I) who killed James, son of Zebedee, and sought to kill Peter (Acts 12:1-5); and a Herod (Agrippa II) who sat in judgment on Paul alongside a Roman governor (Acts 25:13-27). These traditions have been woven together into the passion narrative in different ways in the apocryphal *Gospel of Peter* (where Herod becomes Jesus' chief adversary who crucifies him) and in Luke. Although annoyed by Jesus' silence, and contemptuously mocking him—two details that the other Gospels relate to Jesus' appearance before Pilate—the Lucan Herod confirms Pilate's judgment that Jesus is innocent (Luke 23:14-15). In turn, contact with Jesus heals the enmity that had existed between the Galilean "king" and the Roman, an enmity that may have been caused by Pilate's brutally killing Galileans (Luke 13:1). Once more Jesus has a healing effect even on those who maltreat him.

D. CRUCIFIXION, DEATH, AND BURIAL (23:26-56)

In this section of the passion narrative, Luke is most individualistic. Since he narrates no mocking of Jesus by Roman soldiers after Pilate's sentence, the deliverance of Jesus "up to their will" (23:25) creates the impression that the ones who seize Jesus, take him to Calvary, and

The Passion According to Luke

crucify him are the chief priests, the Jewish rulers, and the people—the last plural subject mentioned (23:13). Eventually, however, we hear of soldiers (23:36), presumably Roman; and the people are shown as following Jesus, without hostility, lamenting. Thus Luke alone among the passion narrators portrays a segment of Jews who are not disciples of Jesus but who are touched by his suffering and death. Jesus addresses these "daughters of Jerusalem," not in reference to his own impending fate, but to the catastrophe that awaits them. They belong to a city that has killed the prophets and refused all Jesus' overtures of grace, a city already destined to be dashed to the ground and trodden by Gentiles (13:34-35; 19:41-44; 21:20-24). Elsewhere, Luke shows great reluctance in having Jesus speak harshly; if he permits that here in threatening words borrowed from Isaiah (54:1-4) and Hosea (10:8), Luke is probably constrained by the factuality of the destruction of Jerusalem that has already taken place at Roman hands by the time he writes.

The contrast in Jesus' attitudes is heightened by the first words he speaks upon coming to the place of the Skull: "Father, forgive them for they know not what they do."[4] This hint that the Jewish chief priests and scribes acted out of ignorance, which is reiterated in Acts (3:17), runs against the general NT judgment of deliberate blindness and malevolence on the part of the Jewish authorities involved in the crucifixion. It constitutes not only a more humane understanding of the complex responsibilities for the death of Jesus (pp. 148–50 above) but also a directive for the gracious treatment of one's enemies that has often been simply called "Christian." There are many who would come after Jesus, beginning with Stephen (Acts 7:60), who would find hope in facing unjust brutality by repeating the prayer of the Lucan Jesus.

Three groups (but not the people) mock the crucified Jesus in response to his forgiving words: the rulers, the soldiers, and *one* of the two criminals crucified with him. In a major departure from the Synoptic tradition, the other criminal in Luke acknowledges the justice of his own sentence and confesses the innocence of one whom he addresses intimately as "Jesus"—an address used elsewhere in the Gospels in a friendly manner only by the blind beggar of Jericho. And the suffering Jesus responds with greater generosity than the petitioner requests, for Jesus will not simply remember the man after entering

[4] See note 3, p. 177 above.

Christ in the Gospels of the Liturgical Year

into his kingdom;[5] he will take the man with him this very day. The oft-used observation that the "good thief" ultimately stole the kingdom is not too far from the truth.

In the last hours of Jesus' life (the sixth to the ninth hours), darkness comes over the earth (which Luke explains as a failing of the sun or as an eclipse, which technically is not possible at Passover time), but it does not obscure the confidence of the dying Jesus. His last words are not those of abandonment (Mark/Matthew) or those of triumph (John) but words of trust: "Father, into your hands I commend my spirit." Adapted from Psalm 31:5-6 (especially as phrased in the Greek Bible), these words, like those in which he forgave his enemies, have offered many a way of meeting death in peace. Once again, the first of the followers of Jesus on this path was the martyr Stephen (Acts 7:59). Luke places the rending of the Temple veil before Jesus' death, not after (Mark/Matthew); for only acts of grace will follow the death of Jesus. The first is a final affirmation of the innocence of Jesus drawn from a centurion, so that timewise on either side of the cross a Roman governor and a Roman soldier have made the same declaration of not guilty. Then the Jewish multitude who followed Jesus to Calvary and looked on (Luke 23:27, 31) is moved to repentance, so that the people return home beating their breasts. A sign of goodness is evoked even from the midst of the Sanhedrin, as Joseph of Arimathea, a saintly member of that body who had not consented to the purpose or the deed of crucifying Jesus, asks for the body of Jesus in order to render the required burial service. If the daughters of Jerusalem wept over Jesus on the way to Calvary, providing the mourning required for burial, the women of Galilee (alongside Jesus' male acquaintances!) look on the burial from a distance (23:49, 55) and prepare spices to complete the burial. The words that will ultimately be addressed to the Galilean women will not be words of warning such as those addressed to the Jerusalem women but words of joy—their burial ministrations will prove unnecessary, for Jesus is among the living, not among the dead (24:1, 5). It has often been critically observed that

---

[5] Of the two attested readings for Luke 23:42, "When you come in your kingdom" and "When you come into your kingdom," the second is probably more original. Later scribes would have been troubled by the realization that the kingdom of God was not brought about immediately by the death of Jesus and would have shifted the focus to the parousia which is involved in the first translation.

The Passion According to Luke

the cross bears for Luke none of the atoning value that it had for Paul. Lucan crucifixion, however, is clearly a moment of God's forgiveness and of healing grace through and by Jesus. The theological language may be different, but the atoning effects are the same.

Chapter 20

The Passion According to John

This passion narrative is read in the liturgy every year on Good Friday, but not without context; for the Johannine Gospel is read daily in the preceding three weeks of Lent and throughout the subsequent Easter Season. Such a context is important for understanding the passion since the Jesus who comes at last to his hour (John 13:1) in the Fourth Gospel is a different dramatic character from the Jesus of the Synoptic passion narratives. He is a Jesus conscious of his preexistence. Through death, therefore, he is returning to a state he has temporarily left during his stay in this world (17:5). He is not a victim at the mercy of his opponents since he has freely chosen to lay down his life with the utter certitude that he will take it up again (10:17-18). If there is an element of struggle in the passion, it is a struggle without suspense, for the Satanic prince of this world has no power over Jesus (14:30); indeed, Jesus has already conquered the world (16:33). Since the Johannine Jesus is omniscient (2:25; 6:6; etc.), he cannot be caught off guard by what will happen in the passion. He had chosen Judas knowing that Judas was going to betray him (6:70-71) and has himself sent Judas off on his evil mission (13:27-30).[1]

A. THE ARREST OF JESUS IN THE GARDEN (18:1-12)
Thus, when the passion scene opens in the garden (18:1), Jesus is not surprised by Judas and the arresting party, as he is in the Marcan account of Gethsemane. Rather he goes forth to meet Judas whom he has been expecting (18:4). And with an ironical touch, John tells us that Judas comes equipped with lanterns and torches. Judas has

---

[1] The reader may be puzzled by my description of the *Johannine* Jesus, since it may resemble the only picture of Jesus he or she has ever known. But that is because it is the Johannine Jesus that has dominated in Christian piety. The Synoptic Jesus does not show any clear awareness of preexistence, is not so emphatically knowing, etc.

preferred darkness to the light which has come into the world (3:19); when he left Jesus it was truly night (13:30), and now he needs artificial light. The Jesus who confronts Judas has not been prostrate in the dust of Gethsemane, praying that this hour and this cup pass from him, as in the Synoptic tradition; for such an attitude would not be conceivable on the part of the Johannine Jesus. He and the Father are one (10:30); he has specifically rejected any prayer that the Father should save him from this hour (12:27); he is eager to drink the cup the Father has given him (18:11). If there is to be prostration in the dust of the garden, that is the fate not of Jesus but of the Roman soldiers and the Jewish police who come to arrest him. These representatives of worldly power, civil and religious, are struck down when Jesus uses the divine name "I AM" (18:6), in order graphically to show the reader that no one can take Jesus' life from him unless he permits it (10:18). Yet, these soldiers and police have power over Jesus' followers who remain in this world (17:15), and so Jesus protects his own by asking that they be let go (18:8), exhibiting for them a care quite consonant with his prayer in 17:9ff.

B. INTERROGATION BY ANNAS;
PETER'S DENIAL (18:13-27)

The Jewish "trial" of Jesus is also quite different in the Fourth Gospel; for it is not a formal procedure before Caiaphas, the high priest, as in Mark/Matthew, but a police interrogation before Annas, Caiaphas' father-in-law. It is an investigation to see whether Jesus admits anything revolutionary in his movement or his teaching (18:19)—anything that could determine whether Jesus was to be handed over for trial by the Romans. In this interrogation a supremely self-confident Jesus easily outpoints Annas (18:20-21), so that his captors are aggravated to the point of abusing him (18:22). The interrogation leaves Annas, not Jesus, with the embarrassing and unanswered question (18:23).

And while Jesus is showing his innocence, his best-known follower, Simon Peter, is showing weakness. The Fourth Gospel catches the full drama of Peter's behavior, since only here is *Peter* identified as the one who cut off the servant's ear in the garden (18:10). Now he wants to deny that he was even in the garden (18:26-27). Also, the fourth evangelist, more than the others, stresses the simultaneity of Peter's denials and Jesus' self-defense. In 16:32 Jesus had said: "An hour is coming . . . for you to be scattered, each on his own, leaving me all alone."

Peter is not yet among those scattered, but he certainly has left Jesus alone.

Again, only in the Fourth Gospel does "another disciple" have a role in the drama of Peter's denial (18:15), presumably "the disciple whom Jesus loved." Whoever he was historically,[2] he was *the* witness par excellence for the Johannine community (19:35; 21:24). If he was someone relatively unknown to other Christian communities, i.e., not one of the Twelve, the fourth evangelist wants all the more to show that his community's patron and hero was present during Jesus' hour of return to the Father (13:1—the Beloved Disciple appears only in chaps. 13ff.), at least, at those crucial scenes at which any other disciple was present: at the Last Supper (13:23-26), in the process against Jesus (18:15-16), at the crucifixion (19:26-27), at the empty tomb (20:2-10), and at the appearance of the risen Jesus (21:7, 20-23). In each scene he is introduced almost as a foil to Simon Peter, the apostolic witness best known to the church at large; and in each the Beloved Disciple comes off more favorably than Peter. He is quicker to see, to understand, and to believe precisely because he has a primacy in Jesus' love, which is a mark of true discipleship. Thus, the fourth evangelist tells us that his Gospel has behind it a trustworthy and even preeminent authority, a message meant perhaps as a reply to other Christians scandalized by the uniqueness of this community's tradition about Jesus, so markedly different from the Marcan-based Synoptic tradition which was popularly thought to have had Peter as its apostolic authority.

C. ROMAN TRIAL (18:28–19:16A)

When the evangelist turns the stage spotlight from Peter's denials back to the continuing process against Jesus, his scenario for the Roman trial is revealed as a striking artistic conception. This is not at all the Synoptic scenario of a Jesus silent before a Pilate who is interrogating him in the presence of his accusers, the Jewish priests. Rather, it is an

---

[2] The late second-century identification of this disciple (never named in the Fourth Gospel) as John son of Zebedee is probably too simplified. More likely he was a companion of Jesus not named in the other Gospels but very important and idealized in the memory of the community whose tradition is preserved in the Fourth Gospel. He had been the model vehicle of the Paraclete/Spirit in bearing witness. For a fuller treatment, see my book *The Community of the Beloved Disciple* (New York: Paulist, 1981).

The Passion According to John

elaborate front-and-back-stage setting, with the priests in the crowd outside, Jesus inside, and Pilate shuttling back and forth between them. As he moves from one stage to the other, Pilate is like a chameleon, taking on the different coloration of the parties who engage him. Outside there is ceaseless pressure, conniving, and outcry; inside there is calm and penetrating dialogue. Not at all silent (cf. Mark 15:5), the Johannine Jesus is an eloquent spokesman, answering the false charges of political complicity that will be brought against his memory during the years to come (not the least by modern fiction writers who want to make him a first-century Che Guevara or by scholars who attribute to him Zealot motives). He will not refuse the title of "The King of the Jews" if Pilate wants to put it that way; but the real reason he came into this world was *not* to be a king (as might be construed from the Jerusalem Bible)—it was to bear witness to the truth (18:37).

So eloquent and self-assured is Jesus that we can scarcely speak of Pilate's trial of Jesus in the Fourth Gospel; it is Pilate who is put on trial to see whether he is of the truth. Pilate may think he has the power to try Jesus, but he is calmly told that he has no independent authority over Jesus (19:10-11). It is not Jesus who fears Pilate; it is Pilate who is afraid of Jesus, the Son of God (19:7-8). The real question is not what will happen to Jesus who controls his own destiny, but whether Pilate will betray himself by bowing to the outcry of the very people he is supposed to govern (19:12). The price he exacts from them by way of an insincere allegiance to Caesar (19:15) is a face-saving device for a man who knows the truth about Jesus but has failed to bear witness to it (18:37-38).

The artistry of the evangelist is never better displayed than in his device of moving the scourging and mockery of Jesus to the center of the Roman trial (19:1-5). In the Marcan/Matthean tradition the scourging was part of the sentence and immediately preceded the journey to Calvary after Jesus had been condemned. The purple cloak in which he was mocked was stripped off before he set out for the place of execution (Mark 15:16-20). But John makes the scourging and mockery a prelude to the climactic moment of having Jesus brought from inside the praetorium to encounter the crowd outside—the mid-moment of the trial, breaking Pilate's shuttle, where all three parties meet in center stage. In all the Gospels the cries to crucify Jesus represent a self-judgment on the part of the onlookers; but no other evangelist highlights the harshness of the cry so effectively as does the fourth evangelist when he makes it a response to Pilate's *Ecce homo*. In its origins "The Man" may reflect an ancient christological title for Jesus, something akin to "Son of Man"; but in the Johannine drama it has had the effect on countless readers of making the rejection of Jesus an action literally inhumane. Moreover, since the Jesus who is rejected wears the mantle and crown of a king, this rejection, combined with preference for Caesar, is portrayed as an abandonment by the Jews of their own messianic hopes.

Here I must beg the reader's indulgence for an aside. One cannot disguise a hostility toward "the Jews" in the Johannine passion narrative, neither by softening the translation to "Judeans" or "Judaists," nor by explaining that John often speaks of "the Jews" when the context implies that the authorities (i.e., the chief priests) alone were involved. By deliberately speaking of "the Jews" the fourth evangelist is spreading to the synagogues of his own time the blame that an earlier tradition placed on the authorities. He is not the first to do this, for the oldest extant Christian writing speaks of "the Jews who killed both the Lord Jesus and the prophets" (1 Thess 2:14-15). But John is the most insistent NT writer in this usage. Why? Because he and/or his confreres have suffered from synagogue persecution. They have been driven out of the synagogue for professing that Jesus is the Messiah (9:22; 12:42). Within a few decades of the composition of John there was introduced into synagogue prayer (*Shemoneh Esreh* or the Eighteen Benedictions) a curse against deviants from Judaism, including followers of Jesus. This was an initial example of an attitude that is still with us today: in the view of many Jews, no matter how true and long one's Jewish lineage may be, one ceases to be a Jew when one confesses Jesus to be the Messiah. At the end of the first century, expulsion from the synagogue seemingly exposed Christians to Roman investigation and punishment, even death—Jews were tolerated by the Romans; but who were these Christians whom Jews disclaimed? The fourth evangelist may well be alluding to this painful outcome in 16:2: "They will put you out of the synagogues; indeed, the hour is coming when whoever kills you will think he is offering service to God." The context of mutual hostility between the Johannine community and the synagogue must be taken into account when proclaiming the Johannine passion narrative in the Good Friday liturgy.[3]

---

[3] See the cautions about preaching on p. 150 above.

The Passion According to John

But let us return from this aside to the closing lines of John's account of the Roman process against Jesus. Pilate wrings from the priests a denial of their royal messianic hopes in favor of allegiance to the pitiful Tiberius, brooding on the cliffs of Capri (19:15). After that, Pilate hands Jesus over "to them" (to the priests) to be crucified (19:16a).

D. CRUCIFIXION, DEATH, AND BURIAL (19:16B-42)

There is no Simon of Cyrene in the Fourth Gospel; the Johannine Jesus carries his own cross (19:17) as a continuing sign that he lays down his own life (10:18). The crucifixion in John consists of a series of short vignettes, some of them similar to Synoptic episodes, but now vehicles of peculiarly Johannine theology.

All four Gospels mention that a charge (*titulus*) listing Jesus as a would-be "King of the Jews" was fastened on the cross, but only John sees here the dramatic possibilities of a proclamation. Pilate has already presented Jesus to his people as king (19:14), only to have him rejected (19:16). Now, in all the pertinent languages of the empire, Hebrew, Latin, and Greek (19:20), Pilate reaffirms the kingship of Jesus and does so with Roman legal precision (19:22). In spite of the objection of the chief priests, the representative of the greatest power on earth has verified that Jesus is king for every passerby to see. The Johannine understanding of the crucifixion is beautifully caught by a line that Christians interpolated into Psalm 106:10, a line known already in the second century A.D.: "The Lord reigns from the wood [of the cross]."

The other Gospels make implicit allusion to Psalm 22:19 in describing the division of Jesus' garments; John makes the allusion explicit, but with particular attention to the seamless tunic which was not divided (19:23-24). His free interpretation of the psalm in order to highlight the tunic has suggested to some scholars a symbolism based on the seamless tunic of the high priest (described in Josephus). John would then be presenting Jesus on the cross not only as a king but also as a priest, a theme in harmony with the consecration language of 17:19. Others see the seamless tunic as a symbol of unity.

In the Marcan/Matthean tradition the women who followed Jesus watched from afar; and none of the disciples was present, for they had fled (cf. Mark 14:50). John's picture is quite different. Not only are the women placed at the foot of the cross, but the Mother of Jesus is included among them, together with the Beloved Disciple (19:25-26).

These are two figures whom John names only by title (cf. 2:1); they meet at last at the moment of Jesus' death. Each was a historical person, but the evangelist is not interested primarily in their historical identity; he is interested in their symbolism. In Mark 3:31-35 (Matt 12:46-50) when his "mother and brothers" come asking for him, Jesus asks, "Who are my mother and my brothers?" He answers this question in terms of discipleship: "Whoever does the will of God is brother and sister and mother to me." In John the dying Jesus leaves his natural mother as the mother of the Beloved Disciple, and that disciple is designated as her son, thus becoming Jesus' brother. Jesus has constituted a family of preeminent disciples,[4] and the Johannine community is already in existence at the cross (which becomes the birthplace of the church).

In 19:29-30 a sponge full of common wine is placed on hyssop and offered to Jesus, an episode recalling the Marcan/Matthean incident where the sponge was placed on a reed and offered to him before he died. By mentioning hyssop, fern-like and certainly less suitable than a reed, John is again playing on symbolism, for in Exodus 12:22 hyssop was used to sprinkle the blood of the paschal lamb on the doorposts of the Israelite houses. Jesus is sentenced to death at noon (19:14), the very hour on Passover Eve when the priests begin to slaughter the paschal lambs in the Temple precincts. In his death he gives meaning to that mysterious acclamation of John the Baptist uttered when Jesus made his first public appearance: "Behold the Lamb of God who takes away the sin of the world" (1:29).

For the fourth evangelist even the very human cry "I thirst" (19:28) must be set in the context of Jesus' sovereign control of his own destiny. Jesus utters it "aware that all was now finished, in order to bring the Scripture to its complete fulfillment." And when he takes the wine, he declares, "It is finished," and he hands over his spirit. How different is this calm scene, of Jesus' laying down his life when ready, from the tortured atmosphere of the last words in Mark/Matthew: "My God, my God, why have you forsaken me?" And even the

---

[4] Besides being symbolized as the mother of the Beloved Disciple, when the context of the whole Bible is taken into account, the Johannine figure of the Mother of the Messiah may evoke *Israel* or Lady Zion, the people of God to whom the Messiah is born, and *Eve*, the "woman" of Genesis 2:23 and her offspring (cf. Rev 12:18).

The Passion According to John

formula, "bowing his head, he handed over the spirit" (19:30), may be redolent of Johannine theology. More than the other Gospels John preserves the ancient Christian understanding that the communication of the Holy Spirit, i.e., the Spirit of Jesus, was an intimate part of the death and resurrection. The Fourth Gospel (7:39) is insistent that the Spirit is not a reality for Jesus' followers until then. John dramatizes this by having Jesus breathe his Holy Spirit forth on his disciples (including members of the Twelve: 20:24) as his first act when he appears on Easter Sunday evening (20:22). Here John may be suggesting by way of symbolic anticipation that Jesus handed over his Spirit to his followers at the foot of the cross, in particular to the two followers (the Mother and the Beloved Disciple) idealized by the Johannine community as their antecedents.

If Jesus has died in both a sovereign and life-giving manner, these traits do not disappear from the narrative with his death—the dead body is the body of a king and it continues his salvific work. The latter trait is apparent in 19:31-37. The other Gospels mark Jesus' death with miraculous signs in the ambiance: the Temple curtain is torn; tombs open and bodies of the saints come forth; and an expression of faith is evoked from a Roman centurion. But the Fourth Gospel localizes the sign in the body of Jesus itself: when the side of Jesus is pierced, there comes forth blood and water (19:34). In 7:38-39 we heard: "From within him shall flow rivers of living water," with the explanation that the water symbolized the Spirit which would be given when Jesus had been glorified. That is now fulfilled, for the admixture of blood to the water is the sign that Jesus has passed from this world to the Father and has been glorified (12:23; 13:1). It is not impossible that the fourth evangelist intends here a reference not only to the gift of the Spirit but also to the two channels (baptism and the eucharist) through which the Spirit had been communicated to the believers of his own community, with water signifying baptism, and blood the eucharist (3:5; 6:53, 63). The added touch that no bone of Jesus was broken (19:33, 36) is seemingly still another echo of the theme of Jesus as the paschal lamb (Exod 12:10).

The burial of Jesus is narrated in all four Gospels, but here once more John goes his own way in order to stress the sovereignty of Jesus. Not only the traditional Joseph of Arimathea but also the exclusively Johannine character Nicodemus appears on the scene. He was attracted by Jesus during the ministry, yet scarcely with enough understanding to make of him a disciple (3:1-10; 7:50-52). Now, when Jesus' disciples have been scattered (16:32), Nicodemus comes forward with courage to perform the burial duties. The words of Jesus are beginning to come true: "When I am lifted up from the earth, I shall draw all men to myself" (12:32). And this is no burial like that in the Synoptic tradition, without anointing and aromatic oils (cf. Mark 16:1; Luke 23:55-56). Rather Jesus is buried as befits a king, with a staggering amount of myrrh and aloes, bound in cloth wrappings impregnated with aromatic oils (19:39-40).

Thus, from beginning to end the narrative has been consistent: it is the passion of a sovereign king who has overcome the world. It is the passion narrative to which the *Vexilla Regis* is the appropriate response.

Chapter 21

Diverse Portrayals of the Crucified Jesus

A common position in biblical scholarship today[1] is that the Gospels
were the product of development over a long period of time and so
are not *literal* accounts of the words and deeds of Jesus, even though
based on memories and traditions of such words and deeds. Apostolic
faith and preaching has reshaped those memories, as has also the
individual viewpoint of each evangelist who selected, synthesized,
and explicated the traditions that came down to him.[2] All of this
means that while there is one Jesus at the font of the four canonical
Gospels, each evangelist knows a different facet of him and presents a
different picture. We have seen this verified in an acute way in the
different Gospel portraits of the crucified Jesus. Since Matthew differs
only slightly from Mark in the passion narrative (at least in portraying
the role of Jesus), we can speak practically of three different portraits:
those of Mark, Luke, and John. Let me describe those portraits briefly,
and then turn to the question of truth.

Mark portrays a stark human abandonment of Jesus which is
reversed by God dramatically at the end. From the moment Jesus
moves to the Mount of Olives, the behavior of the disciples is nega-
tively portrayed. While Jesus prays, they fall asleep three times. Judas
betrays him and Peter curses, denying knowledge of him. All flee,
with the last one leaving even his clothes behind in order to get away

---

[1] For Roman Catholics this is the official position of their church phrased by the
Pontifical Biblical Commission in its 1964 statement on "The Historical Truth of the
Gospels." For the essential portion of that document, see my *Biblical Reflections on
Crises Facing the Church* (New York: Paulist, 1975), 111–15.

[2] In the Biblical Commission document referred to in the preceding footnote a
distinction is made between the apostolic preachers who have been eyewitnesses
and the evangelists who had to depend on previous tradition. Most scholars,
Catholic and Protestant, think that no one of the evangelists was himself an eyewitness of the ministry of Jesus.

Christ in the Gospels of the Liturgical Year

from Jesus—the opposite of leaving all things to follow him. Both Jewish and Roman judges are presented as cynical. Jesus hangs on the cross for six hours, three of which are filled with human mockery, while in the second three the land is covered with darkness. Jesus' only word from the cross is "My God, my God, why have you forsaken me?" and even that plaintive cry is met with derision. Yet, as Jesus breathes his last, God acts to confirm His Son. The trial before the Jewish Sanhedrin had concerned Jesus' threat to destroy the Temple and his claim to be the messianic Son of the Blessed One. At Jesus' death the veil of the Temple is rent, and a Roman centurion confesses, "Truly this was God's Son." After the cross it is possible, then, to see that Jesus was not a false prophet.

Luke's portrayal is quite different. The disciples appear in a more sympathetic light, for they have remained faithful to Jesus in his trials (22:28). In Gethsemane if they fall asleep (once not thrice), it is because of sorrow. Even enemies fare better; for no false witnesses are produced by the Jewish authorities, and three times Pilate acknowledges that Jesus is not guilty. The people are on Jesus' side, grieving over what has been done to him. Jesus himself is less anguished by his fate than by his concern for others. He heals the slave's ear at the time of the arrest; on the road to Calvary he worries about the fate of the women; he forgives those who crucified him; and he promises Paradise to the penitent "thief" (a figure peculiar to Luke). The crucifixion becomes the occasion of divine forgiveness and care; and Jesus dies tranquilly praying, "Father, into your hands I commend my spirit."

John's passion narrative presents a sovereign Jesus who has defiantly announced, "I lay down my life and I take it up again; no one takes it from me" (10:17-18). When Roman soldiers and Jewish police come to arrest him, they fall to the earth powerless as he speaks the divine phrase, "I AM." In the garden he does not pray to be delivered from the hour of trial and death, as he does in the other Gospels, for the hour is the whole purpose of his life (12:27). His self-assurance is an offense to the high priest (18:22); and Pilate is afraid before the Son of God who states, "You have no power over me" (19:8, 11). No Simon of Cyrene appears, for the Jesus of John carries his own cross. His royalty is proclaimed in three languages and confirmed by Pilate. Unlike the portrayal in other Gospels, Jesus is not alone on Calvary, for at the foot of the cross stand the Beloved Disciple and the Mother of Jesus. He relates these two highly symbolic figures to each other as son and mother, thus leaving behind a family of believing disciples. He does not cry out, "My God, why have you forsaken me?" because the Father is always with him (16:32). Rather his final words are a solemn decision, "It is finished"—only when he has decided does he hand over his spirit. Even in death he dispenses life as water flows from within him (see 7:38-39). His burial is not unprepared as in the other Gospels; rather he lies amidst 100 pounds of spices as befits a king.

When these different passion narratives are read side-by-side, one should not be upset by the contrast or ask which view of Jesus is more correct: the Marcan Jesus who plumbs the depths of abandonment only to be vindicated, the Lucan Jesus who worries about others and gently dispenses forgiveness, or the Johannine Jesus who reigns victoriously from the cross in control of all that happens. All three are given to us by the inspiring Spirit, and no one of them exhausts the meaning of Jesus. It is as if one walks around a large diamond to look at it from three different angles. A true picture of the whole emerges only because the viewpoints are different. In presenting two diverse views of the crucified Jesus every Holy Week, one on Palm/Passion Sunday, one on Good Friday, the church is bearing witness to that truth and making it possible for people with very different spiritual needs to find meaning in the cross. There are moments in the lives of most Christians when they need desperately to cry out with the Marcan/ Matthean Jesus, "My God, my God, why have you forsaken me?" and to find, as Jesus did, that despite human appearances God is listening and can reverse tragedy. At other moments, meaning in suffering may be linked to being able to say with the Lucan Jesus, "Father, forgive them for they know not what they do," and being able to entrust oneself confidently to God's hands. There are still other moments where with Johannine faith we must see that suffering and evil have no real power over God's Son or over those whom he enables to become God's children. To choose one portrayal of the crucified Jesus in a manner that would exclude the other portrayals or to harmonize all the Gospel portrayals into one would deprive the cross of much of its meaning. It is important that some be able to see the head bowed in dejection, while others observe the arms outstretched in forgiveness, and still others perceive in the title on the cross the proclamation of a reigning king.

A Risen Christ in Eastertime

Essays on the Gospel Narratives of the Resurrection

Chapters 22–26

Chapter 22

The Resurrection in Mark (16:1-8; 16:9-20)

In some ways Mark remains the most difficult Gospel. Although in seminary courses it may well be the most frequently taught, it is surely the least familiar of the four Gospels to many Christians, especially to Catholics. It was scarcely ever read on Sunday in the pre–Vatican II lectionary; and in citations of passages shared by the Synoptic Gospels, Matthew, functioning as "the church's Gospel," was quoted by preference.[1] Even among scholars who have studied Mark with great intensity, it remains a conundrum, producing little or no consensus as to sources, locale, or goals. The terse Marcan style, which leaves much unexplained, has been an open invitation for imaginative theorizing.[2]

Mark 16, the chapter pertinent to the resurrection, is a prime example of how since the second century Mark has confounded attempts at understanding. Only the first eight verses of the chapter are safely attested as having belonged to the original Gospel. Yet 16:8, which follows an authoritative angelic instruction to speak of the import of the resurrection to the disciples and Peter, has the women who were so instructed "say nothing to anyone for they were afraid." With great difficulty scholars have come up with a grammatical parallel for the abrupt phrasing of this ending, but that parallel does not solve the issue of how what is related in 16:8 constitutes a suitable conclusion to what began in 1:1 as "The Good News of Jesus Christ." How is it good news that the women were afraid to tell anyone of Jesus' resurrection? Textual witnesses of Mark that do not terminate with 16:8 offer three

---

[1] The fact that before 1960 Catholics were officially taught that Matthew either directly or indirectly (in translation) was written by an eyewitness member of the Twelve was also a factor.

[2] The range of views is illustrated by the thesis of a few, but important, scholars that canonical Mark is a censored, bowdlerized version of an esoteric gospel of less sober caliber, as seen in the *Secret Gospel of Mark*, mentioned in a letter of Clement of Alexandria. H. Koester who holds this view dates canonical Mark to around 180!

variant continuations, only one of which has enough frequency to be considered traditional. That one, known as the "Long Ending," is Mark 16:9-20, which appears in all Catholic and most Protestant Bibles (sometimes in the latter in smaller print or as a footnote in order to indicate textual doubt).

Since liturgically Mark 16:1-8 and the most widely attested ending (16:9-20) tend to be read as separate pericopes,[3] I think it best in this series to treat 16:1-8 as if Mark intended to end the Gospel there.[4] Following the treatment of 16:1-8, I shall ask how 16:9-20 makes sense as part of the canonical text of Mark.[5]

MARK 16:1-8: THE WOMEN AT THE TOMB

The principal characters in this scene are the women: Mary Magdalene, Mary of James, and Salome. We were introduced to these three in 15:40-41 (where the second Mary was designated as "of James the less [younger] and of Joses"). There they were identified as women who had followed Jesus when he was in Galilee and ministered to him, and who were now at a distance observing the death of Jesus on the cross. In so describing them, Mark kept them clearly distinct from "his disciples" and/or "the Twelve" who were companions of Jesus at the Last Supper (14:12, 17), who went with him to Gethsemane on the Mount of Olives (14:26, 32), and all of whom fled when he was arrested (14:50). What would Mark have us think of these women?[6] Mark insists that Jesus died alone, abandoned by all his disciples. While these women were not among the disciples who abandoned him, their presence distant from the cross could have been of no

---

[3] In the B year Mark 16:1-8 is the selection for the Easter Vigil and (as alternative) for the morning Easter Mass. Mark 16:9-15 is read on Saturday in Easter week, and 16:15-20 on Ascension Thursday in the B year.

[4] The Marcan situation which involves manuscript evidence differs from that of John. There it is purely a scholarly hypothesis to treat John 20 as the end of the Gospel, for there is no ancient manuscript that lacks John 21.

[5] The Council of Trent insisted on its list of books "as sacred and canonical in their entirety *with all their parts* according to the text usually read in the Catholic Church and as they are in the ancient Latin Vulgate." Discussions clarified that Mark 16:9-20 was included among the "parts." Yet that Tridentine statement about canonicity does not settle the issue of whether Mark wrote 16:9-20.

[6] While without doubt the two groups are kept distinct in the passion narrative, scholars dispute whether in Mark "disciples" ever includes such women followers. In Matthew the term does not, but Mark is less clear.

consolation to him. The women had not been put through the same test as the disciples who were physically closer to him in Gethsemane and failed. Are the women positive models to the Christian readers? Or are they those who once followed him in Galilee but are now passive onlookers? Or have they not failed simply because they have not been tested?

The second Marcan reference to them during the passion (15:47) does not answer these questions. Joseph of Arimathea, "who was himself looking for the kingdom of God," whether or not he was a disciple,[7] did a pious act by getting permission from Pilate to take Jesus' body and bury it. Mark tells us that "Mary Magdalene and Mary of Joses saw where Jesus was laid." Why they did not participate in Joseph's burial of Jesus is never explained and so the impression of uninvolved onlookers persists.

To an extent the ambiguity about the women is partially resolved in the scene we are discussing when Mark reports that after the Sabbath was past (thus sometime after approximately 6 P.M. on Saturday) the women at last get involved on Jesus' behalf, for they buy spices in order to go and anoint him.[8] In Mark 14:8 Jesus revealed that the anointing of his body by an unnamed woman had been a preparation for his forthcoming burial. This plan of the three women to anoint Jesus after burial will be the occasion for revealing his resurrection.

Mark gives a second time-reference which fixes the moment when the women acted on their intention; it was "very early on the first day of the week." Throughout the Marcan passion narrative there has been an extraordinary sequence of precise three-hour time intervals: the story began with "evening" on the first day of the unleavened bread when Jesus ate the supper with his disciples (14:12, 17); it continued through cockcrow when Peter concluded his denials (14:72) and a

---

[7] In *CBQ* 50 (1988): 233–45 I argued that in Mark's understanding this member of the Sanhedrin was not a disciple at the time of Jesus' death (even if he may have become one later)—that may explain why the women could not join Joseph in the burial.

[8] There is considerable scholarly discussion as to whether the intent to anoint a corpse several days after burial is historically plausible. I wish to express the caution that Mark would have wanted his account to be plausible about such an incidental. He is a better guide to plausibility in burial practices of the first century than are 20th-century scholars who base their judgments on the very limited available knowledge about burial in that period.

The Resurrection in Mark

morning hour when Jesus was given over to Pilate (15:1); and it culminated with the third, sixth, and ninth hours as he hung on the cross (15:25, 33; i.e., 9 A.M., noon, 3 P.M.); only at "evening" was Jesus at last buried (15:42).

Not without plausibility scholars have suggested that such time precisions mean that already within Mark's experience there were set times of commemorative prayers as Christians recalled the death of the Lord. The references in 16:1-2 to the end of the Sabbath and to the early hour on the first day of the week may be part of the same picture.[9] The further specification that "the sun had risen" may be a symbolic reference to the resurrection having already taken place. Mark 8:22-26 shows a symbolic interest in seeing and blindness, and that at least makes possible a symbolic interest in light and darkness.

In 16:3-4 the women pose a rhetorical question to themselves as to who will roll away the stone that has been placed at the door of the tomb, and we are reminded that this was a very large stone. The picture helps to reinforce the contrast between human incapacity and God's power. When Mark reports that the women saw the stone already rolled back, he is using the passive to indicate divine action. God has undone the sealing that the Sanhedrin member Joseph of Arimathea so carefully placed (15:46).

As the women look inside the tomb, they see a young man sitting on the right side (a place of dignity) clothed with a white robe. He is surely a divine spokesman;[10] and the amazement that greets him is typical of the reaction to the appearance of angels. In addition, however, this reaction at the end of the Marcan Gospel constitutes an inclusion with the amazement that greeted Jesus when he drove out

---

[9] There are psalm references to morning (early, hour of wakening) as a time of prayer and of awareness of God (17:15; 30:6; 59:17; 101:8). Mark's descriptions of the day of burial as the day before the Sabbath (15:42), of the Sabbath as being past (16:1), and of the first day of the week (16:2) fulfill Jesus' predictions of resurrection "after three days" (8:31; 9:31; 10:34). Yet it is significant that the tomb stories do not refer to "the third day" but to "the first day of the week." How early, without abandoning their reverence for the Sabbath, did Jewish Christians begin to give reverence to the next day, the first of the week, because it was associated with the Lord's resurrection?

[10] Despite the imaginative attempts of some scholars to identify him with the young man who fled away naked from Gethsemane (14:51-52), Matthew 28:2 and Luke 24:23 were correct in understanding Mark to refer to an angelic appearance (also John 20:12).

Christ in the Gospels of the Liturgical Year

an evil spirit at the beginning of the Gospel (1:25-27). There the demon addressed him as "Jesus the Nazarene" (1:24), and so it is not surprising in the present scene to hear the heavenly appearance in the tomb tell the women that he knows that they are seeking "Jesus the Nazarene." This makes the reader certain that the same person who at the beginning of the Gospel manifested his power over evil is the one in whom God now manifests His power over death. From beginning to end Satan has been defeated by Jesus the Nazarene.

From the initial act of Jesus' power and throughout his ministry, those attracted to him could not fully recognize or believe in his divine identity because he had not yet suffered on the cross (8:31-33; 9:31-32). Now at last the angelic youth can add the crucial identification of Jesus the Nazarene, namely, "the one who was crucified." It is only of Jesus the Nazarene who has died on the cross that the triumphal affirmation "He has been raised" (16:6) makes sense in God's plan. The women have been inside the tomb looking about. Yet it is not tautological that having said, "He has been raised," the heavenly youth goes on to say: "He is not here; see the place where they laid him."[11] The significance of the empty tomb in terms of the resurrection of the one who was crucified is not a matter of simple observation. Because of the youth's message the women now know that their well-meaning search for Jesus was in vain.

The Marcan scene, however, is more than a revelation of the resurrection, for 16:7 reports a commission given to the women by the heavenly youth—a commission that makes clear that the risen, crucified Jesus of Nazareth has still more to do. At the beginning of the passion Jesus predicted the loss of faith (*skandalizein*) and scattering of all his disciples who had come with him to the Last Supper. This prediction was not without a ray of hope, however: "But after I am raised up, I will go before you to Galilee" (14:28). The angelic youth harks back to that promise: "Go tell his disciples and Peter that he is going before you to Galilee; there you will see him as he told you" (16:7).[12] The disciples may have utterly failed even to the point where one would-be follower fled away naked (14:52) and Peter cursed Jesus,

---

[11] Genesis 5:24 reports that Enoch was not found because God had translated him (to the other world), but we are not told that Enoch had died. There is no silence about Jesus' death.

[12] In 16:5-7 Mark supplies a double inclusion, one inclusion with the beginning of the whole Gospel (1:24-27) and one with the beginning of the passion (14:27-28).

The Resurrection in Mark

swearing that he did not even know this man (14:71). Yet Mark indicates that this failure can be overcome if the disciples go back to Galilee where Jesus called them at the beginning of the story (1:14-20—still another inclusion).[13] Thus the Marcan readers are not left in total suspense about the fate of Jesus' disciples: he has no intention of losing them permanently. In 10:32 Jesus went before his disciples on the road to Jerusalem while warning them that there the Son of Man would be given over, condemned to death, killed, and after three days be raised up. All his words have proved true, and now he will go before them back to Galilee and there reunite them. Those who were "scattered" (14:27) by the events of the passion at Jerusalem will once more become a community when they return to the place where they were first called together as disciples. This will happen because God will make them see Jesus the Nazarene raised from the dead, the victor over crucifixion whom they had committed themselves to follow.

If the angelic message in 16:7 concerns the disciples and Peter, Mark's primary attention is still centered on the women who had been given this angelic revelation. Their reaction (16:8) has to be a total surprise to the readers. Instead of going forth to the disciples to proclaim with joy that Jesus had been raised and has positive plans for them in Galilee, the women flee from the tomb overcome with trembling, amazement, and fear. They tell nothing to anyone. Inevitably scholars have speculated about the reasons for the silence, at times offering suggestions that have little to do with Mark's expressed line of thought;[14] yet there is where the answer lies. Throughout the Gospel Mark has shown how those who followed Jesus failed because they did not understand that Jesus had to suffer or because they were unwilling to accompany him

---

[13] Nothing in Mark suggests that this geographical direction is meant to support Galilean Christianity over Jerusalem Christianity. (After all, in the early years of post-resurrectional Christianity Peter, mentioned specifically here, was associated with Jerusalem Christianity and no longer with Galilee.) Nor is there much to support the thesis that Mark related Galilee to the Gentile mission as Matthew 4:15 does. The specific mention of Peter who failed outstandingly in the passion shows that "Galilee" is meant to reverse the fate of the disciples during the passion. I do not exclude the added possibility that Mark's use of the place name is meant to remind the reader of all that Jesus taught and said there in the presence of his disciples.

[14] Surely Mark is not interested in explaining why the empty tomb story has appeared so late in Christian tradition or in suppressing the memory of a resurrection appearance to the women because they could not serve as legal witnesses.

Christ in the Gospels of the Liturgical Year

into his passion. Because of the when, where, and how of the appearance of these three women in the passion story (after the death, watching from a distance), readers would get the impression that they had escaped the great trial. Above I have described their coming to the tomb to anoint Jesus as their first act of involvement in the passion. Here, although they have received the revelation of the risen Lord and an angelic commission to proclaim him, they fail. The final words with which Mark describes their failure are: "For they were afraid." This uncomplimentary portrait is in harmony with Mark's somber insistence that none can escape suffering in the following of Jesus.

Amidst Mark's readers surely there were some who had been tested by persecution and had failed. They could find encouragement in the story of Jesus' own disciples, all of whom failed during the passion. But others among Mark's readers would not have been so tested. There is a parallel between them and the women who appear on the scene only after the crucifixion and observe his death without having become involved even in his burial. Like the women they are will-inclined, but after they hear the proclamation of the resurrection and receive a commission to proclaim what has happened to Jesus, they too can fail if they become afraid. Mark's enduring warning, then, would be that not even the resurrection guarantees true faith in Jesus' followers, for the resurrection cannot be appropriated unless one has been tried. People may say that they believe firmly in the risen Christ, but they must realize existentially in their own lives that the one they are following is none other than Jesus the Nazarene who was *crucified*. Mark who has been somber in describing discipleship throughout the passion remains somber about the requirements of discipleship after the resurrection.

MARK 16:9-20 (THE "LONG ENDING"):
THREE APPEARANCES OF JESUS

That grammatically this addition is awkwardly attached to Mark 16:1-8 is obvious from the way 16:9 begins: "Now, having risen early on the first day of the week, he appeared first to Mary Magdalene from whom he had thrown out seven demons." Although the "early on the first day of the week" *partially* echoes Mark 16:1,[15] the readers are

---

[15] "Partially" because the wording for "first" is different, and because the chronological indication in Mark 16:1 refers to the time of the visit to the empty tomb, while here the reference is to a time *before* that, when Jesus had risen.

introduced to Magdalene as if she had not hitherto been encountered as one of the main protagonists in the preceding verses. Moreover, the readers are not introduced to the unnamed "he"; the Jesus who is meant was not an active subject previously in 16:1-8, for there the "he" was the heavenly young man who interpreted the empty tomb.

More important than grammatical awkwardness in the joining is the theological suitability of an appearance to Magdalene. Mark 16:8 left her fleeing in fear and trembling, disobediently silent, failing to communicate the angel's directive to the disciples. Whoever added 16:9 had to assume that Mark did not deny hope to Magdalene despite her behavior.[16] In that assumption he was surely correct: if Mark could report a promised appearance in Galilee to disciples who had fled abandoning the Lord himself when he was arrested, and to a Peter who had denied and cursed the Lord, he could not have been less optimistic about Jesus' mercy to a woman who had failed to obey an angel. Indeed, the way Magdalene is identified makes sense precisely on that score. Jesus had already delivered her from demons (see Luke 8:2); he would scarcely abandon her now.

This appearance of Jesus to Magdalene[17]—literally, his becoming visible—gives her the courage to do the very thing that the angel had previously commanded: she goes to tell "those who had been with him" (the Twelve [Eleven]; Mark 3:14; 16:14), who were mourning and weeping. In describing the reaction of these disciples to Magdalene's message, the author of the Long Ending shows that he shares the pessimistic view of Jesus' followers that characterizes Mark. He reports (16:11) that when these disciples heard that Jesus was alive and had been seen by Magdalene, they were unbelieving.

Disbelief does not defeat the risen Lord, for afterwards he appears "in another form" to two *of them* as they are going into the country-

---

[16] The issue of relating Mark 16:1-8 and the Long Ending is important, for readers of copies of Mark would scarcely be expected to know that two different hands had composed 16:1-8 and 16:9-20 when they were sequential on the same page.

[17] Matthew 28:9-10 and John 20:14 narrate an appearance to Magdalene although the wording of those accounts is not the same as the Long Ending's. I do not plan to debate here the relationship of the Long Ending to the other Gospels. Did its composer have a copy of all or some of the other Gospels before him; or did he sometimes draw on memories of the other Gospels that he had read or heard previously; or did he draw independently on traditions similar to those that had been employed in the other Gospels?

Christ in the Gospels of the Liturgical Year

side.[18] The reference to "another form" tells us how Christians came to explain why Jesus could not be easily recognized. Evidently, however, such a different appearance is enough to overcome previous disbelief, for the two return (to the city of Jerusalem) to tell the rest of the disciples. Just as they had not believed Magdalene, the others do not believe these two. Thus the Long Ending presents us with a remarkable sequence where only an encounter with the risen Jesus himself overcomes previous failure to believe. The harshness of Jesus' rebuke to "the rest" of the disciples (who clearly include the Eleven) for their disbelief and hardness of heart (16:14) is intelligible in light of the reason offered: "They had not believed those who had seen him (after he had been) raised." The community that is reading or hearing Mark consists of people who have to believe those who saw the risen Jesus, and the Long Ending is insisting that such faith was demanded by Jesus even of "those whom he also named apostles" (Mark 3:14 [variant reading]).

When Jesus makes himself visible to the Eleven, they are at table. In other Gospels the appearance of the risen Lord at meals has a eucharistic import,[19] but Mark 16:14 does nothing to emphasize that. If the eucharistic connection was known to the readers of the Long Ending, the rebuke by Jesus about obduracy and disbelief could have been seen as a comment on the failure of those who took part in the eucharistic meal to discern the presence of Jesus (somewhat as in 1 Cor 11:20-34, especially 11:29).

Be that as it may, the primacy in the Long Ending's account of this third appearance of Jesus centers on another feature characteristic of Gospel resurrection stories, namely, the commissioning of those who now become apostles. In Mark 16:15 it is both startling and encouraging that those who have just been upbraided for lack of faith and hardness of heart are now entrusted with preaching the gospel to the whole world. What better way to show that God's grace and not human merit is a primary element in the Good News proclaimed by Jesus. By preaching the risen Christ to others, the Eleven will be strengthened in their faith. Jesus' directive, "Going into the whole world, preach the gospel to every creature," is even more comprehensive than the close

---

[18] This appearance is similar to Luke's story of the two disciples on the road to Emmaus, but once again the wording is not the same.

[19] See the discussion of the meal of bread and fish in John 21:9 (p. 260 below).

The Resurrection in Mark

parallel in Matthew 28:19, "Going, make disciples of all nations." Mark 1:1 identified this writing as "The gospel of Jesus Christ, the Son of God"; and it is that gospel with its christological content that is to be preached by the disciples, for it has within itself the power to change all creation. Through this preaching the risen Lord establishes the authority he has won over all things.

The effect of the preaching is described in 16:16: "The person who believes and is baptized will be saved, but the person who does not believe will be condemned." In this the Long Ending resembles Johannine theology wherein Jesus provokes judgment as people are forced to choose between light and darkness: "The person who believes in him is not condemned, but the person who does not believe is condemned already" (John 3:18).[20] The church situation envisaged by the Long Ending is one where those sent out by Jesus carry on his work and the proper response of faith has to be sealed by baptism in order to bring salvation (see 1 Pet 3:21). The harsh fate that punishes the refusal to believe is partially explicable from the indication in the following verse (Mark 16:17) that the preaching of the gospel will be accompanied by persuasive signs, so that rejection reflects obduracy. Nevertheless, to preach in our times this statement which dualistically equates belief in Christ with salvation and disbelief with condemnation requires caution. Today disbelief flows from many factors including unconvincing signs, e.g., the proclamation of Christ by some who scarcely resemble him.

In the promise that "Signs will accompany those who believe," Mark 16:17 again is close to Johannine theology: "The one who believes in me will do the works that I do and greater" (John 14:12). These signs show that the power as well as the life of the risen Jesus is given to those who believe in his name. Yet since the proclamation of these disciples is "to all creation," the manifestation of that power is wider than during Jesus' ministry. Of the five signs that Mark 16:17-18 enunciates, only the first (casting out demons) and the last (laying hands on the sick and healing them) were characteristic of the Marcan Jesus' own ministry (Mark 1:25-26; 3:11-12, 22; 7:32-33; 8:25). Prodigies resembling the five signs are portrayed in the accounts in Acts of what

[20] In John the judgment is in the present time and is provoked by Jesus himself; in the Long Ending the judgment is future and is provoked by those whom Jesus sends out.

the followers of Jesus accomplish after they receive the Holy Spirit and begin their mission. Paul drives out a possessing spirit in Acts 16:16-18. Speaking in new tongues occurs at Pentecost in Acts 2:4-13 (see 10:46). As for picking up serpents and drinking something deadly without harm, one may think of Acts 28:3-6 where a viper fastens on Paul's hand and hangs from it without his suffering harm.[21] Both Peter and Paul use their hands to heal the sick (Acts 3:7; 28:8). Whether or not the composer of the Long Ending knew Acts directly, he certainly knew traditions about how the emissaries of the risen Christ manifested the power that he had over all creation.

The Long Ending of Mark has developed this third appearance at greater length than the first two because the readers derive their faith from the proclamation by the disciples to whom Jesus appeared. The commissioning of these disciples is the concluding action of "the Lord Jesus"[22] on earth; accordingly in 16:19 he is now taken up to heaven and seated at the right of God. Here the Long Ending is close in sequence, but not in wording, to Luke 24:36-52 where, appearing to the Eleven (24:33, 36) in the general context of a meal (24:41), Jesus predicted that there would be preaching in his name to all the nations (24:47), and then having gone out to Bethany, he was taken up to heaven.

The doubts that the disciples once had (Mark 16:13-14) have now been totally overcome, and they obey by going forth and preaching everywhere (16:20). True to his promise the Lord, even though enthroned in heaven, *works with them* confirming "the word" through the signs that follow the disciples.[23] This sense of divine reinforcement was what gave courage to martyrs, as we see in Justin, *Apology* 1.45:

> This mighty word his apostles, going forth from Jerusalem, preached everywhere. And although death is decreed for those who teach or at all confess the name of Christ, we everywhere both embrace and teach it.

---

[21] See also Luke 10:19: "Behold I have given you authority to tread on serpents and scorpions, and over all the power of the enemy; and nothing shall harm you."

[22] There is some textual doubt about this phrase; it would constitute with the dubious Luke 24:3 the only Gospel instances of a title found in Paul and Acts.

[23] This is not far from the description of "the word" in Hebrews 2:3-4: "Announced first by the Lord, it was attested to us by those who had heard him, while God also witnessed to it by signs and wonders and varied acts of power."

The Resurrection in Mark

Chapter 23

The Resurrection in Matthew (27:62–28:20)

One might assume that a resurrection narrative should start with the women coming to the tomb. Certainly the person who divided the Gospels into chapters felt that way, for in every Gospel that is precisely where a new chapter begins. Thus Matthew 28:1 tells us how Mary Magdalene and the other Mary went to see the sepulcher. In three Gospels I have no quarrel with that manner of beginning resurrection narratives; for what precedes Mark 16:1; Luke 24:1; and John 20:1, respectively, is the story of the burial which is transitional from the crucifixion account to the resurrection.[1] Matthew, however, differs from the others in that, having terminated the burial in 27:61, he has an intervening story in 27:62-66 concerning the guard placed at the sepulcher. That is an integral part of the resurrection story, for elements from it recur in 28:2-4, 11-15; and so we must begin our discussion of the Matthean resurrection narrative not with 28:1, but with 27:62.

That perception is extremely important for understanding the structure of the Matthean narrative. In addition to the transitional episode of the burial that leads to it, four episodes may be distinguished in the narrative, thus a total of five:

(1) [27:57-61: Burial by Joseph of Arimathea, a disciple, with the women present.]

(2) 27:62-66: Chief priests and Pharisees place guards at sepulcher.

(3) 28:1-10: Women come to sepulcher; angel of the Lord descends and frightens the guards, revealing to the women that Jesus is risen; they are to tell disciples that Jesus is going to Galilee, Jesus appears to the women.

---

[1] A partial exception is an intermediary half-verse in Luke 23:56b which pertains to the women resting on the Sabbath.

(4) 28:11-15: Guards bribed by chief priests and assembled elders to lie that the disciples stole the body.

(5) 28:16-20: Appearance of Jesus to the eleven disciples and his commissioning them to go to all nations.

In this structure episodes 1, 3, and 5 concern those favorable to Jesus: (1) a disciple and the women, (3) the women are to tell the disciples, (5) appearance to the disciples. Episodes 2 and 4 concern hostile Jewish authorities and the Roman guards they employ. It is noteworthy that in this artistic arrangement the middle scene (3) mentions all three groups: the women, the guards, and the disciples. One is encouraged in this analysis by a detection of the same alternation in the fivefold structure of episodes in the Matthean infancy narrative.[2] That opening of the Gospel offers many parallels in thought, wording, and popular motifs to the conclusion of the Gospel constituted by the resurrection narrative—an inclusion by which Matthew begins and ends in the same way.

EPISODE IN 27:62-66: CHIEF PRIESTS AND PHARISEES PLACE A GUARD AT THE SEPULCHER

The burial in 27:57-61 was a compassionate action by a disciple, with the women followers of Jesus sitting in attendance opposite the sepulcher; now Matthew turns to malevolent attention paid to the sepulcher. While other Gospels would terminate with the crucifixion scene the hostility by the chief priests and Jewish rulers toward Jesus,[3]

---

[2] The five-part structure of the infancy narrative of Matthew 1:18–2:23 may be sketched thus:
1. 1:18-25: Revelation by an angel of the Lord to Joseph about Jesus' conception, instructing him to recognize Jesus as his son.
2. 2:1-12: The magi come from the East to worship the King of the Jews, only to encounter a *hostile* Herod with the chief priests and scribes. The magi worship Jesus.
3. 2:13-15: Revelation by the angel of the Lord to Joseph to take the child and his mother to Egypt and thus preserve the child's life.
4. 2:16-18: Herod kills the male children of Bethlehem in an attempt to kill Jesus.
5. 2:19-23: Revelation by the angel of the Lord to Joseph that those who sought the child's life are dead and he should return to Nazareth.
Notice that 1, 3, and 5 are positive, while 2 and 4 are negative.

[3] John's post-resurrectional "fear of the Jews" is more general; Acts shows the Jewish leaders still hostile towards Peter and Paul.

The Resurrection in Matthew

Matthew carries it over to the resurrection and uses it to fill in the Sabbath between Jesus' death and burial (late on Friday) and the opening of the tomb (beginning of Sunday). In the infancy narrative that opens Matthew, on hearing of the birth of the King of the Jews, the secular ruler (Herod) worked with the chief priests and the scribes to kill him and thus to prevent even the beginning of his career. At the end of the Gospel, the chief priests and the Pharisees or elders (27:62; 28:12) work with the secular ruler (Pilate) to prevent the survival of his ministry. God will frustrate the armed might of these authorities; and at the end of the resurrection story, as at the end of the infancy story, Jesus emerges triumphant—a lesson of encouragement to Matthew's readers (and to us).

The material in this episode is peculiar to Matthew (even as was the infancy story) and like much popular narrative ignores certain implausibilities. Three times Jesus predicted to his disciples his suffering, violent death, and resurrection on the third day (16:21; 17:22-23; 20:17-19). The disciples never gave evidence of having understood what he meant. Here, however, the chief priests know that Jesus predicted, "After three days I will rise again"; and they understand perfectly what he meant.[4] Consequently, they want the sepulcher made secure until the third day to frustrate Jesus' prophecy. In the Sanhedrin trial of Jesus the issues were his ability to destroy the Temple and whether he was the Messiah, the Son of God; but now the interest has shifted to the veracity of the resurrection claim. Jesus is called by his accusers "a deceiver," a description that will become common in later Jewish polemic against him. The skepticism of the authorities, plus their allegation that his disciples will steal the body (repeated in 28:13), suggests that we may have here an issue that Matthew was facing when writing his Gospel. Although during the ministry of Jesus "the chief priests and the Pharisees" were the target of his parable of the vineyard, as the tenants from whom the vineyard would be taken away (Matt 21:45), the Pharisees were noticeably absent during the passion narrative, for they played little direct role in the death of Jesus. They have reappeared here because in the experience of Matthew's church they were the chief opponents and undoubtedly were skeptics

---

[4] In Matthew 2:3 Herod too was instantly perceptive about the danger presented to him by the birth of the King of the Jews.

Christ in the Gospels of the Liturgical Year

about the resurrection of Jesus. This episode has been drawn from a context of apologetics and polemics.

When the core of this popular narrative was taken over into Matthew's Gospel, it gained another dimension: the inability of human power to frustrate God's plan. In their attempt to prevent the resurrection (even if they describe it as a fraud), the chief authorities of the Jews enlist the help of the governing power, addressing their request to Pilate as *kyrios* (Matthean irony). Pilate's affirmative response has often been misunderstood to mean: "You have a guard [of your own]; go and make it secure as you know how." Yet 28:14 suggests that no Jewish guard under the control of the chief priests is meant, for there the priests offer to placate the governor and keep the soldiers of the guard out of trouble. Rather, Pilate's response should be translated: "You have the guard [you just asked for]"—in other words a grant of Roman soldiers. Thus the governing and religious authorities conspire together against the resurrection of Jesus, even as in the infancy narrative Herod conspired with the chief priests and scribes against the life of the Messiah (2:4, 20 ["*Those* who sought the child's life"]). Despite the use of armed force, neither group of earthly powers proves successful. Sealing the stone and setting the guard will be infantile precautions against the power that God is about to release.

EPISODE IN 28:1-10: THE WOMEN AT THE SEPULCHER; THE ANGEL OF THE LORD AND HIS REVELATION; JESUS APPEARS TO THE WOMEN

Jesus was often accused of violating the Sabbath; perhaps by deliberate irony Matthew places on the Sabbath the effort of the chief priests and the Pharisees to block the resurrection. As soon as the Sabbath is over (approximately 6 P.M. on Saturday) and the first day of the week is beginning, Mary Magdalene and the other Mary set out to see the sepulcher.[5] (Nothing is said about coming to anoint Jesus as in Mark and Luke; the guards, peculiar to Matthew, would never permit that.)

---

[5] An early hour (about dawn) is mentioned in Mark 16:2; Luke 24:1; and John 20:1, although with the contrary indications that "the sun had risen" in Mark and that it was "still dark" in John. There is no such indication in Matthew who has excised both the Marcan references to the morning. What he writes is that the first day of the week was beginning, and by our reckoning that would be about 7–8 P.M. on Saturday.

The Resurrection in Matthew

What they actually see is a stunning series of events narrated by no other Gospel. First of all there is an earthquake. This is harmonious with what Matthew *alone* describes as occurring when Jesus died (27:51b-53): "The earth quaked; and the rocks were split; and the tombs were opened; and many bodies of the saints who had fallen asleep were raised. . . ." Matthew, once more with access to popular storytelling traditions about the resurrection, seeks to convey the wider importance of what God has done for Jesus. In the infancy narrative as "the King of the Jews" was born, his star was visible at its rising (in the East), something seen by the Gentile magi astronomers. When Jesus died with the charge "The King of the Jews" written on the cross over his head, the earth quaked, pouring the dead out of their tombs, something seen by the Gentile centurion and the soldiers with him. And now to herald Jesus' resurrection the earth quakes once more. The main focus of the passion narrative has been on the role of Jesus in the salvation history of Israel; but Matthew wishes to signal that Jesus' role from birth through death to resurrection is of cosmic importance, shaking the foundations of the world and raising even those long dead.

The vivid and imaginative Matthean description catches the apocalyptic aspect of the resurrection. In addition to the earthquake at the sepulcher, an angel of the Lord descends from heaven and rolls back the stone—once more something peculiar to Matthew. The appearance of the angel fits the apocalyptic context: he is "like lightning," even as the great angel who came to reveal to Daniel the last times had "a face like lightning" (Dan 10:6). His garment is "white as snow," even as Daniel's Ancient of Days who judges the nations had a garment white as snow (Dan 7:9; cf. Matt 17:2). The power of God has intervened definitively at the sepulcher of Jesus, and before it the human powers who had conspired to frustrate the resurrection are as nothing. In fear the guards are shaken even as the earth was, and they become "as if they were dead" (28:4). This is truly ironical: Jesus lives and those set to prevent that are as if dead.

The first action of the angel of the Lord whose arrival has been heralded by the earthquake is to roll back the stone and thus undo the ineffectual sealing placed on it by the order of the chief priests (27:66). Some scholars have thought that Matthew is implying that the resurrection took place at this moment, or (more soberly, since he does not mention the resurrection here) that his popular source described the resurrection at this moment. In fact, the second-century, apocryphal *Gospel of Peter* (9:35–10:42) places a highly imaginative description of the resurrection precisely at this juncture. Probably, however, *Peter* represents a more developed dramatization of the type of popular account that influenced Matthew. Matthew's silence about the resurrection itself, similar to the silence in the other canonical Gospels, suggests that in more sophisticated circles it was understood that the resurrection could not be described, for it was an event that touched the other world beyond time and space.[6] When Matthew's angel rolls back the stone, he does so not to provide an exit for the resurrection but to make it possible to see that Jesus was no longer in the place where he once lay (28:6) and that therefore the resurrection had already taken place.

The next task of Matthew's "angel of the Lord" is to interpret the emptiness of the sepulcher. The title that Matthew uses for this angel interpreter[7] reminds us that "the angel of the Lord" served as a revealer and interpreter in the Matthean infancy narrative as well. There (but not since) the angel of the Lord appeared three times. First, in 1:20 this angel explained that Mary's pregnancy (which otherwise would have been misinterpreted) stemmed from the Holy Spirit. So also here the angel explains that the empty sepulcher (which "the Jews" will misinterpret as a result of stealing the body) stems from Jesus' having been raised from the dead (28:7). In his second and third appearances in the Matthean infancy narrative (2:13, 19), the angel of the Lord told Joseph what to do in response to the tremendous events that had taken place. So also here the angel of the Lord gives the women instruction to go quickly and tell the disciples that Jesus has been raised. Those disciples of Jesus forsook him and fled when he was arrested (26:56); and Peter, the one exception who hesitantly tried to continue with Jesus by following at a distance (26:58), denied him three times and cursed him (26:69-75, especially 26:74). Yet they are still in God's plan and are to receive the revelation about the resurrection from the women. These women (whom Matthew does *not* call

---

[6] What is entirely in this world and not beyond time and space is the empty tomb, and that is described on the first day of the week by all four evangelists.

[7] Luke 24:22-23 makes clear that the "two men" (*andres*) of 24:4 were angels; John 20:12 has two angels. Mark 16:5 speaks of a "young man" (*neaniskos*) who in my judgment is to be interpreted as an angel.

The Resurrection in Matthew

disciples), although present at Golgotha, hitherto had only the passive role of looking on the death of Jesus from afar (27:55) and sitting opposite the sepulcher when he was buried (27:61). Now they are rewarded for their initiative in coming to see the sepulcher by being made the first human proclaimers of the resurrection[8] and the intermediaries through whom the faith of the disciples will be rekindled. Many phrases in this description ("Do not be afraid"; "Go quickly"; "They departed quickly . . . fear and great joy") stem from the stereotypic language of angelic announcements in the OT and are found also in the angelic announcements of the infancy narratives.[9] Nevertheless, Matthew is surely presenting virtues that his Christian readers should imitate in receiving and sharing the news of the risen Lord; they are being invited to go quickly with reverential fear and great joy to tell others.

In a further reward to the women who are joyfully obedient to the angel, Jesus himself appears to them. If we may judge from 1 Corinthians 15:5ff., a list of the appearances of the risen Jesus associated with official preaching (see 1 Cor 15:11-12) concentrated mostly on the apostolic recipients (Cephas [Peter], the Twelve, James, Paul); but that does not mean that the other appearances did not occur or were not remembered. Indeed in popular circles, appearances to those who were not part of church leadership may have been of great interest and have received vivid narrative development. In any case, John 20:11-18 (in a more developed form), Mark 16:9, and Matthew 28:9-10 record an appearance to Mary Magdalene (and in Matthew to "the other Mary" 28:1).[10] The reaction of the women to the sight of the risen Jesus is interesting. They come up (a verb Matthew often uses for an action ex-

---

[8] Matthew 28:7 has the women instructed to tell the disciples, "He has been raised from the dead," an element absent from the instruction to them in Mark 16:7. The concluding clause in the instruction of Matthew 28:7 adds solemnity: "Behold, I have told you."

[9] R. E. Brown, *The Birth of the Messiah* (New Updated Ed.; Garden City, New York: Doubleday, 1993), 155–59.

[10] Because Matthew 28:9-10 is heavily Matthean in style, there have been attempts to deny that there was pre-Gospel tradition behind this appearance and to explain it simply as creative Matthean filling out of Marcan silence. Since I find no compelling evidence that John's account of a similar appearance is a rewriting of Mark, it is far easier to suppose a pre-Gospel tradition that each evangelist has rewritten in his own way.

Christ in the Gospels of the Liturgical Year

pressing awe) and worship him. Certainly in that reaction they serve as a model for how Christians should respect the presence of the Lord. Furthermore, they clutch his feet (in the Johannine parallel Jesus has to warn Mary Magdalene, "Do not cling to me"). While such a gesture may underline the reality of Jesus' body and thus have an apologetic function, it also expresses human affection for Jesus—probably an important element in popular appearance narratives. Jesus' message to the women repeats that given to them by the angel. Seemingly, then, in these nonapostolic appearances revelation was not an important factor. Nevertheless, a minor element in the message in 28:10 is interesting. While the angel told the women to report to Jesus' disciples (28:7), here the message is to go to Jesus' *brothers*. A new status will emerge for those who hear and believe in the resurrection: they become God's children and thus the brothers and sisters of Jesus.[11]

EPISODE IN 28:11-15: THE GUARDS; THE SESSION OF THE CHIEF PRIESTS AND THE ELDERS; THE BRIBE AND THE FALSEHOOD

Matthew now returns to the story of the guard, just as in the infancy narrative he resumed the story of Herod after he had stopped to tell how the magi frustrated Herod's plan. Although the chief priests hear all that had taken place and therefore how an angel of the Lord descended from heaven and opened the sepulcher, they do not cease their opposition; they do not repent and come to believe. Earlier (26:3-5, 14-15) the chief priests and elders gathered and took counsel on how to arrest Jesus secretly and kill him; and they paid Judas silver pieces to hand Jesus over. They also sought false testimony to convict Jesus (26:59). A similar process of paying silver pieces and using falsehood is followed here. (One may wonder whether Matthew does not hint at their future punishment, for the silver pieces they paid to Judas came back to haunt them [27:5-6]; and the silver paid to the guards is not much nobler than the blood money paid to Judas.) The last mention of these Jewish authorities (28:15) has them *teaching* the soldiers to lie; the last mention of Jesus (28:20) will have him telling his disciples to teach all nations whatever he has commanded.

---

[11] See also John 20:17 (p. 248 below) for the use of "brothers" for disciples (20:18), and Matthew 12:49; 25:40.

The Resurrection in Matthew

This picture of plotting, a bribe, deliberate falsehood, and a promise to placate is surely a reflection of popular prejudice showing how early Christians attributed malevolence to those who opposed them. While in individual instances of such opposition to Christians there may indeed have been malevolence, Matthew's hostile use of "the Jews" is a generalization that goes beyond historical incidents and reflects antagonism and rumors circulating among ordinary folk. In the more sensitive interreligious relations of our own times, such a broad portrayal of the Jewish authorities as scheming liars and the generalization of the lie as one circulated among "the Jews" should make Christians uneasy. But the period in which this harsh polemic was developed did not share our sensitivities. We have clear instances of Jews hating other Jews over religious issues; the Essenes pictured the Sadducee high priest at Jerusalem as one who embodied deceit; and the high priest did not hesitate to crucify Pharisees and seek to kill the Essene leader. If Acts is to be believed, Jewish authorities would have been pleased to have Christian apostles like Peter and Paul executed. In such a context, when a false explanation of the empty tomb of Jesus circulated among some Jews, it is understandable (even if not to be approved) that ordinary Christians would universalize the attitude and regard it as a knowing falsehood. Indeed, if one may judge from the apocryphal *Gospel of Peter* 8:28–11:49,[12] that bitterness toward Jews in less-controlled, popular Christian circles was stronger than what appears in the more formalized canonical Gospels. One aspect of Matthew's story remains an important lesson. He is implying the futility of the nasty apologetics that has developed in some Jewish circles against the resurrection. Christians may learn that hostile apologetics on either side is futile and does little to further the religious cause that one deems right.

EPISODE IN 28:16-20: THE APPEARANCE OF JESUS
TO THE DISCIPLES ON A MOUNTAIN IN GALILEE
The final scene shifts from Jerusalem to Galilee—the "Galilee of the Gentiles" as Matthew 4:15 describes the land where Jesus began his

[12] There the Jewish elders and scribes are themselves at the tomb and therefore seemingly observe the opening of the tomb and the resurrection itself. They acknowledge themselves guilty of great sin before God in concocting a lie about this, but they persuade Pilate to join in.

Christ in the Gospels of the Liturgical Year

ministry and first called his disciples (4:18-22). Jesus had predicted at the beginning of the passion that, although the disciples would be scattered, after he was raised up he would go before them to Galilee (26:32). The Galilee directive was reiterated at the sepulcher both by the angel of the Lord and by the risen Jesus (28:7, 10) with the added promise that there the disciples (now become his "brothers") would see him. Now at "the mountain" he fulfills the promise. Matthew does not think of a specific geographical mountain but rather of the mountain where Jesus sat when he taught the disciples the Sermon on the Mount (5:1) and the mountain where he was transfigured before Peter, James, and John (17:1). Just as on Mount Sinai or Horeb, Moses encountered God and received from him the Law, so on a mountain during the ministry the disciples had seen the glory of God in the transfigured Jesus and received from him an interpretation of the Law: "You have heard it said but I say to you."[13] The disciples who now come to this mountain once more have already learned from the women that here they are to see Jesus. It is not surprising, then, that despite their dismal history of failure in the passion, they worship the risen Jesus as soon as they see him (28:17), even as the women had done (28:9). At the beginning of the Gospel the Gentile magi came and fell down and worshiped him; at the end his Jewish followers (the women) and disciples render the same worship.

The motif of doubt recurs frequently in appearances of Jesus recounted in the various Gospels; and here while all the disciples worship, some doubt. These are members of the Twelve (or with Matthew's greater precision, of the Eleven); they heard Jesus' threefold prediction of the resurrection during his ministry; they heard his promise to go before them to Galilee, and they heard that promise reiterated by the women; yet some doubt. This doubt may have an apologetic dimension, showing that even the disciples were not anxious to believe and were certainly not credulous; they had to be convinced. More important, the doubt would remind the readers that, even after the resurrection, faith is not a facile response. It might also encourage them that Jesus is not repelled by doubt, for he now comes close to the disciples to speak. Doubting or not, they have worshiped him, and he responds to them.

[13] See Matthew 5:21-22, 27-28, 31-32, 33-34, 38-39, 43-44.

The Resurrection in Matthew

If appearance stories point back by insisting that the risen one is truly the Jesus who was crucified and buried, some of them also point forward to the mission that the resurrection must produce, reflecting an insistence on sharing with others what God has done. Scholars recognize this by speaking of church-founding appearances. In Mark 16:14-15, Matthew, Luke, and John there is such an appearance to members of the Twelve that makes them apostles, i.e., those sent to proclaim the resurrection. The sending is based on Jesus' own status, showing that as Jesus carried on God's work, the apostles carry on Jesus' work. This relationship is phrased in Matthew 28:18-19: "All authority [or power] in heaven and on earth has been given to me; go therefore. . . ."[14] Such wording echoes Daniel 7:14 where authority is given in heaven by the Ancient of Days to a son of man "so that peoples of all nations and languages would serve him." Thus the eschatological and apocalyptic atmosphere established by the earthquake and the appearance of the angel of the Lord at the sepulcher continues on the mountain in Galilee. The authority of the church is delegated from Jesus who has been elevated[15] and has authority in heaven and on earth; the mission that flows from it will touch all nations. It is entrusted to the Eleven, even though some doubted. We are left to suspect that the word of Jesus solved the doubt, and that by proclaiming to others, their faith was strengthened.

The wording of the mission given to the Eleven is significant: "Going therefore, make disciples of all nations." Jesus already had authority during his public ministry (7:29; 9:8; 11:27; 21:23); but when he sent the Twelve out at that time (10:5-6), he instructed them: "Go not among the nations [Gentiles], and enter no town of the Samaritans; but go rather to the lost sheep of the house of Israel." Now the risen Jesus with full eschatological power ("All authority") sends them out to all the nations. Israel is not excluded (see 23:34); but the progression

[14] The functional equivalent is John 20:21, "As the Father has sent me, so do I send you." Notice that the sayings of the risen Jesus tend to be parallel in meaning and function but not in words. This raises the issue of whether the post-resurrectional revelations were in words or by detectable intention that found different wording in different communities.

[15] Although Matthew does not use the language of elevation, one may suppose that here, as elsewhere in the NT, resurrection concerns more than a point of departure (from the sepulcher or tomb); it involves a destination, namely, to glory with God.

Christ in the Gospels of the Liturgical Year

in these two commands, one in the ministry and one after the resurrection, embodies the experience of Matthean Christianity. Jesus himself spoke only to Jews (15:24); and at first so did those who had been with him in the public ministry as they went out after the resurrection to proclaim the kingdom. Yet in the first two decades of church development they discovered that the plan of God was wider.[16] At the beginning of the Gospel Matthew signaled the wide extension of God's plan by writing of Gentile magi who came to Jerusalem—the fulfillment of an OT dream (Isa 2:2-4). Now, however, it becomes clear that the apostles cannot simply wait for the Gentiles to come; they must go out to them. And if in the ministry the chief Jewish followers of Jesus (the Twelve) were called disciples, that privilege and title is to be extended to all nations.

This mission to make disciples of the nations is to be accompanied and accomplished by baptism. Elsewhere in the NT baptism is in the name of Jesus (Acts 2:38; 10:48; 1 Cor 6:11; etc.); but here at the end of that Gospel which the subsequent church made her own catechism we find the triadic formula: "In the name of the Father, and of the Son, and of the Holy Spirit"—undoubtedly the formula in use in Matthew's community when he wrote. Instances in Paul and elsewhere show that very quickly believers in Jesus acknowledged that God the Father was the source and goal of all that Jesus said and did. The Holy Spirit was quickly related to the continuance of Jesus' work within the believer and within the church. Thus while belief in Jesus (his name, who he was) was the first essential component of baptismal profession, the Father and the Spirit were brought into that confession to articulate the larger picture to which believers committed themselves. By a century after Matthew's time an expansion of articulated belief about the Father, the Son, and the Holy Spirit produced a creed divided into articles centered on those three divine agents. This baptismal creed of the Roman church we know as the Apostles' Creed. In other words, the Matthean formula which seems to stand at the terminus of NT baptismal development also represents a beginning in the custom of professing at baptism a formula that enshrines what Christians believe the triune God has done. This formula describes the fullness of divine action to which the acceptance of baptism is the response.

---

[16] See the dramatization of this for Peter in Acts 10.

The Resurrection in Matthew

The baptizing of the nations by the disciples is to be accompanied by their teaching all that Jesus had commanded. Several times Matthew has summed up Jesus' activity in terms of his teaching (4:23; 9:35; 11:1), and that task is now passed on to the Eleven. Their teaching is not to be new or their own, but "all that I commanded you." This is Exodus language (7:2; 23:22; etc.) for what God commanded Israel and so is perfectly appropriate in the final directive of the lawgiver of the new covenant.

The solemn last words of Jesus in Matthew (28:20), "Behold, I am with you all days to the end of time [*aiōn*: age, world],"[17] echo the first words ever spoken about him in the beginning of the Gospel (1:23), "Behold the virgin shall conceive and bear a son and they will name him Emmanuel, which means 'God with us.'" The resurrection is for Matthew evidence not only that God was with Jesus who conquered death but also that in Jesus God's abiding presence is with all those who are baptized in the name of the Father, and of the Son, and of the Holy Spirit and who observe all that Jesus has commanded, as taught by the disciples. In Isaiah 41:10 God promised his people Israel: "Do not be afraid: I am with you." Here the promise is reiterated to an enlarged people including Gentiles who have come to know Him in Jesus Christ. Earthly powers represented by the secular ruler, the chief priests, and the scribes/elders tried to prevent the plan of God both at the conception/birth of Jesus and at his crucifixion/resurrection. They were unsuccessful then, and they will be equally unsuccessful in preventing it till the end of time.[18]

---

[17] The eschatological sweep of the last words of Jesus is brought out by the repetition of "all": "all authority"; "all nations"; "all that I command"; and "all days."

[18] In 17:17 Jesus asked a faithless and perverse generation, "How long am I to be with you?" Here he answers that question for those who are his disciples: "all days."

Christ in the Gospels of the Liturgical Year

Chapter 24

The Resurrection in Luke
(24:1-53; Acts 1:1-12)

The most architectonic of the evangelists, Luke gives a geographical framework to his expansive two-volume narrative of Jesus and of the Spirit. The narrative begins in the Jerusalem Temple among Jews (Luke 1:5-8) and ends in Rome with the directive that future evangelization should concentrate on the Gentiles (Acts 28:28). The hinge that joins the story of Jesus from Nazareth to the story of the Spirit who guides the mission to the ends of the earth is a crucial series of events that take place in Jerusalem, namely, Jesus' passion, death, resurrection, and sending of the Spirit. The first part of that hinge series (Jesus' passion and death) is recounted at the end of Luke's first volume (Gospel of Luke 22–23); the last part of the hinge series (sending of the Spirit) is recounted at the beginning of Luke's second volume (Acts 2). The resurrection, involving appearances of the risen Jesus in Jerusalem,[1] is so pivotal, however, that it is recounted both at the end of the Gospel and the beginning of Acts. As a Jerusalem event at the end of the Gospel, it constitutes an inclusion with the beginning of that Gospel, so that the story both starts and ends in the Jerusalem Temple (see Luke 24:53). As a Jerusalem event at the beginning of Acts, it functions as a counterpoise to the ending in Rome, so that the book becomes a story of how Christianity moved from Jerusalem to Rome, from Jews to Gentiles.

A further indication of the import of the Jerusalem setting of the Lucan resurrection account is found when we consider the geographical motif of journey that governs almost two-thirds of the Lucan Gospel.

---

[1] Luke is the only Gospel that has no room for appearances in Galilee, an especially significant fact if one thinks that Luke knew Mark (16:7).

We hear in Luke 9:51: "When the days approached for his being taken up, he set his face to go to Jerusalem." One can distinguish three stages in this great journey to Jerusalem. (1) The movement from Galilee to Jerusalem runs from 9:51 to 19:27 (with reminders in 10:38; 13:22; 17:11; 18:31). (2) The entry into Jerusalem and a rejection there (particularly at the Temple) that eventually causes Jesus to be put to death on the cross runs from 19:28 to 23:56. (3) The raising of Jesus and his being taken from this world to heaven culminates the Gospel (24:1-53) and is reused to open Acts (1:1-12) so that the heavenly ascent is described twice (Luke 24:51; Acts 1:9). The journey of Jesus from Galilee to Jerusalem ends in heaven; that constitutes a promise that the journey of his disciples to the ends of the earth (Acts 1:8) will also end in heaven.

Giving more detailed attention to this last stage involving the resurrection and ascension, we find that from the viewpoint of time it consists of two sections, while geographically there are four episodes:

A. Easter Sunday Events
 (1) 24:1-12: The women and Peter visit the empty tomb.
 (2) 24:13-35: Two disciples going to Emmaus encounter Jesus.
 (3) 24:36-53: Jesus appears to the Eleven gathered in Jerusalem and is taken to heaven from Bethany; they return to Jerusalem, blessing God in the Temple.

B. Appearances during Forty Days
 (4) Acts 1:1-12: Jesus instructs the apostles to wait in Jerusalem for the Spirit but ultimately to be his witnesses to the end of the earth; he is taken to heaven from Mount Olivet.

In the course of considering the episodes one by one, we shall be sorely tempted to compare Luke to Mark in Episode 1 to observe the Lucan adaptations, and to compare Luke to John in Episode 3 since only these two Gospels share an Easter Sunday evening appearance of Jesus to the disciples gathered in Jerusalem. Nevertheless throughout this volume I have to read each Gospel as a unit without intrusive appeals to other Gospels for knowledge that the Gospel under consideration does not convey. This insistence allows us to hear the Gospel in a way that resembles how the first audience must have heard it since they scarcely had the comparative material supplied by the other Gospels. It also facilitates appreciation of the inner consistency of the

Lucan Gospel, especially of how the resurrection chapter (24) echoes motifs in the chapters (1–2) dealing with the infancy.

Although Luke begins the account on the first day of the week (24:1), his opening picks up on a transitional sentence that concluded the burial. Luke told us not only that the Galilean women saw how Jesus' body was laid in the tomb (23:55) but also that they went back to prepare spices and myrrh and then rested on the Sabbath according to the commandment (23:56).[2] In reporting that, while Luke did not identify by name the women from Galilee, he made their good intentions amply clear. They did not assist in the burial because they had at hand no prepared spices, and their delay until Sunday was dictated by their obedience to the commandment of Sabbath rest. Luke's story of Jesus' birth was replete with references to how those involved were law-observant (1:6, 8-9; 2:21-25, 37, 39, 41-42), and that motif returns at his death. From the beginning to the end of Jesus' life on earth, there was no break with the commandments that God had given to the people of Israel.[3]

The fact that the women come at the crack of dawn on the first day after the Sabbath with the spices they had prepared (24:1) catches their eagerness to render loving service. In describing the growing perplexity of these women when they reach and enter the tomb, Luke makes an elegant play on their finding what they did not expect (the tomb open, for the stone had been rolled back—Luke's first mention of the stone!) and their not finding what they did expect (the body of the Lord Jesus). Fear is added to perplexity when suddenly there are standing alongside them two angelic men in dazzling apparel.[4] At the beginning of the Gospel (Luke 2:9) an angel of the Lord was suddenly standing

---

[2] Functionally, then, both Luke and Matthew interpose a Sabbath event between Jesus' burial on Friday and the finding of the empty tomb on Sunday; but Matthew's story of obtaining a guard for the tomb (27:62-66) is long enough to constitute an episode in itself.

[3] Eventually Luke will come to the issue of Christian nonobservance of the food laws. On that issue Peter will be instructed by new divine revelation in Acts 10:9-16; even then, however, partial and respectful observance will be included in Acts 15:29.

[4] Although Luke 24:4 speaks of "two men," their clothing suggests heavenly origin; and 24:23 identifies them as angels. See Acts 10:30; Daniel 8:15.

alongside the shepherds to explain the significance of what had happened at Bethlehem; at the end the same divine assistance is supplied to explain the significance of what had happened at the Place of the Skull (Calvary) and at the tomb. The birth of Jesus brought joy; the death brought sorrow; but both are manifestations of divine glory (see 24:26). Fearful (24:5), even as were the shepherds (2:9), the women bow to the ground. The question the two "men" address to the women, "Why do you seek the living among the dead?" is a rhetorical revelation that despite the crucifixion Jesus lives. In the better manuscripts of Luke the angels go on to a more prosaic proclamation: "He is not here but has been raised." That Jesus is not here the women can see with their eyes; that this is because God has raised Jesus they must take on faith. The two angels go on to rebuke implicitly the women's lack of spontaneous understanding that resurrection had to be the denouement of crucifixion: in Galilee Jesus had given a detailed outline of the fate of the Son of Man, including resurrection on the third day.[5] Moreover, since Jesus' words involved a "must," that fate was divinely ordained—an ordination that made the passion intelligible and the resurrection inevitable.

Brought to recall Jesus' prediction (24:8), the women show they have spontaneity by immediately acting. That Jesus lives is the heart of the Gospel, and the good news can never simply be received and kept. The women go back from the tomb to tell the Eleven and "all the rest" (24:9). Luke does not specify who the latter are, but presumably they include the two disciples who are to set out for Emmaus in the next episode. In 24:11 Luke will tell his readers of the contemptuous reception given the women's report; but first (24:10) he stops to identify belatedly these Galilean women who "stood from afar" at the crucifixion, observed the burial, and now with their spices have visited the tomb emptied by the resurrection. Lucan readers should recognize the first named, Mary Magdalene, for alone among the Gospels Luke has introduced her during the public ministry of Jesus. She was one of the women whom Jesus had healed of evil spirits and infirmities; in particular, from Magdalene seven demons had gone out (8:2). The second woman, Joanna, the wife of Chuza, Herod's steward (a possible trans-

---

[5] The form given to Jesus' words by the angels in 24:6-7 is an amalgam of several statements by the Lucan Jesus: 9:22, 44; 18:31-33.

lation of *epitropos* in 8:3), was one of the same group. (The "Mary of James" listed third by Luke 24:10 has not previously been mentioned, and no identification is given for "the other women.") The fact that Mary Magdalene and Joanna were companions of the Twelve in Galilee (8:1-3) in the following of Jesus makes it all the more startling that now their story of the empty tomb and the angelic explanation is treated by the Eleven as if it were silly chatter that need not be believed.[6] The women, although slow to understand, had believed the explanation of the angelic men who reminded them of Jesus' prediction; the Eleven refuse belief even though the women's account must have reminded them of the prediction. Luke 24:10 underlines their obduracy by reporting that the women "kept telling" the apostles about what had happened—an unusual touch in a Gospel that is so gentle on the Twelve/Eleven.

A footnote to this episode is supplied by 24:12 which reports that one of the Eleven, Peter (evidently deciding to test the women's story), ran to the tomb to peer in.[7] The fact that Peter sees only the burial wrappings[8] and not the body of Jesus confirms at least part of the women's story. Yet Peter is not said to have concluded that the other part of their story was true, namely, that Jesus had been raised from the dead; for he returns from the tomb not with joy but with amazement. Did the fact that he did not see angelic men there make him doubt? The rest of the chapter will be devoted by Luke to appearances of the risen Jesus that will overcome disbelief among the Eleven and "all the rest" who were with them. And in a passing reference (24:34) we shall hear that Peter (Simon) was the recipient of a special appearance.

[6] Commentaries often explain that generally the testimony of women was not given credence, but the situation here is aggravated because of the close past relationship of the apostles to these women. According to Luke 24:34 the Eleven did accept the report of Simon (Peter); yet Peter had seen the risen Lord and these women had not.

[7] This verse is found both in the best copies and the oldest manuscript of Luke. It should not be omitted despite verbal similarity to John 20:3-4. A later passage, Luke 24:24, suggests that Peter was not alone: "Some of those who were with us went off to the tomb and found it just as the women said."

[8] Earlier (23:53) Luke reported that Jesus was wrapped in a shroud (*sindōn*); here he speaks of burial wrappings (*othonia*). Even if Luke derived these reports from different sources, readers would be meant to see the terms as equivalent, or to think of the shroud as part of the burial wrappings.

The Resurrection in Luke

EPISODE IN LUKE 24:13-35:
TWO DISCIPLES ON THE ROAD TO EMMAUS

In many ways this story, very Lucan in style, has no parallel among the other Gospels.[9] The longest of all the canonical resurrection stories, its length provides the risen Jesus an opportunity to offer revelatory teaching that shows how the entire passion and resurrection fit into God's plan contained in the Scriptures. A connection with the first episode (the women and Peter at the tomb) is established by the information that the second occurs on the same day and that the dramatis personae are "two of them," i.e., of those who had heard the women's story and refused to believe.[10] (Perhaps disbelief is illustrated by their decision to leave Jerusalem despite the report that the Lord had risen there.) The naming of Emmaus as their destination and the specification of the distance as seven miles (60 stadia) lend realism to the story—even if those details have caused interpreters trouble ever since in identifying a plausible place that would jibe with the distance.[11]

Picturesque too is Luke's having the two men discussing "all these things that had occurred [in relation to Jesus]" at the very instant that "Jesus himself" appears to them (24:14-15). It is a dramatic moment when the main figure of all these episodes, who thus far has been the subject of revelation and discussion, at last comes on the scene, and even more dramatic because he is not recognized. That the risen Jesus is different is noted in several Gospels (pp. 205, 247, 258), but Luke's way of explaining it relates the problem to the disciples whose "eyes were held back from recognizing him" (24:16). By the casual atmosphere he gives to the encounter, Luke implies how the two must have

---

[9] Scholars classify it as a tale, or legend, or circumstantial narrative. Leaving aside the pejorative tone in some of those classifications, we must recognize dramatization in the Lucan narrative. The only parallel in the story line is in the Marcan Appendix (16:12-13): "After these things [the appearance to Magdalene; her report to those who had been with him], he appeared in another form to two of them walking, going into the country. Having gone back, they announced it to the rest; but they did not believe them." Some would argue that this is close to the pre-Gospel tradition that Luke dramatized.

[10] Only in 24:18, with the naming of one of them as Cleopas, does it become clear that these are not members of the Eleven.

[11] Some manuscripts and Church Fathers read "160 stadia" (= 18.4 miles), a distance comparable to the 20 miles from Jerusalem to Amwas (Ammaous Nicopolis) near Latrun. There is rabbinic evidence suggesting the presence of Christians at Emmaus.

Christ in the Gospels of the Liturgical Year

looked on Jesus: happening by, perhaps a Passover pilgrim (24:18) leaving Jerusalem to return home, and wanting to share their company on the road, he shows interest in their conversation. When they start to answer him, they stop walking and confront him with dismay, as Cleopas[12] demands rhetorically how this man, who has been in Jerusalem, can be so singularly ignorant of what has been happening there. The simple artistic staging of the episode continues in 24:19 as the stranger asks "What things?" opening the way for a dramatic recounting of the passion of Jesus of Nazareth,[13] "a prophetic man mighty in deed and word before God and all the people" (24:19-20). In his first public appearance at Nazareth, Jesus spoke of himself as a prophet (4:24); later as Jesus set himself to go to Jerusalem the reason he offered was that no prophet should perish at a distance from Jerusalem (13:33); here his followers clearly acknowledge him to have had that role. Yet (unusual for Luke) there is also a note of disillusionment: "We were hoping that he was the one who was going to redeem Israel"—a disappointment all the more startling when we remember that Zechariah, father of the Baptist, had praised God: "He has visited and accomplished redemption for His people" (1:68); and Anna, having seen the child Jesus, spoke of him to all who were awaiting the redemption of Israel (2:38). Cleopas, who gives voice to this disappointment about Jesus, is one of those who were with the Eleven when Magdalene and the other women reported the resurrection of Jesus (24:9), and previously the Eleven had been congratulated by Jesus for having continued with him in his trials (22:28). The cross has turned fidelity into discouragement! Yet the women's message was not totally without effect, for Cleopas mentions it as a counterindication to the loss of hope. The women were reminded by the two angels

[12] Perhaps Luke considered it dramatic to postpone the naming of characters in these episodes until the narrative is advanced (only in 24:10 were the women named). The many attempts to name the other disciple (e.g., Peter) are in vain and counterproductive to the Lucan emphasis in the story.

[13] The concise summary of the passion (with parallels in the sermons in Acts, e.g., 2:22-23) has the statement: "Our chief priests and rulers gave him over to a sentence of death, and they crucified him." It refutes the claim that, because Luke's account of the Jewish trial of Jesus has no formal sentence of condemnation (22:71), Luke did not blame the Jewish authorities for the death of Jesus (see also Acts 2:36; 3:13; 4:10). Typically Lucan is the contrast between the authorities (negative) and "all the people" (positive).

The Resurrection in Luke

that Jesus had said the Son of Man would rise on the third day (24:7), and this is the third day (24:21). Cleopas then recounts the substance of the first episode involving the visit of the women and of "some of those who were with us" to the empty tomb (24:22-24)[14]—all this with a glimmer of hope but no real faith.

Still unrecognized, the stranger begins to answer the implicit objections to believing that Jesus was the redeemer of Israel (24:25)—not objections raised by the enemies of Jesus among the Jewish authorities but objections raised by those who have been following him. Those who are "foolish and slow of heart to believe all the prophets had foretold" are disciples! The "all" is in one way typical Lucan generalization (see Acts 24:14), but in another way it was only by combining various passages from the prophets[15] that Christians could reconcile with God's plan their picture of a suffering Messiah who was also exalted (24:26: "the Messiah had to suffer these things and [so] to enter his glory"). Already at the beginning of the Gospel (Luke 3:22) the combination of a messianic exaltation psalm (Ps 2:7) and a Suffering Servant passage (Isa 42:1) implicitly set the pattern for this, as God spoke about Jesus at the baptism. The theme of a Messiah having to suffer first will continue in Luke 24:46 and in the Christian preaching of Acts 3:18; 17:3; 26:23. Evidently the idea that one crucified as a wrongdoer could be a glorious king was very difficult for the early Christians to accept—in pre-Christian Judaism there was no clear expectation of a suffering Messiah—and so it was a focal point in hermeneutical reflections on the Jewish Scriptures.[16] While we can be

[14] In the present sequence 24:22-24 is a summary of what has already been narrated, but some scholars see it as the kind of nucleus that Luke developed into the longer narrative. Although Mark 16:1-8 does not mention the appearance of Jesus (to the women) at the tomb, only Luke explicitly excludes appearances at the tomb.

[15] Luke/Acts uses a Jewish designation for the biblical books (the Law and the Prophets; see 24:27) wherein what we call the historical books (from Joshua through Kings) are the Former Prophets, and the writing prophets are the Latter Prophets. Thus the dynastic oracle in 2 Samuel 7:11-16, promising an eternal throne to the kings of the House of David (the basis of the expectation of "the Messiah" understood as the unique or final anointed Davidic king) and the Isaian description of the Suffering Servant (Israel, but understood by Christians to be Jesus) would be part of what "all the prophets" had foretold.

[16] Early Christians shared contemporary Jewish hermeneutics whereby the prophets were thought to have spoken of the distant future, specifically of what

Christ in the Gospels of the Liturgical Year

certain that in the explanations offered by the risen Jesus from 24:25 on we are hearing phrases from early Christian preaching about Jesus, Luke would suggest strongly that Jesus himself initiated this use of Scripture, beginning with Moses and all the prophets to articulate his understanding of himself (24:27). As can be seen from the description of the Teacher of Righteousness in the Dead Sea Scrolls, such a proceeding would be normal for a Jewish religious figure of the time.

Luke's admirable storytelling technique is apparent in 24:28-29 as the disciples struggle to get this intriguing stranger to stay with them at the village of Emmaus, to dine and spend the night. His opening up of the Scriptures during the journey may have made their hearts burn within them (as they acknowledge later in 24:32), but they still have not recognized him. Yet their appeal for him "to stay" shows that they have not lost the instinct of discipleship, and now at table with them Jesus makes the gesture of breaking bread that finally opens their eyes. As soon as they recognize that it is Jesus, he disappears from their sight (24:31). From analogies in their own mythology, pagan readers of this story would surely grasp that a divine figure had disguised himself and visited with mortals. Luke's Christian readers, however, are to learn more from the episode, as the commentary supplied by the two disciples (speaking to each other in 24:32 or to the Eleven in 24:35) makes clear.

First, even though exposition of the Scriptures by Jesus did not bring about recognition, reflection on the scriptural exposition set their hearts on fire and prepared them for recognition. Second, they recognized him in the breaking of the bread. While one may contend that Jesus had a characteristic way of doing this so that the disciples were recognizing a familiar style, more is involved. Whether used nominally or verbally, breaking bread is a Lucan expression (Acts 2:42, 46; 20:7, 11; 27:35) generally thought to refer to a eucharistic meal. That connotation here is strengthened by the similarity in describing what Jesus did at the last meal (Last Supper) that he ate with his disciples and what he does here. Comparing the two, we see the plausibility that

---

was now happening. For Christians it was not so much that the Scriptures were thought to throw light on Jesus; rather Jesus was thought to bring out the meaning of the Scriptures. While undoubtedly some of the arguments based on Scripture were honed in debates with nonbelieving Jews, the primary goal in appealing to the Scriptures was to supply understanding to believers.

The Resurrection in Luke

Luke wanted his readers to understand that it was in a eucharistic action that Jesus was recognized:

22:19: "Having taken bread, having given thanks [*eucharistein*], he broke and gave it to them, saying, 'This is my body which is given for you.'"

24:30: "Having taken bread, he blessed (it or God); and having broken, he gave it about to them."

(The issue is not whether Jesus actually celebrated a eucharist with the two disciples at Emmaus but how Luke is using the story to instruct his readers.)

Taken in this way, the episode in 24:13-35 would have supplied important instruction. These readers might have reflected to themselves nostalgically that a half-century before in a nearby land there were people fortunate enough to have seen the risen Jesus with their own eyes: "Would that we had been there!" Luke is reporting that those who were in that enviable situation and saw him could not truly know Jesus until the Scriptures were expounded and they recognized him in the eucharistic meal. The Christians of Luke's time had the Scriptures and the breaking of the bread—those same means of knowing the Lord. So have Christians ever since, for the Scriptures and the eucharist are the essential components of our Sunday service. In the matter of encountering the risen Jesus *with faith*, a past generation is not more privileged than the present one.

* * *

As a transition from this episode to the next, Luke 24:33 recounts that "at that same hour" when Jesus disappeared, the two disciples returned to Jerusalem where they found gathered together "the Eleven and those with them." We remember that when the women came back from the tomb after encountering the angelic men, they made their report to "the Eleven and all the rest" (24:9). At the end of these first two episodes Luke illustrates the duty of sharing "the good news" of the risen Lord with others, while at the same time showing the centrality of the apostles in Jerusalem who are now about to see the risen Lord themselves.[17]

---

[17] Luke uses time indications to bind together the episodes in this chapter but ignores the formidable chronological difficulties in this overly long first day of the

The truly curious factor is that before the two disciples can make their report, the Eleven have their own news: "In reality the Lord has been raised and has appeared to Simon" (24:34).[18] The "in reality" means that the Eleven presume that the two returning disciples know no more than when they left, namely, that both the women and Peter had found an empty tomb and that the women claimed to have seen angels who announced that Jesus was risen. All doubts that the Eleven had about those earlier reports have been resolved while the two disciples were away, for the Lord has been seen by Simon (Peter). Surely Luke is combining different traditions here, and the sentence that affirms the appearance to Simon may be a form of the very old preaching formula found in 1 Corinthians 15:5 which lists the appearance to Cephas (Peter) first. But in the present sequence the sentence has the effect of showing that the apostolic faith in the risen Lord is not based on a story about an empty tomb or even on the message of angels; it is based on an actual encounter with Jesus. The two disciples may have known the risen Lord because they recognized him in the breaking of the bread, but Simon (and through him the Eleven) knows the Lord because he has seen him.

EPISODE IN LUKE 24:36-53:
THE ELEVEN[19] GATHERED IN JERUSALEM

This episode is a literary unit in the sense that it narrates one appearance of the risen Jesus to one group in the Jerusalem area. Yet there are minor shifts of locale that suggest a subdivision: 24:36-49 takes place where the Eleven and the others are gathered together; 26:50-53 takes place as they go out to Bethany and return to the Jerusalem Temple.

(a) 24:36-49: *The appearance of Jesus at the place where the Eleven had gathered and eaten.* In 24:33 we were told that two disciples returned

---

week—formidable even if for convenience Luke has ceased employing a Jewish reckoning wherein the day ends at sunset. It was already toward evening, with the day far gone (24:29), when the two disciples reclined with Jesus at table. The meal plus the long journey back on foot would make their finding the Eleven very late.

[18] This is so curious that Codex Bezae attributes the statement to the two disciples, leading to the conclusion that Simon (Peter) was the unnamed disciple alongside Cleopas on the road to Emmaus (note 12 above).

[19] Technically the group includes "the Eleven and those with them" (24:34). However, since "those with them" are never identified here (cf. Acts 1:14) and they play no distinct role, I shall refer simply to the Eleven throughout the episode.

from Emmaus to find their colleagues gathered, but were not told where. The presence of food (24:41-42) suggests that this is a place where the Eleven had eaten. Presumably the tradition about the site of Jesus' appearance in Jerusalem was vague,[20] and Luke may have avoided imaginative specification to make it possible for his readers to relate the scene to their own house-church meetings. The greeting "Peace to you" uttered by the risen Jesus would be appropriate to that setting since it became an inter-Christian greeting.[21]

At the beginning of the episode there is a strong Lucan effort to make clear that Jesus is not a spirit or a ghost but has a real body (he can eat), indeed the same body that was crucified (his hands and feet are marked in a visible way). It may well be that Luke wrote this scene with apologetic intent. He may have sought to refute nonbelievers who rejected the resurrection (24:39: "It really is I!") and/or to correct incipient Christian gnostics or docetists who denied that there was a bodily element to Jesus' victory over death (24:39 "No spirit/ghost has flesh and bones as you see me having"). Interestingly, in the Lucan sequence the Eleven who believe that Jesus has been raised (24:34) have doubts in their hearts (24:38) and even disbelieve (24:41)[22] when Jesus insists on his bodily reality. Others detect a more didactic goal in the passage: Christians expecting their own bodily resurrection may have sought more knowledge about it through reflection on the risen body of Jesus.

---

[20] John 20:19, 26 has a comparable resurrection appearance take place in a site where the doors were shut. Mark 16:14 has Jesus appearing to the Eleven while they were reclining at table. Acts 2:1 sets the Pentecost scene where the Twelve (Eleven plus Matthias) were "all together in the same place." The idea that the resurrection appearances and descent of the Spirit took place in the large upper room where Jesus ate the Passover meal with his disciples (Luke 22:12-14) is a guess of later harmonization.

[21] See John 20:19, 26 and the frequent use of "Peace" in Paul's greetings to churches. This expression and other verses in this episode are omitted in Codex Bezae and some witnesses of the Western textual tradition; but today there is an increasing tendency to regard the disputed passages as authentically Lucan.

[22] Typically Lucan is the softening of the disbelief as "because of joy"; cf. the disciples' "sleeping from sorrow" in 22:45. Here Luke uses *dialogismoi* ("doubts, negative thoughts") to describe what is in the hearts of the Eleven. In the infancy narrative (2:35) Simon recognized that in the future Jesus would play a judicial role: "The negative thoughts of many hearts will be revealed."

Christ in the Gospels of the Liturgical Year

In any case Luke offers the most materially realistic view of the body of the risen Jesus found in the NT. Some modern scholars judge his presentation excessively naive; but that may be because they themselves do not accept the reality of the bodily resurrection, a reality on which I think all the pertinent NT writers would agree. Within the agreement, however, there may well have been a difference on the material properties that the NT writers would attribute to the risen body of Jesus. Paul's notion of a *spiritual* body to be possessed by the risen Christian (presumably based on his experience of the risen Jesus) is related to his thesis that "flesh and blood cannot inherit the kingdom of God" (1 Cor 15:50). This seems quite different from Luke's insistence on Jesus' flesh and bones. Nevertheless, one should acknowledge that Luke's primary interest is in the identity of the risen Jesus ("It really is I"), so that having the Eleven recognize the bodily aspect of Jesus in the eating of the fish (24:42-43) is not too different from having the two disciples at Emmaus recognize Jesus in the breaking of the bread. An important part of the risen Jesus' identity is his continuity with his corporeal existence during the ministry. That Luke is not naive is illustrated by Acts 10:40-41: "God raised him on the third day and granted that he should be manifest not to all the people but to us witnesses, chosen beforehand by God, who ate and drank with him after his resurrection from the dead." Despite the earthly properties of eating and drinking attributed to the risen Jesus, Luke recognized that there were different properties since he could not be seen by all.

Having assured the Eleven of his identity, Jesus proceeds (24:44-46) to use exactly the same pedagogy with them that he used in the previous episode with the two disciples. He explains the things written about him in the Scriptures and how they show that the Messiah had to suffer and be raised from the dead.[23] In Luke's view the interpretation of the Scriptures is an essential element in understanding the passion and resurrection. In that Luke is not far from the tradition

---

[23] What is different here is Jesus' contention that during his time with them (the public ministry) he already told them, "All the things written about me in the Law of Moses and the Prophets and the Psalms must be fulfilled." There is no such verbatim statement of Jesus recorded in Luke's Gospel; yet the claim that both the word of Jesus and the Scriptures support what occurred in the passion is very powerful.

reported by Paul in 1 Corinthians 15:3-5 which describes as "according to the Scriptures" the death, burial, and resurrection.

The scene now turns to a commissioning, a common feature in the resurrection narratives (pp. 205–7, 218–19, 250), even if it is phrased in different terms by the various evangelists. What is unique is that Luke brings the commissioning under the same scriptural imperative as the passion and resurrection. Not only is it written that the Messiah should suffer and rise; it is written "that in his name repentance for the forgiveness of sins be proclaimed to all nations, beginning from Jerusalem. You are witnesses of this" (24:47-48).[24] Since the proclamation beginning from Jerusalem will be described in Acts, in the Lucan outlook the Scriptures contain already the whole of God's plan narrated in the two-volume work (Gospel, Acts), describing the work of Jesus and that of the Spirit. The emphasis that this repentance (*metanoia*) or total change of mind for forgiveness of sins will be proclaimed (verbal form related to *kerygma*) *in Jesus' name* suggests that both preaching and baptizing are envisaged as part of the commission. For instance in Acts 2:38 *metanoia* and being baptized in the name of Jesus are joined as the basic demands imposed on those who accept the preaching of Peter about Jesus.[25] Meeting these demands will lead to the gift of the Holy Spirit. Similarly in the passage we are discussing the risen Jesus follows his prediction about *metanoia* for the forgiveness of sins with a demand that the Eleven take note: "I am sending [*apostellein*] the promise of my Father on you" (24:49). They are to stay in Jerusalem until they are clothed with power from on high. All these themes will be picked up at the beginning of Acts, making clear that Jesus is speaking of the gift of the Holy Spirit. Acts 1:4-5 speaks of *the promise of the Father* in relation to baptism with the Holy Spirit; Acts 1:8 has Jesus telling the Eleven that when the Holy Spirit comes upon them, they shall be his *witnesses*

---

[24] Luke does not indicate what biblical passages he has in mind as backing for this mission to the Gentiles. Perhaps he thinks of various prophetic passages about the Gentiles coming to know God; but those passages envision the nations coming to Jerusalem, not an Israelite mission to them. Acts 2:16-21 has Peter citing Joel 2:28-32 (3:1-5) about the outpouring of the Spirit on all flesh.

[25] See also the joining of preaching the good news (*euangelizesthai*) with baptism in the name of Jesus in Acts 8:12. There are many references in Acts to preaching, to healing, or to baptism being done in the name of Jesus.

from Jerusalem to the ends of the earth; Acts 2:33 refers to their "having received from the Father *the promise* of the Holy Spirit." Some of the other Gospel commissions have the disciples themselves sent; indeed that is how they became apostles (i.e., those sent). Yet in Luke the Holy Spirit is the one sent, for that Spirit empowers the apostolic mission (Acts 15:28: "It has seemed good to the Holy Spirit and to us"). In the Lucan infancy narrative the Holy Spirit coming upon Mary as the power of the Most High brought about the conception of God's Son (1:35). At the beginning of the public ministry Jesus returned in the power of the Spirit into Galilee (4:14). At the beginning of Acts the apostles will be clothed with power when the Holy Spirit comes on them (1:8).

When one looks back at what the two disciples learned from the risen Jesus on the road to Emmaus and on what the Eleven learned in Jerusalem, beyond the assurance that Jesus had conquered death and was raised bodily, there is a remarkable message that would speak meaningfully to the communities addressed by Luke in the late first century. The demand for the *metanoia* of which Jesus speaks was placed on these Christians when the good news about Jesus was proclaimed to them; and they were baptized in the name of Jesus, which was the occasion of their receiving the Holy Spirit. The Scriptures were explained to them, with the meaning of the Law and the Prophets (and the Psalms) being enlightened through what God had done in Jesus and in the church by the Spirit. These Christians gathered together, greeting one another with "Peace to you"; and through the eyes of faith they saw that Jesus was present in the breaking of the bread. In short, Luke's Christian readers could have found much of their Christian life laid out for them by the risen Jesus.

(b) 24:50-53: *Leading the Eleven to Bethany, Jesus ascends to heaven; the Eleven return to the Jerusalem Temple.* The movement to Bethany (the purpose of which is not clarified by Luke) may have belonged to the pre-Gospel tradition. (Acts, by speaking of the Mount of Olives, will clothe the site of the ascension with OT echoes.) In the Gospel opening, after the priest Zechariah received an annunciation of the birth of John the Baptist from the angel Gabriel, he was unable to speak to the people and bless them as they expected (Luke 1:10, 21-22). At the end of the Gospel Jesus blesses the Eleven in a priestly manner. We see that when we compare Luke's description of Jesus in 24:50, "Having lifted up his hands, he blessed them," with the description of the saintly high priest

Simon II in Sirach 50:20: "He lifted up his hands over all the congregation of Israel to pronounce the blessing of the Lord with his lips."

This blessing marks the departure of Jesus as he is taken up to heaven. On the mount of the transfiguration (9:30) Moses and Elijah (two figures who in Jewish tradition were taken up bodily into heaven) appeared in glory and spoke to Jesus of his exodus. Now, like those predecessors, Jesus makes his exodus. As Jesus is taken up, he completes the journey to Jerusalem that he began shortly after the transfiguration "when the days approached for his being taken up" (9:51).[26] Sirach 50:21 describes the reaction of the people to the priestly blessing of Simon II: "They bowed down in worship." Similarly Luke 24:52 describes the reaction of the Eleven to Jesus' blessing and ascension: "They worshiped him."

Then with great joy they return to Jerusalem where they are constantly in the Temple. This matches the promise of joy given to Zechariah in that Temple at the beginning of the Gospel (1:14). The last Greek words in the Gospel tell us what the Eleven do in the Temple: They bless God. No Gospel ends its account of the good news on a more beautiful note or on one that is more challenging for the Christians of all times as they come together in their own communities.

EPISODE IN ACTS 1:1-12:
JESUS' PARTING INSTRUCTIONS TO HIS APOSTLES;
ASCENT TO HEAVEN

At the beginning of Acts, Luke takes pains to relate his second volume to his first,[27] which, he says, ended on the day Jesus was taken up after he had instructed his apostles through the Holy Spirit. In Acts 1:9 Luke will tell us again that Jesus was taken up to heaven; and such duplication has puzzled scholars even to the point of their postulating that another hand added one of the two accounts. Rather, Luke is

---

[26] Many commentators think it unusual that Luke includes an ascension scene in his resurrection account (but see Mark 16:19 which includes sitting at God's right). Yet an element in this ascension is the termination of Jesus' earthly appearances, a concept known to Paul who lists Jesus' appearance to him as the last of all (1 Cor 15:8). Luke is giving OT coloring to the idea of a final appearance that existed before the Gospels were written.

[27] Since I am concerned only with the resurrection features of this narrative, I leave aside the issue of the identity of Theophilus.

using the resurrection appearances and the ascension as what I have called a hinge. From the stance of the Gospel the resurrection-ascension terminates visibly all that Jesus began to do and teach (Acts 1:1); from the stance of Acts it will prepare the apostles to be witnesses for Jesus to the ends of the earth (1:8). His using the ascension twice shows once more that despite the concreteness of his descriptions Luke has no naive understanding of what he is describing. The going of Jesus to God after death is timeless from the viewpoint of God; but there is a sequence from the viewpoint of those whose lives it touched.

In the opening description in Acts (1:1-2) two minor features are noteworthy, for they strengthen the connection between Luke's two volumes. First, there is a reference to the first volume (the Gospel) as describing what Jesus *began* to do and teach. If the verb is meant literally, Luke sees Jesus as continuing spiritually his activity in Acts, even though he has ascended into heaven. Second, Jesus is said to have instructed his chosen apostles through the Holy Spirit before he was taken up (in the first volume). Thus while Luke will describe the coming of the Holy Spirit in Acts 2, he recognizes that the Spirit was already active in Jesus' interpretation of Scripture and commissioning of the apostles as described in Luke 24.

On the other hand, Acts 1:3 tells us something we would never have expected from the Gospel, namely, that for forty days after his passion and death Jesus made appearances to his apostles. The reference to Jesus giving "many proofs" showing that he was alive and speaking to the apostles of the kingdom of God suggests that Luke is thinking of the type of appearance narrated in the episode we have just considered (24:36-49), where Jesus showed his hands and feet and ate fish to prove that it was he and not a ghost, and where he instructed the Eleven about the Scriptures and the future preaching of *metanoia*. In making the apostles the recipients of more than one appearance Luke may be reflecting an early tradition similar to that in 1 Corinthians 15:5-8 where among the six persons or groups to whom Jesus appeared are listed Cephas (Peter), the Twelve, and Paul.[28] As I pointed out in footnote 26, such traditions set a time limit after which Jesus did

---

[28] Despite the claim of some scholars that Luke considered only the Twelve apostles, he calls Paul an apostle in Acts 14:14. It is not clear whether Luke would extend the term to others mentioned in the 1 Corinthians list, e.g., James the brother of the Lord and "all the apostles [beyond the Twelve]."

The Resurrection in Luke

not appear, although the limit Paul cites is considerably longer than either of the two Lucan limits ("the same day" in Luke 24; forty days in Acts). The role of the forty days becomes clear when we reflect on Luke's predilection for architectonic arrangement, noted at the beginning of this chapter. In Luke 4:1-2 Jesus was led by the Spirit to spend forty days in the desert, after which he returned in the power of the Spirit to begin his ministry in Galilee (4:14). By way of balance it is appropriate that Acts too begins with a forty-day preparatory period. In both instances Luke is evoking the forty years in the desert during which God prepared Israel for entrance into the Promised Land. This imagery fits well with the way in which the beginning of Acts symbolically associates the beginnings of the Christian community with the beginnings of Israel, e.g., the completion of the number twelve (Acts 1:15-26) so that the Christian parallel to the twelve Israelite patriarchs may be made perfect; also the Sinai symbolism in the description of the Pentecost event (wind, fire, Pentecost as the feast of the giving of the Law to Israel). The God who called Israel so long before to be His covenanted people is following the same patterns in His renewal of the covenant through Jesus Christ.

Moving on from his general introduction in Acts 1:1-3, Luke proceeds to describe appearances in which Jesus addresses himself directly to his apostles. In the first (1:4-5)[29] Jesus calls attention to the fact that the message he gives them (not to distance themselves from Jerusalem but to wait for the promise of the Father) is one that they already heard from him (see Luke 24:49). Yet here he makes the clarifying addition that the promise of the Father is to be fulfilled when they are baptized in the Holy Spirit not many days from now. Thus the risen Jesus reminds his apostles not only of what *he* said when he appeared to them at Easter but of what John the Baptist said at the beginning of the ministry when he contrasted his own baptizing with water and the coming baptism in the Holy Spirit and fire (Luke 3:16).[30] From the

---

[29] The context supplied by 1:4 depends on the translation given to *synalizomenos*, whether it means "being assembled with," or "dwelling with," or "eating with." If the last, we have another instance of the meal setting that is common in resurrection appearances. If the first, we have another vaguely described meeting of the Eleven/Twelve, similar to the one that will follow in 1:6 (also Luke 24:33).

[30] Acts 1:5 does not repeat the "in fire" phrase of the Baptist, but the Pentecost baptism of the apostles in the Holy Spirit will be accompanied by "tongues as of fire" (Acts 2:3).

beginning to the end of his first volume, Luke prepared for the coming of the Spirit that would mark the second volume.

In another appearance (Acts 1:6-8) Jesus goes beyond reminders to supply an important revelation. Both during the public ministry and after the resurrection Jesus spoke of the kingdom of God (Luke 4:43; Acts 1:3); and now his disciples, gathered together, ask about that kingdom which they understand as a kingdom to be restored to Israel. Their understanding is not illogical: the raising of Jesus showed that God had definitively intervened in history and that Jesus is the Messiah (Luke 24:26), i.e., the anointed king of the House of David who was expected to reestablish the Davidic kingdom. Thus in their question the apostles are vocalizing an understanding that would have been shared by many who heard (of) Jesus of Nazareth. Scholars debate endlessly about Jesus' own view of the kingdom of God. The differing views in the NT are explained more easily if Jesus was never lucidly specific about the extent to which the kingdom would be visible and/or invisible, about whether it would come soon (in this generation) or in the less definite future, about whether it would exist in this world and/or in the next.[31] Be that as it may, here Luke presents that side of Jesus' teaching that makes sense of the two-volume Lucan work and of the worldwide missionary thrust so prominent in the second volume. If the risen Jesus were going to bring about the kingdom immediately as part of the end of the world, there would be no point to writing books for future readers,[32] or to embarking on a mission that would not have time to reach the ends of the earth. The firm answer that Luke reports from the risen Jesus, "It is not for you to know the times or the seasons that the Father has set by His own authority," defuses chronological speculation about God's final intervention, and has been reiterated by the church at large ever since as a response to sectarians in each generation who spend time and religious energy calculating the time of the second coming. It is much more important that Jesus' followers,

[31] Although divine, Jesus was truly human; and so many wonder whether he had exact knowledge of such things. They point to a saying of Jesus which has parallels to his statement here but which Mark 13:32 places in the public ministry: "Of that day or that hour no one knows, not even the angels in heaven, nor the Son, but only the Father."

[32] It is not accidental that the first Christian writing (before 70) consists of letters addressed to the immediate present, and that only about 70 and the fall of Jerusalem do we get a more permanent literature that may envision future readers.

The Resurrection in Luke

empowered by the Holy Spirit, spend their time and energy bearing witness to him.

Luke uses Jesus' emphasis on witness to present (Acts 1:8) the outline of this second volume that he is writing. Acts 2–7 will concern the witness borne in Jerusalem culminating in Stephen's witness by his blood. Acts 8–12 will concern events of a decisive nature occurring chiefly in Samaria and Judea, culminating with both Peter and Paul leaving Jerusalem for more distant places.[33] Acts 13–28 will concern the great mission to the Gentiles starting out from Antioch and ending in Rome, and thus to the ends of the earth.[34]

Having thus prepared his apostles in detail for the future, Jesus is taken up to heaven (Acts 1:9). Here Luke is even more graphic than in 24:51, for this time a cloud intervenes to take him from their sight. (This is similar to the cloud of divine presence mentioned by Luke 9:34-35 at the transfiguration.) Two men in white suddenly are standing there to interpret the event for Jesus' followers, even as two (angelic) men in dazzling apparel were standing by the empty tomb to interpret that for the women (24:4-7). Their interpretation of the ascension gains eschatological coloring from information that Luke supplies as the episode ends in Acts 1:12, namely, that this ascension takes place on the Mount called Olivet.[35] The most prominent scriptural reference to the Mount of Olives comes at the end of the prophetic collection, in Zechariah 14:4-21 where we are told that God will come there with his holy ones to exercise the great judgment and to manifest his kingship

[33] Others would apply the "Judea and Samaria" section of Jesus' words to Acts 8–10, regarding chapter 10 as the terminus since there a Gentile is converted. Yet the action in chapters 11–12 is largely in Judea. That Luke has fashioned Jesus' words from his own plan for the book becomes apparent when we realize that, although the apostles are supposed to have received this directive at the beginning, the spread of Christianity to the Samaritans and the Gentiles utterly astounds some when it takes place, and there are debates about whether this is justified. Moreover, although the apostles are told to be the witnesses who follow this itinerary, the Twelve (except Peter and John) largely remain in Jerusalem, and others are responsible for the spreading witness.

[34] The *Psalms of Solomon* 8:15 associates Rome with "the ends of earth."

[35] Presumably, then, the gathering of the disciples in Acts 1:6, to whom Jesus speaks, also takes place on the Mount, for we are not told that they went out to this site—contrast Luke 24:50: "Jesus led them out as far as Bethany." Clearly there was a tradition about Jesus' departure for heaven from this area east of Jerusalem, but Acts plays on its theological possibilities.

Christ in the Gospels of the Liturgical Year

over all the earth. No wonder then that at this place the two men can give the assurance that Jesus, taken up this way, "will come (back) in the same way as you saw him going" (Acts 1:11). The cloud that takes Jesus from their sight is related to that coming, for Luke 21:27 promised that "they will see the Son of Man coming in a cloud with power and great glory."

It is interesting how the revelation given by the Lucan angels pertains to our times. Many liberal Christians, confusing the simple biblical description with the deeper underlying reality, reject the second coming as simplistic; often this leads them to think that by good endeavor and social justice they will build the kingdom in this world. Luke's narratives of the appearances of the risen Jesus insist that it really is God's kingdom; only He can establish it and He will do that through His Son. By ignoring God's authority human endeavor, no matter how religiously benevolent, will build another Tower of Babel rather than the kingdom. On the other hand, those who believe in God's activity and spend their time looking up to heaven for the second coming, as if they could calculate it, are really also rejecting God's authority in which only He knows the times and the seasons. The ironic question of the two heavenly speakers, "Men of Galilee, why do you stand peering into heaven?" (Acts 1:11), constitutes advice that there is little danger of missing the second coming (no matter what it consists in). Therefore it makes little sense to seek to gain mastery of the times and seasons as if God could be controlled. Matthew ends his account of the resurrection with the assurance that Jesus is with us all days till the end of time; Luke, who twice describes Jesus' departure, ends the resurrection story with the assurance that he will come back just as surely as he left. Meanwhile, there is the promise of the Father, the Holy Spirit.

The Resurrection in Luke

Chapter 25

The Resurrection in John 20
—A Series of Diverse Reactions

John is a Gospel of encounters: Nicodemus, the Samaritan woman at the well, the cripple at Bethesda, the man born blind, Mary and Martha, and even Pilate. One after the other they have made their entrance onto the Johannine stage to encounter Jesus, the light come into the world; and in so doing they have judged themselves by whether or not they continue to come to the light or turn away and prefer darkness (John 3:19-21). It is not surprising, then, that the principal Johannine account of the appearances of the risen Jesus becomes a series of encounters illustrating different faith reactions.

The following arrangement of four episodes can be observed:

(1) 20:1-10: Reactions of Simon Peter and the Beloved Disciple
(2) 20:11-18: Reaction of Mary Magdalene
(3) 20:19-23: Reaction of Disciples
(4) 20:24-29: Reaction of Thomas

The first pair of episodes takes place in relation to the tomb, early on Easter Sunday morning; the second pair of episodes takes place where the disciples are gathered, first on Easter Sunday evening and then a week later. Although the respective characters in the episodes are interrelated, the reaction of one does not influence the reaction of the other. The total scenario reminds us that in the range of belief there are different degrees of readiness and different factors that cause people to come to faith.

EPISODE IN 20:1-10: REACTIONS OF SIMON PETER
AND THE BELOVED DISCIPLE

In all four Gospels women come to the empty tomb on the first day of the week, but only in John does Mary Magdalene visit the tomb twice. The second visit (John 20:11ff.) is the one that has major parallels to

Christ in the Gospels of the Liturgical Year

the other Gospel accounts; the first visit functions mostly to set the stage for the story of Simon Peter and the Beloved Disciple. Even in such a stage setting, however, there are Johannine touches. As in Mark and Luke, Mary Magdalene[1] comes "early," but only in John do we have the added indication that "it was still dark." In this Gospel where light and darkness play such a role, darkness lasts until someone believes in the risen Jesus. We are not told why Magdalene comes to the tomb;[2] but her alarmed reaction of racing off to tell the two disciples, "They took the Lord from the tomb, and we do not know where they put him!" (the first of the three times she stresses this), suggests a personal attachment to Jesus—an attachment the Good Shepherd will draw on later in the scene. Her immediate conclusion that Jesus' body has been stolen, a conclusion reached seemingly without entering the tomb, is peculiar to John. Matthew 28:13-15 attributes to "the Jews" the calumny that Jesus' disciples stole the body; but Mary Magdalene jumps to the conclusion that Jesus' "enemies" have done this, for she reports to *disciples* that others have stolen the body. Later (20:19) we shall hear of doors being closed "for fear of the Jews." This has been a Gospel shaped by antagonism between the followers of Jesus and the synagogue, and that hostile context carries over to the resurrection account.

The two disciples who respond to Magdalene's report about the tomb are Simon Peter and the Beloved Disciple. The latter figure, never mentioned as such during the first part of the Gospel which describes Jesus' public ministry, has appeared with startling frequency in the second part when "the hour has come for Jesus to pass from this world to the Father" (13:1). He belongs to that context where "having loved his own who were in the world, Jesus loved them to the end." Before John 20 this disciple has appeared at the Last Supper next to Jesus, in the high priest's courtyard next to Simon Peter, and near the

---

[1] That Mary Magdalene was not alone is suggested by her "we" in 20:2. However, since she is the sole recipient of the appearance of Jesus in 20:11-18 (and in that John may be closer to original tradition than Matthew 28:9-10 where "the other Mary" also sees the risen Jesus), any others who went to the tomb with Magdalene tend to fade into the background in John's understanding of the tradition. John is fascinated by the dramatic possibilities of individuals, even if a group is present.

[2] In Mark and Luke she comes to anoint the body; in Matthew, to see the sepulcher guarded by soldiers.

The Resurrection in John 20

cross of Jesus next to Jesus' mother. These contexts have been recounted in detail by the Synoptic evangelists who, however, never seem to have seen the presence of this disciple; for them he is the invisible man. The present instance is no exception: Luke 24:12 tells us that Peter arose and ran to the tomb, looked in, saw the linen cloths, and went home wondering.[3] Luke gives no indication of the companion disciple who features so prominently in John. Yet Luke 24:24 may give us a key to this enigma: "Some of those who were with us went to the tomb and found it just as the women said." In other words Luke knows of several disciples going to the tomb, and yet is capable earlier of mentioning only Peter because the others were not important as witnesses. The one whom John calls the disciple whom Jesus loved may have been invisible to the Synoptic tradition because he had no great name or rank, whereas his presence was eminently memorable to others who had a different criterion of greatness. For them he had the highest rank of all because Jesus loved him. John 20:2 uses two titles: The first is "the other disciple"; the second is "the disciple whom Jesus loved." The first may have been the way he was evaluated (and therefore forgotten) by other Christians; the second was the way he was known to those who preserved his memory in the Johannine tradition.

John paints artistically the delicate relationship between this disciple and the famous Peter (with whom he has appeared in a situation involving contrast twice before [13:23-24; 18:15-16] and will appear twice more [21:7, 20-22]). That the disciple reached the tomb first but did not enter, allowing Peter to catch up and enter first, has been the subject of imaginative speculation as to who had the greater ecclesiastical dignity. In fact, the arrangement may be dramatic, not theological: his entering last makes the disciple's reaction the culmination of the episode. In any case, neither the arrival nor the entry is the featured point of John's contrast between the two figures. What matters to the evangelist is that they responded differently to what they saw in the tomb, namely, the burial garments and the separate headpiece without

---

[3] This verse in Luke is textually dubious. Some scholars theorize that it was added by a later scribe who copied it from John; others suggest that it was originally part of Luke but excised by a scribe, because, by not mentioning the Beloved Disciple, it seemingly contradicted John. See note 7, p. 225.

the body: The disciple believed, and nothing is said to indicate that Peter believed.[4] In the Pauline list of those to whom the risen Jesus appeared, the name of Cephas (Peter) comes before all others (1 Cor 15:5). But John knows of one who believed in the risen Lord even before an appearance, with a perspicacity that arose from love.

John 20:8 relates this belief to what the disciple saw, namely, the burial garments in an otherwise empty tomb. Because the evangelist takes such care to describe the burial wrappings lying there, with the piece of cloth that covered the head rolled up in a place by itself, many have thought that the configuration of these garments was significant to the disciple, e.g., that they preserved the form of Jesus' body. Others have contended that the presence of the garments caused the disciple to deduce that the body had not been stolen, for grave robbers would scarcely have taken the time to unwrap the corpse and carry it away naked. Such reasoning does not explain why neither Simon Peter nor Mary Magdalene were moved to faith from having seen the garments. A better suggestion involves inner Johannine symbolism. Lazarus came forth from the tomb "bound hand and foot with linen strips and his face wrapped in a cloth" (John 11:44); Jesus has left the same two-fold set of wrappings in the tomb. Lazarus was resuscitated to natural life but would die again and need his burial garments once more. By contrast, the garments left in Jesus' tomb revealed to the disciple that Jesus had been raised to eternal life. The added Johannine comment that "as yet they did not understand the Scripture that Jesus had to rise from the dead" explains Simon Peter's failure to understand, for, as Luke 24:25-27, 32 shows, explanation of the Scriptures helped Jesus' disciples to accept the resurrection. Once more, by contrast, the extraordinary sensitivity of the first one to believe after the resurrection is highlighted since this disciple needed no such help.

[4] I am not impressed by the argument that if John meant that Peter did not believe, he would have mentioned it. John does nothing to denigrate Simon Peter who in his estimation was one of Jesus' "own" whom he loved to the very end (13:1, 36), and who stayed with Jesus when others turned away because he recognized in Jesus the Holy One of God who had the words of eternal life (6:66-69). What John wishes to *emphasize* here is not the failure of Simon Peter to believe but the extraordinary sensitivity of the other disciple, stemming from the love of Jesus, that enables him to believe.

The Resurrection in John 20

In 20:10 we read: "With this the disciples went back home." The evangelist's dramatic preference for individual encounter with Jesus has led him carefully to remove Simon Peter and the Beloved Disciple from the tomb before the episode in which Mary Magdalene comes to faith there. The faith perception by the disciple and Simon Peter's lack of it have no influence on Magdalene whose reaction must be evaluated on its own. Next to Peter, James, John, and Judas, we note that Magdalene is the most frequently mentioned Gospel follower of Jesus (fourteen times in all) and as such is a worthy character for the Johannine stage. In describing Mary's second visit to the tomb, John rejoins the common Christian tradition that she encountered an angelic presence there. Peculiar to John is the artistic touch that carefully positions one angel at the head and the other at the foot of the place where Jesus had lain—a positioning comparable to the careful description in 20:6-7 that positioned separately the burial wrappings and the cloth that had covered Jesus' head. Readers are not meant to ask why these angels were not there when Simon Peter and the Beloved Disciple entered the tomb. John is illustrating different reactions as greater aids to faith are supplied. In the previous episode Magdalene's first impression at the tomb was negative (20:1-2: "They took the Lord from the tomb, and we do not know where they put him"), but it served as a transition to the positive main story of how the Beloved Disciple came to faith (20:3-10). Similarly here, despite the presence of the angels, Magdalene's second impression at the tomb is negative (20:11-13: "They took my Lord away, and I do not know where they put him"), but it serves as a transition to the positive main story where she will come to faith (20:14-18). That development is made possible not by angels but by Jesus himself.

The appearance to Magdalene may have been a very old tradition, despite the absence of women's names from a more official list of witnesses to the resurrection in 1 Corinthians 15:5ff.[5] John has expanded the traditional material into a dramatic encounter. Even though Jesus stands plainly in sight and speaks to Magdalene, she does not recognize him. Jesus' question "Whom [*tina*] are you looking for?" echoes the first words he spoke in this Gospel, for in 1:38, when Jesus turned

---

[5] I discussed this in relation to Matthew 28:9-10 on pp. 214–15 above.

Christ in the Gospels of the Liturgical Year

around and saw two disciples of John the Baptist following, he asked, "What [*ti*] are you looking for?" It is a question that probes discipleship,[6] voiced most recently and tragically (18:4) in the garden across the Kidron to the arresting party brought by Judas to seize Jesus. The disciples of John the Baptist stayed with Jesus and found the Messiah (1:41). The arresting party was hostilely looking for Jesus the Nazorean; they found him but were struck down in judgment (18:6). Magdalene is looking for the dead Jesus; she will find the living Lord.

Although the failure to recognize Jesus is a common feature in Gospel resurrection narratives, the way John dramatizes Magdalene's lack of recognition is unique. Her reiterated supposition that people have carried Jesus off and her consuming concern to know where they have put him now fasten in on one whom she supposes to be the gardener (20:15), that is, the caretaker of the garden in which John 19:41 (alone) has told us Jesus was buried. The depth of Mary's concern can be seen in the question posed to her both by the angels and by the unrecognized Jesus: "Why are you weeping?" a query that gives the impression that tears have blurred her vision to heavenly interventions. The failure to see is overcome only when Jesus calls her by name. In John 10:3, 5 the Good (or really, Model) Shepherd was said to call by name the sheep that belong to him, sheep who will not follow a stranger "because they do not recognize the voice of strangers." Mary's spontaneous reaction to being called by name, namely, her addressing Jesus as "Rabbuni," an endearing term for Teacher, verifies that claim of the Good Shepherd. In the instance of the Beloved Disciple, a faith that stemmed from seeing the now-useless burial clothes represented one form of perceptiveness based on love. A faith that stems from Mary's hearing her name called represents another form: She is one of those of whom Jesus said: "I know my sheep and mine know me" (10:14).

Admixed in Magdalene's recognition and the love it reflects is an all too human element or, as John would phrase it, an element of this

---

[6] The parallelism constituted by a similar question in the opening and closing Gospel scenes takes for granted that both men and women are disciples of Jesus in John—something not necessarily true elsewhere, for in Matthew "disciples" seem to be equated with the Twelve. Discipleship is the only category that is given importance in John, and it is open equally to all who believe and are begotten as children by God.

The Resurrection in John 20

world below. Matthew's account (28:9) of the appearance to the women at the tomb has them clutching Jesus' feet. Something like that may be supposed here, for Jesus tells Mary, "Do not cling to me." She would hold on to his presence, keeping him here below; but he must remind her of the import of both clauses in the evaluation of his followers that he gave at the Last Supper (John 17:14): "They do not belong to the world any more than I belong to the world." When Jesus says to Magdalene, "I am ascending to my Father," he is reiterating where his home is, namely, the world above to which he belongs. When he adds "and to your Father," he is revealing to her that because of her post-resurrectional faith the world to which she now belongs is also above—the heavenly house of Jesus' Father in which there are prepared many mansions (14:2). In indicating that "my Father" is now "your Father,"[7] Jesus is vocalizing in his own words the promise of the Prologue (1:12): "All those who did accept him he empowered to become God's children." That same new status is reflected in Jesus' reference to the disciples as "my brothers" in 20:17 as he sends Mary out to proclaim to them his ascension.[8] If at the beginning of the tomb story, Mary Magdalene (named in full only at the beginning and the end: 20:1 and 18) went to tell the disciples that "They took the Lord from the tomb," at the end of the tomb story she goes to tell them, "I have seen the Lord." She already knew that he was Lord from what he had done in his lifetime, but now she understands the profundity of that title from what he has revealed after his resurrection. He is now more than the "Rabbuni" whom she lovingly recognized when he first called her name. The Beloved Disciple was the first to believe; Magdalene is the first to proclaim *the risen Lord*.[9]

[7] The pattern is found in Ruth 1:16: Urged by Naomi to stay behind in Moab, Ruth insists that, though not an Israelite, she will come to Israel with Naomi; for from this moment, "Your people shall be my people, and your God my God."

[8] On the general use of "brothers" for the disciples, see p. 215 above. The Beloved Disciple already became Jesus' brother at the cross in John 19:26-27 when Jesus said to his mother in reference to the disciple, "Woman, here is your son." We shall see other instances of the priority of the Beloved Disciple in gifts and experiences that ultimately come to the rest of those who believe in Jesus.

[9] In John 21 we shall see that although the Beloved Disciple has a certain priority over Simon Peter in faith and love, he is not made a shepherd of the sheep. Here in chapter 20 his priority in faith does not make him a proclaimer of resurrection faith. The relation of the disciple to Jesus is interior; exteriorly his only service is to

In narrating Jesus' appearance to the group of disciples (as already in the instance of Magdalene's [second] visit to the tomb), John is close to common tradition, for several Gospels describe a commissioning appearance of Jesus to the Twelve or Eleven.[10] Once more, however, John has his own way of arranging the reactions. In 20:1 he gave this setting: "Early on the first day of the week when it was still dark"; in 20:19 he gives this setting: "On the evening of that first day of the week when, for fear of the Jews, the disciples had locked the doors of the place where they were." The darkness has been dispelled since the Beloved Disciple and Mary Magdalene know that the Lord is risen; but fear and hiding still mark the lives of the disciples, despite Magdalene's report to them of what had happened at the tomb. Yet the fact that the disciples have already heard that Magdalene has seen the Lord makes intelligible the absence of doubt when they see Jesus appear.

His "Peace to you" (a statement of fact, not a wish) in 20:19 goes beyond a greeting[11] because of what Jesus proclaimed at the Last Supper: "'Peace' is my farewell to you; my 'peace' is my gift to you; and I do not give it to you as the world gives it"—words Jesus coupled with the statement that if he was going away, he was also "coming back to you" (14:27-28). Next, in 20:20, the risen Jesus shows his disciples his hands and side, with the wound marks inflicted during the crucifixion (as 20:25 will make clear). He thus removes all question of

---

witness (19:35). As for Magdalene, while her proclamation of the risen Lord is (in the language of other NT works) an apostolic role, we should remember that "apostle" is not Johannine terminology.

[10] See Luke 24:36-49; Mark 16:14-18; Matthew 28:16-20; also 1 Corinthians 15:5. John does not define which "disciples" were present; but the absence of Thomas, "one of the Twelve" (John 20:24), suggests that others of the Twelve were among the disciples. John does not demote the Twelve (see 6:67-69 where they have a special attachment to Jesus), but his use of "disciples" is more widely representative of those who would believe in Jesus. If one puts together 20:2, 10, and 18, one might judge that the disciple whom Jesus loved should be present; but one can never anticipate the reappearance of that mysterious figure.

[11] While "Peace to . . ." is a general greeting in rabbinic Hebrew, in biblical Hebrew the *shalom* greeting tends to be confined to solemn, often revelatory moments, e.g., Judges 6:23.

The Resurrection in John 20

his identity[12] and fulfills a Last Supper promise (16:21-22): "You are sad now; but I shall see you again, and your hearts will rejoice with a joy that no one can take from you." In reporting the reaction of the disciples John says that they saw that it was "the Lord," and this use of the standard post-resurrectional title is the closest that John comes to telling us that they believed. Their insight brings them joy, a response that fulfills the goal enunciated by Jesus at the Last Supper (16:24): ". . . in order that your joy may be full."

Jesus repeats "Peace to you" (20:21); this not only further clarifies that we have here no simple greeting, but also suggests that peace is to accompany the disciples in their forthcoming assignments. The first of those is conveyed through a commissioning: "As the Father has sent me [*apostellein*], so do I send you [*pempein*]." While John's stylistic preference for varied vocabulary plays a major role in such an alternation of the verbs "to send," the fact that he does not use the title "apostle" (*apostolos*) may explain why here he does not repeat *apostellein* in reference to the disciples. Nevertheless, this is a commissioning comparable in large part to the apostolic commissioning of the Twelve (Eleven) in Luke 24:46-49; Matthew 28:18-19; and Mark 16:15.[13] The paradigm for the commissioning in John is the Father's sending of Jesus with all that implies by way of purpose, e.g., to bring life, light, truth. Just as the Father was present in the Son during the Son's mission (12:45: "Whoever sees me is seeing him who sent me"), so now must the disciples in their mission manifest the presence of Jesus to the point that whoever sees the disciples sees Jesus who sent them. That is an

---

[12] In Luke 24:37-40 the invitation "See my hands and feet" responds explicitly to questionings that rise in the heart of the disciples who think they are seeing a spirit. While Jesus' showing his hands and side in John 20:20 and inviting Thomas to examine his wounds in 20:27 imply a certain tangible corporality, the fact that Jesus comes and appears in front of the disciples even though the doors are locked (20:19) should make us wary of assuming that John had a crassly physical understanding of the body of the risen Jesus. There is no solid Gospel evidence that the appearance of the risen Jesus to his disciples on earth was other than bodily (and certainly no evidence that his body remained in the grave); yet there is much evidence that this was a different kind of body or one with different properties from the body before death.

[13] I say "in large part" because the other commissionings specify the destination (the world, the Gentiles); in John 20:21 the mission is as wide as that of Jesus' mission from the Father.

Christ in the Gospels of the Liturgical Year

enormous challenge! It was anticipated at the Last Supper (13:20): "Whoever welcomes anyone that I shall send welcomes me, and whoever welcomes me welcomes him who sent me."

Such re-presenting of Jesus on the part of the disciples becomes possible through the gift of the Holy Spirit (20:22). Jesus was designated by John the Baptist as "The one who is to baptize with the Holy Spirit" (1:33);[14] and at the Last Supper he promised to send the Holy Spirit (15:26). That promise is now fulfilled for the disciples when the risen Jesus says to them, "Receive the Holy Spirit."[15] A particular aspect of this gift of the Spirit is signaled by Jesus' breathing on the disciples, a gesture that even in vocabulary is evocative of Genesis 2:7: "The Lord God formed the human being out of the dust of the earth and breathed into his nostrils the breath of life." We should be aware that "spirit, wind, breath" often represent the same vocabulary cluster, for that makes intelligible the passionate exclamation of Ezekiel 37:9: "From the four winds come, O spirit, and breathe into these slain that they may come to life." This motif is repeated close to NT times by Wisdom 15:11: "The One who fashioned [the human being] and breathed into him a living spirit." Just as in the first creation God's breath brought into existence a human being in his image and likeness, so now Jesus' gift of his own Holy Spirit makes the disciples God's children in the likeness of the Son. Now they are born of Spirit (John 3:5). The breath of God in Genesis gave life; the breath of Jesus gives eternal life.

In addition John relates Jesus' gift of the Spirit to the power over sin: "If you forgive people's sins, their sins are forgiven; if you hold them, they are held fast." Jesus was sent as the Lamb of God to take away the sin of the world (John 1:29; see also 1 John 2:1-2); he now shares that power with his disciples. The description of this power as

---

[14] The gift of the Holy Spirit in 20:22 is connected in the next verse with the forgiveness of sins; notice that before John the Baptist's description of Jesus cited above, he described him as "the Lamb of God who takes away the sin of the world" (1:29).

[15] At Jesus' death his Spirit was given over to the Beloved Disciple and to the mother of Jesus (who had now become the mother of the disciple) as they stood near the cross (John 19:26-27). Notice that in many aspects of the complex of resurrection/ascension/gift-of-the-Spirit the Beloved Disciple has priority over the other disciples in John. Different NT works will deal with that complex in different ways, e.g., Acts 2 has still another moment for the giving of the Spirit (Pentecost).

including both forgiveness and binding is related to the fact that the coming of Jesus produces a *krisis* or judgment as to whether people will opt for darkness or light, so that some are condemned and some are not (John 3:18-21). If Jesus so mirrored God that when people met him they were forced to self-judgment, his disciples must so mirror Jesus that those who encounter them are provoked to a similar *krisis*. At the Last Supper (17:18) Jesus spoke more specifically than here of sending his disciples *into the world*; in that context he spoke both of the world hating them (17:14) and of the world believing because of them (17:21). The provoking of *krisis* or self-judgment is not the total range of the forgiveness and binding of sin granted in John 20:23,[16] but it is an aspect that John would not have us overlook. To represent Christ to a degree that forces people to make a decision in their lives is a tremendous empowerment.

EPISODE IN 20:24-29: REACTION OF THOMAS

In a transitional verse (20:24) John tells the reader that Thomas the Twin[17] was absent. He has been portrayed in John 11:16 and 14:5 as a figure not easily persuaded. The disciples who saw the risen Jesus in 20:19-23 give to Thomas exactly the same report that Mary Magdalene had given to them (20:18): "We have seen the Lord." On the basis of Magdalene's report the disciples did not doubt when Jesus appeared to them; but Thomas is adamant in his refusal to believe on the basis of their word. He wants to probe the wounds of Jesus in order to be sure. Other evangelists mention doubt on the part of the disciples after the resurrection (Matt 28:17; Luke 24:11, 41; Mark 16:11, 14); only John dramatizes that doubt so personally in an individual. Thomas' words, "If I do not see . . . and put my finger . . ., I shall never believe," reflect an attitude condemned by Jesus in John 4:48: "Unless you

---

[16] Patristic writers will see the power over sin granted in John 20:23 as being exercised in baptism; later writers and the Council of Trent will see it applied in the sacrament of penance and will specify that this exercise of the power is not granted to all Christians. As legitimate as these specifications are, there is no requirement to think that the evangelist had them in mind. Our concern here is to understand this power in light of the overall Gospel context dealing with sin and judgment.

[17] It is not clear why the evangelist takes the trouble to explain the meaning of the Semitic form underlying "Thomas." Some have speculated that he was Jesus' twin in appearance; in gnostic speculation he becomes the recipient of special revelations.

Christ in the Gospels of the Liturgical Year

people can see signs and wonders you never believe." The Jesus of John does not reject the possibility that miracles lead people to faith, but he does reject miracles demanded as an absolute condition.

That "after eight days" Jesus appears in the same place (once more with the doors locked) may indicate that there was already a reverence for Sundays in the Johannine community. (Indeed in the same decade of the 90s in which the Gospel of John was written we find a reference to "the Lord's Day" in Revelation 1:10.[18]) There is a touch of Johannine irony in having the time and circumstances of the appearance to the disciples the same as those of the appearance to Thomas. Jesus' "Peace to you" is repeated despite Thomas' antecedent doubts! Knowing what Thomas has said (even as he had shown previous knowledge of what was in the human heart [2:25]), Jesus invites Thomas to examine his hands and side—an invitation that turns the tables on Thomas by probing him. Scholars have debated whether in fact Thomas physically probed the risen body. Surely, on the basis of Johannine theology, however, if Thomas had examined and touched Jesus' body, he would have persisted in a disbelief that he had already demonstrated and would have ceased to be a disciple. The words of Jesus as he challenges Thomas should be taken literally: "Do not persist in your disbelief, but become a believer." Thomas accepts that directive, does not touch Jesus, and so professes faith.

The final irony of the Gospel is that the disciple who doubted the most gives expression to the highest evaluation of Jesus uttered in any gospel: "My Lord and my God." At the beginning of the Gospel the evangelist told the readers that the Word was God (1:1). Now by an inclusion he has shown how difficult it was for Jesus' followers to come to such an insight. Thomas has been remembered in Christian imagery as the doubter par excellence; yet the last words of Jesus to him in response to his confession of faith are an enviable encomium, "You have believed."

---

[18] It is not unlikely, even if unprovable, that the eucharist would have been celebrated on a Sunday thus designated, and that would mean the presence of the risen Lord. Less certain is the interpretation of "after eight days" as the first evidence of a Christian theology of the eighth day (*ogdoad*), illustrated later in the *Epistle of Barnabas* 15:9: "We celebrate with gladness the eighth day in which Jesus also rose from the dead, and having appeared, ascended into heaven."

If the Gospel narrative ended at that point, we would have been satisfied that in chapter 20 we had seen four different reactions to the risen Jesus. Much to our surprise Jesus and the evangelist are interested in a fifth reaction. The Beloved Disciple believed when he saw the garments left in the tomb; Mary Magdalene believed when she heard the voice of the risen Jesus call her name; the disciples believed when they saw the risen Jesus and realized that it was the Lord; Thomas believed when challenged by the risen Jesus to carry out a disbelieving program of probing. The final praise for belief, however, is extended by Jesus to those who have believed without seeing garments or bodily presence. In the Johannine portrait no greater praise can be given to Jesus than "My Lord and my God"; no greater praise can be given to Jesus' followers than "Blessed are those who have not seen and yet have believed." Through that faith the prophecy of Hosea 2:25 (23) is fulfilled: A people that was formerly not a people has said, "You are my God." Or, in the words the evangelist uses to describe the purpose of his Gospel, through that faith the followers of Jesus "have life in his name" (John 20:31).

Chapter 26

The Resurrection in John 21
—Missionary and Pastoral Directives for the Church

The Easter season stretches from Holy Saturday to Pentecost. The church thus enables us to realize that Jesus' emergence from the dead and from the tomb, his ascent to God, his glorification, and the gift of the Spirit are all one mystery. The evangelists, however, for narrative purposes and from the viewpoint of the human beings living in time who are involved in the story, have to describe as taking place on different occasions the various aspects of that one great resurrection mystery. John 20:1 portrays Jesus as already having risen when Mary Magdalene comes to the now empty tomb "early on the first day of the week, while it was still dark." When later in the day Jesus appears to Mary Magdalene, he says to her (20:17), "I am ascending to my Father and your Father, to my God and your God." On the evening of that same day when he appears to the disciples, he breathes on them and says (20:22), "Receive the Holy Spirit."[1] The gift of the Spirit is one of the church-founding aspects of the resurrection.

The presence in John of another chapter (21) involving an appearance of Jesus is also related to the issue of church-founding. Most critical scholars recognize that chapter 21, following upon the conclusion of the Gospel in 20:30-31, is an editorial (or redactional) addition to the Gospel. In fact, despite the editorial seams (21:1, 14) that facilitate the joining of John 20 and 21, the appearance of Jesus in John 21 seems totally independent of the appearances in John 20; for the disciples act as if they had never seen Jesus before. While all that analysis of composition is important in the total exegetical picture,

---

[1] Luke for his own structural purposes stretches out the description: ascension to heaven takes place either on Easter Sunday evening (Luke 24:51) or 40 days later (Acts 1:3, 9-10), and the gift of the Spirit takes place on Pentecost (50 days after Passover).

the interpretation of a Gospel in the liturgical context must work with the text *as it now stands*.[2] Accordingly I shall read the appearance in John 21 as granted to those who have seen the risen Lord and received the gift of the Spirit in John 20, just as the account reads in the Bible without critical presuppositions. Also I suggest that the appearance in John 21 can be understood more profoundly if one keeps in mind the context supplied by the whole Gospel,[3] and leaves aside the possibility that this may be an independently appended chapter.

Although all the events in chapter 21 take place in the one site on the one morning as a sequential series, the editorial remark in 21:14 offers justification for speaking of two parts, consisting of 21:1-14 and 21:15-24. The final verse (21:25) is a conclusion to the whole Gospel and does not apply specifically to the resurrection appearance. For convenience' sake we shall work with four subdivisions:

(1) 21:1-8: The Appearance of Jesus at the Sea of Tiberias and the Miraculous Catch of Fish
(2) 21:9-14: The Meal of Bread and Fish
(3) 21:15-19: Jesus and Simon Peter
(4) 21:20-24: Jesus and the Beloved Disciple

If one looks back to John 20, the same fascination with reactions to the risen Jesus by individuals (here: by the disciples, Simon Peter, the Beloved Disciple) is attested; but now the symbolism of action and message is more developed, as we shall see below.

EPISODE IN 21:1-8:
THE APPEARANCE OF JESUS AT THE SEA OF TIBERIAS AND THE MIRACULOUS CATCH OF FISH
The last time Jesus was in Galilee at this sea with his disciples was on the occasion of the multiplication of the loaves (John 6), and that event is implicitly recalled in this chapter. In John 6:67-70 Simon Peter took the initiative in speaking for the Twelve; here again he takes the initiative in proposing to go fishing, and arouses the others to go with him.

---

[2] This approach is valid for more than liturgical purposes. No matter how likely our reconstruction of Fourth Gospel composition, the only known form of John has chapter 21 after 20. On the principle that such an order made sense to the one who produced it, we should comment on it.

[3] This approach was stressed above in chapter 4.

Christ in the Gospels of the Liturgical Year

Of the seven disciples listed, one reminds us of the beginning of the Gospel, for Nathaniel from Cana in Galilee (last mentioned in John 1:45-51) reappears here. Four more are members of the Twelve: Simon Peter, Thomas, and the sons of Zebedee. It is astonishing that these members of the Twelve who saw the risen Jesus in Jerusalem,[4] were sent out by him, and received the Holy Spirit as a grant of power over sin (20:21-23) are now simply fishing in Galilee. In particular, Thomas had a special encounter with the risen Jesus whom he confessed as Lord and God, but now gives no evidence of having been changed dramatically. John 21 has the effect of warning the readers that a move from belief in the risen Jesus to action based on that belief cannot be taken for granted. Disciples who came to believe in Jesus in John 20 are now engaged in ordinary activity without a sign of transformation.

In any case the disciples are unsuccessful in their fishing, for they catch nothing all night (21:3). Then at dawn Jesus is suddenly present on the shore—a description with a hint of mysteriousness. Though they have seen the risen Jesus twice before and though Thomas was invited to probe physically Jesus' hands and side, the disciples do not recognize him.[5] This failure to recognize, since it shows limitation on the part of those who *saw* the risen Jesus, may underline the beatitude uttered by Jesus to Thomas in 20:29: "Blessed are those who have *not* seen and yet have believed."

Thus far in John there has been recounted no scene where men fishing by the lake were called by Jesus to be his disciples and made "fishers of men." That scene was placed at the beginning of the Gospel by Mark (1:16-20; Matt 4:18-22) as the first major initiative of Jesus' ministry. Luke 5:1-11 has combined with that account a story of how, although Simon and the others had fished all night and caught nothing, they let down their nets at Jesus' instruction and caught so many fish that their nets were breaking. In other words, besides the common Synoptic symbolism whereby the disciples are made fishers of people, Luke's miraculous catch stresses that the mission guided by Jesus will

---

[4] The scene in John 20:19-23 presumably involved members of the Twelve (note 10, p. 249).

[5] This nonrecognition that we have encountered in several resurrection appearances also served apologetically: it militated against the thesis that the disciples were credulous and looking for the resurrection so that they might have identified another person as Jesus.

The Resurrection in John 21

be extraordinarily abundant. Placed at the beginning of the Gospel, this Synoptic treatment is predictive of a future that will come only when the public ministry of Jesus is over. John offers his form of the miraculous-catch story[6] after the resurrection with a much more immediate focus. The disciples were sent out by the risen Jesus in 20:21; yet they have resumed the fishing trade. Jesus now uses that trade to symbolize what they must begin to do. As in Luke, Jesus' assistance reverses human incapability to make a catch: so many are the fish caught in John 21 that the disciples cannot haul in the net.

The miraculous catch brings about recognition of the risen Jesus in a pattern that has some similarity to the recognition process in John 20. In that previous chapter we saw a sequence of reactions: the Beloved Disciple believed first, simply on the evidence of the garments in the tomb (20:8). So also here he is the first to recognize the Lord, simply on the evidence of the catch (21:7). In John 20, although she did not recognize Jesus at first, Mary Magdalene was the next person to know him when she heard him call her by name and seemingly she went to clutch him (20:16-17). Here, through the Beloved Disciple as intermediary,[7] Simon Peter hears that it is the Lord and immediately jumps into the sea to go to Jesus on the land. No interpreter is certain what John means precisely when he writes in 21:7 of Simon Peter adjusting garments over his nakedness before he springs into the sea. Besides the more obvious meaning that he donned a garment when he previously had nothing on, his action could mean that he belted or tucked in the only garment he had on over his naked body. Perhaps the purpose of the description is to have Peter show respect before Jesus. In any case the Johannine scene portrays Peter's spontaneity and love of the Lord—a motif Jesus will pick up later in the dialogue with Peter (21:15-17).

---

[6] Many scholars think that the miraculous-catch story has a more original locus in Luke, i.e., that it was a ministry story which John has placed after the resurrection. The fact that Luke adds it to a Marcan context suggests to me that it was a free-floating story without a fixed locus and that Luke has inserted it where he thought best. Whether John's post-resurrectional context is more original depends on whether the appearance of Jesus to Peter was integrally connected to it, rather than joined to it by John.

[7] See also John 13:23-26; 18:15-16.

Christ in the Gospels of the Liturgical Year

EPISODE IN 21:9-14:
THE MEAL OF BREAD AND FISH

Although this episode introduces a new topic centered on a meal, what happens is intrinsically linked to the catch of fish and will fill out the missionary symbolism of that catch. In 20:20 the disciples came to experience the reality of the risen Lord only after the Beloved Disciple and Mary Magdalene. So also here the disciples, not knowing that it is Jesus, have carried on the fishing chore of dragging the net full of fish toward the shore. When they arrive they see a charcoal fire already burning, with fish and bread on it. Jesus, to them still a stranger, asks for fish from the fresh catch; and Simon Peter, knowing that this is a command of *the Lord*, hastens to drag the net ashore. The symbolism of the catch is now forcefully emphasized by enumerating 153 large fish; yet, we are told, the net is not broken. Scholars have exercised great ingenuity in explaining the number. It may simply be a touch to underline the eyewitness quality of the scene (see 21:24); it may represent the total number of different species of fish known to Greek zoologists (as suggested by Jerome: in that case its function is to symbolize the universality of the mission); or it may be a play on the numerical value of the names in Ezekiel 47:10 where fishermen stand on the shore of the Dead Sea from *Engedi* to *Eneglaim*, spreading their nets, and there are as many fish in the Sea enriched by the stream from the Temple as there are in the Mediterranean (in which case John is showing the fulfillment of OT eschatological prophecy). What is certain is that the number and size of the fish show how successful the disciples can be with Jesus' help. One is reminded of John 4:37-38 where Jesus sends disciples to reap an abundant harvest that they did not sow. The symbolism of the net that has not been torn has also been the subject of scholarly discussion. In John 17:19-20 Jesus prays for the oneness of those who believe in him through the word of those whom he sends out, and so the untorn net may symbolize the unity of those "caught" by the disciples whom the risen Jesus has sent out (20:21).[8]

---

[8] Other passages dealing with unity include John 10:16 where the "Good Shepherd" says that he has other sheep not of this fold, and that he has to bring them so that there will be one sheep herd, one shepherd. This passage is relevant for chapter 21 because in 21:15-17 Jesus uses the image of shepherding once more. A possible parallel for the net that was not torn may be the tunic of Jesus that was not torn or divided (19:23-24), which many see as a symbol of unity.

The Resurrection in John 21

Granted all these reported details of the catch, it is truly astounding that the disciples have not recognized the Lord. John 21:12 (somewhat hesitantly) at last attributes knowledge to them as Jesus invites them, "Come and eat your breakfast." (Is it by chance that these last words spoken by Jesus to the disciples in John are an invitation even as were the first words spoken by Jesus to them in 1:39: "Come and see"?[9]) Other recounted appearances of the risen Jesus are associated with meals: Luke 24:30, 42; perhaps Acts 1:4; Acts 10:41; Mark 16:14. Luke (p. 230 above) stressed a eucharistic aspect in the meal of the risen Jesus with the two disciples at Emmaus (24:30-35: they knew him in the breaking of the bread). John 21:12-13 seems to fit into that ambiance. The disciples know Jesus as the Lord in the context of a meal; and we are told that Jesus came and took bread and gave it to them, and similarly the fish. The last time he was at this lake Jesus took the loaves; and when he had given thanks (*eucharistein*), he distributed it to those seated, and likewise the fish (John 6:11). That scene of the multiplication of the loaves was interpreted eucharistically in John 6:51b-58: "The bread that I shall give for the life of the world is my flesh. . . . If you do not eat the flesh of the Son of Man and drink his blood, you have no life in you." Thus there is reason to think that the readers of John might well reflect on their own eucharists as they read how the risen Jesus fed the disciples at the lake and might be challenged to recognize that it is the risen Lord who is present in those eucharists.

EPISODE IN 21:15-19: JESUS AND SIMON PETER
Tradition (Luke 24:34; 1 Cor 15:5) has it that, among those who would be apostolic preachers of the resurrection, Simon, called Cephas or Peter, was the first to see the risen Jesus. That appearance to Simon is nowhere recounted in the Gospels; yet hidden beneath the surface of John 21 the story may still be present in terms of an appearance in Galilee to Peter when he was fishing. This appearance may have included the questioning of Peter by Jesus and a commissioning of him to support or care for others.[10] What is fascinating in the sequence of

[9] Notice, however, that there are different Greek words for "Come" in the two passages.
[10] Some would relate to John 21:15-17 other sayings of Jesus to Peter now scattered through the Gospels. Matthew 16:16-18, where Peter is made the rock on which the church will be built, is often thought to have had originally a post-resurrectional

Christ in the Gospels of the Liturgical Year

chapter 21 is the shift of topic. Peter was part of the group of disciples who made the huge catch of fish; thus he was part of the general apostolic mission that would bring in large numbers of believers. But now Jesus speaks to him alone *about sheep*! The catching of fish is an apt image for an evangelizing mission; but to picture the ongoing care of those brought in by that mission one has to change the image. We call this care of those already converted "pastoral," precisely because of the set use of flock and sheep in this connection. Thus the readers of John 21 are invited to see in Peter the combination of missionary and pastor.[11]

If we are familiar with Johannine language, several factors in the dialogue of 21:15-17 stand out. Jesus addresses Peter as "Simon, son of John." The only other time Jesus addressed him thus was in 1:42 when Jesus gave him the name "Cephas (which means Peter)." In other words, in John this is an address that leads to an identification, either by name (as in 1:42) or by role (here). The role of shepherding the sheep, like the name Peter, signifies this man's special identity in the Christian community.

Before this role is assigned, Peter is asked three times: "Do you love me?";[12] or more precisely, the first time Jesus asks, "Do you love me more than these?" If "these" refers to the other disciples who did not recognize Jesus in the meal (and who now seem almost to have disappeared from the scene), then we are reminded of Simon Peter's boastful reaction in 13:37 at the Last Supper. There, after Jesus warned of the impossibility of following him to the cross, Peter objected, "Lord, why can't I follow you now? I will lay down my life for you."

---

context. A related saying in Luke 22:31-32, where Jesus prays for Simon that his faith will not fail and that when he has turned he will strengthen his brothers, is difficult to fit into a post-resurrectional context.

[11] In the genuine Pauline letters Paul emerges as a missionary; but in the post–Pauline Pastorals (1–2 Timothy, Titus) we see Paul wrestling with permanent church structure. Thus a movement from missionary to pastor is attested in the remembrance of Paul as well as of Peter.

[12] The verb is alternated thus: in Jesus' three questions: *agapan, agapan, philein*; in Peter's response: *philein, philein, philein*. Similarly there is alternation in the verbs that govern the sheep ("to feed, pasture": *boskein, poimainein, boskein*), and in the noun for sheep (*arnion, probaton, probation*). Older commentators, overly influenced by classical Greek, sought precise shades of meaning in these choices; rather they are simply stylistic variations.

Against that background Peter might now have claimed to love the risen Jesus more than the others, for there is no greater love than the willingness to lay down one's life for one's friend (15:13). Moreover, in the present chapter, Peter hastened to Jesus from the boat while the other disciples did not recognize him and stayed in the boat. Does Peter still think of himself as the most loving? From his response it is now apparent that Peter has been chastened by the failure he manifested in denying Jesus; for he does not compare his love with that of the other disciples[13] but confines himself to a simple, personal affirmation of love. Even in that affirmation Peter trusts himself to Jesus' knowledge. Previously, when Simon Peter boasted about his willingness to follow Jesus even unto death, Jesus showed that he knew Peter better than Peter knew himself by predicting three denials before cockcrow. Now, although Simon Peter believes with all his heart that he loves Jesus in total fidelity, all that he is willing to claim is: "You know that I love you."

There is no doubt, then, that the threefold pattern and some of the context of the questions and answers in 21:15-17 are set over against the pattern of the threefold denial of Jesus by Peter in the high priest's court (18:15-18, 25-27). It is noteworthy that in the three Synoptic Gospels, when the cock crowed, we were told that Peter recalled Jesus' predictions of three denials before cockcrow (Mark 14:72; Matt 26:75; Luke 22:61); but that was not said in John. Perhaps we are meant to think that only here after the resurrection Peter is reminded of Jesus' prediction by being questioned three times.

Yet the dialogue between the risen Jesus and Simon Peter has a more immediate purpose than Peter's repentance. A major pastoral role is being assigned to him—indeed a role that in Johannine theology is highly unexpected. Those scholars who have worked with the Johannine Epistles and have sought to read between the lines of the Fourth Gospel in order to reconstruct the life of the Johannine community[14] have noticed the lack of titles customarily used for NT church authori-

[13] Most scholars understand "more than these" personally, i.e., "more than these disciples do"; but another possible understanding is to take "these" as a neuter accusative: "Do you love me more than you love these things [i.e., your ordinary pursuits like fishing]?" Then, Jesus would be asking Peter to leave his ordinary life and devote himself to serving the followers of Jesus.

[14] See, for instance, R. E. Brown, *The Community of the Beloved Disciple* (New York: Paulist, 1979) and the bibliography cited therein.

Christ in the Gospels of the Liturgical Year

ties. In 1 Corinthians 12:28 Paul states, "God has appointed in the church first apostles, second prophets, third teachers"; yet the whole Johannine corpus calls none apostles, mentions among Christians only those prophets who are false (1 John 4:1), and states that the readers have no need of anyone to teach them (1 John 2:27). 3 John 9 shows a dislike for a man named Diotrephes who likes to put himself first (in authority) in a local church. To this depreciation of human authorities one must add the evidence of John 10. In the 80s the image of shepherding a flock was in use in several NT areas as a symbol for the work of the presbyter-bishops.[15] Yet in John 10 Jesus identifies *himself* as the model shepherd, the sole gate by which one should enter the sheepfold, so that anyone who does not enter by that gate is a thief and a robber (10:1, 7). Is the assignment of a shepherding role to Simon Peter symbolic of a change in Johannine attitude? By tradition Simon Peter was regarded as the first of the Twelve and the granting of authority to him by Jesus at the end of John (indeed, in an appended chapter) could suggest the latterly realization by the Johannine community that without human shepherds the community would split up (along the lines attested in 1 John 2:19).

In any case, if John 21:15-17 is a modification of the sole shepherd role assigned to Jesus in John 10, careful qualifications are incorporated in John 21 to make certain that Johannine values are preserved. No pastoral assignment is made without the assurance that Simon Peter loves Jesus. The model disciple of this community is the one whom Jesus loves. The Paraclete/Spirit is promised to those who love Jesus and keep his commands (14:15). Thus the mutual love that exists between Jesus and the believers is a most important factor in this community's life, and that criterion is applied to anyone who would exercise pastoral care. Ours is a time when people quarrel over who should have authority in the church with the "have-nots" polarized against the "haves." The argument is advanced that to hold pastoral office is a human right or at least the right of all who are baptized. John's primary concern is of quite a different sort. The one who would care for the sheep must first show love for Jesus, even to the point of laying down life itself for him (as we shall see below). That criterion is a challenge both to the "haves" and the "have-nots."

---

[15] Acts 20:17, 28; 1 Peter 5:1-4; see also Ephesians 4:11 (apostles, prophets, evangelists, *pastors*, teachers).

The Resurrection in John 21

Another qualification is imposed by the dialogue of John 21:15-17. Even though Peter is charged with caring for the sheep, Jesus continues to speak of those as "my lambs, my sheep." The flock never passes into the proprietorship of the human shepherd; no one can ever take the place of Jesus. Speaking of himself as the model shepherd, Jesus claimed, "I know mine, and mine know me" (10:14). His was a voice that the sheep would recognize as he called them by name (10:3, 5, 16). The priority of a personal relationship to Jesus on the part of those who constitute the flock is not neglected now that a human structure of authority is being established. Only Jesus can use the word "mine," even though Peter feeds the sheep. Inevitably in the course of decades and centuries the church would take on coloring and values from a secular society where visible authority is most important and where such authority tends to be possessive. The language of the Johannine Jesus serves as a leavening corrective against all tendencies, however well-intentioned, of those in authority to speak of "my people, my parishioners."

What Peter is told to do is to feed or care for the sheep. Because the king in OT imagery was described as a shepherd, the task of pasturing the flock was often understood to involve ruling.[16] Yet the notion of ruling authority has at most a minor place in Jesus' commission to Simon Peter. In chapter 10, which describes the role of the good or model shepherd, Jesus never talks about ruling. The role of the shepherd is to lead the sheep out to pasture, to know them personally so that they feel close to him, and especially to lay down his life for the sheep (10:11, 15). At the Last Supper Peter boasted that he would be willing to lay down his life for Jesus (13:37-38), but he failed miserably when challenged to do so. Evidently Jesus has not forgotten that preamble to Peter's denials, and so in the context of commissioning him to feed the sheep Jesus now warns Peter about death (21:18-19). If Peter is given care of the sheep, he will be required to lay down his life. The description of Peter's stretching out his hands, being fastened with a belt, and being led forcibly to where he would not go is surely a reference to a penal death (21:19: "The kind of death by which Peter was to glorify God"). Perhaps more specifically it is a reference to Peter's crucifixion. In either case, the likely date at which this is being

---

[16] This is illustrated by the use of *poimainein* (note 12 above) in the Septuagint of 2 Samuel 5:2; 1 Chronicles 17:6.

Christ in the Gospels of the Liturgical Year

written is after Peter had glorified God as a martyr, so that John knows that Peter's following Jesus to death—an aborted action on Good Friday—was eventually verified on Vatican Hill. The Simon Peter of John 21 who three times states, "Lord, you know that I love you," keeps his word by laying down his life for the one whom he loves, as an essential part of the care of the sheep assigned to him. In that action he obeyed the last words ever spoken to him by Jesus: "Follow me" (21:19b, 22). Such behavior was far more important in the Johannine estimation of Peter as shepherding than the issue of how much power Peter had over the sheep.

EPISODE IN 21:20-24:
JESUS AND THE BELOVED DISCIPLE

Despite the dialogue just discussed and the unique pastoral role given to Peter, he is not the most important follower of Jesus in Johannine thought. The disciple whom Jesus loved was mentioned early in the scene as the first to recognize Jesus and the one to inform Peter. We now discover that this disciple is still present. Indeed it is interesting that this disciple was left without an introduction when first named (21:7) but is now introduced as the figure who had lain on Jesus' breast at the Last Supper (21:20). The scene with Simon Peter reminded us of the boasts made by him at the Last Supper and his subsequent three-fold denial of Jesus; a more intimate relationship to Jesus is recalled for the Beloved Disciple.

The readers would almost have forgotten the presence of this disciple; now suddenly he is mentioned as following Jesus and Peter, but seemingly standing behind. Is that positioning a way of hinting that in the estimation of the larger church it is Peter the shepherd who would stand in front? Peter himself raises the question, "What about this man?" Curiously this disciple to whom no pastoral authority over the flock has been assigned is a subject of concern to the human figure who has just received authority. Is this because the Beloved Disciple really does not fit easily into a value system established by authority? In these last verses of the Gospel we find peculiarly Johannine values exemplified in a striking way. To be a disciple whom Jesus loves is in the end more important than to be assigned church authority! If Peter has a primacy of pastoral care, this disciple has another primacy bestowed by Jesus' love.

Peter is to die a martyr's death, but Jesus has a destiny for this disciple that is less dramatic but more enduring. The play on the

The Resurrection in John 21

265

disciple's remaining until Jesus comes is a final literary touch in a Gospel that has played with double-meaning terms throughout as a way of showing how human beings misunderstand, because they think on the level of this world which is below while God's world is above. Even some of the Johannine community ("the brothers" of 21:23) have misunderstood this final play on words. They thought that when Jesus said, "Suppose I would like him to remain until I come," he meant that the disciple would not die. But John 21:23 tells us with absolute assurance that Jesus did not mean that—an assurance that probably indicates that the disciple was already dead. Why then did Jesus even raise the issue of the disciple's remaining? A modern biblical critic may use this passage to discuss Jesus' knowledge of the time of the second coming and may point to Mark 13:32 which says that even the Son does not know of that day or that hour.[17] Yet while limitations in Jesus' earthly knowledge may well explain the historical origin of the saying in John 21, this Gospel where Jesus is virtually omniscient can scarcely be interpreted as implying a limitation on Jesus' part. Does the Johannine answer as to why Jesus made the statement[18] lie in the dual nature of the Beloved Disciple? John 21:24 clearly presents him as a historical person who gave witness; as such he died and did not remain until Jesus comes. At most he remains on in his witness and in the written tradition preserved in the Fourth Gospel. Yet in another sense the Beloved Disciple represents the perfect disciple—the *kind* of disciple that Jesus loves. If Peter embodies church authority, this disciple embodies all those who, although they may not be commissioned to care for the sheep, are deeply loved by Jesus because they love him and keep his commandments. In that sense, the kind of disciple whom Jesus loves will remain until Jesus comes. If the last words of Jesus in Matthew (28:20) are that he will be with us to the end of time, the last words of Jesus in John may be affirming the final fruit of the resurrection: a believing community of Christians will remain until Jesus returns.

---

[17] See also Mark 9:1: Some of Jesus' contemporaries will not taste death before they see the kingdom of God come in power.

[18] Some speculation about Johannine thought is justified here because, although John rejects a misunderstanding, he does not explain in what sense the saying conveys truth.

Christ in the Gospels of the Liturgical Year

A Once-and-Coming Spirit at Pentecost

Essays on the Liturgical Readings
between Easter and Pentecost,
Taken from the Acts of the Apostles and from the Gospel
According to John

Chapters 27–32

Chapter 27

Introduction Explaining this Treatment of the Liturgical Season

For several reasons the season between Easter and Pentecost is more complex than the other liturgical seasons on which I have reflected. The only consistent readings for this seven-week period are from the Acts of the Apostles (beginning with 2:14), which supplies the pericopes for the first reading of the weekday and Sunday Masses. The weekday selections constitute the longest sequential reading in the Mass lectionary from any book of the Bible outside the Gospels. Yet there is an apparent illogicality in this arrangement: The coming of the Spirit is described in Acts 2:1-11 (the passage read on the feast of Pentecost), and yet the rest of Acts is read before and not after Pentecost. Thus in the liturgical period when we are readying ourselves for the coming of the Spirit, we read what happened in the early church once the Spirit had come!

The weekday readings from the Acts of the Apostles (henceforth simply called Acts) are perfectly sequential, running from chapter 2 to the end (chap. 28).[1] Yet the selections are not proportionately distributed throughout Acts, for there is a clear bias toward the earlier part of the book. Of the forty-two weekday readings only the last three are taken from the final one-quarter of Acts (following 21:15) when Paul is seized and tried in Jerusalem and Caesarea and then sent to Rome. By comparison fourteen readings are taken from the first quarter of Acts (chaps. 2 through 7) describing the life of the church in Jerusalem up to the stoning of Stephen.[2] Thus there is far greater emphasis on the

---

[1] The sequence is broken only on Ascension Thursday; on that feast (in some regions celebrated on Sunday) the first reading is the account of the ascension in Acts 1:1-11, and the Gospel reading is from the conclusion of Matthew (A year), of Mark (B), or of Luke (C).

[2] Or, to count in another way, eleven readings are taken from the first four chapters (2 through 5); two readings are taken from the last four chapters (25 through 28).

history of the first Christian community rather than on the career per se of the great apostle. True, nineteen readings are taken from the section of Acts that concern the missionary travels of Paul from the time he sets out from Antioch until he returns to Jerusalem to be arrested (13:4–21:15). Yet even in those the selection shows a minimum interest in the travels and a maximum interest in what happened in the communities that Paul converted. Thus it is fair to say that in the readings from Acts on weekdays between Easter and Pentecost the emphasis is on the life story of the early church, Jewish (Jerusalem) and Gentile (Antioch and Pauline)—a life story the beginnings of which will be described on Pentecost.

In previous chapters I commented on the Gospel passages of the various seasons, but they are more complex here. The weekday Gospel readings of the First Week after Easter (the octave) recount the appearances of the risen Jesus, and I have already made them the subject of reflection in *A Risen Christ at Eastertime* (chaps. 22–26 above). For the weekdays after Easter from the Second Week on, the church reads sequentially from the Gospel according to John, beginning with chapter 3. Yet there are large gaps as the lectionary skips from chapter 3 to 6 to 10 (dialogue with Nicodemus, multiplication of the loaves, Good Shepherd, etc.), with the longest and most sequential set of readings (nineteen) devoted to the Last Supper (chaps. 13–17). From a strictly exegetical viewpoint it would be difficult to write detailed sequential reflections on such selections unless one chose to ignore all the intervening material. Moreover, I have already written for Liturgical Press *The Gospel and Epistles of John—A Concise Commentary*, and it would be of little interest simply to excise from that. As will become apparent, however, I shall not ignore the Gospel readings from John, even though my primary concentration will be on Acts. Just as there was an apparent illogicality in reading in this pre-Pentecost season selections from Acts that in the story line follow the original Pentecost, so also there is an apparent illogicality in reading in this post-Easter season Johannine selections that in the story line precede Jesus' death. Yet it is at the Last Supper that the Johannine Jesus speaks of the coming of the Paraclete.

I have been speaking about weekday readings. Would it not be of more help if I concentrated on Sunday readings? Since most clergy give brief homilies at weekday Masses, I am not sure that concentration on Sundays would be more helpful to them. But there is another reason why it may be more helpful to laity and clergy alike to concentrate on the weekday cycle as a way of making the Sunday readings intelligible. (What follows is a bit complicated, but my analysis will provide a good overview.) In this season the Sunday readings are also from Acts and John although, of course, since there are fewer Sunday readings, the selection is more limited.[3] In a certain sense the Sunday readings are a pale reflection of the wealth of the weekday readings.

Let me illustrate that claim. In any given year only five selections from Acts are read on the Sundays between Easter and Ascension. If one surveys the fifteen passages from Acts read in the course of the three-year cycle of Sundays, relatively few are not included in the forty-two weekday selections that are read every year.[4] As for Gospel readings, because the first two Sundays always recount resurrection appearances, in any given year only four selections from John's account of the public ministry of Jesus are read on the Sundays between Easter and Pentecost. If one surveys the twelve passages from John read in the course of the three-year cycle of Sundays, really only two are not included in the thirty-six weekday selections that are read every year.[5] Thus if I reflect on the weekday readings, I shall for all practical purposes have covered the Sunday readings, no matter which of the three liturgical years (A, B, C) it happens to be. Since my chapters, like the weekday order, will be strictly sequential, those who are interested primarily in a given Sunday's readings need only to look at headings of the chapters to find where that particular pericope is discussed (within the larger context that would be necessary for intelligibility in any case).

Despite the apparent illogicalities I have mentioned above, theological reflection enables us to see that there really is good sense in the

---

[3] I refer to the first and third readings of each Sunday Mass. The Sunday readings from Acts and John are sequential from the Third Sunday on, but only within the given year (A, B, or C). A special case is presented by the Acts readings 1:12-14 and 1:15-17, 20-26 (A and B) of the last Sunday after Easter which are chosen as a sequence to Ascension Thursday. I remind readers that in *A Risen Christ at Eastertime* I treated the appearance of the Lord in Acts 1:1-12, which includes the ascension.

[4] Namely, Acts 2:42-47 (A: Second Sunday); 5:12-16 (C: Second Sunday); 8:14-17 (A: Sixth Sunday); 9:26-31 (B: Fifth Sunday); 10:25-48 (B: Sixth Sunday).

[5] Namely, John 13:31-33a, 34-35 (C: Fifth Sunday), and 14:15-21 (A: Fifth Sunday). Notice how the John readings of the Fourth Sunday, 10:1-11 (A) and 10:11-18 (B), are dealt with on Monday of the Fourth Week.

Introduction Explaining this Treatment of the Liturgical Season

lectionary pattern of reading from Acts and John at this season. Let me explain this first in relation to the readings from Acts that describe the aftermath of the gift of the Spirit. The mystery of the resurrection that we celebrate on Easter is complex. In one action that goes beyond earthly time Jesus is victorious over death, emerges from the tomb, returns to his Father, and gives the Spirit to those who believe in him. From the viewpoint of the first followers who continued to live on within time these actions were spread out: They found the tomb empty on Sunday morning; the risen Lord appeared to them on that day or subsequently; the termination of the appearances caused them to realize that Jesus was now permanently with God; and they received the Spirit. Yet the timeless character from God's viewpoint has left its mark in the NT reports, for without embarrassment the same event is described as having taken place at different times. If one reads Hebrews 9:11-28, one gets the impression that Jesus ascended from the cross with his blood directly into heaven, even as Luke 23:43 has the dying Christ say on Good Friday, "*This day* you will be with me in Paradise." According to John 20:17 ("I am ascending to my Father and your Father"), Jesus seems to have begun his ascent to the Father on Easter Sunday in the daytime before he appears to the disciples at night. According to Luke 24:51 he ascended on Easter Sunday night, and according to Acts 1:3, 10 he ascended some forty days after Easter. Now in all these accounts the same basic action of going to God's presence, terminating Jesus' existence on earth, is involved; but it is described in different ways with different theological nuances.

The same may be said of the gift of the Spirit by the victorious Jesus. Once again it is an event that surpasses time, and accordingly is described at different moments in different NT narratives. In John Jesus is victorious already when he is raised up on the cross (12:31-33), and before his death he has already fulfilled all things given him by God (19:28). Thus, as he dies he gives over the Spirit to the community of special disciples at the foot of the cross (19:30), and from his dead body come forth water and blood symbolizing the gift of the Spirit (19:34; 7:38-39). Yet also in John on Easter Sunday night to "the disciples" (i.e., presumably to others than those at the cross, for this group seems to include members of the Twelve) Jesus can say, "Receive the Holy Spirit" (20:22). And, of course, Acts 2:1-4 has the Spirit come in power fifty days after Easter. Given such variation it is not illogical for the lectionary to describe immediately after Easter the life of the

Christian community called into being by the risen Jesus, gift of the Spirit. The church need not wait until the feast of Pentecost when it will solemnly celebrate that gift. Theologically it knows that the gift of the Spirit is part of an Easter mystery that goes beyond time.

As we turn to the use of the Gospel of John, we must remember that all the Gospels are written from a post-resurrectional viewpoint. They differ only in the extent in which the memories of the ministry have been rewritten from that vantage, ranging in the order (from the least extent to the most) Mark, Luke, Matthew, John. In the three-year cycle the church reads from the first three of those, one Gospel per year. Thus for the most part it reads the Gospel accounts of the ministry after Pentecost. But it has chosen to read sections of John's account of the ministry every year after Easter, thus tacitly giving recognition that it is the Gospel with the most pronounced post-resurrectional reinterpretation.[6] In particular, there is no theological difficulty about reading John's account of the Last Supper after Easter because Jesus' discourse recounted in that context is addressed to Christians of all times and places, i.e., those who constitute "his own." Despite the localization on the night before Jesus died, the Johannine Jesus says, "I am no longer in the world" (17:11)—a clear indication that the evangelist was writing these words from the viewpoint of a Jesus already victorious and on his way to the Father. In other words the liturgy is actually respecting the evangelist's mindset in placing Johannine material after Easter.

How is it possible to reflect on Acts and yet take cognizance of the Johannine readings? They are complementary. Acts describes the external or visible career of Christianity from the first preaching to Jews in Jerusalem until Paul arrives in Rome, the capital of the Gentile world. The proclamation about Jesus that began among Jews has its future among Gentiles: "They will listen" (28:28). The author sees the working out of the presence of the Spirit in actions of historical persons in geographically diverse places. The Gospel of John sees the working of the Spirit in the internal life of Christians. This eternal life is given in baptism (Discourse with Nicodemus in chap. 3), nourished by the food of eternal life (Bread of Life Discourse in chap. 6), and

---

[6] This custom of reading portions of John after Easter is very ancient, as old as the fourth century in some liturgies.

Introduction Explaining this Treatment of the Liturgical Season

cared for by the Good Shepherd (chap. 10). The intimate words of Jesus to his own in the Last Discourse concern the love commandment, the Paraclete, union with him and the Father—in other words all the constitutive elements of that life. To simplify, although both authors believe that Christian life manifests the Spirit, the author of Acts shows the Spirit at work in the external course of history, while the author of John shows the Spirit at work in the inner existence of the disciple. In what follows I shall reflect on the story of Acts and, in lesser space, point to the complementarity of the Johannine readings.

Chapter 28

The Church Begins in Jerusalem
(Acts 2:14-41)

The first two weekday readings after Easter and the readings of the Third and Fourth Sundays of the A year are from this section of Acts that describes Peter's first sermon and the effect it produced. It is a marvelous passage with which to begin our reflections on the church that the Spirit has produced, for it is a masterful summary of Christian essentials.

Before reflecting on it, let me say a few words about the section of Acts 2 that precedes it and that constitutes the reading on Pentecost itself. The Feast of Weeks or Pentecost (so-called because it was celebrated seven weeks or fifty days after Passover) was a pilgrimage feast when pious Jews came from their homes to the Temple or central shrine in Jerusalem. The historical nucleus of what is described in Acts 2:1-13 is seemingly that on the next pilgrimage feast after Jesus' death and resurrection his Galilean disciples and his family came to Jerusalem and that, while they were there, the presence of the Spirit was charismatically manifested as they began to speak in tongues. This was seen as a sign that they should proclaim publicly what God had done in Jesus.

Acts has re-presented that nucleus with theological insight, highlighting its central place in the Christian history of salvation. In that presentation the meaning of Pentecost plays a key role. It was an agricultural feast celebrated in May or June as a way of giving thanks to God for the wheat or grain harvest; but like the other pastoral or agricultural feasts of the Jews it had acquired another meaning, recalling what God had done for the chosen people in their history.[1] The

---

[1] In the case of other feasts, namely, Passover/Unleavened Bread and Tabernacles (Tents, Booths), the OT itself records the salvific history applications, respectively the exodus and the desert wandering on the way to the Promised Land. In the OT

deliverance from Egypt was commemorated at Passover. About a month and a half later in the Exodus account (19:1) of that deliverance the Israelites arrived at Sinai; and so Pentecost, occurring about a month and a half after Passover, became the commemoration of God's giving the covenant to Israel at Sinai—the moment when Israel was called to be God's own people.

In depicting God's appearance at Sinai, Exodus 19 includes thunder and smoke; and the Jewish writer Philo (contemporary with the NT) describes angels taking what God said to Moses on the mountaintop and carrying it out on tongues to the people on the plain below. Acts, with its description of the sound of a mighty wind and tongues as of fire, echoes that imagery, and thus presents the Pentecost in Jerusalem as the renewal of God's covenant, once more calling a people to be God's own. According to Exodus, in the Sinai covenant the people who heard the invitation to be God's own and accepted it were Israelites. After Sinai in biblical language the other nations remained "no people." Acts 2:9-11, with its broad sweep from the extremities of the Roman Empire (Parthians, Medes, and Elamites) to Rome itself, describes the nationalities who at Pentecost observed and heard what was effected by the Spirit at the Jerusalem renewal of the covenant. Thus Acts anticipates the broad reach of the evangelizing that has now begun, an evangelizing that will ultimately make even the Gentiles God's own people (Acts 28:28).[2] In the Christian estimation what happened at this Pentecost is more momentous and wider reaching than what happened at the first Pentecost at Sinai.

---

no salvific history meaning is supplied for Weeks (Pentecost), but in later rabbinical writings the meaning given above is attested. Thanks to the pre-Christian *Book of Jubilees* and the Dead Sea Scrolls, we now have evidence that this meaning was known in Jesus' time.

[2] A possibility is that the list describes the areas evangelized by missionaries from the Jerusalem church (as distinct from areas evangelized from other centers like Antioch, e.g., through the journeys of Paul). In Acts 2:5 Luke describes the people from these areas as devout Jews, an identification that fits the pilgrimage feast context. Yet in the total context of the book, which describes the gradual extension of the mission from Jews to Gentiles, we may be meant to see here an anticipation that all from these nations (2:17: "all flesh") would be invited and accept. In the language of the letter associated with the chief apostle of the Jerusalem church, a letter addressed to people from areas listed in Acts 2:9-11, those who were once "no people" become God's people (1 Pet 2:10).

Christ in the Gospels of the Liturgical Year

Reaction to the disciples who have received the Spirit speaking in tongues—ecstatic behavior that looks to observers like drunkenness—causes Peter to deliver the first Christian sermon, a sermon that Acts conceives of as the fundamental presentation of the gospel.[3]

PETER'S SERMON (ACTS 2:14-36)
Peter interprets the action of the Spirit at Pentecost as the fulfillment of the signs of the last days foretold by the prophet Joel. In the immediate context the hearers have seen some startling things (and perhaps we are to think not only of the mighty wind and tongues of fire but also of the darkening of the sun at Jesus' death [Luke 23:44]); yet it still required faith to see that Jesus had introduced the last times. That is a message throughout the NT and still a message today. The world around us, even in nominally Christian areas, is less and less inclined to think that Christianity proclaims anything earth-shattering. People relying on physical sight are apt to question whether the coming of Jesus really changed anything in the world since there is still war, oppression, poverty, and suffering. Yet we Christians still believe and proclaim that there are radical new possibilities for life that did not exist before, for "whoever calls on the name of the Lord shall be saved" (Acts 2:21). As Jesus himself did, the first Christian preacher challenges human self-sufficiency with a proclamation of both the need of God's grace and the possibility of receiving it.

Worth noting is the fact that Peter makes this proclamation in what we would call OT terms, thus affirming the basic consistency of what God has done in Jesus Christ with what the God of Israel did for and promised to the people of the covenant. Long centuries after God first called the Hebrew slaves and made them the people of Israel, their self-understanding would be tested as to whether anything had really changed because of that calling, especially when they lost the land

---

[3] In these reflections I do not plan to enter into detailed issues of historicity: Did Peter actually deliver a sermon on Pentecost itself? What did he say? The sermon in Acts is obviously composed by the author of the book, but did he have a tradition about the nucleus of the apostolic preaching? The speaking in tongues should make us cautious in our judgment. At an early level or recounting, it was obviously ecstatic, whence the appearance of drunken babbling. It has been reinterpreted in Acts as speaking in other tongues or languages which are understood—a reinterpretation that has not wiped out the earlier tradition.

The Church Begins in Jerusalem

and were carried off into exile. In other words, they lived through beforehand what has often been the Christian experience in the centuries after Jesus. Both they and we have had to have the vision of faith to see God's realities in and through a history where at times God seems to be absent. In part that is why the OT remains an essential element in Christian proclamation. It covers not only the establishment of the covenant but the attempt to live as God's covenanted people over a millennium of ups and downs. The NT alone covers too short a period of time and is too filled with success to give Christians the lessons the OT gives. For centuries in Roman Catholicism the OT (except for verses from the Psalms) was never read on Sundays, leaving us unfamiliar with what was taught so well there. In the aftermath of Vatican II that defect has been corrected, and yet it is disappointing how seldom the OT readings are the subject of the homily. Preachers turn too easily and quickly to the Gospel readings for their topic, even when the very thing that might most challenge their audience is in the OT passage!

In what follows Peter turns from the (OT) Scriptures to tell what God has done in Jesus: a brief summary of his mighty works, crucifixion, and resurrection, culminating in scriptural evidence that he was the Lord and Messiah (2:36). In a certain sense this concentration on christology represents a change from Jesus' own style as narrated in the first half of Luke-Acts. Although in Luke's Gospel both an angel and God testified that Jesus is the Messiah and the Son of God, and the disciples called him Lord, Jesus did not talk directly about himself. He spoke about God's kingdom and its challenge to accepted values. Nevertheless, Acts confirms the evidence of Paul that early preachers shifted the primary focus of their proclamation to Jesus himself, almost as if they could not announce the kingdom without first telling of him through whom the kingdom was made present. The fundamental gospel became centered on the christological identity of Jesus as Messiah and Son of God (see Rom 1:3-4).

I once wrote an essay suggesting that the sermons in Acts might serve as a guide to certain fundamental aspects that should be included in Christian preaching today.[4] That holds true not only for the already-mentioned insistence on the OT but also for this emphasis on

---

[4] "The Preaching Described in Acts and Early Christian Doctrinal Priorities," reprinted in my *Biblical Exegesis and Church Doctrine* (New York: Paulist, 1985), 135–46.

Christ in the Gospels of the Liturgical Year

christology. There are many things that need to be called to people's attention (morality, social justice, family issues, etc.), but preaching is not really Christian unless it is rooted in Jesus Christ. It is discouraging to hear sermons in Christian churches where, despite the value of the message, Jesus is scarcely mentioned. In Catholic circles this should be kept in mind when preaching the difficult demands of Christian living. Psychologically, as a matter of persuasive procedure, it may not be wise simply to root those demands in authoritative church teaching without going the further step of showing that the church teaching itself is rooted in what the Lord Jesus proclaimed. There are those who will simply shrug off church teaching as a matter of opinion, but would not so easily dismiss the issue if it were shown them that Jesus Christ, the Son of God, was no less exacting than his church.

THE RESPONSE (ACTS 2:37-41)

Having presented this model of Christian preaching, Acts now dramatizes in question and answer form the fundamentals of accepting the gospel. What must be done once people believe the proclamation that God has made the crucified Jesus Lord and Messiah (2:36-37)? Peter states specific requirements and then makes a promise. The first demand is to "repent." In the first half of Luke-Acts the public ministry of Jesus begins with John the Baptist preaching "a baptism of repentance" (Luke 3:3: *metanoia*); Mark 1:4 mentions the baptism of repentance in relation to John, and then (1:14-15) has Jesus come and begin preaching: "Repent and believe in the gospel" (see Luke 5:32). Here, then, Acts is carefully showing continuity between the beginning of the public ministry of Jesus and the beginning of the church, between the first demand of the proclamation of the kingdom and the first demand of apostolic preaching. Literally the Greek verb *metanoein* (*meta* = "across, over"; *noein* = "to think") means "to change one's mind, way of thinking, outlook." The traditional translation, "to repent," indicates the necessity of a change of lifestyle and direction for those who are conscious of being sinners, i.e., of being turned away from God. They must turn around toward God. But the gospel is preached also to religious people who have sought to serve God. A demand to "repent" often will not make an impression on them; they will think of it as a demand for others who are just beginning. Only when it is translated literally as a demand to change one's mind will its offensiveness penetrate. Generally religious people do not like to change their minds, for they already know what God wants. (In recent Catholic life we should remember that the greatest protest about the changes introduced by Vatican Council II came from the most observant Catholics!) If we look at the public ministry, we see that rarely, if at all, was Jesus found offensive by those who are portrayed as sinners. The religious people were the ones who found him offensive, precisely because through his parables and actions he was challenging whether their views really were God's views. Sometimes when I explain this orally, I can see people nodding their heads as they think of certain religious people who need to change their minds. That is too easy: We must be convinced that we need to change as much as those others. Moreover, the summons to "change your minds" because the kingdom of God is at hand, although presented at the beginning of Jesus' ministry and the beginning of the apostolic mission, cannot fully be met by a once-for-all-time response. Many times in our lives we must be willing to change our minds as a new presentation of God's will confronts us. One cannot come to Christ without responding to the challenge, "Change your minds"; one cannot remain alive and fruitful in Christ without responding to the same challenge.[5]

Second, Peter demands, "Be baptized . . . for the forgiveness of your sins" (Acts 2:38b). Although John the Baptist insisted that people receive the baptism of repentance, Jesus did not; in the first three Gospels during his whole ministry he is never shown as baptizing anyone.[6] Forgiveness of sins was through the power of his word. In one way Acts is showing continuity: Jesus' power over sin remains. But now it is exercised through baptism, and so in his second demand Peter goes beyond the pattern of Jesus' lifetime. The time of the church is beginning.

Baptism is looked at in different ways in the different books of the NT, and our theology of baptism represents an amalgamation from

[5] See R. D. Witherup, *Conversion in the New Testament* (Zacchaeus Studies NT; Collegeville, MN: Liturgical Press, 1994).

[6] Once in John (3:22) he is said to baptize, but that is corrected and denied in 4:2. In a post-resurrectional appearance the Matthean Jesus tells the Eleven (the Twelve minus Judas) to make disciples of all nations, baptizing them (Matt 28:19). Not only is there no reason to think that the readers of Acts would have known Matthew's Gospel; but also, as I explained in *A Risen Christ at Eastertime* (above, pp. 218–20), that Matthean scene embodies the retrospective experience of the Matthean community toward the end of the first century.

those different views.[7] (I shall return to that below when I discuss baptism in John 3.) Baptism as a public action is important for our reflection here: Peter is portrayed as asking people to make a visible and verifiable profession of their acceptance of Jesus. This is tantamount to asking people to "join up." For someone who would eventually be compared, rightly or wrongly, to other founders of religions, Jesus was remarkably "unorganizational." True, he is reported as calling a few people (particularly the Twelve) to leave their work and follow him, but otherwise he seems to have been content to leave without follow-up those who encountered him and were visibly moved by what he did and said. He does not try to organize them or put specific continuing demands on them. The Gospels tell us with vague generalization that they went back to their towns and villages and reported enthusiastically what they had seen and heard. But there is no evidence of their forming "Jesus groups" in his lifetime. After the resurrection, however, his followers show an instinct to gather and hold together those whom they convince about Jesus; and their demanding an identifying sign like baptism is the first step in that process of gathering. Indeed, we have little evidence in early Christian missionary endeavor of people being free to say, "I now believe in Jesus," and then walking off on their own—they are made part of a community. This is important theologically. Peter is telling people that they can be saved, but not simply as individuals. The basic Israelite concept is that God chose to save *a people*, and the renewal of the covenant on Pentecost has not changed that. There is a collective aspect to salvation, and one is saved as part of God's people. The importance of the church is a direct derivative from the importance of Israel.

Once again Acts is almost prescient in anticipating what should be part of our understanding of Christian essentials today. We all know that there is a division among Christian churches. Yet there may be a more dangerous division among Christians. I have often thought that in the twenty-first century the deepest chasm experienced in Christianity may be between those who, although they worship in various churches, think "church" is important, and those for whom Christianity is really

---

[7] We must recognize that the first Christians did not understand from the very beginning all the implications of what they believed and did, and the different books of the NT often show different stages of understanding.

The Church Begins in Jerusalem

281

a matter of "Jesus and me," without any concept of being saved as part of a people or church.

Third, Peter specifies that baptism must be "in the name of Jesus Christ." The fact that John the Baptist baptized and that Jesus himself was baptized by John was surely an important factor in moving the followers of Jesus to insist on baptism; yet Acts 18:24–19:7 contends that there was a clear distinction between the baptism of John and baptism "in the name of the Lord Jesus" (19:5). We are not certain about procedures in the earliest Christian baptism; but most likely "in the name of" means that the one being baptized confessed who Jesus was (and in that sense spoke his name),[8] e.g., "Jesus is Lord"; "Jesus is the Messiah (Christ)"; "Jesus is the Son of God"; "Jesus is the Son of Man."[9] Such baptismal confessions would explain why titles were so commonly applied to Jesus in the NT. From the very beginning the identity of Jesus' followers was established by what they believed and professed about Jesus. (Our later creeds are an enlarged expression of the faith expressed at baptism.) This was a startling difference from Judaism; for although one could call Jews "disciples of Moses" (John 9:28), no one would ever think of defining them by what they believed about the personal identity of Moses. The need to give expression to the centrality of Jesus in the new covenant made Christianity a creedal religion in a manner dissimilar to Judaism.

Here again I see Acts giving us valuable guidance about Christian fundamentals. I have often thought it would be a fascinating exercise some Sunday to ask everyone in church to write on a slip of paper one sentence explaining what a Christian is. My suspicion is that many of the responses would consist of behavioral descriptions, e.g., a Christian is one who practices love of neighbor. True, one cannot be much of a Christian without behaving as Jesus taught, but behavior is not

---

[8] This early, of course, we are not reading about infant baptism; and so it is less likely that the person conducting the baptism had to say the formula over the persons being baptized: They could speak for themselves. As I explained in *A Risen Christ at Eastertime*, the use of the triadic formula in Matthew 28:19 would have been a later development giving a fuller picture of God's plan of salvation.

[9] John 9:35-38 may be echoing a baptismal ceremony in that church: a question from the baptizer, "Do you believe in the Son of Man?"; a responding question from the one to be baptized, "Who is he that I may believe?"; a response from the baptizer "Jesus"; a response from the one who is to be baptized, "Lord, I believe"; and then an act of worship.

Christ in the Gospels of the Liturgical Year

sufficiently defining: Christians are not the only ones who exhibit love toward each other. It would be fascinating to know how many would answer that a Christian is one who believes that Jesus is the Christ. That, of course, is both the most ancient and basic definition. We may well need to reiterate today what seemed so obvious to our original ancestors in the faith.

Fourth, after spelling out the demands on those who believe in Jesus, in 2:38-39 Peter makes a promise: "You shall receive the gift of the Holy Spirit, for the promise is . . . to as many as the Lord God calls." (The last clause reminds us that although there is a challenge to the hearers to change their lives, the priority in conversion belongs to God.[10]) Peter and his companions have received the Holy Spirit, and now they promise that the same Holy Spirit will be given to all believers. In terms of the fundamentals of Christian life there will be no second-class citizens, and the same equality in receiving the gift of the Spirit will prove true when the first Gentiles are baptized (Acts 10:44-48). That there was no privileged class in what really mattered was an enormously attractive factor in evangelizing, and even in today's church it is worth emphasizing. Inevitably when the church received more structure, different roles were assigned to individuals; and some were ordained, i.e., put in a certain order. Such specialization, necessary as it was, has produced envy and bickering in the church. We can see that already in 1 Corinthians 12. Some are apostles, some are prophets, some are teachers, etc.; and in order to overcome the fact that those who have one gift envy those who have another, Paul has to stress that these are all gifts of one and the same Spirit, meant to build up the one body into which all are baptized. The same holds true today when we bicker over who can hold which roles in the church. These roles may be visibly important in terms of public prestige and even power. But we need to be reminded that they all pale when compared to the basic gift given to all: baptism and the Holy Spirit. When we stand before the throne of God and church offices are no more, our dignity will depend on the extent to which we have remained faithful to our common baptismal calling and have lived by the one Spirit given to all.

---

[10] Acts 2:40 is sometimes translated, "Save yourselves from this crooked generation"; but from a theological viewpoint the passive is better rendered literally: "Be saved." People cannot save themselves; they can respond to God's saving grace.

The Church Begins in Jerusalem

Chapter 29

The Jerusalem Church of One Mind
(Acts 2:42–5:42)

Acts has told us that many of those who heard Peter's sermons met his demands and were baptized (about three thousand people!). Now the author turns to describe how they lived. The memories he reports are highly selective, so that we have as much a theology of the early church as a history. First, he summarizes under four headings the relations of Christians[1] with one another (2:42-47) and then, in a continuous narrative highlighting Peter and John, their relations to others (3:1–5:42). Historically the setting would be the first years in Jerusalem, from Jesus' death and resurrection (A.D. 30 or 33) until about 36—a period that, surely with idealization, he describes as the time when the believers were of one mind (1:14; 2:46; 4:24; 5:12). Liturgically, six readings from this section of Acts are found in the different cycles of the Second, Third, and Fourth Sundays of Easter, and nine consecutive readings constitute pericopes on weekdays of the First and Second Week of Easter.

FOUR CHARACTERISTICS SUMMARIZING RELATIONS
AMONG BELIEVERS (ACTS 2:42-47)

One of the notable marks of Acts, especially in the first part, is to give brief summaries of the early Christian situation, generalizing what is happening. The present section constitutes an admirable summary of how ideally the first believers in Jesus related to one another. Singled

---

[1] I am aware that throughout these early chapters of Acts, which treat of immediately post-resurrectional Jerusalem, to speak of Christians or Christianity is an anachronism; no designation had as yet been found for those who believed in Jesus. If the author of Acts is historically correct, it was at Antioch (seemingly in the late 30s) that the believers were first called Christians. Yet having noted that, for the sake of simplicity I shall anticipate the terminology.

out are four features[2] that I shall treat in this order: *koinōnia*, prayers, breaking of the bread, and apostles' teaching.

Koinōnia (Fellowship, Communion). In chapter 28 above, I pointed out that, although in his public ministry Jesus showed little interest in a formally distinct society, his followers by introducing baptism showed a remarkable drive toward having believers "join up." Those who believed belonged to a group. The wide distribution in the NT of the term *koinōnia* (related to *koinos*, "common" as in Koinē Greek), shows that those who were baptized felt strongly that they had much in common. Sometimes it is translated as "fellowship," although that is a rather weak term. More literally it is "communion," i.e., the spirit that binds people together, or "community," i.e., the grouping produced by that spirit. Indeed, *koinōnia* may reflect in Greek an early Semitic name for the Jewish group of believers in Jesus, comparable to the self-designation of the Jewish Dead Sea Scrolls group as the *Yahad*, "the oneness, unity."[3]

An important aspect of the *koinōnia* described in Acts 2:44-47; 5:1-11 is voluntary sharing of goods among the members of the community. While the idealism of Acts probably exaggerates in referring to "all goods," the fact that there were common goods among the Dead Sea Scrolls group shows that a picture of sharing is plausible for a Jewish group convinced that the last times had begun and that this world's

---

[2] The selection is made from the later vantage point of the author: features that have been the most important and enduring. There is an idealization, not in the crude sense of creating a fictional picture, but in holding up the primitive community as embodying what a Christian community should be. In the first five chapters of Acts equal time is not given to the problems and faults of the Jerusalem community.

[3] Another early name may have been "the Way," e.g., Acts 24:14: "According to the Way . . . I worship the God of our Fathers" (also Acts 9:2; 19:9, 23; 22:4; 24:22). This was also a Dead Sea Scrolls self-designation: "When these people join the community (*Yahad*), they . . . go into the wilderness to prepare the way of the Lord." This reflects the idealism of the return of Israel from exile (Isa 40:3), when Israel came along the way prepared by God to the Promised Land. The designation that became the most popular, i.e., *ekklēsia*, "church," plausibly reflects the first exodus in which Israel came into being, for in Deuteronomy 23:2 the Greek OT rendered *qāhāl*, "assembly," by *ekklēsia* to describe Israel in the desert as "the church of the Lord."

The Jerusalem Church of One Mind

wealth has lost its meaning.[4] Sharing goods and livelihood bind people together closely—a person really makes a commitment when he or she puts funds into a common bank account with someone else. Part of the goal of the Jerusalem community's sharing was that there might be no members who were totally impoverished. The actual result, however, may have been that most of the community were relatively poor. Paul refers several times to the poor (Christians) in Jerusalem for whom he was collecting money (Rom 15:26; Gal 2:10; 1 Cor 16:1-3). The willingness of Gentiles in distant churches to share some of their wealth with the Jewish Christians in Jerusalem was for Paul a tangible proof of the *koinōnia* that bound Christians together.

Of course, *koinōnia* was a wider concept than the sharing of goods; it involved common faith and common salvation. How intrinsic it was to Christianity is exemplified in Galatians 2:9 where Paul deems the outcome of the discussion in Jerusalem *ca.* A.D. 49 about the fate of the Gentile churches to have been a great success because at the end the leaders of the Jerusalem church gave to him and Barnabas the right hand of *koinōnia*. For Paul it would have been against the very notion of the one Lord and the one Spirit if the *koinōnia* between the Jewish and the Gentile churches had been broken. Only toward the end of the NT period do we get clear evidence that the Christian *koinōnia* has been broken. The author of 1 John sees the necessity of having *koinōnia* "with us" in order to have *koinōnia* with the Father and the Holy Spirit, and he considers "those who went out from us" to be the antichrists (1:3; 2:18-19).

As with other aspects of Acts' portrayal of the early church, the notion of *koinōnia* needs emphasis in our time. There is, first of all, the great scandal of Christians living in churches that have broken *koinōnia* with each other; and the whole purpose of ecumenism is to see if we can regain that communion. And a more immediate scandal is our sudden tendency within Roman Catholicism to break the

---

[4] More than other Gospels Luke is insistent that wealth is an obstacle to the acceptance of Jesus' standards and that the rich are endangered (1:53; 6:24; 12:20-21; 16:22-23). Sometimes it is contended that Luke has deeschatologized Christianity in the sense that he has recognized that Christians do not know the times or seasons for the final intervention of God's rule/kingdom (Acts 1:7). That does not mean that he has given up his hope for the second coming or lost his estimation of values consonant with a theology in which this world is not a lasting entity.

Christ in the Gospels of the Liturgical Year

koinōnia. For centuries after the sixteenth-century Reformation we took pride (somewhat gloatingly) in the fact that Catholics were united while the Protestant churches seemed to splinter over and over again. Yet now after the twentieth-century self-reformation at Vatican II, we are splintering. On the ultraconservative extreme there is the movement of Archbishop Lefebvre which is convinced that it is remaining faithful to the church by breaking from the Bishop of Rome. On the liberal extreme there are small conventicles attempting to celebrate the eucharist without ordained clergy, thinking they are reduplicating the life of the early communities. Often this is justified by the claim "We are the church" (probably with the supposition that the clergy or hierarchy are claiming to be the church). Should not all Catholic Christians recognize that they can claim no more than that they are *part* of the church—part of a much larger *koinōnia* that includes the presiding presence of the bishop[5] (and for the whole church, the presiding presence of the Bishop of Rome)? Breaking from that *koinōnia* is scarcely reduplicating the values of the early church.

Prayers. Praying for each other was another aspect of *koinōnia*, and the Pauline letters bear eloquent testimony to his constant prayer for the communities he founded. Here, since we are considering the description of the first Christians in Acts, it might be fruitful to reflect on what kind of prayer forms were used by those Jews who came to believe in Jesus. Of course, since they did not cease to be Jewish in their worship, they continued to say prayers that they had known previously. When Mark wrote, the primacy of the basic Jewish confession, the *Shema* ("Hear, O Israel, the Lord our God, the Lord is one"), was still being inculcated even for Gentiles (12:29). I share the view of many scholars that the hymns of the Lucan infancy narrative, the Magnificat, the Benedictus, the Gloria, and the Nunc Dimittis, were early Christian compositions that Luke took over and adapted in placing them on the lips of the first characters of his Gospel. Like the Jewish hymns of this time (as exemplified in the Books of the Maccabees and the Dead Sea

---

[5] At the beginning of the second century Ignatius of Antioch is an eloquent exponent of this: "Make sure that no step affecting the church is ever taken without the bishop" (*Smyrnaeans* 8:1); "I must count you blessed who are united with your bishop, just as the church is united with Jesus Christ" (*Ephesians* 5:1); "You must never act independently of your bishop and presbyters" (*Magnesians* 7:1).

The Jerusalem Church of One Mind

Scrolls) they are a pastiche of OT echoes. They celebrate what God has done in Jesus; yet they are not christological in the sense of giving details from the life of Jesus. (Contrast the hymns of Phil 2:6-11; Col 1:15-20; John 1:1-18.) The Benedictus is a marvelous example: Something tremendous has happened; but it is described in terms of Abraham, David, the biblical ancestors, and the prophets.[6]

In addition to these common Jewish prayer patterns the early Christians adopted Jesus' own prayer style, still visible in the Lord's Prayer which is preserved in different forms in Matthew 6:9-13 and Luke 11:2-4; but, of course, some petitions of the Lord's Prayer echo petitions of synagogue prayers. It is important to notice the eschatological tone of that prayer which asks the heavenly Father to cause the divine name to be praised (hallowed), to bring about the kingdom, and to make the divine will all-effective on earth—in other words, which asks God to bring in the endtime. Then the prayer turns to the share of the Christians in the endtime: to be forgiven in the judgment, not to be led into the fearsome trial, and to escape the power of the Evil One.[7] This eschatological tone of Christian prayer is intimately linked to a fervent expectation that Christ would come again soon. A very ancient Christian prayer transcribed from Aramaic, *Maranatha*, "Our Lord, come," has the same tone and is more specifically christological. And indeed inevitably Christian prayer did center on recalling and praising what Jesus had done, a development one is tempted to associate with the increasing Christian awareness of distinctiveness from other Jews.

Breaking Bread. Acts portrays early Christians like Peter and John going frequently, or even daily, to the Temple to pray at the regular hours (2:46; 3:1; 5:12, 21, 42). This implies that the first Jews who believed in Jesus saw no rupture in their ordinary worship pattern. The "breaking of bread" (presumably the eucharist) would, then, have been in addition to and not in place of the sacrifices and worship of

---

[6] In my judgment 1:76-77 represents Luke's adaptation to the context.

[7] See "The Pater Noster as an Eschatological Prayer" in my *New Testament Essays* (New York: Paulist, 1982 reprint), 217–53, for the idea that *peirasmos* originally referred to the trial of the endtime (not simply to daily temptation), and for the fact that *epiousios*, the word that most often has been translated as "daily," may not mean that.

Christ in the Gospels of the Liturgical Year

Israel. Notice the sequence in 2:46: "Day by day attending the Temple together and breaking bread in their homes." How did the first Christians interpret the eucharist? Paul, writing in the mid-50s (1 Cor 11:23-26), mentions a eucharistic pattern that was handed on to him (presumably, therefore, from the 30s) and says, "As often as you eat this bread and drink this cup, you proclaim the Lord's death until he comes." The recalling of the Lord's death *may* echo the Jewish pattern of Passover re-presentation (Hebrew: *zikkārôn*; Greek: *anamnēsis*), making present again the great salvific act, now shifted from the exodus to the crucifixion/resurrection. The "until he comes" reflects the eschatological outlook we saw above in the Lord's Prayer and *Maranatha*. Attached, however, to a sacred meal it may have a special Jewish background. In the Dead Sea Scrolls community there was left vacant at the sacred repast a place for the Messiah in case God should raise him up during the meal. The thought that Jesus would come back at the celebration of the eucharist may be related to the tradition that the risen Jesus showed himself present at meals (Luke 24:30, 41; John 21:9-13; Mark 16:14), so that his disciples recognized him in the breaking of the bread (Luke 24:35). As we reflect on these different details, we can find the background of much of the later theology of the eucharist, e.g., the celebration of the eucharist as a sacrifice can be related to recalling the death of the Lord, and the concept of the real presence of Christ in the eucharist can be related to believing that the risen Lord appeared at meals and would return again at the sacred meal.

A Jewish pattern may also have affected the Christian choice of a time for eating the eucharistic meal. Undoubtedly, the discovery of the empty tomb early Sunday morning helped to fix Christian attention on what by the end of the first century would be known as "the Lord's Day." Yet the choice of Sunday may have also been facilitated by the pattern of the Jewish Sabbath which ended at sundown on Saturday. Before sundown Jews who believed in Jesus did not have extensive freedom of movement; but when the Sabbath was over (Saturday evening), they would have been free to come from a distance to assemble in the house of another believer to break the bread. This may explain why the ancient Christian memory is of a celebration on the night between Saturday and Sunday. Such a eucharistic assembly would be a major manifestation of *koinōnia* and eventually help to make Christians feel distinct from other Jews.

The Jerusalem Church of One Mind

Teaching of the Apostles. Authoritative for all Jews were the Scriptures, in particular the Law and the Prophets; this would have been true for the first followers of Jesus as well. Thus, early Christian teaching would for the most part have been Jewish teaching.[8] Points where Jesus modified or differed from the Law or from the Pharisee interpretation of the Law were remembered and became the nucleus of a special teaching. As they passed this on, the Christian preachers would have made their own application to situations that Jesus had not encountered; and the content stemming from Jesus in the teaching would have been expanded by apostolic teaching. (See the example of two instructions on marriage and divorce, one from the Lord and one from Paul, in 1 Cor 7:10, 12.) This teaching of Jesus and of the apostles, while secondary to the teaching of the Jewish Scriptures, was more authoritative in regard to the specific points it touched. When such teaching was committed to writing, these writings had within themselves the possibility of becoming a second set of Scriptures (the NT).[9] An understanding of the dynamics of distinctive Christian thought is very useful today as we seek to emphasize that the OT (i.e., the Law and the Prophets) is not simply an interesting prelude to the really important NT, but the basic presupposition of the NT with which we must be familiar to be fully Christian. In reflecting on the four characteristics of relations among Christians that Acts mentions, I have emphasized two aspects of the picture: continuity with Judaism, and the distinctive features that marked off the community of Jews who believed in Jesus from the rest of Jews. These aspects were in tension, pulling in opposite directions: The first held the Christians close to their fellow Jews who met in the synagogues; the second gave to the

---

[8] This fact is sometimes overlooked by those who search out NT theology or ethics. The points of unique importance mentioned in the NT are like the tip of the iceberg, the bulk of which is the unmentioned, presupposed teaching of Israel.

[9] The gathering of writings was a part of the canon-forming process particularly active in the late second century. During the same period a somewhat similar process within rabbinic Judaism produced the Mishna, a second set of teachings alongside the Scriptures. Thus by the end of the second century both those who believed in Jesus and the Jews who did not had written authoritative supplements to the Law and the Prophets. The different character of the two writings (one a collection of stories about Jesus and the early church, letters to the churches, and an apocalypse; the other a collection of legal interpretations) reflects essential differences in the respective religious focuses.

Christ in the Gospels of the Liturgical Year

Christian *koinōnia* identity and the potentiality of self-sufficiency. External factors of rejection and reaction, however, would have to take place before Christians would constitute a distinguishably separate religious group, and that development will be the subject of later chapters of Acts. Before that we should consider three chapters in which Acts describes the earliest interactions of those who now believed in Jesus with their fellow Jews.

NARRATIVES HIGHLIGHTING THE RELATIONS OF EARLY CHRISTIANS TO OTHERS (ACTS 3:1–5:42)
In these chapters Acts will use the actions of Peter and John to focus narratives that involve the first Jewish believers in Jesus with their Jerusalem neighbors who do not share that belief, a relationship that will produce more conversions and much opposition.

Acts 3:1-26: A Healing and the Preaching that Follows. In 2:43 Acts mentions in passing that many wonders and signs were done through the apostles; in 2:46 it was said that day by day they attended the Temple together. Those summary statements were meant to prepare the way for the account in 3:1-10 of the healing that takes place when Peter and John go up to the Temple. The story is told with a real sense of drama. The lapidary statement of Peter catches the spirit of the Christian self-understanding that what we have to offer is different from what the world, even at its best, can give: "Silver and gold I have none, but what I have, I give you: In the name of Jesus Christ of Nazareth, walk." Luke's Gospel showed Jesus beginning his ministry by manifesting the healing power of God's rule (kingdom) to the amazement of all (4:31-37); Acts has the clear intention of showing that Peter and the apostles carried on the same work with the same power. The healing is "in the name of Jesus Christ of Nazareth," i.e., worked through the power of the heavenly Christ, not through any self-sufficiency of the apostles. And yet there is more in this reference to "the name" than we may first notice. We have heard that believers had to be baptized "in the name of Jesus." To know a person's name is to know his identity; to know that Jesus is the Messiah, the Lord, the Son of God is to know his christological identity. There is power in the knowledge of that name (christological identity), and faith in it opens access to that power: "By faith in his name, his name has made this [lame] man strong" (Acts 3:16). Respect for the personal name of God

The Jerusalem Church of One Mind

(YHWH or Yahweh) and the awesome power it possessed caused Jews not to mention it publicly. (In Jewish legend when the Pharaoh kept questioning Moses as to who was this God who demanded that the people be let go, the exasperated Moses finally used the name of God; and the Pharaoh was struck to the ground.[10]) Christians developed a similar awe for the name given to Jesus, as we see in Philippians 2:9-11: "Therefore God has highly exalted him and graciously bestowed on him the name that is above every other name, so that at the name possessed by Jesus every knee should bow in heaven, on earth, and under the earth, and every tongue confess that Jesus Christ is Lord."

The Lucan account of Jesus' ministry combined his healings and his words; here in a similar pattern Peter's healing is followed by a sermon (Acts 3:11-26). The author idealizes the situation by speaking of those who see and hear as "all the people" (3:9) or "the people" (3:12). This sermon is presented as an embodiment of how preachers presented Jesus to Jews. As with Peter's sermon on Pentecost, it amalgamates OT echoes and what God has done in Jesus. If the Pentecost sermon began its challenge with the prophecy of Joel that was seen to be fulfilled in what was happening, this sermon will terminate (3:22-26) with a challenge based on the promise of Moses in Deuteronomy 18:15-19 that God would raise up a prophet like him who must be listened to. In 3:19 the demand to "repent" or "change one's mind" (*metanoein*) appears once more, but now there is greater specification. The Jews of Jerusalem delivered up and denied Jesus the servant of God in the presence of Pilate who had decided to release him (3:13); they denied the Holy and Just One and asked for a murderer (3:14: Barabbas). Yet they acted in ignorance as did their rulers,[11] and accordingly they are being offered this chance to change. Ours is a time when because of past tragedies we are trying to learn not to generalize

---

[10] In anti-Christian Jewish polemical stories in circulation by the end of the second century, the (evil) power of Jesus was attributed to the fact that he had gone to Egypt, learned magic, and had the divine name sewn into his thigh.

[11] The language of Acts echoes the Lucan account of the passion: There Pilate could find no guilt in Jesus and wanted to release him (Luke 23:4, 14-15, 20-22); Barabbas was said to have committed murder (23:19, 25); the centurion confessed Jesus to be just (23:47); and Jesus prayed for those who crucify him, "Father, forgive them; for they know not what they do" (23:34a). In my *The Death of the Messiah* (2 vols.; New York: Doubleday, 1994), 2.§40, I argue that 23:34a, although missing from many manuscripts of Luke, is more likely genuine.

Christ in the Gospels of the Liturgical Year

responsibility for evil actions, and so it is painful to see in the NT the generalizing of Jewish responsibility for the execution of Jesus (here literally: "men [*andres*] of Israel"; Matt 27:25: "all the people"; 1 Thess 2:14-15: "the Jews who killed both the Lord Jesus and the prophets"). Luke-Acts, at least, shows some sensibilities on the subject by showing that not all the people were against Jesus (Luke 23:27, 48) and that those who were did not consciously choose to do something evil (also Acts 13:27).[12] In face of the apostolic preaching, however, ignorance is no longer an excuse, and change of mind/heart is necessary if they are to receive Jesus as the Messiah when he is sent back from heaven (Acts 3:19-21). The story that follows will maintain that many of the people did change, but most of the Jewish leaders did not. In the late 50s Paul confidently foresaw that the salvation that had come to the Gentiles would make those who went by the name Israel jealous and ultimately lead to their full inclusion (Rom 11:11-12). By the time Acts was written (80s or 90s of the first century?), the situation had hardened. Acts will end its story in Rome with the very harsh judgment that, as Isaiah foretold, this people will never hear or understand, and therefore the salvation wrought by God in Christ has been sent to the Gentiles who will listen (28:25-29). Of course, the author of Acts did not mean that from this moment on Christians would no longer receive into the church Jews who came to believe in Christ, but he no longer expected the mission to the Jews to bear much fruit.

Acts 4:1-31: The Antagonism of the Sanhedrin and the Apostolic Refusal to Yield. The apostolic preaching and its success (4:4: five thousand) is portrayed as stirring up the wrath of the priests and the Sadducees who arrest Peter and John. Jesus' own attitude toward resurrection had aroused the opposition of the Sadducees "who say there is no resurrection" (Luke 20:27-38), and so Acts is once more creating a parallelism between Jesus and the apostles in having the Sadducees disturbed that Peter and John have been proclaiming in Jesus the resurrection from the dead (Acts 4:2). A meeting of the Sanhedrin consisting of rulers, elders, scribes, and chief priests is convened against them (4:5-6), just as a Sanhedrin of the elders of the people, and chief priests and scribes was convened against Jesus (Luke 22:66). (In neither

---

[12] Notice also the thesis in Romans 10:3 that it was out of ignorance that Israel according to the flesh did not submit to God's righteousness in Christ.

The Jerusalem Church of One Mind

case are the Pharisees mentioned as having been directly involved, and that may be historical.) They focus on the miracle, demanding, "By what name did you do this?"—a question that prepares for the response of Peter emphasizing anew what we have already heard: "by the name of Jesus Christ of Nazareth whom you crucified, whom God raised from the dead. . . . There is no other name under heaven given to the human race by which we must be saved" (Acts 4:10, 12).

Luke did not report in his Gospel the annoyed wonderment of the people of Nazareth that Jesus, who was only a carpenter, could teach wisely (Mark 6:1-3). That omission may have been prompted by Luke's attested reluctance to report what was derogatory of Jesus. By way of compensation Acts 4:13 reports the annoyed wonderment of the authorities at the boldness of the religious proclamation of the apostles who were not formally educated in religious matters or the Law of Moses.[13] Trapped by the clear factuality of the healing that had been performed, the Sanhedrin authorities blusteringly cut short any debate by arbitrarily ordering Peter and John not to speak in the name of Jesus (4:18). This prepares for an unforgettably defiant response of Peter (4:19-20). Less than two months before, Peter in the high priest's house had denied Jesus three times; now before a battery of chief priests he cannot be silent about Christ. Among the Gospels Luke alone (22:31-32) had Jesus pray that, although Satan desired to sift Peter and the others like wheat, his faith would not fail and he would turn and strengthen his brethren. Here we see the prayer fulfilled as Peter and John emerge unyielding from the Sanhedrin to report to their fellow believers what has happened—a report that consists of a triumphal prayer of praise to God (Acts 4:24-30) comparing the forces that had been aligned in Jerusalem against Jesus (Herod and Pilate, the Gentiles and the "peoples" of Israel) to the forces now uttering threats against his followers. In a literary flourish this prayer is described as shaking the place where they are. They are all filled with the Holy Spirit and, thus strengthened, proceed to speak the word of God with boldness (4:31). Matthew (27:51; 28:2) had the earth quake as a manifestation of supportive divine power when Jesus died and rose; Acts has it quake as the Holy Spirit manifests God's supporting presence in the commu-

---

[13] Through the centuries many have used the reference in Acts 4:13 to the apostles as being untrained in letters to portray them as illiterate. That is unnecessary.

Christ in the Gospels of the Liturgical Year

nity of believers. Peter's catalyzing role in this fulfills Jesus' promise to him in Luke 22:32.

Acts 4:32–5:11: Another Description of the Relations among Believers. After Peter's initial sermon on Pentecost to the Jerusalem populace, Acts (2:41-47) stopped to summarize how those who listened and believed related to one another as a community. Now again (4:32-35), as a demonstration that they were of one heart and soul, we are given a summary description emphasizing some of the same features, especially that they held things in common (*koinos*). This time, however, the summary is followed by two examples. The first involves Joseph, surnamed by the apostles Barnabas, who sold a field and brought the money to the apostles to contribute to the common fund. Besides exemplifying positively the spirit of *koinōnia*, this reference prepares for future narrative. Barnabas is a Levite, and Acts 6:7 will tell us that many priests came to believe; thus the faith would make its way even among those most opposed to Jesus. Moreover, Barnabas is from Cyprus; and when later at Antioch he becomes a missionary with Paul, they will first go to Cyprus (13:1-4).

The other example, involving Ananias and Sapphira (5:1-11), is negative and illustrates divine punishment of those who violated the purity of the early community. It does not constitute a reading in the Easter season, perhaps a tacit recognition that God's striking people dead is too chilling for modern religious sensibilities. Yet no story illustrates better the Israelite mentality of the early believers. The Twelve were meant to sit on thrones judging the tribes of Israel (Luke 22:30); here judgment is exercised on the renewed Israel through Peter. In the OT (Josh 7) Israel's attempt to enter victoriously beyond Jericho into the heart of the Promised Land was frustrated because Achan had secretly hidden for himself goods that were to be dedicated to God. His deception caused God to judge that Israel had sinned and needed purification, for the people had to be perfect. Only when Achan was put to death and his goods burned could Israel proceed as the people of God. So also the renewed Israel has been profaned by the deceptive holding back of goods which were claimed to have been contributed to the common fund. Satan entered into Judas, one of the Twelve, to give Jesus over (Luke 22:3-4); and now he has entered into the heart of Ananias, a believer in Jesus, to be deceptive in relation to the Holy Spirit that has brought this community of believers into being (Acts 5:3). Such impurity must be eradicated, and that can be accomplished only

The Jerusalem Church of One Mind

by the judgment of Peter which brings about the fatal action of God. (We are very close here to an early understanding of the power to bind and to loose!) It is in describing the fear produced by this intervention that Acts uses the term "church" for the first time (5:11). Obviously the author does not think that such an act of judgment is alien to the nature of the church. We might wonder how he would react to the church's omission of the reading in an Eastertime lectionary that contains all the surrounding passages.

Acts 5:12-42: The Second Confrontation with the Sanhedrin. The author of Luke-Acts likes to pair passages symmetrically in order to convey the intensification of an issue, and that is true in this second confrontation of the apostles with the Sanhedrin. No longer one healing, but many signs and wonders are involved. People even from the surrounding villages begin to bring their sick to be cured by the apostles, especially by Peter. Once again the high priests and the Sadducees have the apostles arrested but are frustrated when an angel of the Lord releases them so that they return to the Temple—a release all the more ironical because the Sadducees do not believe in angels. Thus the Sanhedrin session called to discuss the apostles has to have them arrested again. As with the arrest of Jesus (Luke 22:6) care has to be taken not to arouse the people (Acts 5:26). When the high priest indignantly recalls that the apostles had been charged not to teach in Jesus' name, again Peter expresses his defiance with a memorable line: "We must obey God rather than human beings" and then gives a christological sermon as though he hoped to convert the Sanhedrin (Acts 5:30-32). The infuriation reaches the point of wanting to kill the apostles (5:33), when the Pharisee Gamaliel I intervenes. Scholars have debated endlessly whether this part of the scene is historical.[14] At least it does not lack chronological verisimilitude, for the great Gamaliel lived in Jerusalem at this time. Far more important, however, is the place of the scene in the Lucan storyline. Acts has not mentioned Pharisees as opposed to the followers of Jesus; and now it has Gamaliel the Pharisee advocating tolerance for them. Later (23:6-9) Acts will have

---

[14] There are anachronisms in Gamaliel's speech, e.g., he mentions Theudas' revolt and "after him Judas the Galilean." If this Sanhedrin session took place around A.D. 36, Theudas' revolt had not yet taken place, and Judas' revolt had taken place thirty years before.

the Pharisees supporting tolerance for Paul over against the Sadducees. Reference to Gamaliel is harmonious in another way, for Acts (22:3) will present Paul as having studied with this great teacher of the Law who here is depicted as a fair-minded man. Offering examples of other movements that failed, Gamaliel summarizes the situation, "If this work be from human beings, it will fail; if it is from God, you will not be able to overthrow it."[15] (It may not be true that every religious movement that is of human origin fails; nevertheless, the church would have been wiser many times in its history if it had used Gamaliel's principle to judge new developments in Christianity rather than reacting in a hostile manner too quickly.) Gamaliel's advice carries the day. Although the apostles are beaten, they are let go; and tacitly the Sanhedrin adopts the policy of leaving them alone as they continue every day to preach Christ publicly and privately (5:42).

Brief Reflections on John 3 and John 6

As explained in chapter 27 above, I do not plan to comment on the passages from John in themselves, but only as they are related to the Acts readings in the Easter season. Acts describes the external or visible history of early Christian life. Working through Jesus' words, John gives a theological insight into the internal relations of Christians to Jesus. In the liturgical weeks when the Acts readings discussed in chapters 28 and 29 are being read on weekdays, the Gospel selections are from John 3 and John 6.[16] In Acts we heard Peter's challenge to those who would be the first Christians, a challenge to be baptized and receive the Holy Spirit. In the description of their lives as a community we heard of the breaking of the bread as part of the koinōnia that held them together. It is no accident that the accompanying readings from John 3 deal with being born again of water and Spirit, and those from John 6 deal with eating the bread of life. Acts plays out its story against the background of opposition from the chief priests and the members of the Sanhedrin. John 3 consists largely of a dialogue with

---

[15] Acts 23:6-9 will show Pharisees siding with the Christian position on resurrection against the Sadducees, but that is not offered by Gamaliel in the present situation as the reason for toleration.

[16] The selections from John 6 overlap into the Third Week of Easter.

Nicodemus, a member of the Sanhedrin who does not understand Jesus; John 6, set in a synagogue, involves a debate over Scripture with Jews who think Jesus' claims are impossible.

John 3. This first great dialogue/discourse in John deals with the most basic gift that the Son of Man has brought from heaven to earth, eternal life.[17] The opening verses are the only reference in John to "the kingdom of God," which is a central theme of Jesus throughout the Synoptic Gospels. John immediately translates that motif into the language of eternal life which is a central theme in the Fourth Gospel. This simple and yet profound image is based on the all-important fact that Jesus is God's only, unique Son, a dignity never possessed by anyone before or after. In particular Jesus is compared to Moses who, after going up the mountain to speak with God, came down to reveal God's will. Jesus as God's Son was already with God and had only to come down to reveal. A human parent possesses earthly life (a life that ends in death); God has eternal life. Human beings receive earthly life from their parents; Jesus, as God's Son, has eternal life from the heavenly Father. As the Word-become-flesh, he and he alone can give this eternal life to those whose human life he shares. Those who believe in him receive it.

To Nicodemus who approaches him as a teacher from God[18] Jesus explains how this takes place. For eternal life even as for earthly life begetting or birth is necessary, yet from God above, not from earthly parents. This is a radical challenge to the Judaism of which Nicodemus is a leading representative, a Judaism for which membership in the

---

[17] To understand the uniqueness of John among the Gospels it is necessary to recognize that the others never refer to a previous life that the Son shared with the Father; they are never specific about an incarnation. Whereas for them Jesus is the Son of Man during his earthly ministry and will come back from heaven as the Son of Man at the end of time, for John Jesus on earth has already come from heaven as the Son of Man. Please note: I am not saying that the first three evangelists deny or would deny an incarnation, but simply that there is nothing in their writings that shows they were aware of it. An awareness is found, however, in other non-Gospel passages in the NT (Philippians [probably]; Colossians; Hebrews).

[18] He thinks Jesus has been raised up by God whereas Jesus has actually come from God. A commentary on the Gospel will explain the many plays on Greek words in this passage, e.g., the same word means "begetting by" (a father) and "born from" (a mother); the same word means "again" and "from above"; the same word means "wind" and "spirit."

chosen people of God comes from birth from a Jewish mother. To that Jesus responds that flesh begets only flesh, so that the identity or status of one's earthly parents makes no difference whatsoever so far as relationship to God is concerned—it takes the Spirit to beget spirit. And so begetting/birth from God above is a begetting/birth of water and Spirit.

In discussing baptism in Acts, I commented that there are many different NT theologies of baptism. John sees it as a birth through which the Spirit gives God's very life; consequently those believers begotten/born of water and Spirit are God's own children. In the Synoptic Gospels we hear that one has to become like a little child to inherit the kingdom; John has radicalized that idea to an insistence on being born from God as a child.

Nicodemus, of course, does not understand how this can be (3:9) because he thinks on an earthly level and does not recognize that it is one from heaven who speaks to him. In the dialogue that follows (which now becomes a monologue) Jesus explains in various ways the great sweep of descent from heaven and return to heaven (through being lifted up on the cross) involved in the incarnation. Others may emphasize judgment at the end of time; but for John, since God manifested love by giving the only Son to come among us, that coming constitutes judgment. People must decide either for the light that has come into the world or for darkness.

The sudden switch to a setting involving JBap (3:22ff.) helps to specify that what Jesus has been speaking about does involve baptism, hitherto not mentioned by name. Indeed we are told that Jesus himself baptized. As mentioned in chapter 28 above, in the Synoptic Gospels we are never told that Jesus baptized anyone; and his command to others to baptize (Matt 28:19) comes only after the resurrection. Consequently one could get the impression that baptism, which is an extremely important part of church life, was quite foreign to Jesus' own life and practice. The Fourth Gospel brings baptism as a begetting/birth of water and Spirit very much into the context of Jesus' life since it is one of the first issues he introduces when he discusses the purpose of his coming. Thus no longer can there be a dichotomy between what Jesus said and did and what the church says and does; one continues the other.

John 6. The same may be said about the eucharist. The three Synoptic Gospels localize the eucharistic action of Jesus at the Last Supper

The Jerusalem Church of One Mind

before he dies and have a specific reference to the shedding of his blood which will take place the next day. Paul sees the eucharist as recalling the death of the Lord until he comes. That magnificent conception leaves difficulties. Is the eucharist so attached to Jesus' death that it is unrelated to what he did earlier during his public ministry, and once again do we have a dichotomy between what he normally did and what is central in church life? How often should one recall or make present the death of the Lord? Once a year the Jewish Passover recalled the great delivering action of the God of Israel; should Christians follow that pattern?[19] In a sense John answers those questions. The eucharistic teaching comes as a commentary on the multiplication of the loaves and thus is intimately related to what Jesus did in his ministry. The eucharist is not explicitly related to Jesus' death but is treated as food, the bread of life, and thus should be received frequently.

Chapter 6 begins with the multiplication of the loaves and the walking on the water, a combined scene in which John is substantially close to the Synoptic account(s). There is an echo of the miracles of Moses during the exodus (manna, walking dryshod through the sea), but John's young lad with barley loaves heightens the secondary similarity to the Elijah/Elisha miracle pattern (2 Kgs 4:42-44). The peculiarly Johannine contribution comes the next day when implicitly the evangelist answers the intriguing question that haunts readers of the Synoptics: What happened to those people for whom Jesus worked miracles? Did the miracle change their lives? Did they become believers?

John indicates that those for whom the bread was multiplied really saw no profound significance beyond that it was a good way to get bread. While John certainly thought that there was a multiplication of physical loaves, he now has to make clear that the Son of Man who has come down from above did not do so to satisfy physical hunger. People who have loaves multiplied for them will become physically hungry again; he has come to give a heavenly bread that people will eat and never again become hungry. In 4:14 Jesus spoke to the Samaritan woman of his ability to give water that people would drink and never

---

[19] Interestingly in the Roman Catholic liturgy only one Mass is designated as the celebration of the Lord's Supper, namely, the Mass celebrated on Holy Thursday.

Christ in the Gospels of the Liturgical Year

thirst again, and here the Johannine Jesus is completing the picture of eternal food and drink. In discussing John 3, I explained that the Gospel employs the imagery of a birth from above that gives eternal life even as birth from parents gives earthly life. Once born, those with earthly life have to take physical food and drink to remain alive; once born, those with eternal life have to take eternal food and drink to remain alive.

Jesus' remarks on the bread of life, we are finally told (6:59), were given in a synagogue; and indeed we can understand the sermon better if we know how homilies were composed at this period. The basic pattern was a detailed exposition of a passage from the Pentateuch of Moses illustrated by a supporting passage from the Prophets. In debating with him about what he had done in multiplying loaves and what importance he had, the crowd supplies the biblical text, "He gave them bread from heaven to eat" (John 6:31; see Exod 16:4, 15) which they interpret as: Moses gave our ancestors the manna to eat. (Once again, as in chapter 3, the dignity of Jesus will be made clear by comparison with Moses.) Jesus denies their interpretation: The "He" is the heavenly Father not Moses; the tense of the verb is "gives," not "gave";[20] and the bread from heaven is not the manna because those who ate that bread died. The true bread is Jesus who comes down from heaven so that people may eat and never die.

Already in the OT God's revelation (specifically the Law) was compared to a well of water and to food, and people were warned that it is not by physical bread alone that they live but by every word that comes from the mouth of God. In that vein Jesus first presents himself as the bread of life come down from heaven in the sense of embodying divine revelation that people must believe (6:35, 40; notice that in 6:35-50 there is little emphasis on eating the bread of life).[21] The prophetic quotation that supports Jesus' exegesis is "They shall all be taught by God" (6:45; from Isa 54:13), which is literally true since Jesus who is doing this teaching is the Word-become-flesh, and "the Word

---

[20] The exegesis behind this particular point seems to be based on the ability to read a form of Hebrew *ntn* (the root for "give") as either a past indicative or a present participle.

[21] I am deliberately simplifying by stressing revelation as the main theme in 6:35-50 and the eucharist as the main theme in 6:51-58. The interweaving is more complicated.

The Jerusalem Church of One Mind

was God." The "Jews" murmur at him (even as their ancestors murmured at Moses in the desert): Jesus cannot have come down from heaven because they know his parents. As with Nicodemus this reflects a misunderstanding on the part of those who think on an earthly level; the parent of whom Jesus is speaking is the heavenly Father.

In 6:51-58 the bread of life takes on another dimension as the language shifts to eating and drinking, to flesh and blood. "The bread that I shall give is my flesh for the life of the world" is quite close to the Lucan Last Supper declaration, "This is my body which is given for you,"[22] and may well have been the Johannine eucharistic formula. To this there is another Jewish objection, parallel to the one in the first part of the discourse, as if Jesus was offering his tangible flesh in a cannibalistic way. But Jesus insists that his flesh is truly food and his blood truly drink (not on a crassly carnal level, of course: 6:63).

Acts has told us of the eucharistic breaking of the bread as an element in Christian *koinōnia*; John in a poetic way has laid out for us the basic elements that can make the Christian eucharistic celebration nourishing. If the service of the word feeds us with divine revelation as the bread of life, and the service of the sacrament feeds us with the flesh and blood of Christ, the life with which we are endowed at baptism will remain.

---

[22] An underlying Semitic *bśr* was rendered more literally in some Greek-speaking communities as *sarx* ("flesh") and more idiomatically in others as *sōma* ("body").

Chapter 30

Diversity in the Jerusalem Church; Expansion to Judea and Samaria (Acts 6–9)

After the Sanhedrin session at which Gamaliel spoke (*ca.* A.D. 36?), Acts begins an era in which, except for the brief period in which a Jewish king ruled Judea (Herod Agrippa I; A.D. 41–44; Acts 12:1-23), the branch of the Jerusalem church closely associated with the Twelve was not persecuted.[1] That period would come to an end in A.D. 62 when James, the brother of the Lord and leader of the Jerusalem church, was put to death.[2] Thus, according to the implicit indications of Acts, for some twenty years (A.D. 36–40, 45–62) the main Christian leaders could have functioned with Jerusalem as a base without attempts by the Jewish authorities to have them exterminated. This is not implausible, for we have indications that Paul could go to Jerusalem within those years and see some of the "pillars of the church" without any indication of secrecy. However, the removal of the external threat did not mean that all was well. Suddenly, after speaking of the church as being of one mind, at the beginning of chapter 6 Acts tells us about a hostile division among Jerusalem Christians, a division that will bring persecution on a segment of them (not those closely associated with the apostles) and lead eventually to a great missionary enterprise.

---

[1] To forestall an objection, let me point out that the Hellenist branch of the Jerusalem church (e.g., Stephen) was persecuted; but Acts 8:1 maintains that in that persecution and expulsion the "apostles" were not bothered, and for Acts "apostles" refers to the Twelve (exception 14:14).

[2] This James, who was not one of the Twelve, was closely connected with them, whether or not Luke would have considered him an apostle. For Paul "apostle" was a wider term and included (besides himself) a major figure like James of Jerusalem (Gal 1:19).

DIVERSITY IN THE JERUSALEM CHURCH AND ITS EFFECTS (ACTS 6:1–7:60)

Selections from this section of Acts serve as lectionary readings on three weekdays at the end of the second week of Easter and the beginning of the Third Week; and on two Sundays (Fifth, Seventh, A and C respectively).

Acts 6:1-6: Divisive Behavior within the Jerusalem Church. Probably here Acts draws on an old tradition, and the account is sketchy. (Was the source sketchy or did the author choose not to dwell on such an unpleasantry in a church that he has told us was of one mind?) The division manifests itself in an area that Acts has lauded several times: the common goods. Now, however, this feature is no longer a sign of *koinōnia*, for two groups of Jewish believers within the Jerusalem community are fighting over the common goods. Why? The designation of one group as Hellenists (Greek-like) and the Greek names of their leaders (6:5) suggest that they were Jews (in one case a proselyte or convert to Judaism) who spoke (only?) Greek and who were raised as children acculturated to Greco-Roman civilization. Deductively by contrast, then, the other group called the Hebrews would have spoken Aramaic or Hebrew (sometimes as well as Greek) and have been more culturally Jewish in outlook.[3] Beyond the cultural difference apparently there was also a theological difference. The apostles, who were clearly Hebrew Christians, did not let their faith in Jesus stop them from worshiping in the Temple (Acts 2:46; 3:1; 5:12, 21). However, Stephen, who will become the Hellenist leader, speaks as if the Temple has no more meaning (7:48-50). In fact, we know that Jews of this period were sharply divided over the claim that the Jerusalem Temple was the sole place on earth at which sacrifice could be offered to God; and so it is not improbable that Jews of opposite persuasion on that issue may have become believers in Jesus. Some of them would have regarded that faith as a catalyst toward the demise of the importance of Temple cult. In any case the disagreement among these Jerusalem Christians has been translated into finances (as have many inner church fights ever

---

[3] Paul, who probably knew Hebrew or Aramaic as well as Greek, considered himself a Hebrew (2 Cor 11:22; Phil 3:5) in his strict preconversional behavior as a Jew, whether or not that designation meant the same to him as it did to the author of Acts.

Christ in the Gospels of the Liturgical Year

since) because the Hebrews (surely the larger group) were attempting to force the Hellenists to conformity by shutting off common funds from the Hellenist widows, who presumably were totally dependent on this support.

In order to deal with this situation the Twelve summoned "the multitude" of the disciples (perhaps a technical name for those who could vote) to settle the issue. In this session the Twelve avoided the obvious, simple solutions. Although Hebrews themselves, they did not simply side with the Hebrews and demand that the Hellenists either conform or leave. Moreover, they refused to take over the administration of the common goods; specifically they did not wish to involve themselves in waiting on or serving[4] tables in order to ensure a fair distribution of food. Rather they wished to allow the Hellenists to have their own leaders and administrators of the common goods.

This brief scene offers Christians of today important subjects for reflection. *First*, nowhere do we see more clearly the unique role of the Twelve.[5] A symbolic group at the beginning of the renewed Israel (even as the twelve sons of Jacob/Israel were esteemed as the originators of the twelve tribes), the Twelve have the eschatological function of purifying and maintaining the wholeness of God's people. They are once and for all, never replaced; there are only twelve thrones of judgment and they are to have them. Here the concern of the Twelve for the whole of the renewed Israel is exemplified in their refusing to take a partisan position. They preserve the *koinōnia* by their solution, for the Hellenists are to remain as fully recognized brothers and sisters in

---

[4] Because the verb "to wait on, serve" in Acts 6:2 is *diakonein*, this scene has come to be interpreted as the establishment of the first deacons. The position of the Hellenist leaders who are selected in this scene is not similar to that of the deacons described in the Pastoral Letters. If one wants to be anachronistic and apply a later ecclesiastical term to their role, these administrators would be closer to bishops than to deacons.

[5] It needs to be emphasized that in the total NT picture "the Twelve" and "apostles" are not simply equatable terms even though the Twelve were also apostles. The apostles (a larger group than the Twelve as the distinction in 1 Corinthians 15:5, 7 makes lucidly clear when it distinguishes between "the Twelve" and "all the apostles") are commissioned to proclaim the risen Lord and gather believers. In the traditional theology bishops are "successors of the apostles" (not "successors of the Twelve" as such) because they inherit the care of the churches that emerged from the apostolic mission.

Diversity in the Jerusalem Church; Expansion to Judea and Samaria

Christ. Peter is normally the spokesman of the Twelve, and in the church today the symbolic functioning of the Twelve is represented by the successor of Peter when the papacy is at its best. There are always factions in the church who want their opponents excommunicated or suppressed because they are not "true Catholics" or "true Christians." But the successor of Peter, who symbolizes the unity of the whole people of God, has as a principal task to hold the *koinōnia* together. One of his great glories is to keep people in the church and not let them be driven out.

Second, in reality the acceptance of the suggestion made by the Twelve was a decision in the early church for pluralism and an appropriation of what we have come to call today "the hierarchy of doctrine." The cultural and theological differences that existed in Jerusalem between the Hebrews and the Hellenists were implicitly being judged as less important than their common belief in Jesus. That same instinct will manifest itself later when it comes to the issue of whether circumcised believers can accept uncircumcised believers as equally and truly Christian. From the beginning Christianity has not gloried in uniformity except in basics, e.g., the christological identity of Jesus as uniquely embodying God's presence. Most believers in Jesus decided very early that it was better to tolerate differences of practices and of theological attitudes rather than to destroy the *koinōnia.*

Third, the scene illustrates certain factors about the nature and origins of church structure. No blueprint had come from Jesus showing how the community of those who believed in him was to be administered. By the time described in Acts 6 (*ca.* A.D. 36?) believers are increasing in numbers and are arguing with one another—two sociological factors that always produce a need for defining leadership more clearly. The Twelve refuse to become administrators for local groups; yet such administrators now need to be appointed. Accordingly we hear of the seven who become the administrators for the Hellenist believers. Probably administrators also emerge for the Hebrew Christian community at the same time; henceforth (Acts 11:30; 12:17; 15:2, 4, 6, 13, 22, 23; 21:18) James the brother of the Lord and the elders (presbyters) shall appear as authorities in Jerusalem, alongside the apostles. The choice of administrators in 6:6 is done in the context of praying and the laying on of hands. Too often when modern Christians think of church structure, they take a simple, not to say simplistic, view. On the ultraliberal end of the Christian spectrum, church structure is seen simply as a sociological development that can be changed by voting. On the ultraconservative end of the spectrum church structure is seen to have been established by Jesus and no changes are permissible. Precisely because Jesus did not leave blueprints, church structure developed to meet needs; and so sociological factors have played a role. Yet in Christian self-understanding the Holy Spirit given by the risen Christ guided the church in the way it developed, so that structure came to embody Jesus Christ's will for his church. (For that reason, certain basic aspects of the structure are believed by Christians to be unchangeable.) In other words, on the analogy of the incarnation, there is both the human and the divine in the church and its structure. A recognition of that will allow adaptations in church structure to meet the needs of our day without giving us the sense that each generation is free to reinvent the church.

Fourth, as depicted in Acts the Twelve made a good proposal—"the multitude" of the Jerusalem community recognized that by expressing approval. Nevertheless, as we are about to see, the decision had unexpected results that caused those in authority in Jerusalem many problems. Certainly none of those present at this meeting could have foreseen how far their decision would lead the church. (We should always recognize that with any major decision in the church the results are likely to go beyond what was foreseen and that often there is no way to stop at a point we judge prudent the thrust of what we have begun.) Let us now look at the aftermath.

Acts 6:7–7:60: Effects of Keeping the Hellenists within the Christian Communion. In keeping the Hellenists within the Christian *koinōnia* the Jerusalem community now becomes responsible for the actions and preaching of the Hellenist leaders. The chief priests and the Sanhedrin had implicitly decided to extend grudging tolerance to those who believed in the risen Christ (even though technically they were forbidden to speak in the name of Jesus); but that did not mean they would tolerate attacks on the Temple from believers in Jesus any more than they tolerated it from other Jews.[6] The first-ranking among the Hellenists,

---

[6] The Jewish writer Josephus speaks of various sects of the Jews (Sadducees, Pharisees, Essenes); and presumably the believers of Jesus would have been considered another, annoying variety, even if they did not think of themselves in this category (Acts 24:14).

Diversity in the Jerusalem Church; Expansion to Judea and Samaria

Stephen, stirs up opposition at a Jerusalem synagogue attended largely by foreign Jews. They drag him before a Sanhedrin and level a charge about the message he is preaching—not that Jesus is risen (the previous issue that had disturbed the Sanhedrin about the Twelve), but that Jesus would destroy the Temple. Interestingly, although in the trial of Jesus Mark and Matthew had false witnesses charge Jesus with saying that he would destroy the Temple sanctuary (Mark: "made with hands"), Luke omitted that charge against Jesus. Did the evangelist want to lead his readers to a more subtle understanding, namely, that what was destructive to the Temple in Jesus' proclamation became apparent only after his lifetime and then through those believers, like the Hellenists, who saw the more radical implications of Jesus' message?[7] In his long speech (Acts 7:2-53) in response to the Temple charge Stephen will phrase those radical implications in the climactic statement: "The Most High does not dwell in houses made with hands" (7:48).

Although Acts gives us speeches of Peter and Paul, none is so grand as the speech of Stephen. Is that because the Christianity that exists in the author's lifetime has now followed the path of Stephen in terms of rejection of the Temple rather than that of Peter and Paul, both of whom are described as worshiping in the Temple? Stephen's survey of the salvation history from the patriarch Abraham to Israel's entrance into the Promised Land under Moses and Joshua has fascinated scholars since elements in it do not seem to reflect standard OT understanding. Some have even proposed that we have here reflections of a Samaritan background harmonious with the mission in Samaria that will soon be undertaken by the Hellenists. That discussion is too technical for our interests here, especially since only the last three verses of the speech (7:51-53) are read in the post-Easter lectionary. Those verses are astoundingly polemic from a prisoner in the dock, for Stephen accuses his hearers of giving over and murdering Jesus the just one even as

[7] We are uncertain of the logic because the charge against Stephen in Acts 6:13 (as against Jesus in Mark and Matthew) is attributed to false witnesses. Why are the witnesses called false? Since the finale of Stephen's defense speech seems to offer a basis for accusing him of opposition toward the Temple and having radical ideas about the Law, it is unlikely that we are meant to think that the witnesses simply invented the charge. Perhaps they may have oversimplified the causality as if Jesus (or some of the Christians) planned personally to do physical damage to the Temple.

their fathers persecuted the prophets. Not surprisingly this accusation brings the rage against Stephen to the boiling point, and he is cast out of the city and stoned to death (7:54-60). Both the Sunday and weekday lectionaries contain the account of this death; and the scene is truly significant, not only because Stephen is the first Christian martyr, but also because the death of Stephen in Acts matches so closely the death of Jesus in Luke. Both accounts speak of the Son of Man (standing/seated) at the right hand of God (Luke 22:69; Acts 7:56); both have a prayer for the forgiveness of those who are effecting this execution (Luke 23:34; Acts 7:60); both have the dying figure commend his spirit heavenward (Luke 23:46; Acts 7:59). In the figure of Peter Acts has shown continuity with Jesus' ministry of healing and preaching; in the figure of Stephen Acts has shown continuity with Jesus' death. And just as Jesus' death was not the end because the apostles would receive his Spirit to carry on the work, the death of Stephen is not the end, for observing is a young man named Saul (7:58). He consents to the death (8:1), but in God's providence he will continue the work of Stephen.

EXPANSION TO JUDEA AND SAMARIA; HELLENIST MISSION; CONVERSION OF SAUL; PETER'S ACTIVITIES (ACTS 8:1–9:43)

Selections from this section of Acts serve as lectionary readings on four weekdays at the end of the Third Week of Easter; and on two Sundays (Fifth, Sixth, B and A respectively).

Acts 8:1-40: The Hellenist Mission. In a complicated description that involves the phrase "all were scattered," Acts 8:1 now tells us that a selective persecution followed the death of Stephen. The Hellenists were scattered; the apostles (and seemingly the Hebrew Christians) were not, presumably because they did not propagandize against the Temple as the Hellenists did. In this persecution a ferocious agent is Saul whose conversion will be dramatically recounted in the next chapter. Acts 1:8 laid out the divine plan of evangelization: "You shall be my witnesses in Jerusalem and in all Judea and Samaria, and to the ends of the earth."[8] We have heard of witness (*martyria*) borne in

---

[8] Acts presents these as the risen Jesus' words; but that must be understood correctly, for the book goes on to show that the disciples had no awareness that they had been informed of such a plan. In terms of origin most scholars would think

Jerusalem culminating with the martyrdom of Stephen; now we are to hear about preaching in the next two regions as the Hellenists are scattered throughout Judea and Samaria. The picture of the spread of Christianity is highly selective; in 9:2, 10 we shall find a reference to Christian believers in Damascus without being told how they got there! Nevertheless it is interesting to reflect on the simplified picture in Acts 8.

First, such a basic step as moving outside Jerusalem to preach to a wider audience is not the result of planning but of persecution. Aspects of that picture will be true of many new missions throughout the ages: External pressure will cause Christians to see an area or means of evangelization that would not have occurred to them, and occasionally a harsh disaster will be turned into an opportunity. Thus once again Acts shows us that from the very start Christianity was not governed by a blueprint but by the Spirit.

Second, those who are expelled and become the missionaries to areas outside Jerusalem are the Hellenists, the more radical Christians in terms of their relation to Jewish Temple worship. Missionary activity in itself might have been neutral in the attitude it inculcated toward Judaism, but with the Hellenists as spokesmen it was bound to have a centrifugal force. Their converts to Jesus would have no deep attachment to features of Jewish worship; and where they encountered opposition from Jews who did not believe in Jesus, they would have felt less obligated to preserve a Christian attachment to the Jewish synagogues.

Third, the Hellenists, who differed from Hebrews (whether or not the latter had come to faith in Jesus), seemingly felt less obligated to preach Jesus only or even chiefly to Jews. Acts 8:5 tells us they went to the Samaritans; and 11:19-20 indicates that in Phoenica, Cyprus, and Antioch, although at first they spoke the word only to Jews, some preached to Gentiles. The instinct to go to Samaria is interesting. One of the major differences between Samaritans and Jews was that the former did not accept the Jerusalem Temple as the only place of worship. Since the Christian Hellenists were Jews who did not believe

_____

that the material available to the author of Acts, writing some fifty years after the early evangelizing, enabled him to detect a geographical expansion; and he has used that expansion as a plan for the book. He would have looked on this procedure as discovering what Christ had willed for his church, whence the attribution of it to the risen Jesus.

Christ in the Gospels of the Liturgical Year

that God dwelt in houses made with hands, they were ideally suited to preach Jesus Christ to an area that might well have been hostile to Hebrew Christians who kept going to the Temple. (Many think that there is a Hellenist strain in John, the only Gospel where Jesus goes into Samaria and gains Samaritan followers. In John 4:21 we may be hearing the type of preaching done in Samaria by the Hellenists, for it speaks of an hour "when you will worship the Father neither on this mountain [Gerizim, the Samaritan holy place] nor in Jerusalem.")

In any case the Hellenist proclamation of the good news to the Samaritans is highly successful. Yet the net of proclamation attracts Simon Magus, a figure who later became a subject of speculation, figuring in legend as the great adversary of Christianity. Does the author of Acts include the story of his defeat because already when Acts was being written gnostics were active who made Simon a hero?[9] Interestingly, the one to confront Simon is Peter, not Philip the Hellenist successor of Stephen. The Jerusalem church has heard of the Hellenist success and sent Peter and John that they might receive the Holy Spirit. (One suspects that this is bowdlerizing the basic purpose of the apostolic visitation, namely, to verify whether the conversion of such outsiders as the Samaritans is reconcilable with Jesus' proclamation.) The impression is created in Acts that granting the Spirit required the collaborative presence of the Twelve. Simon wants their power and offers money for it (thus forever immortalizing his name in the designation "simony"). Peter challenges him to repent; yet unlike Stephen's prayer for his adversaries, this promotion of repentance is qualified as to whether Simon can really change his heart (8:22-23). That qualification may have fed the later legends. The experience in Samaria is pictured as influencing Peter and John because on their way back to Jerusalem they preached the gospel to Samaritans (8:25).

Acts 8:26-40 supplies another example of Hellenist evangelization, this time in the southern part of Judea rather than the north, again manifesting geographical spread. The fact that the Ethiopian eunuch has come to Jerusalem to worship and is reading Isaiah gives the impression of a foreign Jew from an exotic region in Africa (one of "the ends of the earth," whether modern Ethiopia or Nubia to the

---

[9] The designation of Simon as "the Power of God called Great" sounds as if he was one of the gnostic emanations that stand between the distant, hidden God and human beings. Is the author's categorizing him as a *magus* a contemptuous classification of a gnostic teacher?

Diversity in the Jerusalem Church; Expansion to Judea and Samaria

south of Egypt is envisaged). Philip the Hellenist's ability to interpret the prophet in order to explain Christ to the eunuch is a continuation of the risen Jesus' interpreting the Scriptures for his disciples (Luke 24:27, 44-45). Deuteronomy 23:2(1) would rule out the admission of the castrated into the community of Israel, but Philip has no hesitation about meeting the eunuch's request to be baptized into the community of the renewed Israel. That openness prepares us for the admission of Gentiles, and by way of transition Acts stops here to tell us about Saul/Paul who would be the great emissary to the Gentiles.

Acts 9:1-30: The Conversion of Saul. Besides narrating the account of the conversion here, the author will report it twice more from Paul's lips in his speeches of self-defense (22:3-21; 26:2-23).[10] In those later versions the vocation of Paul to evangelize the Gentiles will be blended into the conversion account. Here the author is content to move in stages: Ananias who cures and baptizes him is told of the future mission, but not Saul himself. Yet clearly it is because of all that is to be accomplished through this "vessel of election" (9:15) that Acts is so interested in recounting his dramatic conversion effected by Jesus himself.[11] The dramatic touches of the story are superb, e.g., the personalizing of Saul's hostility in 9:4, "Saul, Saul, why do you persecute me?" The reluctance of Ananias to have anything to do with Saul despite the Lord's instruction highlights the metamorphosis of Saul from a truly fearsome persecutor. Acts is very careful to report that this great missionary received the Holy Spirit (9:17); for his proclamation will eventually be as potent as was that of Peter and the others who received the Spirit at Pentecost. In chapter 28 above I wrote about the importance of christological belief; in significant harmony with that Acts sums up the new convert's preaching as "Jesus is the Son of God" (9:20). Acts also lays the basis for the future activity of Barnabas with Paul by telling us that it was Barnabas who supported Saul

[10] Only the first of the three is read in the lectionary of this season between Easter and Pentecost.

[11] The risen Jesus appeared on earth to the Twelve and then departed to heaven whence he now speaks to Saul. Does that mean that the author of Acts posits a qualitative difference of status between the Twelve and Paul in terms of their relationship to Christ? 1 Corinthians 15:5-8, from Paul himself, would give the impression that there was no difference in the appearances of the risen Jesus to Peter or the Twelve and the appearance to Paul (other than time: they are listed first, he is last).

Christ in the Gospels of the Liturgical Year

against those in Jerusalem who could not believe that the persecutor had now changed. Evidently under the constraint of actual history, Acts postpones the most famous activities of Saul/Paul by telling us that he went back to Tarsus (9:30); his great mission will be described later after the author tells us more about Peter.[12]

Acts 9:31-43: Peter's Activities. The first of the Twelve was the spokesman of apostolic missionary activity in Jerusalem (Acts 2–5); now that the church has been spreading to Judea and Samaria[13] the Hellenists and Saul have taken center stage (with Peter invoked chiefly to face Simon Magus). Beginning in 9:31, however, Peter returns to the fore, first for his missionary work in Lydda and Joppa and then (10:1ff.) for his pivotal role in bringing Gentiles into the *koinōnia*. (The first element really prepares for the second.) Previously we have seen that in the name of Jesus Peter could heal and preach. Acts now reiterates this parallelism, for the cure of Aeneas at Lydda with the command to rise echoes closely Jesus' cure of the paralyzed man (Luke 5:24-26). Even more closely the revivification of Tabitha resembles Jesus' action in raising the daughter of Jairus (Luke 8:49-56).[14] No power has been withheld from the church, not even the power over death itself. Now, however, we are about to move beyond the parallels to Jesus' ministry to a new area, the Gentiles. The Lucan Gospel account of Jesus began and ended in the Jerusalem Temple. What Peter does next will eventually take Christianity outside Judaism to Rome as representative of the ends of the earth.

Brief Reflections on John 10 and John 12

In the week (the Fourth of Easter) just after the lectionary offers selections from Acts 6–9, its Gospel selections are from John 10 and 12.[15]

---

[12] The overlapping of the two figures helps to show that the same gospel was preached by both.

[13] Having listed Judea and Samaria as the next stage after Jerusalem in 1:8, the author of Acts is careful to signpost that geographical expansion (chaps. 8–9) by mentioning Judea and Samaria in 8:1 and 9:31.

[14] The order "Tabitha, rise" in Acts 9:40 is remarkably like *"Talitha cum(i)"* in the parallel Marcan account (5:41).

[15] The Fourth Sunday of Easter, where the readings in all three cycles are from John 10, is sometimes called Good Shepherd Sunday.

We saw in Acts 6 how a divided community created the need for an administrative leadership, and how persecution drove the Hellenists out of Jerusalem to begin a mission to the Samaritan outsiders. It is quite appropriate, then, to turn to Gospel readings from John that deal with shepherding the flock and other sheep not of this fold.

Structures of authority developed gradually in the early church. Shortly after the selection of local administrators for the Hellenist Christians, James and the elders are portrayed as the leaders of the Jerusalem Hebrew Christian community. Acts 14:23 has Paul appointing presbyters in the churches, and 20:28 has him tell the presbyters of Ephesus to shepherd the flock in which the Holy Spirit has made them overseers. Reading John against that background supplies an interesting corrective of the long-term dangers inherent in such structuring. Figures given authority in the church tend to become all important in the eyes of those whom they were meant to serve; their presence is immediate, and often it seems that Jesus is reached chiefly through them and their activities. For John the immediacy of Jesus is crucially important because only he can give God's life. At the end of the first century when the language of shepherds was widespread for those in charge of churches, the Johannine insistence that Jesus is the good or model shepherd and that all others are thieves and bandits is challenging. The sheep should heed only the divine shepherd. True, in the Johannine context the words are addressed to the Jews and so the primary attack may be on the leadership of the synagogues, but such language is bound to have a dynamism in making Christians qualify the role of their own leaders.

Later in John 21:15-17 we see a shepherding role of feeding the sheep entrusted to Simon Peter, a human being; but even then the sheep are not his—only Jesus can call them "my sheep." The shepherding image in the OT is sometimes used to symbolize the ruling power of the king. Yet Jesus as the model shepherd does not speak of his authority or of ruling. He speaks of his intimate knowledge of his sheep and of an ability to call each by name so that they will recognize him when he leads them to pasture. Jesus speaks also of his willingness to lay down his life for the sheep lest they be snatched by the wolf. This is what makes shepherding truly pastoral. Accordingly, in chapter 21 when Simon Peter is appointed to feed the sheep, Jesus signifies how Peter will die a martyr's death, a death that qualifies him as a shepherd according to the Good Shepherd's standards. Thus, while for a church that has strongly articulated structure Acts supplies evidence of that necessary development as early as apostolic times, John offers a critique that helps to ensure that structure does not interfere with an immediate relationship between Jesus and the believers that is at the heart of Christianity.

John 10:16 indicates that Jesus has other sheep that are not of this fold and that he wishes to bring them into the one flock under the one shepherd. Most likely, given the distinctiveness that surrounds the Beloved Disciple (the model of the Johannine community) in the Fourth Gospel, and the constant contrast between that disciple and Simon Peter, the Johannine community was not entirely one with churches that considered the Twelve as their patrons—a situation that has some similarity to the difficult relationship between the Hebrew and Hellenist Christians in Acts. On the importance of the *koinōnia* or oneness of the church both Acts and John agree. As indicated in reflections above, this ideal remains of paramount importance for relationships not only among the Christian churches but even within a church like the Roman Catholic. The tendency to divide over issues must be confronted by the stated demand of Jesus to be the one shepherd over the one flock.

As we judge what is essential for unity and what are tolerable diversities, we must come back to the criterion of christology put forth by Peter in Acts when he insisted on baptism in the name of Jesus, i.e., the confession of who Jesus is. There are other essential Christian beliefs, but they must be evaluated by their interrelationship with the all-essential belief in Christ. That is harmonious with the weekday lectionary passage John 12:44-50 where Jesus states that those who believe in him are really believing in the God who sent him and that judgment will be based on such faith. Those who see Jesus and refuse belief are judging themselves. The majority of people in the world today are not Christians: They do not believe in Jesus, and indeed many can be said not to have seen him. They have their own struggle with light and darkness, and their salvation is entrusted to the all-gracious God whose ultimate goal is salvific (see 12:47). As for Christians, as we seek the grace to constitute the one flock under the one shepherd, our immediate concern must be for our fellow believers—to be sure that the faith we profess in Christ is what is demanded in Acts and John.

Diversity in the Jerusalem Church; Expansion to Judea and Samaria

Chapter 31

Outreach to the Gentiles; the Church of Antioch (Acts 10–14)

Gradually the author of Acts shifts attention to the mission to the Gentiles. In chapter 10 Peter is led by the Spirit to baptize Cornelius (and his household), a pious God-fearer, i.e., a Gentile who participates in synagogue prayers and accepts the moral demands of Judaism. In 11:20 we are told that the Hellenists began preaching to the Greek-speaking Gentiles. In 13:4ff. the mission of Barnabas and Saul from Antioch is described, a mission that first preaches to the Jews in the synagogues but gradually turns to the Gentiles.

THE CONVERSION OF THE GENTILE CORNELIUS (ACTS 10:1–11:18)

In Acts 10 the author as a third-person reporter recounts what happened; in Acts 11 Peter in his own first-person report repeats what happened as he defends his behavior before the Jerusalem Christians. (As with Paul's repetitions of the story of his conversion, the duplication signals that this is an account of pivotal importance.) Selections from the first part of this section are read on the B Sunday of the Sixth Week of Easter, while 11:1-18 is read on the Monday of the Fourth Week of Easter. In other words the lectionary is satisfied with an overall impression of what was involved. Actually there are six subdivisions in the Acts narrative: (a) 10:1-8: The pious Roman centurion Cornelius receives a vision of an angel of God at Caesarea telling him to send to Joppa for Simon called Peter; (b) 10:9-16: At Joppa Peter receives a vision telling him that foods traditionally considered ritually unclean are in fact not unclean; (c) 10:17-23a: Pondering the vision, Peter receives the men sent by Cornelius who ask him to come to Cornelius' house; (d) 10:23b-33: Cornelius receives Peter and explains that he was told to send for him; (e) 10:34-49: Peter preaches a sermon, and the Holy Spirit comes upon the uncircumcised present, so that Peter commands them to be baptized; (f) 11:1-18: Returning to Jerusalem, Peter has to account for his boldness in baptizing Gentiles.[1]

Because there are heavenly revelations both to Cornelius and Peter, readers are meant to recognize that what occurs here is uniquely God's will. Such an emphasis was probably necessary because of the controversial nature of the two issues involved: Were Christians bound by the Jewish rules for kosher foods? Should the Gentiles be received without first becoming Jews (i.e., being circumcised)? The post-Easter lectionary ignores the former, perhaps because those who shaped the lectionary did not think the issue of enduring import. Yet here we have a major break from Jewish practice, a break supported not by a Hellenist radical but by the first of the Twelve. Gradually the extent to which new wine cannot be put into old wine skins (Luke 5:37) is becoming apparent. Often modern Jewish and Christian scholars, studying the history of this early period and regretting the great rift that opened between Christianity and Judaism, suggest that if in the first century there had been more tolerance and understanding on both sides, the split could have been avoided. Some indications in the NT, however, suggest that the radical implications of Jesus were really irreconcilable with major tenets and practices of Judaism.

Lectionary (and indeed general Christian) attention is focused on the second issue: Did Gentiles have to be circumcised to receive baptism and the grace of Christ? Notice that the issue concerns Gentiles. So far as I know the NT does not debate whether Jewish Christian parents should have their sons circumcised. Not even Paul, who faces over and over again this issue with the Gentiles, ever states explicitly what a Jewish Christian should do. I would assume that most Jewish Christians did (and should have) circumcised their sons in order to continue to receive the special privileges of being Jews. That would have become problematic theologically only if they thought that circumcision was necessary along with baptism for someone to become a child of God and part of God's people newly chosen in Jesus Christ.

Implicitly or explicitly those who insisted that Gentiles needed to be circumcised (i.e., become Jews) were maintaining that being a Jew

---

[1] The lectionary is concerned with small portions of (d) and (e) and the whole of (f).

Outreach to the Gentiles; the Church of Antioch

had primacy over faith in Christ in terms of God's grace. Peter is pictured as rejecting that in his speech and action in 10:34-49. Scholars debate whether the author of Acts is historical in presenting Peter as the first to accept uncircumcised Gentiles into the Christian *koinōnia*. One may argue from 11:20 that the Hellenists were the first to do this, and clearly later Paul was the greatest spokesman for the practice. Yet since Paul mentions Peter (or Kephas) at Antioch dealing with Gentiles (Gal 2:11-12) and at Corinth (1 Cor 9:5), what may underlie Acts is the memory that among the Jerusalem leaders Peter was foremost in displaying such openness, whence the ability of Peter or his image to appeal to both sides of the Christian community.[2] From what is described here, we may reflect on several issues of relevance to Christians today.

First, as incredible as it may seem, such a fundamental issue as whether one should proclaim the kingdom to Gentiles and whether they had to become Jews was not detectably an issue solved by Jesus in his lifetime.[3] There are those today on both extremes of the ecclesiastical spectrum (ultraliberal, ultraconservative) who think they can appeal to the words or deeds of Jesus to solve any question in the church (parochial, diocesan, or universal). If Jesus did not solve the most fundamental question of the Christian mission, we may well doubt that his recorded words solve most of our subsequent debated problems in the church.

Second, Peter is not presented as solving the problem by his own initiative or wisdom. He says in Acts 10:28 that God has shown him that he should not consider others unclean. Moreover, from the fact that Cornelius has received a vision from God Peter concludes that God shows no partiality (10:34). The reason Peter offers for not forbidding the uncircumcised Cornelius to be baptized is that the Holy Spirit has come upon him (10:47).[4] In other words we have another instance of

[2] Paul (Gal 2:7) speaks of Peter's having been entrusted with the gospel to the circumcised; yet a letter attributed to him, 1 Peter, is clearly written to Gentile Christians (2:10: "You were once no people").

[3] The stories of the Syrophoenician woman who asked to have her daughter healed and of the Roman centurion whose faith Jesus praised are of exceptional character and do not really settle the problem.

[4] Some today would try to solve a modern issue about "baptism in the Spirit" (as distinct from baptism in water) from the sequence in Acts. That is not possible. According to his purpose and interests the author of Acts shows: (a) the Twelve

Christians facing an unforeseen problem and solving it, not by appeal to a previous blueprint for the church, but by insight (gained from the Holy Spirit) as to what Christ wanted for the church.

Third, the radical character of what Peter has done and proclaimed is challenged in 11:3 by confreres in the church of Jerusalem: "Why did you go to the uncircumcised and eat with them?" It is not clear whether at heart this Christian "circumcision party" was altogether opposed to converting Gentiles to belief in Christ or was simply insisting that Gentiles could be converted only after they had become Jews.[5] One may imagine this group appealing to Abraham and Moses as proof that the Scriptures demanded circumcision and arguing there was no evidence that Jesus had ever changed the requirement for circumcision.[6] Peter answers the circumcision party by telling about his visions and the coming of the Spirit upon Cornelius' household. This existential argument silences the circumcision party (for the moment) and leads to the acceptance of Gentiles into existing Jewish Christian groups (11:18). But the issue has not been fully resolved, as Acts will show us after it has depicted an active mission to Gentiles.

---

and those together with them receiving the Spirit without (ever) being baptized in water; (b) people being baptized (in water) and then receiving the gift of the Spirit (2:38; 19:5-6); (c) people receiving the Spirit before being baptized in water (here); (d) people having been baptized in water (with the baptism of John) who never even knew that there was a Holy Spirit (18:24–19:7).

[5] Similarly, as we shall see, among those Jewish Christians open to converting Gentiles to Christ without demanding circumcision there were differences, e.g., as to whether the Gentiles should be required to accept some Jewish practices. Since Gentile Christians took on the coloring of the Jewish Christians who converted them, I have maintained that it is utterly useless to speak of Gentile Christianity and Jewish Christianity as if these referred to two different theological stances. In terms of relations to Judaism there was a whole range of theological stances in Jewish Christianity and a matching range in Gentile Christianity.

[6] Jewish Christians who invoked the authority of James objected to Peter's eating with Gentiles (Gal 2:12) and thus, apparently, to his eating food that could be considered ritually unclean. Would not that objection be contrary to what Jesus had said? Mark 7:19 (alone) interprets Jesus' words to mean that he declared all foods clean. That is probably a post-resurrectional insight, gained after Christians had moved in that direction. Consequently, at least from the viewpoint of chronology, Acts is plausible in having Peter discover this (through revelation) a number of years after Jesus' death.

Outreach to the Gentiles; the Church of Antioch

DEVELOPMENTS AT ANTIOCH AND JERUSALEM
(ACTS 11:19–12:25)

(From this section only what happens at Antioch is narrated in the lectionary, in the Fifth Week of Easter; in my reflections, however, I shall include some of what happened at Jerusalem for it supplies background for what follows.) Perhaps as part of his technique of handling simultaneity, the author now picks up the story of the Hellenist Christians broken off in chapter 8 when he described the scattering from Jerusalem that sent them to Samaria. Belatedly we are told that they went also to Phoenicia, Cyprus, and Antioch (in Syria), preaching at first only to Jews but then gradually to Gentiles as well. This may be a tacit way of acknowledging that, although a Hebrew Christian like Peter did accept a Gentile household into the community, the really aggressive effort to convert Gentiles began with the Hellenists. When Jerusalem heard this, Barnabas was sent to Antioch to check on the development; and he approved it (11:22-23).[7] This becomes the occasion of bringing to Antioch Saul, last heard of in 9:30. Thus, while the Jerusalem church in the person of Peter is taking the first steps toward admitting a few Gentiles, Antioch develops as a second great Christian center, more vibrantly involved in mission. It is in this second center that believers in Jesus, who are now both Jews and Gentiles, receive the name "Christians" by which they will henceforth be known (11:26).

The development of the Antioch base is a grace because Jerusalem and Judea are hit particularly hard by a famine foretold by Agabus (11:27-30) and by persecution in a changed political situation where direct Roman rule had been replaced by a Jewish kingdom (12:1-23; under Herod Agrippa I: A.D. 41–44). The famine offers the Antiochene Christians a chance to display *koinōnia* by sharing goods with the poorer believers in Judea; the persecution offers the Jerusalem Christians an opportunity to bear witness by martyrdom, for James, son of Zebedee and brother of John, is put to death.[8] There is no move toward replacing James as there was when Judas' betrayal left the

---

[7] Nevertheless, his approval will not be enough when all the implications of the mission become apparent, and Acts 15 will tell us how at Jerusalem he and Paul had to give an account of what had happened.

[8] This is James the Greater who in legend went to Spain (venerated at Compostela) and evidently came back again to Judea soon enough to die about A.D. 41! He must be kept distinct from another member of the Twelve, James son of Alphaeus (about whom we know nothing), and above all from a third James, the brother of the Lord

Christ in the Gospels of the Liturgical Year

sacred number of the Twelve incomplete. That is because, as I have explained, the Twelve are not to be a continuous group in history but a once-for-all-time symbol. There are only twelve thrones to judge the tribes of Israel (Luke 22:30; Matt 19:28), and it is to one of those that by his fidelity to Christ James has now gone. Acts 12:3, 11 associates the Jewish people with the anti-Christian hostility of Herod, whereas hitherto in Luke-Acts there was a tendency to distinguish between the Jewish people (more favorable to Jesus) and their rulers. Readers are being prepared for a situation in which Judaism and Christianity are not only distinct but hostile.

Great danger threatens when Peter is arrested; but God intervenes through an angel to release him, even as God intervened by an angel to release him when he was arrested by the Sanhedrin (5:19). Later an earthquake will free Paul when he is in prison in Philippi (16:26). These divine interventions show God's care for the great spokesmen of the gospel.[9] That Peter, after his escape from Herod, went to another place (Acts 12:17) has given rise to the imaginative, but probably wrong, tradition that at this juncture Peter went to Rome and founded the church there. That Peter, as he left Jerusalem, sent word to James has been interpreted, also wrongly, as his passing the control of the church (and even the primacy) to James. This thesis fails to distinguish between the roles of the two men: Peter, the first of the Twelve to see the risen Jesus, is always named first among them; there is no evidence that Peter was ever local administrator of the Jerusalem church—a role of administration rejected for the Twelve in Acts 6:2. Probably as soon as there was an administrative role created for the Hebrew element of the Jerusalem church, James held it, not illogically because he was related to Jesus by family ties.[10] In any case Peter's departure from

who is a dominant figure in the Jerusalem church and is not a member of the Twelve. Unfortunately the sanctoral cycle of the liturgy tends to confuse the latter two.

[9] In the light of such tradition, one can imagine later Christian puzzlement when neither Peter nor Paul escaped Nero's arrest at Rome where they were executed. Would some have judged that the emperor was more powerful than Christ? Perhaps that is why a book like the Apocalypse had to stress so firmly that the Lamb could and would conquer the beast representing imperial power.

[10] The dominant Gospel evidence is that the "brothers" of Jesus were not disciples during his lifetime (Mark 3:31-35; 6:3-4; John 7:5); but the risen Jesus appeared to James (1 Cor 15:7), and James was an apostle in Jerusalem at the time of Paul's conversion (Gal 1:19; *ca.* A.D. 36).

Outreach to the Gentiles; the Church of Antioch

Jerusalem was not a permanent one; he had returned by the time of the meeting in that city described in Acts 15 (*ca*. A.D. 49). Acts finishes the colorful story of the frustrated persecution by describing (12:23) the horrible death of being eaten by worms visited by God on King Herod Agrippa in A.D. 44. It is quite similar to the death of the great enemy of Israel, King Antiochus Epiphanes, in 2 Maccabees 9:9. Both accounts are theological interpretations of sudden death: Those who dare to raise their hand against God's people face divine punishment.

The stories of famine and persecution at Jerusalem end on a triumphal note: The persecutor has fallen; God's word grows and multiplies, and Barnabas and Saul bring John Mark back with them to Antioch (12:24-25).

THE MISSION OF BARNABAS AND SAUL/PAUL FROM ANTIOCH (ACTS 13:1–14:28)

The lectionary of the Fourth and Fifth Weeks of Easter shows greater interest in this section than in what has immediately preceded: two Sunday (C cycle) and six weekday readings. Here Acts begins (13:1-5) with a short description of the church of Antioch. If Jerusalem has the apostles (i.e., the Twelve), Antioch has prophets and teachers. It is scarcely accidental that Paul, whose mission would begin from Antioch, speaks of the leading charisms or gifts of the Spirit thus: "God has appointed in the church first apostles, second prophets, third teachers . . ." (1 Cor 12:28). Acts places Barnabas and Saul among the prophets and teachers, although Paul thought of himself as an apostle. Notice that Barnabas is listed first and Saul last; only during the mission will the order be reversed to Paul and Barnabas (e.g., 13:43) and the name Paul begin to be used consistently in place of Saul. In other words, in the mission the great proclaimer of the gospel will find his status and identity.

We are told that the Antiochene prophets and teachers were "performing a liturgical service [*leitourgein*] to the Lord and fasting." In Luke 5:34-35 Jesus says that the guests do not fast while the bridegroom is with them; but the days will come when the bridegroom will be taken away and then they will fast. Those days have now come and fasting has become a part of the early church life known to Luke. What did the liturgical service consist of? Was it a eucharist? Although the NT never gives a clear picture of any follower of Jesus presiding at the eucharist, in the light of "Do this in commemoration of me" addressed to the Twelve in the Lucan account of the Last Supper (22:19), there is no reason to doubt that members of the Twelve presided. But who presided at Antioch where the Twelve were not present? About the turn of the first century *Didache* 10:7 depicts a situation where prophets celebrated the eucharist, and that may have been the custom earlier as well. In this context of prayer and fasting, hands are laid on Barnabas and Saul. We should not anachronistically speak of this as an ordination; it is a commissioning by the church of Antioch for a mission that is often counted as the first of three Pauline journeys and dated to A.D. 46–49.

Along with John Mark, Barnabas and Saul go to Cyprus, Barnabas' home territory; and they speak in the Jewish synagogues. Since in his own writings Paul speaks of converting Gentiles, scholars have wondered whether Acts is accurate here. But the Pauline letters are to churches evangelized in later missionary journeys at a time when Paul had turned to converting Gentiles—a development that may have stemmed from experiment if he found (as Acts indicates) he was more successful with them.[11] That in fact he was involved with synagogues at some time in his missionary activity is strongly suggested by his statement in 2 Corinthians 11:24: "Five times I received from the Jews thirty-nine lashes." Saul's encountering in Cyprus and besting the false prophet and magus, Bar-Jesus, sets up a certain parallelism with Peter's encountering Simon Magus in Samaria. The enemies of the gospel are not simply earthly forces (as Paul will state clearly in his own letters).

Moving on from Cyprus to Asia Minor may have been a more adventurous extension of the mission than Acts indicates, and perhaps that is what caused John Mark to depart and go to Jerusalem (Acts 13:13). A later reference to this (15:37-39) shows that the behavior of John Mark left a bad memory with Paul. The author makes what happened in Asia Minor at Antioch of Pisidia almost an exemplar of the Pauline mission. Acts 13:16-41 gives a synagogue sermon of Paul (henceforth so named) that in its appeal to the OT and summary of what God did in Jesus is not unlike the sermons that Acts earlier

---

[11] To the end, Acts will continue to show Paul, when he arrives at a new site, speaking first to Jews. That is dubious: Romans 1:16 indicates that in the general proclamation of the gospel Jews came first, but 11:13 characterizes Paul's own apostolate as "to the Gentiles."

Outreach to the Gentiles; the Church of Antioch

attributed to Peter.[12] Thus we get a picture of a consistent message preached by the two great figures who dominate the story of the early church, Peter and Paul. (From Paul's own words [Gal 2:14] we know that these two men did not always agree in their application of the gospel. Yet when it came to the essential message about Jesus, Paul associates himself with Cephas [Peter] and the Twelve [and James!] in a common preaching and a common demand for belief [1 Cor 15:3-11].) Acts 13:42-43 reports a generally favorable reaction to the sermon, but 13:44-49 shows that on the following Sabbath there was hostility from the Jews so that Paul and Barnabas shifted their appeal to the Gentiles. The Jewish hostility continued until they were driven from Pisidia—a rebuff that evidently did not discourage them: "The disciples were filled with joy and the Holy Spirit" (13:52). Much the same thing is reported in Iconium (Acts 14:1-7).

In Lystra (14:8-11) Paul is depicted as healing a man crippled from birth just as Peter healed a cripple in 3:1-10, so that readers are now assured that the healing power of Jesus that was passed on to Peter in dealing with the Jews of Jerusalem has been passed on to Paul as well in dealing with Gentiles. The vivid Gentile reaction, hailing Barnabas and Paul as the gods Zeus and Hermes, catches the ethos of a different world where the message of the one God (14:15-18) has not really taken root, making it all the more difficult to preach Christ. (On this slender evidence, by the way, is based much speculation about the appearance of Paul as short and slight.) This time the hostility aroused by the Jews leads to the stoning of Paul and leaving him for dead. In his own writing Paul will speak eloquently about his suffering for Christ, including being stoned (e.g., 2 Cor 11:23-27); and Acts has incorporated some of that suffering in its presentation as well. In a passing phrase Acts 14:23 has Paul and Barnabas, when they revisited the cities of Asia Minor, appointing presbyters (or elders) in every

---

[12] Undoubtedly the author of Acts composed the speech attributed to Paul; yet the composition is not alien to Pauline thought about Christ attested in his letters. For instance, Acts 13:23 relates Jesus to David's posterity and 13:33 makes God's raising Jesus the moment of saying, "You are my Son; today I have begotten you." In writing to the Romans (1:3-4) Paul speaks of the one who was "descended from David according to the flesh and designated Son of God in power according to the Spirit of holiness by resurrection from the dead." In Acts 13:39 there is justification language similar to that of the Pauline letters.

Christ in the Gospels of the Liturgical Year

church. Many doubt that this form of structure existed so early.[13] At least we may deduce from Acts that by the last third of the first century when the work was written, presbyters existed in these churches and their status was seen as part of the Pauline heritage. The journey ends with a return of Paul and Barnabas to Antioch in Syria and a report to this church that had sent them forth: "God had opened a door of faith to the Gentiles" (14:26-27).

Brief Reflections on John 13–16

In a certain sense the history recounted in Acts 10–14 makes the church whole: Jews and Gentiles coming in numbers to believe in Christ. The lectionary accompanies that story with Gospel readings from Jesus' words to "his own" (John 13:1) at the Last Supper—words set on the night before he died but clearly reaching out to believers of all times and places, telling them how to remain Jesus' own. Nowhere in the lectionary of this season is the pattern of external happenings in Acts and internal life in John clearer.

The weekday selection of the Johannine Jesus' final words (Fourth Week of Easter) begins in 13:16 with the basic reminder that the servant is not greater than the master and must be willing to render the humble service that the master has just demonstrated in washing his disciples' feet. But that admonition is not accepted by the one among them who will lift up his heel against Jesus. In the light of what we have heard in Acts, this is a sober reminder that all the problems were not over when, having struggled with external opposition (Jewish and pagan), Paul and Barnabas made many converts. From the time of Jesus' death to the church today there is always danger from within, with Judas as the example of those (in or out of authority) who are not willing to remain humble disciples.

The main tone of the Last Discourse, however, is more encouraging, as the next Last Supper passage used by the lectionary (John 13:31-35; Fifth Sunday, C cycle) shows us. The Jesus who speaks is already

[13] Presbyters are never mentioned in the undisputed Pauline letters; the appointment of presbyters is a major issue only in the post-Pauline Pastoral Epistles. Yet *episkopoi* and *diakonoi* are mentioned in Philippians 1:2, and arguments from silence about what church structure(s) existed in Paul's lifetime are very uncertain.

glorified and will be further glorified by returning to the Father; those who keep his commandment to love one another will be truly his disciples and share in that glory. In 14:1-6 (weekday sequence) Jesus promises that there are many rooms in his Father's house where he is going to prepare the way for them. We have been reading in Acts of the lateral spread of the church on earth, but the Johannine Jesus is more interested in the vertical relation of those whom he is leaving behind on earth to his heavenly Father. If *koinōnia* with one another is a major concern of Acts, union with God is a major concern of the Last Discourse. As one who shares God's eternal life and earthly human life, Jesus is the embodiment of that union; he is the way. The disciples want to be shown the Father; yet in the long time they have been with Jesus, they have not recognized the extent to which the Father and he indwell and are one (14:8-11). If in Romans 1:13 harvesting fruit means converting people to Christ, the image of the vine and the branches in John 15 puts its emphasis on relationship to Jesus. He is the vine and one bears fruit by getting increased life from him. Disciples must participate and remain in the love that binds the Father and the Son; and as he leaves them behind, they must manifest that love as they live together. Jesus reiterates, "This I command you, to love one another" (15:17).

In the words that Jesus speaks to his own in these chapters, we encounter a major factor that influenced the church's decision to select the Johannine Last Discourse as the Gospel readings for this season. In chapter 27 I pointed to the paradox that we are preparing for Pentecost, and yet the story of Acts that supplies the first readings tells us what happened *after* Pentecost and the coming of the Spirit. The paradox is partially resolved because the Last Discourse in John has five passages where Jesus speaks of the coming of the Paraclete,[14] the Spirit of Truth; and the church can use them in the lectionary of Fifth and Sixth Weeks of Easter to prepare for the feast of the Spirit which is now only a few days away. From the viewpoint of Christians today, Acts' story of the original Pentecost and what happened afterwards in the development of the early church is past history. However, each generation in its own life must relive the coming of the Spirit, and the Johannine Jesus' words have the power to make that possible.

---

[14] 14:15-17; 14:25-26; 15:26-27; 16:7-11; 16:12-14.

In these brief reflections on John 13–16, then, let me concentrate on the unique Johannine presentation of the Paraclete, a title given to the Holy Spirit only in the Fourth Gospel. The Greek *paraklētos* means literally "one called alongside," and a standard use of the term was for one called alongside to help in a legal situation: a defense attorney. This notion is present in some of the words used to translate *paraklētos*, namely, "advocate, counselor." There is a legal tone to some of what Jesus says about the Paraclete; yet the picture is more exactly that of a prosecuting attorney. Jesus himself is going to be crucified and die; in the eyes of the world he will be judged, found guilty, and convicted. Yet after his death, the Paraclete will come and reverse the sentence by convicting the world and proving Jesus' innocence (16:8-11). He will show that Jesus did not sin; rather the world sinned by not believing in him. He is the one who is righteousness, as is shown by the fact that he is not in the grave but with the Father. The judgment that put him to death did not defeat him; ironically it defeated his great adversary, the Prince of this world.

In a famous passage (Job 19:25) Job knows that he will go to death judged heinously guilty by all because of the sufferings visited on him; yet he knows that his vindicator lives, namely, the angel who will stand on his grave and show to all that he was innocent. That vindicating angelic spirit has the role of a paraclete, and Jesus now looks for the Holy Spirit as his Paraclete. We have seen in Acts divine interventions to prove the righteousness of Peter and Paul when they were accused; and as we look for the coming of the Spirit, we look for one whose task is to be certain that ultimately injustice and evil cannot overcome those who believe.

Yet there is another role for "one called alongside": Sometimes those who suffer or are lonely need to call in someone to console and comfort them. That aspect of the Paraclete is caught by the translation "Comforter" (as in Holy Comforter), "Consoler." In the context of the Last Supper Jesus' disciples are sorrowful because he is departing; what should console them is the promise that someone just like Jesus is coming to take his place. Here we touch on a major emphasis in the Johannine presentation of the Paraclete: the likeness of the Spirit to Jesus that enables the Spirit to substitute for Jesus.[15] (That is why the

---

[15] Intrinsic to that notion is the idea that the Paraclete is personal. The common Greek term for "Spirit," *pneuma*, is neuter; and therefore in many NT passages

Outreach to the Gentiles; the Church of Antioch

Paraclete Spirit cannot come until Jesus departs.) Both come forth from the Father; both are given by the Father, or sent by the Father; both are rejected by the world. The Johannine Jesus claims to have nothing on his own; whatever he does or says is what he has heard or seen with the Father. The Paraclete will speak nothing on his own; he will take what belongs to Jesus and declare it; he will speak only what he hears (John 16:13-15). When Jesus is on earth and the Father in heaven, whoever sees Jesus sees the Father. When Jesus has gone to the Father, whoever listens to the Paraclete will be listening to Jesus. In short what Jesus is to the Father, the Paraclete is to Jesus. Thus in many ways the Paraclete fulfills Jesus' promise to return.

In one extraordinary passage (16:7) Jesus says that it is better that he go away, for otherwise the Paraclete will not come. In what possible sense can the presence of the Paraclete be better than the presence of Jesus? Perhaps the solution lies in one major distinction between the presence of Jesus and that of the Paraclete. In Jesus the Word became flesh; the Paraclete is not incarnate. In the one human life of Jesus, visibly, at a definite time and a definite place, God's presence was uniquely in the world; and then corporally Jesus left this world and went to the Father. The Paraclete's presence is not visible, not confined to any one time or place. Rather the Paraclete dwells in everyone who loves Jesus and keeps the commandments, and so his presence is not limited by time (14:15-17). That may be the way in which the coming of the Paraclete is "better." These words of Jesus about the Paraclete illustrate beautifully how the audience to which he speaks at the Last Supper extends beyond those present at that moment. In terms of the presence of God as the Paraclete there are no second-class citizens: The Paraclete is just as present in the modern disciples of Jesus as he was in the first generation.

That fact is particularly important when we consider one of the principal activities of the Paraclete. The Paraclete is the Spirit of Truth who supplies guidance along the way of all truth. The Johannine Jesus had many things to say that his disciples could never understand in his lifetime (16:12); but then the Paraclete comes and takes those things and declares them (16:15). In other words the Paraclete solves the problem of new insights into a past revelation. When God gave the

---

neuter pronouns are employed: The Spirit is spoken of as "it," whether or not that is preserved in English translations. But *paraklētos* is personal (masculine), and the referential pronouns that are used are personal.

Christ in the Gospels of the Liturgical Year

Son, divine revelation was granted in all its completeness: Jesus was the very Word of God. Yet that Word spoke audibly under the limitations of a particular culture and set of issues. How do Christians of other ages get God's guidance for dealing with entirely different issues in a very different culture? Jesus' words make clear that the Paraclete who is present to every time and culture brings no new revelation; rather he takes the revelation of the Word made flesh and declares it anew, facing the things to come. We see from the words of Paul to the presbyters of Ephesus in Acts 20:28-31 that one reason for the establishment of the presbyteral church structure was to protect the faithful from strange perversions of truth. The Pauline Pastoral Epistles also envision presbyter-bishops who hold on to the doctrine they have received as a criterion for judging what is valid in any new approaches. Thus at a time when other churches were developing such an external teaching magisterium to guide all those under pastoral care, John places the emphasis on the indwelling Paraclete, the guide to all truth, given to every believer. There has been a tendency in Christian history to allow one or the other of these approaches to dominate; but as the sole approach each one has drawbacks. Teachers whose only strength is to hold on to the tradition may tend to regard all new ideas as dangerous. The Spirit is a vibrant guide and would seem better adapted to face the things to come; yet when two believers who claim the guidance of the indwelling Paraclete disagree, often neither can see a way in which he or she can be wrong, and the tendency is to split into irreconcilable divisions. By reading John alongside Acts, implicitly the church is reminding itself that guidance for Christians involves an interplay between external instruction by well-grounded teachers and internal movements of the Paraclete. Both factors are essential to enable the church to combine valid tradition and new insights without breaking the *koinōnia*.

The Jesus of the Last Supper who prepares his disciples for the coming of the Spirit is not unrealistic. The world will hate the disciples who have received the Spirit of Truth (15:18-19) which the world cannot accept because it neither sees nor recognizes that Spirit (14:17). The disciples will be expelled from the synagogues and even put to death (16:2-3), a Johannine parallel to some of the treatment of Paul that Acts narrates. Yet because Jesus is with them, they can have peace. "In the world you will have trouble; but take courage I have overcome the world" (16:33).

Outreach to the Gentiles; the Church of Antioch

Chapter 32

The Jerusalem Conference Propels the Church to the Ends of the Earth (Acts 15–28)

If what Paul had done pleased the church at Antioch, it did not please the circumcision party at Jerusalem who now send people to Antioch to challenge the acceptance of Gentiles without circumcision. One might have thought that this issue was settled at Jerusalem earlier (Acts 11) when Peter justified his acceptance of the Gentile Cornelius without circumcision. It was, however, one thing to incorporate into a largely Jewish Christian community a few Gentiles; it was another to be faced with whole churches of Gentiles such as Paul had founded—churches that would have little relation to Judaism other than holding in veneration the Jewish Scriptures.

We can see in Romans 11:13-36 Paul's understanding of what he thought would happen from his Gentile mission: The Gentiles were a wild olive branch grafted on the tree of Israel; and eventually, through envy, all Israel would come to faith in Christ and be saved.

The circumcision party may have been far more realistic in their fears that Paul had begun a process whereby Christianity would become an almost entirely Gentile religion, which of course is what happened. (Ultraconservatives, as distorted as their theology may be, are often more perceptive about the inevitable direction of changes than are the moderates who propose them.) Far from being grafted on the tree of Israel, the Gentile Christians became the tree. To stop that foreseeable catastrophe Paul's opponents attack the principle that Gentiles may be admitted without becoming Jews (i.e., being circumcised). They cause enough trouble that Paul and Barnabas have to go to Jerusalem to debate the issue. What follows is a report of what may be judged the most important meeting or conference[1] ever held in the history of

---

[1] Very often this is called the Council of Jerusalem, but preferably the term "council" is avoided because people tend to confuse it with later ecumenical councils of the church (Nicaea, etc.).

Christianity, for it decided the question of whether Christianity would be a minor Jewish sect or would soon become a separate religion reaching to the ends of the earth.

THE GREAT CRISIS SETTLED BY THE JERUSALEM CONFERENCE (ACTS 15:1-29)

Selections from this chapter of Acts are read on the Sixth Sunday of Easter (C year) and on three days of the Fifth Week.

We are fortunate in having two accounts of the Jerusalem conference, one in Acts 15, the other in Galatians 2; and this double perspective teaches us much about the great personalities of early Christianity. Scholars tend to prefer Paul's own account as an eyewitness and to regard the Acts account as later bowdlerizing. There is no question that Acts presents a simplified and less acrimonious report; but as regards Galatians, we should recognize that a personal account written in self-defense has its own optic that removes it from the realm of the purely objective. For instance, in Galatians 2:1 Paul says, "I went up to Jerusalem with Barnabas, taking Titus along with me"; Acts 15:2 says that "Paul and Barnabas and some others were appointed to go up to Jerusalem." That they went up commissioned by the church of Antioch may very well be the more accurate picture, even though (as part of his self-defense in Galatians) Paul highlights his initiative in cooperating. It is very clear from Acts that those in Jerusalem had the power of decision on the issue. Paul speaks disparagingly of the "so-called pillars" whose reputation meant nothing to him; but, of course, that title implies that their reputation did mean something to others, and in the long run Paul could not stand alone. True, as he claims, he got his gospel (of the freely given grace to the Gentiles) through a revelation from Jesus Christ and would not change it even if an angel told him to do so (Gal 1:8, 11-12); yet he mentions the possibility that he had run in vain (2:2). If that is more than an oratorical touch, he may have been admitting the power of the "pillars": Should they deny his Gentile churches *koinōnia* with the mother church in Jerusalem, there would be a division that negated the very nature of the church. Thus, despite Paul's certitude about the rightness of his evangelizing, the outcome of the Jerusalem meeting for the communities he had evangelized involved uncertainty.

The Jerusalem Conference Propels the Church to the Ends of the Earth

To have brought along Titus, an uncircumcised Gentile (Gal 2:3), was a shrewd maneuver. Probably some of the circumcision party[2] had never seen any of the uncircumcised Gentiles whom they denied to be true Christians; and it is always more difficult to confront others who patently believe in Christ and tell them face-to-face, "You are not Christians because you do not agree with me." Another prudent step by Paul (Gal 2:2) was first to lay out his argument privately before those at Jerusalem who were of repute. First reactions of authorities are often defensive; when they are uttered in private, they can be modified later without loss of face. Some tragedies could have been averted in the post–Vatican II Catholic Church if those eager for change had stayed away from the front page of newspapers. Such "eyeball-to-eyeball" confrontations with authorities usually proved little more than nearsightedness.

The public disputation, however, is the core of the story. Four participants were involved, two predictable and two unpredictable. Predictable were the unnamed spokesmen of the circumcision party who demanded that the Gentiles be circumcised in order to become fully Christian and, on the other extreme, Paul and his companions who argued that to demand circumcision would nullify the dispensation of grace by Christ. Unpredictable were Peter, who as the first of the Twelve had a responsibility toward the whole people of the renewed Israel, and James, who with the elders represented the leadership of the Hebrew Christian community of Jerusalem. Arguments from three of the four participants are reported. Understandably, given the goal of Galatians, Paul's account is centered on his own role, not yielding submission even for a moment and convincing the reputed pillars of the truth of his gospel. Yet Acts gives the least space to Barnabas and Paul (15:12), sandwiching their report between Peter's words (15:6-11) and those of James (15:13-21)—an arrangement creating the impression that it is the last who carried the day. Probably one needs to read between the lines of both accounts. The issue to be discussed was what Paul and Barnabas had done in their missionary activity, and in that sense the conference was centered on Paul. Yet his reasoning was probably implicit in what he had done and was not likely to persuade

---

[2] In place of this more neutral terminology of Acts (which in 15:5 also specifies that they were members of the party of the Pharisees), Paul speaks polemically of "false brethren" spying out the freedom of his treatment of the Gentiles.

Christ in the Gospels of the Liturgical Year

those still undecided; therefore Acts may very well be correct in the proportion it gives to Paul's remarks. Peter's stance favorable to Gentiles was already known at Jerusalem, and so the real suspense may have been centered on what James would say, since he would carry the Jerusalem church with him. Galatians 2:9 recognizes that by listing James ahead of Cephas (Peter) and John as the so-called pillars of the church.

What was the reasoning advanced? Acts says that Barnabas and Paul recounted the signs and wonders done among the Gentiles; Galatians says that Paul related to them the gospel he preached among the Gentiles, which surely meant an account of how such people had come to faith without circumcision. If Galatians 1 is a guide, Paul's self-understanding was that, if God had freely called him while he was persecuting Christians, God's grace was given freely without previous demands. According to Acts Peter's argument was also experiential: Gentiles had to be accepted without distinctions and imposed burdens because God had sent the Holy Spirit on the uncircumcised Cornelius. James' argument in Acts is reasoned and, as might be expected from a conservative Hebrew Christian, draws upon the Law. The prophets foretold that the Gentiles would come, and the Law of Moses allowed uncircumcised Gentiles to live among the people of God provided that they abstained from certain listed pollutions. Unfortunately we do not hear the arguments advanced by the circumcision party, other than the simple statement in Acts 15:5 that the Law of Moses required circumcision.

What is startling is a deafening silence. No one who favors admitting the Gentiles without circumcision mentions the example of Jesus, saying, "Jesus told us to do so." And, of course, the reason is that he never did tell them to do so. Indeed, one may suspect that the only ones likely to have mentioned Jesus would have been those of the circumcision party, arguing precisely that there was no authorization from him for such a radical departure from the Law.[3] This may have

---

[3] The Synoptic Gospels give attention to Jesus' reaching out to tax-collectors and prostitutes. Was part of the reason for preserving that memory an implicit rebuttal of the circumcision position? One could construct the rebuttal thus: Jesus did reach out to those outside the Law, and now in our time the Gentiles are the ones outside the Law. One must recognize, however, that such arguments offer their own difficulties, for they can be used to justify almost any practice.

The Jerusalem Conference Propels the Church to the Ends of the Earth

been the first of many times when those who have resisted change in the church did so by arguing that Jesus never did this, whereas those who promoted change did so on the import of Christ for a situation that the historical Jesus did not encounter. In any case, both Acts and Galatians agree that Peter (and John) and James kept the *koinōnia* with Paul and his Gentile churches. The road was now open for free and effective evangelizing to the ends of the earth. In fact that road would also lead away from Judaism. Whatever non-Christian Jews thought of Christian Jews, they were bound together by having been born into the chosen people. There would be no such ties to Christian Gentiles; and even though the Savior for those Gentiles was a Jew born under the Law, Christianity would soon be looked on as a Gentile religion quite alien to a Judaism for which the Law would become ever more important once the Temple was destroyed.

THE RETURN TO ANTIOCH; WIDER PAULINE MISSIONARY ACTIVITY (ACTS 15:30–21:14)

Reasonably consecutive readings from Acts 16–20 constitute the selections in the lectionary for ten weekdays from the end of the Fifth Week of Easter into the middle of the Seventh Week.

Acts 15:30-39: The Return to Antioch. According to Acts Paul and Barnabas went back to Antioch with Judas and Silas, carrying a letter that made it clear that circumcision was not to be required of Gentile converts. However, the Gentiles were to be required to abstain from four things proscribed by Leviticus 17–18 for aliens living among Israel: meat offered to idols, the eating of blood, the eating of strangled animals (i.e., animals that were not ritually slaughtered), and incestuous unions (*porneia*, "impurity," but here with kin). This is the position that James advocated when he spoke at the Jerusalem conference. When we compare the picture to Paul's account in Galatians 2:11ff., we realize that the history was probably more complicated. A plausible combination of the two sources of information yields something like the following. Paul and Barnabas went back to Antioch with the good news that freedom from circumcision had been recognized. However, struggles developed as to whether Gentile Christians were bound by food laws as were the Jewish Christians who constituted the church alongside them. Paul argued that they were not bound, and Peter participated in this free practice until men from James came demand-

Christ in the Gospels of the Liturgical Year

ing specific practices of the food laws.[4] Peter acceded to James, much to Paul's anger. Probably so also did Barnabas and John Mark; for Acts, which is silent about the struggle between Paul and Peter, reports a quarrel between Paul and those other two figures, so that they would no longer travel together (15:36-40). When Paul set out on another mission, it was Silas he took. In the churches he would convert (where Gentile Christians would have been the majority) the Gentiles were not bound by Jewish food laws, as we see from Paul's letters. Apparently in the area where James of Jerusalem had influence (Acts 15:23: Antioch, Syria, and Cilicia, where presumably Jewish Christians were the majority), the Gentiles were bound. Through the Jerusalem conference the *koinōnia* had been preserved as to what was essential for conversion: Gentiles did not have to become Jews. However, this did not guarantee uniformity of lifestyle. Paul thought that freedom from the food laws was so important that it was an issue of gospel truth (Gal 2:14); apparently others did not think it that important. We can learn a lesson today from this later struggle: Too often there has been an insistence on uniformity. Only with great care should comparable differences, no matter how deeply felt, become a litmus test of true Christianity or true Catholicism.

Acts 15:40–21:14: Wider Pauline Missionary Activity. It is customary to detect in Acts three Pauline missionary journeys, with one journey (A.D. 46–49) before the Jerusalem conference and two after it (A.D. 50–52, 54–58). We are uncertain, however, that the author of Acts made such a division, for it is easy to look on everything from 15:40 to 21:14 as one long journey.[5] What is certain is that, after the Jerusalem decision, Acts describes Paul's major missionary activity as ranging much farther than his first missionary effort. It is now that, after retracing his previous journey, he went to northern Galatia, and crossed over to Greece (Philippi, Thessalonica, Athens, Corinth), coming back to Ephesus in Asia Minor and finally back to Antioch. Then setting out once more from Antioch he went to Ephesus for two years and from

[4] Galatians 2:12. Scholars are divided on whether the men from James included Judas and Silas bringing the letter mentioned in Acts.
[5] Only one extremely brief passage (18:22-24) would encourage us to divide it. In any case, the division into journeys is entirely based on Acts, not on Paul's own expressed memories, even though he could supply a chronological calculation of his visits to Jerusalem (Gal 2:1).

The Jerusalem Conference Propels the Church to the Ends of the Earth

there he wrote to some of the churches just mentioned (probably Galatians, Philippians, and part of the Corinthian correspondence). Subsequent travels brought him to Macedonia and Corinth, travels that offered an occasion for the writing of the rest of the Corinthian correspondence and the letter to the Romans. It is almost as if the Jerusalem decision made possible the most creative time of Paul's life.

The narrative begins with the circumcision of Timothy in Acts 16:1-5, the reliability of which action is questioned by many scholars. They think it inconceivable that Paul would have changed his stance on circumcision even to win converts. However, if Timothy was looked on as a Jew, we have no clear evidence that Paul would have wanted Jewish Christians to give up circumcision. The words in Galatians 5:2, "If you receive circumcision, Christ will be of no advantage to you," are addressed to Gentiles. Romans 9:4-5 speaks of the privileges of Paul's "kinsmen according to the flesh," the Israelites: To them belong the sonship, the glory, the covenants, the giving of the Law, the worship, the promises, the patriarchs. Why deprive Timothy of this birthright? At least some Christians must have thought that way, and this disputable issue is indicative of how complex it must have been to be a Jew who believed in Jesus.

Paul's vision of the man of Macedonia in 16:9-10 that causes him to cross over to Greece is seen by the author of Acts as a divinely inspired moment. The spread of Christian faith to Europe is presented almost as manifest destiny; and in retrospect the tremendous contributions of two thousand years of European Christianity would justify that judgment. Far more than the author of Acts could have dreamed, the appeal of the man of Macedonia ultimately brought Christianity to ends of the earth that in the first century were not even known to exist. Some on other continents who were evangelized from Europe complain that they were indoctrinated with an alien culture. Yet Europeanization would probably have happened in any case; and the fact that the cross of Christ was planted alongside the banner of the respective king was potentially a helpful corrective—both to abuses that existed before Europeans came (that are sometimes forgotten) and to the abuses they brought.

The evangelizing at Philippi (16:11-40) shows us some of the best and the worst of a mission among Gentiles. The generous openness and support of Lydia, a Gentile devotee of Jewish worship, is a model for the Christian household. On the other hand, the legal and financial problems presented by the girl who had a spirit of divination remind us that Paul was dealing with an alien, superstitious world. As the account continues, the miraculous opening of the prison echoes scenes of Peter's miraculous release from prison and shows that God is with his emissary to the Gentiles. The complexity of Paul's trial because he is a Roman citizen illustrates how the early Christians, in order to survive, had to use every available means, including Roman law.

At Thessalonica (17:1-9) Paul runs into the same kind of Jewish opposition that marred his mission in Asia Minor before the Jerusalem conference. The list of charges against Paul and his supporters in 17:6-7 resembles the list of charges against Jesus before Pilate in Luke 23:2—a list found only in Luke.[6] Before we finish, we shall see other resemblances between the treatment of Jesus and the treatment of Paul, undoubtedly a parallelism that fit the theology of Luke-Acts. Jewish opposition forces Paul to go on to Beroea where in an interesting gesture of evenhandedness the author tells us that the Jews were nobler and less contentious. But the Jews from Thessalonica follow, and so Paul pushes on to Athens (17:15).

Just as the author of Acts exhibited a sense of destiny when Paul crossed to Europe, he shows an appreciation of what Athens meant to Greek culture in recounting Paul's stay there. He supplies a dramatic context of Epicurean and Stoic philosophers (17:18) who try to fit this new teaching into their categories. The author knows about the agora or public square (17:17) and the hill of the Areopagus (17:19); and the sermon delivered there by Paul draws on an awareness of the many temples and statues of the city. The play on the altar to an unknown god and the philosophical and poetic quotations offer a cultured approach to the message about Christ, quite unlike the gambits of the other sermons in Acts. The master-touch in the scene may be the reaction to this eloquence from the cosmopolitan audience: Some mock; others put Paul off; some believe. Paul will go from here directly to Corinth, and in 1 Corinthians 2:1-2 he describes what may have been a lesson learned: "When I came to you proclaiming the mystery of God, I did not come with lofty words or wisdom. For I decided to know nothing among you except Jesus Christ and him crucified."

[6] The more formal character of the Roman trial of Jesus in Luke probably stems from the familiarity of the author with Roman procedures against individual Christians in his own time.

The Jerusalem Conference Propels the Church to the Ends of the Earth

By comparing Athens to other great cities in the Roman Empire of the first century one can evaluate strengths and priorities in the Christian mission. Athens was the center of culture, philosophy, and art; Paul's message had only limited success there, and we are told of no other early mission to the city. Alexandria was the center of learning with its magnificent library tradition; the eloquent preacher Apollos came from there (Acts 18:24), but otherwise (and despite later legends) we know of no pre-70 Christian missionary activity there. Rome was the seat of imperial power and ruled the world. There was a successful Christian mission in the capital by the 40s; Paul could address plural house churches there before 60; various NT writings are thought to have been addressed to or sent by the church of Rome; and ultimately Peter and Paul would die there. Why greater attention to Rome than to Athens or Alexandria? An answer detectable beneath the symbolism may be that Christians were realists; neither Athens the museum nor Alexandria the library could sway the world, and so the powerful city that did was a better target.

Paul's stay at Corinth (18:1-18) has an added interest because of the later correspondence that he would direct to that church (causing us to know more about it than about any other Pauline church) and because characters like Aquila and Priscilla (Prisca) will feature in that correspondence. These two figures who had come from Rome (probably already as Christians) will eventually go back to Rome and be part of Paul's contacts ("coworkers in Christ Jesus") with that city before he ever gets there (Rom 16:3). Since we have already heard of Silas and Timothy, we can see Paul forming a circle of colleagues and friends who would be in contact with him all his life. Just as the disciples of Jesus carried on the master's work, the coworkers of Paul would continue the apostle's work and literature in the post-Pauline period. The reference to tent-making at the beginning of Paul's stay at Corinth reminds us of the indication in his letters that he normally supported himself and did not ask his hearers for personal financial help (also Acts 20:33-35). Once again we see Jewish hostility so that Paul is brought before the tribunal of the Roman proconsul Gallio—a figure whose presence at Corinth supplies a most important key for dating Paul's mission there to A.D. 51–52. The unwillingness of the Roman official to get involved in Jewish religious questions is part of the general picture given of the pre-Nero period when Rome was not yet hostile to Christians as such. The tribunal or *bēma* of Corinth has recently been excavated and may be seen in the agora or market, a reminder of how Christianity was now being proclaimed in places and before people verifiably historical.

Once Paul leaves Corinth, Acts crowds into a few verses (that may even be confused) a return through Ephesus and Caesarea to Jerusalem (18:22a?) and back to Ephesus. The lectionary skips even that brief report and follows Acts 18:24–19:40 in concentrating on scenes in Ephesus, another great center of Pauline activity (more than two years) and of future importance for the church. Here the author tells us of Apollos from Alexandria and others who believed in Jesus but had received only the baptism of John and knew nothing of the Holy Spirit. Little enlightenment is given about how such a situation could exist—were these evangelized by some who knew Jesus during the ministry but left Palestine before the crucifixion and resurrection? Acts has told us before and tells us again of Paul's struggles with synagogue Jews and with devotees of pagan deities, divination, and magic; but this is one of the few times that it hints at a confrontation with competing Christian preachers, a struggle that has a major place in much of the Pauline correspondence.

Alas, such conflicts offer us background for our church situation today where Christians are struggling not only with a secular world that looks on faith in Christ as an antiquated superstition but also with each other over different presentations of the gospel. Acts 19:11-17 piques our interest with a portrait of Paul the miracle-worker and of Jewish exorcists attempting to drive out evil spirits using the name of Jesus—another reminder of how closely the ministry of the early church resembled the ministry of Jesus. Several times previously in Acts when describing the success of the ministry, the author stopped to report that the word of God increased or grew (6:7; 12:24), and now he repeats that refrain (19:20). It signals that alongside Jerusalem and Antioch, Christianity has now another great center, Ephesus, and that Paul's ministry has been blessed even as was the ministry of the Twelve.

Acts 19:21 is the first indication of Paul's ultimate plan to go to Rome via Greece and Jerusalem, an important anticipation for how the book will end. The lectionary skips over the colorful account of the silversmiths' riot centered on Artemis or Diana of the Ephesians (19:23-40) as well as the travels through Macedonia to Troas where Paul raised the dead to life (20:1-12). It would be of interest to know if Paul's

The Jerusalem Conference Propels the Church to the Ends of the Earth

breaking bread in 20:11 means that he presided at the eucharist. What does appear in full in the lectionary is the eloquent farewell sermon given at Miletus to the presbyters of the church of Ephesus (20:17-38). Earlier I mentioned the problem of whether Acts' account of Paul appointing presbyters on his first missionary journey was anachronistic, and that same issue has been raised here. Nevertheless this sermon has great value as a guide to how the author of Acts sees the presbyters inheriting the care of the church from Paul. In the Pastoral Epistles there is information suggesting that, after going to Rome and being released from prison, Paul came back to Asia Minor in the mid 60s. Acts betrays no knowledge of this, so that the sermon constitutes Paul's final directives to those whom he will never see again (20:25, 38).[7] It begins with an *apologia pro vita sua* (20:18-21) as Paul reflects on how he has served the Lord; this yields to foreboding about the imprisonment and afflictions he must now undergo. This man who first encountered the profession of Christ in Jerusalem some twenty years before at the trial and stoning of Stephen is being led by the Spirit to return to that city where he will be put on trial amidst cries for his death (see 22:22). In this portentous context Paul admonishes the presbyters he is leaving behind to be shepherds of the flock in which the Holy Spirit has made them overseers (20:28: *episkopos*).[8]

As we can see from 1 Peter 5:1-4, the comparison of the presbyters to shepherds of the flock was well established in the late first century. Although that image contains within it a note of authority, the real emphasis is on the obligation to take care of the flock and not let it be ravaged—in short, what we mean by "*pastoral* care," a terminology derived from shepherding. The most pressing danger, as also in the Pastoral Epistles, is false teaching: "those who speak perverse things so as to draw away disciples" (Acts 20:30). Subsequently churches with strong doctrinal emphasis have found in such a passage the roots of a

[7] This portion of Acts resembles the context of the Pastoral Epistles where the time of Paul's departure has come (2 Tim 4:6-8). In fact both Acts and the Pastorals (in that order) were most likely written after Paul's death. Many scholars think that of the existing correspondence Romans was the last letter actually written by Paul and contains his last preserved thoughts.

[8] *Episkopos*, literally "one who oversees," is the Greek word for bishop. Once more we are close to the atmosphere of the Pastorals where there are groups of presbyter-bishops in the post-Pauline churches, i.e., presbyters who oversee the community's life and teaching.

Christ in the Gospels of the Liturgical Year

teaching magisterium that is vigilant against error. In this context Paul stresses that he supported himself, coveting no one's silver and gold (20:33-35), and indeed elsewhere in the NT advice to presbyters warns against a corrupting love of money (1 Pet 5:2; Titus 1:7; 1 Tim 3:3), an enduring temptation since the presbyters managed the common funds. After this farewell at Miletus, Acts (21:1-14) tells us more briefly of other dramatic farewells at Tyre and Caesarea, with the supernatural warnings of impending doom growing more intense.

ARREST AT JERUSALEM; IMPRISONMENT;
SENT TO ROME FOR JUDGMENT (ACTS 21:15–28:31)

Clearly then it is with a sense of approaching climax that we read finally that Paul went up to Jerusalem. His report of success among the Gentiles (presumably accompanied by the collection of money for the Christian poor of Judea of which we learn from the letters) is welcomed by James and the elders who match his claims with reports of their own successes among the Jews. Even Acts, which unlike Paul's letters has not signaled his expectation of a less than enthusiastic reception by the Jerusalem Christian authorities, cannot disguise the negative feelings raised by rumors about what Paul has been teaching.[9] (Evidently the nasty habit of misjudging one's fellow Christians based on hearsay without personally verifying the facts goes back to Christian beginnings.)

The well-intentioned plan to have Paul show his loyalty to Judaism by purifying himself and going to the Temple (21:24) fails when fanatics start a riot claiming that he has defiled the holy place by bringing Gentiles into it. Paul is saved from the crowd only by the intervention of a Roman tribune with soldiers who arrest him. The lectionary ignores all this as well as Paul's speech of defense (22:3-21) in which he recounts his conversion. After the readings from Paul's speech to the Ephesian elders at Miletus in Acts 20, the lectionary picks up Paul's story with 22:30; 23:6-11 when he stands before the Sanhedrin and arouses dissent between the Sadducees and Pharisees over the

---

[9] We can deduce from Paul's letters that he never taught the Gentiles to follow admonitions such as those found in the apostolic letter of Acts 15:23-29, restricting their freedom, a letter James reminds him of in 21:25. However, we have no evidence that he taught "all the Jews who live among the Gentiles to forsake Moses" (21:21).

The Jerusalem Conference Propels the Church to the Ends of the Earth

resurrection. There are echoes here of Jesus' dealing with the Sadducees over the resurrection (Luke 20:27) and his appearance before the Sanhedrin. The fate of Paul the great disciple is not different from the fate of his master. The parallelism is heightened by the next lectionary selection as it races to end the readings from Acts in the last week of Easter. From the many-chaptered account of Paul's trials and imprisonment, it chooses 25:13-21 where the Roman governor Festus who has inherited Paul as a prisoner brings him before the Herodian king Agrippa II to be heard, even as in Luke's passion (23:6-12) Pilate turns Jesus over to Herod Antipas. Neither Herodian king finds the prisoner guilty.

The last reading in the pre-Pentecost lectionary is appropriately from the last chapter in Acts (28:16-20, 30-31) as Paul comes to Rome after his long and treacherous sea journey. Unfortunately it does not contain the magnificent understatement in 28:14, "And so we came to Rome." This is the ultimate step foreseen by the risen Jesus: "You shall be my witnesses in Jerusalem and Judea and Samaria and *to the ends of the earth.*" By the time Paul came to the capital in the early 60s, Christian communities had been there for about twenty years. But in the flow of the story that has centered on Peter and Paul, the climax comes with the arrival in Rome of the great missionary. The irony is that Roman authorities have sent him there because of his appeal to the emperor, and thus have been responsible for the evangelizing of their own empire. To the very end of its account Acts portrays Paul appealing to the local Jews with the insistence that he has done nothing "against the customs of our fathers."[10] Nevertheless his preaching to them about Jesus has no success, and the last words attributed to him in the book despair of ever getting a hearing from Jews and a firm decision to turn to the Gentiles who will listen. Clearly the author expects the Christian message to be carried out to the whole empire. The summary that ends the book speaks of Paul's preaching two years in Rome with success.

---

[10] Acts 28:21 is important: The author portrays the Jewish community in Jerusalem as being in close contact with the Jewish community in Rome (which may well be factual). That the Jews in Rome have heard nothing hostile about Paul is odd, since in writing to the Romans Paul seems to expect hostility upon arrival from Christians who are particularly attached to Judaism. I have discussed this in *Antioch and Rome* (New York: Paulist, 1982), 111–22.

Christ in the Gospels of the Liturgical Year

Brief Reflections on John 17 and John 21

In the last week of the pre-Pentecost season the lectionary employs as Gospel readings the Johannine Jesus' "high priestly" prayer in John 17 and his last words to Simon Peter and the Beloved Disciple in John 21. The prayer constitutes one of the most exalted pages in the NT as the Johannine Jesus speaks to the Father of the completion of the work assigned him. That work, as we have seen, involves the gift of eternal life, a life centered on the intimate knowledge of the one true God and of Jesus who was sent. Those whom the Father has given Jesus have been entrusted with such revealed knowledge, and Jesus prays for them. His assertion "I do not pray for the world" (17:9) startles us today, especially after Vatican Council II which took a generally positive attitude toward the possibilities offered by the modern world. Yet the distinction Jesus makes about being in the world but not of it (17:14-15) is valid. Although God manifested love for the world in sending the only Son (3:16), by the end of the Gospel the world represents those who have preferred darkness to light. Jesus' own are not part of that world which has a Prince of its own, the evil one. The only one of Jesus' companions who belongs to the world is Judas, the son of destruction (17:12), the one into whom Satan entered (13:2, 27). The rest are protected by the name that the Father has given to Jesus (17:11-12)[11] and that he has revealed to them (17:6, 26).

Throughout the Last Discourse Jesus has been speaking through and beyond his disciples to believers of all time. The prayer makes that explicit in 17:20: "It is not for these alone that I pray but also for those who believe in me through their word." The special focus of this prayer for subsequent believers is "that they all may be one," as Jesus returns to the attitude of the Good Shepherd (10:16). The story we have heard in the readings from Acts stresses *koinōnia* in the face of divisions among Christians; and now John 17:22-23 gives a most realistic reason for Jesus' disciples being one, namely, that "the world

---

[11] We saw that baptism in the name of Jesus probably meant confessing the name by which Jesus' status was acknowledged (Lord, Messiah [Christ], Savior, Son of God, etc.). Sometimes that confession is connected to what happened at the resurrection/exaltation, e.g., "God greatly exalted him and bestowed on him the name that is above every other name . . . Jesus Christ is Lord" (Phil 2:9-11). John is clear that Jesus possessed the name (Son of Man? I AM?) during his earthly life.

The Jerusalem Conference Propels the Church to the Ends of the Earth

may know that you sent me." One of the greatest obstacles to evangelizing others about Jesus is a lack of love among Christians, and so
Jesus prays that the love the Father had for him before the creation of
the world "may be in them and I may be in them" (17:24, 26).

After the prayer the lectionary turns to John 21:15-25. Roughly at the
same lectionary moment when Paul in Acts is speaking his last words
to the presbyters whom he has appointed in the church of Ephesus,
instructing them to keep watch over the flock, Jesus speaks his last
words to Simon Peter instructing him to feed the lambs. As I have
stressed above, this belated introduction of human pastoral care into
the Johannine picture manages to keep alive the ideal of the one Good
Shepherd. The sheep still belong to Jesus, and Simon Peter must show
his care for them by the way he dies. It is ironical that having received
his pastoral assignment Peter's first reaction is typical of many in
church structure ever since: He is worried about the Beloved Disciple
who seems to be a threat because he does not fit in. Jesus' corrective is
sharp and perceptively enduring: "How does that concern you? Your
concern is to follow me." Although Peter is given pastoral authority,
it is of the Beloved Disciple who holds no position in church structure
that Jesus says, "Suppose I would like him to remain until I come"—a
consoling thought for the vast majority whose only position in the
church is to be disciples. A discipleship of love is what really matters
in the eyes of the Johannine Jesus, and that will endure. No wonder
that the evangelist's last words (21:25) about such a Jesus (and the
lectionary's last words in the pre-Pentecostal season) are that all the
books in the world cannot do him justice.

Christ in the Gospels of the Ordinary Sundays

Essays on the Gospel Readings
of the Ordinary Sundays
in the Three-Year Liturgical Cycle

Chapters 33–36

Chapter 33

The Gospel According to Matthew[1]
(Liturgical Year A)

Preliminary Statement

In the final section of this book I want to supply assistance in appreciating the Gospels in the three-year Sunday lectionary. In principle the usage is simple, but there are some complications. I shall be concerned only with the readings on the Ordinary Sundays of the year, not the festal periods of Advent, Christmas, Holy Week, and Easter through to Pentecost, which I have already covered in previous chapters.

How are the Gospels used on the Ordinary Sundays of the year? This question concerns Matthew, Mark, and Luke—the three Synoptic Gospels. (Actually, I also devote a chapter to the usage of John in the days after Christmas and in Lent for the sake of completeness.) For practical purposes one must think of beginning the sequential reading of the three Synoptic Gospels with the Third Sunday of Ordinary Time. In each of the three Gospels this means starting consecutive lectionary readings with Jesus' activities after John the Baptist (JBap) has been removed from public activity because he has been arrested by Herod (starting respectively with Matt 4:12-23 in Year A; Mark 1:14-20 in Year B; Luke 4:14-21 in Year C[2]).

---

[1] A minor point: Lectors in church should be trained to read exactly the title that the lectionary gives to the reading (not "*of* Matthew" or "according to *St.* Matthew" or, worst of all, the cutesy rendering, "The Good News St. Matthew wrote to us"— no NT book was written to us, even though all have meaning for us). These lectionary Gospel titles are the oldest we know, and we should respect them.

[2] Actually on that Sunday the lectionary begins with the Lucan Prologue, 1:1-4, and then follows immediately with 4:14. I shall comment on this in chapter 35, below.

Now no Gospel as it stands in the NT begins there, so why this lack of synchronization between NT and liturgy? Let me devote a paragraph to the complicated answer, which lies in the awkwardness of combining festal and ordinary times in the liturgy. In the NT Matthew and Luke begin with two chapters of infancy narrative; they are read in late Advent, Christmastime, and Epiphany. There follows in the NT the account of the public ministry of JBap (Matt 3:1-12; Luke 3:1-6, which coincide with the opening of Mark [1:1-8]). The liturgy reads that account on the Second Sunday of Advent as part of its thesis that JBap is a key figure in the preparation for the coming of Christ, to be celebrated on Christmas. Then in the NT the three Synoptic Gospels recount the story of the baptism of Jesus; and the liturgy reads this on the feast of the Baptism (Matt 3:13-17 in Year A; Mark 1:7-11 in Year B; Luke 3:15-16, 21-22 in Year C), always celebrated on the Sunday following the Epiphany and thus replacing the First Sunday of Ordinary Time. (The Second Sunday of Ordinary Time respects an old liturgical theme of different epiphanies or manifestations of Jesus.[3]) In the NT the Synoptic Gospels[4] next recount the temptation or testing of Jesus after forty days in the desert (Matt 4:1-11; Mark 1:12-13; Luke 4:1-13), but the lectionary again cedes to an ancient tradition by reading the Gospel accounts of the temptation on the First Sunday of Lent, respectively in Years A, B, and C.[5] All this is why only on the Third Sunday of Ordinary Time the sequential readings of the Synoptic Gospels begin respectively with Matthew 4:12; Mark 1:14; and Luke 4:14. (That sequential reading continues until the First Sunday of Lent and then picks up again after Pentecost.[6])

---

[3] Revealed by a star to the magi (Epiphany proper, often celebrated on Sunday), by a heavenly voice at the baptism (feast of the Baptism), and by Jesus at Cana, who changes water to the best wine (described only in John 2:1-12). Now on the Second Sunday John 1:29-34 is read in Year A; 1:35-42 in B; 2:1-12 in C.

[4] Luke is an exception, for it follows the baptism with a genealogy of Jesus (3:23-38) and only then narrates the temptation. This genealogy is never used in the lectionary.

[5] Similarly, sequence is broken by the custom of assigning accounts of the transfiguration in the Synoptic Gospels to the Second Sunday of Lent in Years A, B, and C respectively.

[6] The number of Sundays of Ordinary Time before Lent runs from five to nine, depending on when Easter occurs. Although we speak of the resumption of Ordinary Sundays after Pentecost, the celebration of Trinity Sunday and (in many

Important Note: I wish to alert *all* who use the Sunday Gospel lectionary—although those whose task is to preach on it may need especially to be put on their guard. It is odd to begin a year's sequential reading of Matthew, or Mark, or Luke on the Third Sunday of the year, especially when one's sense of liturgy has been shaped by the preceding Advent, Christmas, Epiphany, Baptism feasts, and the immediately preceding passage from John.[7] One's tendency is simply to concentrate on the Gospel narrative of the Third Sunday with Jesus at Capernaum, or the Sea of Galilee, or Nazareth, and to proceed without any attention to the fact that this narrative is the entree into a great Gospel that will be one's companion for the rest of the year, and without asking who is this Jesus of whom we hear in the Gospel. In other words, to begin without reflecting on what has gone before and what is going to follow. Rather, on this Third Sunday preachers should proclaim with enthusiasm: "Today we begin to read seriously the Gospel according to Matthew, or Mark, or Luke—one of the four fundamental portrayals of Jesus Christ on which the church bases its understanding of what God's Son was like when he walked on the face of this earth, of the values he would have us live by, and of how he accomplished our salvation."

And to underline that, those whose task is to proclaim the Gospel might ask themselves and the Sunday congregation three basic questions. *First*, do we really understand what we are saying or hearing when we speak Sunday after Sunday of a reading from "the 'Gospel' according to . . ."? Do we understand what a Gospel is and why it was written? (See chap. 4, "Understanding How the Gospels Were Written and Their Use in the Sunday Liturgy," for the answer to this question.) *Second*, do we have any idea what Matthew's Gospel is, or Mark's, or Luke's, why it is distinctive and what it is trying to say? *Third*, how does this Sunday passage lead us into the Gospel and fit its purpose? With adaptation that third question will need to be asked every Ordinary Sunday all year long as a reminder of the answer to

---

places) of Corpus Christi on Sunday delays that resumption for one or two weeks. The number of Ordinary Sundays in the total year varies—the 34th (Christ the King) always being used as the last.

[7] It is even harder to have a sense of beginning John when one starts sequential readings from that Gospel in the middle of Lent. But I shall leave that problem till chapter 36, below.

The Gospel According to Matthew

the first and second questions. It is to help with the second and third questions that I have written here in chapters 33–36 an overview of each Gospel.

* * *

Although modern scholars generally begin their Gospel studies with Mark, the oldest of the written Gospels, Matthew stood first in most ancient biblical witnesses and has been the church's Gospel par excellence. Indeed, Matthew has served as the foundational document of the church, rooting it in the teaching of Jesus—a church built on rock against which the gates of hell would not prevail (only Matt 16:18). Matthew's Sermon on the Mount, the (eight) Beatitudes, and the Lord's Prayer are among the most widely known treasures in the Christian heritage. (It is always awesome to stop and think how impoverished we would be without the contributions peculiar to each Gospel.) Organizational skill and clarity, plus a penchant for unforgettable images, have given this Gospel priority as the church's teaching instrument. Consequently it is no surprise that in the triennial lectionary the church reads Matthew on the Sundays of the first or A Year.

INTRODUCTORY OBSERVATIONS
I have contended above that on the Third Sunday of Ordinary Time, when for all practical purposes we begin reading the Gospel of the liturgical year, besides reflecting on what a Gospel is one should appreciate in a general way what makes the particular Gospel distinctive. Accordingly, at the beginning of each chapter that follows I shall give a summary of information about the Gospel and an outline of the whole,[8] that is, background details meant to enrich the readers' and hearers' understanding.

Matthew was probably written in the period A.D. 80–90 in the vicinity of Antioch in Syria, a major city with a sizable Jewish population. From Jerusalem, Jewish missionaries came to Antioch proclaiming

---

[8] The general outline is important for seeing how individual pericopes fit into the whole. In the outlines and my comments I draw on material in my *Introduction to the New Testament* (New York: Doubleday, 1997). I am grateful to the publisher for permission to reuse. That work would supply readers with much longer treatments of the Gospels than I can provide here.

Christ in the 30s, and they made converts not only among fellow Jews but also among Gentiles. Barnabas and Paul were important figures in the Antioch Christian community by the early 40s (Acts 13:1-3). In the late 40s the mixed Christian community at Antioch was a factor in provoking the opposition of some at Jerusalem to the acceptance of Gentile converts without circumcision. Although the famous meeting at Jerusalem *ca.* A.D. 49 settled that question in the affirmative (Acts 15:1-29; Gal 2:1-10), it did not settle the issue of relations between Jewish and Gentile Christians. Subsequent confrontation at Antioch involved Peter, Paul, and adherents of James (the leader of the Jerusalem church); and apparently a conservative attitude toward the Jewish heritage won out—a position more conservative than Paul's (Gal 2:11-14).

Matthew reflects the situation decades later. Despite the Gospel's echoes of a strongly Jewish-Christian background, there are amid the Christians addressed many Gentiles, perhaps constituting the majority. Although Jesus came only for the lost sheep of the House of Israel (10:5-6; 15:24), by the will of the risen Christ the mission had succeeded in making disciples of all nations (28:19); and these Gentiles had been more willing to listen than those who were originally the tenants of God's vineyard (21:41). In the Gospel's outlook this change from Jews to Gentiles seems to be God's punishment because of the rejection and crucifixion of Jesus (27:25), but Matthew also stresses that the Jewish heritage must be preserved. Most scholars, Catholic and Protestant, agree that the evangelist was not Matthew, one of the Twelve Apostles and an eyewitness of Jesus' ministry, but a Jewish convert of the second or third generation,[9] probably a scribe, "instructed in the kingdom of heaven . . . a householder who brings out of his treasure new things and old" (13:52). The ideal of preserving the old wineskins as well as the new wine (9:17) illustrates the Matthean Jesus' attitude toward the Law. Every small letter and even part of a letter of the Law (jot and tittle) are to remain (5:18), but only as radically interpreted by Jesus: "You have heard it said [by God to Moses], but I say to you" (5:21, etc.). Such new Christian interpretations were more liberal than the views

---

[9] A minority thinks the evangelist was a Gentile. Whether he was Jew or Gentile, it is customary for scholars to keep calling this unknown figure "Matthew." The same custom of traditional name will be followed in regard to the other evangelists in the subsequent chapters.

The Gospel According to Matthew

prevalent in the emerging rabbinic Judaism of the last decades of the first century—rabbis who were in some ways the heirs of the Pharisees of Jesus' time. Accordingly, the Gospel contains a fierce critique of the Pharisees, lapsing at times into polemical exaggeration. Although these Jewish teachers may have succeeded to the chair of Moses (23:2-3), they are insulted as "hypocrites" (23:13, etc.). Probably the antagonism stems in part from the fact that the mixed Jewish and Gentile Christians addressed in the Gospel were no longer welcome in the local Jewish synagogues. This alienation is reflected in the description "their synagogues" (Matt 4:23, etc.) and in Jesus' warning about the fate of some of those whom he sends out: "You will scourge some of them in *your* synagogues" (23:34). A separate Christian entity or even institution had emerged, namely, the enduring church of Jesus founded on Peter as the chief representative of those who proclaimed Jesus as the Messiah, the Son of God (16:18).

To enable Jesus to speak to Christians living in this context Matthew composed a masterful account of the one who was the visible presence of "God with us" (1:23). Having before him what Mark had written as "The gospel of Jesus Christ," Matthew incorporated about 80 percent of that work into his own.[10] Mark had concentrated on what Jesus had done, and to fill out the picture Matthew added a collection of Jesus' teachings (found also in Luke and drawn from a tradition that we call Q). That material he organized into five magnificent sermons, beginning with the Sermon on the Mount, thus contributing in a unique way to the image of Jesus the lawgiver and teacher of the New Covenant, one greater than Moses, who would guide all, Jew and Gentile alike, to God. In a number of places, by a formula such as "This happened in order to fulfill . . .," Matthew calls attention to how what happens in the Gospel matches OT expectations; and the care with which the appropriate OT text is chosen suggests that meticulous, almost bookish study of the Christian tradition has already begun. Finally, Matthew incorporates in his portrait of Jesus narrative material found in no other Gospel, as seen, for instance, in the accounts of Jesus' infancy and death. Characteristic of this material are vivid imagination (dreams, plotting), extraordinary heavenly and earthly

[10] With changes of style and emphasis: Overall Matthew writes with more polish and avoids descriptions of Jesus or the disciples that might appear insufficiently reverent.

Christ in the Gospels of the Liturgical Year

phenomena (angelic interventions, sign of a heavenly star, earth-quakes), and an unusual amount of scriptural influence. Many would suggest that here Matthew is tapping a vein of popular folk tradition about Jesus, less formal than material derived from preaching. To all this the evangelist has brought his own writing skill, developed theology, and remarkable pedagogical sense, so that the Gospel presented first in the NT and the liturgy has become the most influential.

Various methods of dividing Matthew have been proposed, but the outline given on page 354 can help for a basic understanding.

GUIDANCE TO BEGINNING THE SEQUENTIAL USE OF MATTHEW IN THE LECTIONARY

On the Third Sunday of Ordinary Time the lectionary begins the consecutive reading of Matthew with 4:12. In order to understand the Jesus who is described there, let me devote the following three paragraphs to what Matthew 1:1–4:11 has already told us, some of which has been read in the liturgy.

The lectionary separates off Matthew's infancy narrative (chaps. 1–2) for use in the last week of Advent and Christmas. I have already treated these chapters above (chaps. 5–15). What should be remembered from that material is that the evangelist wanted the Gospel account of Jesus' ministry (which begins with Part One: 3:1–7:29) to be introduced by a survey of Israel's history (the genealogy) and a replay of the story of how Joseph brought Israel to Egypt to save it, and how Moses was spared when the wicked ruler (OT: Pharaoh; NT: Herod) tried to kill the male children. What God does in Jesus is new but was substantially anticipated by what God did in and for Israel. The unique Son of God who will come from Galilee to be baptized is the kingly Messiah of the House of David.

Matthew's introductory presentation of JBap (3:1-12) was read in the liturgy on the Second Sunday of Advent. In that passage Matthew was following Mark's opening pattern, with JBap preaching in the wilderness as Isaiah had foretold and baptizing with water in anticipation of the one who would baptize with the Holy Spirit. What might especially be noted for our present purposes is Matthew's insertion of JBap's condemnation of the Pharisees and Sadducees and his threats of destruction (3:7-12). The evangelist thus makes explicable their rejection of JBap, to be reported in 21:25-26, and also Jesus' hostility

The Gospel According to Matthew

Outline of the Gospel according to Matthew

1:1–2:23   **Introduction: Origin and Infancy of Jesus the Messiah:**
1. The who and how of Jesus' identity (1:1-25);
2. The where and whence of Jesus' birth and destiny (2:1-23).

3:1–7:29   **Part One: Proclamation of the Kingdom:**
1. Narrative: Ministry of JBap, baptism of Jesus, the temptations, beginning of the Galilean ministry (3:1–4:25);
2. Discourse: Sermon on the Mount (5:1–7:29).

8:1–10:42   **Part Two: Ministry and Mission in Galilee:**
1. Narrative mixed with short dialogue: Nine miracles consisting of healings, calming a storm, exorcism (8:1–9:38);
2. Discourse: Mission Sermon (10:1-42).

11:1–13:52   **Part Three: Questioning of and Opposition to Jesus:**
1. Narrative setting for teaching and dialogue: Jesus and JBap, woes on disbelievers, thanksgiving for revelation, Sabbath controversies and Jesus' power, Jesus' family (11:1–12:50);
2. Discourse: Sermon in Parables (13:1-52).

13:53–18:35   **Part Four: Christology and Ecclesiology:**
1. Narrative mixed with much dialogue: Rejection at Nazareth, feeding the 5,000 and walking on the water, controversies with the Pharisees, healings, feeding the 4,000, Peter's confession, first passion prediction, transfiguration, second passion prediction (13:53–17:27);
2. Discourse: Sermon on the Church (18:1-35).

19:1–25:46   **Part Five: Journey to and Ministry in Jerusalem:**
1. Narrative mixed with much dialogue: Teaching, judgment parables, third passion prediction, entry to Jerusalem, cleansing the Temple, clashes with authorities (19:1–23:39);
2. Discourse: Eschatological Sermon (24:1–25:46).

26:1–28:20   **Climax: Passion, Death, and Resurrection:**
1. Conspiracy against Jesus, Last Supper (26:1-29);
2. Arrest, Jewish and Roman trials, crucifixion, death (26:30–27:56);
3. Burial, guard at the tomb, opening of tomb, bribing of the guard, resurrection appearances (27:57–28:20).

Christ in the Gospels of the Liturgical Year

toward them. A noteworthy Matthean addition in the account of Jesus' baptism (3:13-17) is designed to deal with an implicit christological problem: JBap recognizes that Jesus who is greater should be doing the baptizing, but Jesus accepts baptism from JBap as part of God's salvific plan related to the kingdom ("righteousness"; see 6:33). Throughout the Gospel this evangelist will be very careful of anything that could detract from the uniquely high status of Jesus.

The testing/temptation of Jesus after forty days and forty nights in the desert (4:1-11—not read in the liturgy until the First Sunday of Lent in Year A) serves a double purpose. First, these temptations, partially shaped from the kinds of testing Jesus underwent during the ministry, illustrate the ways in which the proclamation of God's kingdom might have been diverted, so that it would have become a kingdom according to the standards of this world.[11] Second, they prepare us for the continued opposition of Satan, who regards Jesus' proclamation of the kingdom as a threat to his own power and kingdom. The temptations are prognostic of eventual victory; for after Jesus has demonstrated that he is the Son of God who completely serves God's will, the devil departs and angels wait on Jesus (4:11).

As we now turn to the main concern of this book, the reading of Matthew on Sundays, let me emphasize that what I present below is too brief to constitute even a mini-commentary. It is meant to provide an overview so that the Sunday pericopes can be seen in context and interpreted in the sequence in which Matthew presents them. A helpful way of reading it would be to take what follows section by section (indicated by indented headings) and to reread that section each Sunday covered therein before concentrating on the individual pericope.

JESUS BEGINS GALILEE MINISTRY; CALLS DISCIPLES; SERMON ON THE MOUNT (4:12–7:29; SUNDAYS 3–9)

The consecutive reading of Matthew begins on the Third Sunday of Ordinary Time with 4:12-23, where Jesus goes to Galilee, begins his

---

[11] For instance, using miraculous power for personal convenience (stones to bread) or for aggrandizement (showing off from the Temple pinnacle), or for domination (all the kingdoms of the earth). Jesus' refusals to have his goals distorted are all phrased in quotations from Deuteronomy 6–8, where, during the forty-year testing of Israel in the wilderness, God spoke through Moses to the people, who were tempted to rebel against the divine plan by false worship.

The Gospel According to Matthew

ministry, and calls his first four disciples to become fishers of "men" (= people). To this sequence taken from Mark, Matthew adds a geographical precision relating Capernaum to Zebulun and Naphtali, which prepares for a citation[12] from Isaiah 8:23–9:1 that speaks of "Galilee of the Gentiles." Once more Matthew has in view his mixed congregation with many Gentiles. The summary of the spread of the Gospel (4:24-25), although drawn from Mark, makes a special point that his fame went out "through all Syria," perhaps because the Gospel was written there.

The Sermon on the Mount (5:1–7:29) is Matthew's greatest composition. It weaves together Q material with uniquely Matthean passages into a harmonious masterpiece of ethical and religious teaching. More than any other teacher of morality, the Matthean Jesus instructs with divine power and authority, and by this empowerment makes possible a new existence. There are parallels between Moses and the Matthean Jesus. The OT conveyer of divine revelation encountered God on a mountain; the NT revealer speaks to his disciples on a mountain (Matt 5:1-2). For Christians, next to the Ten Commandments as an expression of God's will, the eight Beatitudes (5:3-12; Sunday 4) have been revered for expressing succinctly the values on which Jesus placed priority. In the comparable Lucan passage (6:20-23) there are only four beatitudes (phrased more concretely: "you who are poor . . . hungry now . . . weep now . . . when people hate you"); and it is likely that Matthew has added spiritualizing phrases ("poor *in spirit* . . . hunger and thirst *for righteousness*") and four spiritual beatitudes (meek, merciful, pure in heart, peacemakers). Seemingly Matthew's community has some people who are not physically poor and hungry; and the evangelist gives assurance that there was an outreach of Jesus to them as well, if they have attitudes attuned to the kingdom. Jesus teaches these beatitudes to the disciples who are to be the salt of the earth and the light of the world (5:13-16; Sunday 5).

The ethics of the new lawgiver (5:17-48; Sundays 6–7) constitutes a remarkable section, not only for the way it has shaped the Christian understanding of Jesus' values but also for its implicit christology. In

---

[12] This is a citation using the formula "That what was spoken by the prophet Isaiah might be fulfilled." Matthew has ten to fourteen such formula citations (more than the other Gospels put together); they reflect the evangelist's careful study of the Scriptures.

Christ in the Gospels of the Liturgical Year

presenting God's demand the Matthean Jesus does not dispense with the Law but asks for a deeper observance that gets to the reason why its demands were formulated, namely, to be "perfect as your heavenly Father is perfect" (5:48). The polemics of Matthew's time are illustrated by the evaluation of Jesus' righteousness as exceeding that of the scribes and Pharisees. In the series of six slightly variant "You have heard it said . . . but I say to you" clauses, Jesus dares explicitly to modify or correct what God said through Moses. He makes the demand of the Law more penetrating (e.g., by prohibiting not only killing but anger, not only adultery but lust); he forbids altogether what the Law allows (no divorce, no oath); and he turns from the Law to its opposite (not retaliation [Deut 19:21] but generosity to offenders; not hating enemies [Deut 7:2] but loving them). In other words the Matthean Jesus, speaking more confidently than any first-century rabbi, implies that he is more authoritative than Moses and seems to legislate with all the assurance of the God of Sinai.

In 6:1-18 (not read on Sunday but on Ash Wednesday) Jesus reshapes the exercise of piety: almsgiving, prayer, fasting. His warnings are not against pious practices but against ostentation. The Lord's Prayer, taken from Q, has been shaped by Matthew partially along the familiar lines of synagogue prayer, for example, the reverential "Our Father who are in heaven." The organization into six petitions reflects Matthew's love of order. The first three, "May your name be hallowed, may your kingdom come, may your will come about on earth as in heaven," are different ways of asking God to bring about the kingdom definitively. (This prayer then, at least in its earlier emphasis, was not far from the tone of *Maranatha*—"Come, Lord Jesus" [1 Cor 16:22; Rev 22:20].) The second three deal with the fate of the petitioners as they anticipate that future moment. The coming of the kingdom will involve the heavenly banquet, and so they ask a share of its food (bread); it will involve judgment, and so they ask forgiveness, assessed by the criterion of forgiving others that Matthew emphasizes (25:45); it will involve a dangerous struggle with Satan, and so they ask to be delivered from the apocalyptic trial and the Evil One.[13]

---

[13] English-speaking Protestants are familiar with an ending of the Lord's Prayer, "For thine is the kingdom, and the power, and the glory, for ever. Amen," which the King James translators took from inferior Greek manuscripts. Although not an original part of Matthew, it was a very early liturgical expansion. In the

The Gospel According to Matthew

There follow further instructions on behavior for the kingdom (6:19–7:27, with 6:24-34 read on Sunday 8, and 7:21-27 on Sunday 9). At our time when a consumer society is very concerned with the best in clothes and food and when a great deal of energy is put into being sure that we have financial security for the future, the Matthean Jesus' challenge not to worry about what to eat, or to wear, or about tomorrow may be even more biting than in his own time. The praise of those who hear Jesus' words (7:24-27) as building a well-founded house almost constitutes a judgment against those who reject him. The "When Jesus finished these words" formula terminates the sermon, with the accompanying theme of astonishment at the authority of Jesus' teaching.

MINISTRY IN GALILEE; MISSION SERMON
(8:1–10:42; SUNDAYS 10–13)
There now follow in chapters 8 and 9 of Matthew three sets of three miracles constituting a total of nine (healings, calming a storm, exorcism), interspersed with dialogues, mostly pertaining to discipleship. Only 9:9-13 is read in the lectionary (Sunday 10): There in an adaptation of the Marcan call of Levi; Jesus calls Matthew, a tax collector. (That change of name had a role in attributing this Gospel to Matthew.) Tax collectors often abused their role by oppressive exaction, but Jesus justifies his selection by announcing that he has come to call sinners, not the righteous. These chapters close with Jesus' observation that the harvest of the crowds needs laborers (9:35-38), and in turn that leads to Jesus' addressing the laborers whom he has chosen.

The Mission Sermon (10:1-42) is set in the context of Jesus' sending out the "disciples" with authority over unclean spirits and the power to heal—Jesus is giving them his power to proclaim the kingdom (compare 10:7 with 4:17). Three portions of the sermon are read in the Sunday lectionary. In the introductory part of 10:1-8 (Sunday 11) Matthew stops to recite the names of the Twelve "Apostles,"[14] thus

"Communion" section of the Roman Catholic Mass, the Lord's Prayer is followed by a short invocation and then a form of that ancient ascription: "For the kingdom, the power, and the glory are yours, now and forever."

[14] It may be observed that Luke 6:13-15 and Acts 1:13 present a list of the Twelve that differs from that in Matthew 10:2-4 (and Mark 3:16-19) in one of the last four names: Thaddaeus in Mark and most manuscripts of Matthew; Lebbaeus in some

relating the mission of the twelve disciples in the midst of the ministry to the apostolic sending after the resurrection (28:16-20). Even before he was crucified Jesus knew that others had a role to play in spreading the good news of the kingdom; and the directives in the sermon have an ongoing force in the Christian mission known to Matthew's readers. In 10:5-6 Jesus warns them not to go to the Gentiles and the Samaritans but to "the lost sheep of the house of Israel." This probably reflects the history of Matthean Christianity, where there was at first almost exclusively a mission to the Jews and only later a mission to the Gentiles.[15] The Matthean Jesus anticipates the kind of persecution that will greet the post-resurrectional apostles, but they are assured divine care (10:26-33; Sunday 12). And their acknowledging Jesus in the face of hostile persecutors guarantees that Jesus will acknowledge them before his heavenly Father. Jesus warns that following him requires difficult choices in relation both to family ties and life (10:37-42; Sunday 13), but generosity will bring a generous reward. The ending of the sermon highlights the salvific importance of the mission: Receiving the missionaries is receiving Jesus, and receiving him is receiving the God who sent him.

QUESTIONING OF AND OPPOSITION TO JESUS;
THE SERMON IN PARABLES
(11:1–13:52; SUNDAYS 14–17)

Two chapters (11:1–12:50), largely of teaching and dialogue, precede the next great sermon. Set in the context of Jesus moving about in Galilean cities, they concern a medley of subjects: Jesus and JBap, woes on disbelievers, thanksgiving for revelation, Sabbath controversies, and Jesus' family. (Although we have not been told that Jesus' disciples returned from their mission, they are with him in 12:2, 49.) The imprisoned JBap has heard of the deeds of the Messiah, and so 11:4-6

Western manuscripts of Matthew; Judas (Jude) in Luke-Acts. Apparently by the time the evangelists wrote, amidst agreement about Jesus' choice of the Twelve, recollection of the minor members was uncertain.

[15] Matthew 28:19: "Make disciples of all nations." The mixing of two time periods in the sermon is easily recognizable: Although Jesus forbids the disciples to go near the Gentiles, he speaks of their being put on trial by Gentile as well as Jewish authorities.

The Gospel According to Matthew

explains that Jesus is the kind of Messiah prophesied by Isaiah.[16] Then (11:7-15) Jesus reveals that JBap is more than a prophet: He is the angelic messenger sent by God to lead Israel to the Promised Land (Exod 23:20) and the Elijah sent to prepare Israel for God's action (Mal 3:1, 23-24). JBap accomplished this by having prepared the way for Jesus, thus becoming the greatest human being ever born before the kingdom of heaven came. Apocalyptic struggle introduces the full coming of the kingdom, and the imprisonment and ultimately the execution of JBap are marks of that. Having spoken about his own identity and that of JBap, in 11:16-19 Jesus criticizes sharply "this generation" for being willing to accept neither.

Next the lectionary skips to 11:25-30 (Sunday 14; also the feast of the Sacred Heart), where Jesus speaks in the style of divine Wisdom by thanking the Father for revelation given to those who are childlike, including those who do not count in this world. This jubilant cry, drawn from Q, represents a type of high christology very close to what we find in John's Gospel, where Jesus calls himself the divine Son to whom the Father has given all things (John 3:35; 5:22, 26-27); no one knows God except that Son (1:18; 14:9) who reveals the Father to the chosen (17:6). And in the "Come to me" invitation to the heavy-laden (Matt 11:28-30), Jesus (like God in Exod 33:14 and Wisdom in Sir 6:23-31) promises rest to those who take on themselves the obligations of the kingdom. These are among the sweetest words ever attributed to Jesus—words that make intelligible Paul's appreciation for "the meekness and gentleness of Christ" (2 Cor 10:1).

The lectionary omits the rest of chapter 11 and all of chapter 12, which set Jesus' teaching in a series of controversies. They have a christological import, since Jesus declares that his presence is greater than the Temple, that the Son of Man is lord of the Sabbath, and that he is acting in the spirit of the prophets. Ominously, the Pharisees react by planning to destroy Jesus. This leads into the Sermon in Parables (13:1-52), which structurally is the center of the Gospel and (since Jesus is not likely to have spoken seven or eight parables on one occasion) illustrates Matthew's pedagogical interest in bringing

---

[16] Matthew 11:2-11, describing how the imprisoned JBap sent envoys to Jesus to ask if he is the one to come, is read on the Third Sunday of Advent in Year A as part of the liturgical motif that JBap is a figure preparatory for the coming of Jesus on Christmas.

together like material. The parables serve as a varied commentary on the rejection of Jesus by the Pharisees in the two preceding chapters. The sermon opens with the parable of the sower and its interpretation (13:1-23; Sunday 15), which emphasizes the different kinds of obstacles and failures encountered by the proclamation of the kingdom. The weeds among the wheat and its interpretation (13:24-43; Sunday 16) seems to move to another level of concern. After the proclamation has won adherents to ("sons of") the kingdom, they will be living together in the world with evil people (who are "sons of" the Evil One). Why not eliminate the evil? Unfortunately that could lead to the good being pulled out as well, and so the separation has to be left to a future judgment by the Son of Man. The Matthean Jesus tends to give erring Christian community members a time to mend their ways (see 18:15-17). The paired parables of the mustard seed and the leaven (Matt 13:31-33) illustrate the present small beginnings of the kingdom and its great future by using examples of extraordinary growth familiar respectively to a man and to a woman. The paired parables of the hidden treasure and the pearl of great price (13:44-46; Sunday 17) stress the great value of the kingdom and the necessity of taking the once-for-all opportunity to gain it, even if that requires selling off everything else. The dragnet and its interpretation (13:47-50) once more postpones the separation of the good and bad in the kingdom till the close of the age. The sermon ends with a summary parable of the householder and the new and old treasure (13:51-52). Those who have understood the parables are like a trained scribe who appreciates the new revelation in Jesus and the old revelation in Moses. The evangelist probably considered himself in this light.

CHRISTOLOGY AND ECCLESIOLOGY
(13:53–18:35; SUNDAYS 18–24)
A great variety of subjects are treated in the mixed narrative and dialogue (13:53–17:27) that precedes the next sermon: rejection at Nazareth, feeding the 5,000 and walking on the water, controversies with the Pharisees, healings, feeding the 4,000, Peter's confession, first passion prediction, transfiguration, second passion prediction. In 13:10-11 Jesus had said that he spoke in parables because the disciples were to know the mysteries of the kingdom of heaven; accordingly, in what now follows Jesus turns his main attention to the disciples from whom the church will develop, especially to Peter the rock on whom

The Gospel According to Matthew

the church will be built. The rejection at Nazareth (13:54-58) helps to explain why Jesus must concentrate on his disciples, since even his townspeople do not accept him.[17] The lack of faith at Nazareth is followed by an account of how Herod killed JBap (14:1-12) and was superstitiously uneasy about Jesus. In an attempt to get away from Herod Jesus withdraws to a lonely place where he feeds the 5,000 and subsequently walks on the water (14:13-33; Sundays 18–19). There are different layers of theological emphasis in these miracles: They echo miracles of Moses (the manna and walking dry-shod through the Red Sea) and of the prophet Elisha (2 Kgs 4:42-44); also the loaves miracle anticipates eucharistic feeding, and the walking on the water is a type of theophany illustrating Jesus' divine identity (note the "I am" ["It is I"] in Matt 14:27). The end of the walking-on-the-water scene is remarkable in Matthew; for in 14:33 the disciples, instead of failing to understand as in Mark 6:52, worship Jesus as "Son of God." Most significant is the scene peculiar to Matthew where Jesus invites Peter to come to him on the water, and as Peter begins to sink, Jesus helps him (14:28-31). This is the first of three instances of special Petrine material in Matthew. Peter's impetuousness, the inadequacy of his faith, and Jesus' individual care to lead Peter further are quite characteristic. As a man of little faith who would sink unless the Lord saved him, Peter is representative of the other disciples; their faith and his in the Son of God gains strength from Jesus' powerful helping hand.

The debate with the Pharisees and scribes from Jerusalem over what defiles (15:1-20) leads Jesus to condemn blind guides who will be rooted out. Moving on to Tyre and Sidon, Jesus heals the daughter of the Canaanite woman (15:21-28; Sunday 20), a story resembling the healing of the centurion's servant boy in 8:5-13. At the Sea of Galilee we are told of the second multiplication of loaves, namely, for the 4,000 (15:32-39). While this may be a preaching variant of the earlier story, the repetition has the effect of emphasizing Jesus' power.

Amid hostile confrontations Jesus rejects the disbelieving request for a sign: The Pharisees and Sadducees cannot interpret the already

---

[17] Matthew shows greater reverence for Jesus and his family than does the parallel in Mark 6:1-6: He does not report that Jesus was a carpenter or was a prophet without honor "among his own relatives." (Matthew's substitution of "son of a carpenter" for Mark's "carpenter" gave rise to the artistic custom of depicting Joseph as a carpenter.)

Christ in the Gospels of the Liturgical Year

present signs of the times. Criticizing his disciples as people who have little faith for they have not fully understood the bread miracles, Jesus warns them against the leaven or teaching of the Pharisees and Sadducees,[18] whom he equates with an evil and adulterous generation. Yet Jesus' disciples have considerable faith, for in 16:13-20 (Sunday 21) Peter confesses that Jesus is the Son of the living God—a revelation from the Father in heaven, not a matter of human reasoning ("flesh and blood"). The revelation to Paul of Jesus' divine sonship is phrased in almost the same language (Gal 1:16). If that revelation constituted Paul an apostle, this one constitutes Peter the rock on which Jesus will build his church, a church that even the gates of hell (probably Satanic destructive power) will not prevail against. The OT background of Peter's acknowledgment of Jesus as the Davidic Messiah, the Son of God, is the prophecy of 2 Samuel 7: David's descendant will reign after him and God will treat him as a son. That promise was provoked by David's desire to build a house or temple for God, and so Jesus' promise to build a church on Peter, who acknowledges him as the fulfillment of the promise to David, is not illogical. Isaiah 22:15-25 describes the establishment of Eliakim as the new prime minister of King Hezekiah of Judah: God places on his shoulder "the *key* of the House of David; he shall *open* . . . and he shall *shut*." The italicized words are echoed in Matthew 16:19 as Jesus gives to Peter the keys of the kingdom, so that whatever he binds/looses on earth is bound/loosed in heaven. Matthew's picture of the exaltation of Peter does not eliminate Jesus' subsequent chastisement of Peter as Satan (16:21-23; Sunday 22), who thinks on a human level because he does not accept the notion of Jesus' suffering in the first of three similar predictions of the passion. This sobering correction leads into directives (16:24-27) to the disciples both about the suffering required for discipleship and about future glory when the Son of Man comes.

The account of the transfiguration (17:1-9; Second Sunday of Lent in Year A) is another step in the Matthean christological sequence pertaining to divine sonship that runs from the angelic annunciation to Joseph that the child was conceived through the Holy Spirit (1:20), through God's revelation about "my Son" (2:15), to the voice from

---

[18] This is not easily reconcilable with 23:2-3, where Jesus says that his disciples are to practice and observe whatever the scribes and the Pharisees tell them because they sit on the chair of Moses.

heaven at the baptism speaking of "my beloved Son" (3:17), to the disciples' recognition after the walking on the water (14:33), culminating in Peter's confession (16:16).

The rest of chapter 17 is not read in the Sunday lectionary. Unfortunately that means the omission of another special Matthean Petrine scene centered on the (Temple?) tax (17:24-27),[19] where Peter is the intermediary in teaching Christians to avoid public offense by paying the tax on a voluntary basis and thus to be peaceable citizens (see Rom 13:6-7; 1 Pet 2:13-16). His role is all the more important if on the Gospel level Matthew is dealing with a problem faced by Christians after Peter was dead.

The Sermon on the Church (18:1-35) gives to a collection of ethical teaching, much of it once addressed to Jesus' disciples, a perspective that makes it strikingly suited to an established church, the type of church that only Matthew has Jesus mention (16:18). Matthew connects ecclesiology and christology, for the apostles are to interpret and teach all that Jesus commanded (28:20). Although a structured church is the context in which the tradition and memory of Jesus are preserved, Matthew recognizes a danger: Any structure set up in this world tends to take its values from the other structures that surround it. This chapter is meant to ensure that those values do not smother the values of Jesus. To readers who struggle with church issues today, this may be the most helpful of the five Matthean sermons; and so those who preach might well interpret the *whole* sermon, even though the Sunday lectionary includes only two excerpts from it. The peculiarly Matthean instructions in 18:15-20 (Sunday 23) are clearly adapted to a church situation, for after the unsuccessful efforts of individuals to win over a reprobate, a report is to be made to the "church" (= local community, unlike the use of "church" in 16:18). The process is designed to prevent too early and frequent use of authority—a danger in any structured community. The quarantine of the recalcitrant reprobate in 18:17 "as a Gentile and tax-collector" sounds very definitive, reinforced by the power to bind and loose in 18:18. Yet we must remember that Matthew's community was a mixed one of Jews and Gentiles, and that Jesus' final instruction was to go out to the Gentiles and teach them

---

[19] It reflects oral tradition, with the finding of the stater coin in the fish's mouth adding almost a folkloric touch.

(28:19). Moreover, Jesus had shown a particular interest in a tax collector named Matthew, inviting him to follow (9:9; 10:3). Therefore, the repudiated Christian may still be the subject of outreach and concern. In 18:21-22 (Sunday 24) Peter is once more a figure of authority getting instruction from Jesus on how he should act. Although he is being a bit "legalistic" in trying to find out how often he should forgive, his offer is quite generous—except for the family circle few people forgive someone seven times. Jesus gives a remarkable answer: seventy-seven, that is, an infinite number of times (cf. Gen 4:24). Christian forgiveness, then, is to imitate the unlimited range of God's forgiveness, as is confirmed by the eloquent parable of the unforgiving servant (18:23-35), which invokes divine judgment on those who refuse to forgive. All this has a very real application in church life, for the number of people who turn away from the church where they have not found forgiveness is legion. Overall, to the extent that churches listen to Jesus speaking to his disciples in this chapter, they will keep his spirit alive instead of memorializing him. Then Matthew 18:20 will be fulfilled: "Where two or three are gathered in my name, there am I in the midst of them."

JOURNEY TO AND MINISTRY IN JERUSALEM
(19:1–25:46; SUNDAYS 25–34)

Leading to the next sermon is a section with vivid narrative mixed with much dialogue (19:1–23:39): teaching, judgment parables, third passion prediction, entry to Jerusalem, cleansing the Temple, clashes with authorities. After Jesus has revealed his intention to found his church and has given instructions about the attitudes that must characterize it, he goes up to Jerusalem, where his predictions about the death and resurrection of the Son of Man will be fulfilled.

The whole of chapter 19 is omitted in the Sunday lectionary, which moves directly to the parable of the workers in the vineyard (20:1-16; Sunday 25), which is peculiar to Matthew. The payment begins with the last hired workers and moves to the first hired, so that it may be seen by those who worked all day long that all are paid the same. The parable illustrates that God's gracious giving is not determined by what is earned—a Matthean example of a major Pauline emphasis.

The entry into Jerusalem (21:1-11) constitutes the reading for the procession with palms on Passion (Palm) Sunday in Year A. It is highlighted by citations of Isaiah 62:11 and Zechariah 9:9 that stress the

The Gospel According to Matthew

meekness and peacefulness of the messianic king.[20] The Sunday lectionary skips over the cleansing of the Temple, the cursing and withering of the fig tree, and the challenge to Jesus' authority by the priests and the elders, answered in terms of JBap (Matt 21:12-27). The peculiarly Matthean parable of the two sons (21:28-32; Sunday 26) compares the authorities to the son who says he will obey the father but does not. Jesus fashions a highly polemic contrast: Tax collectors and harlots who believed JBap will enter the kingdom of God before the authorities. The sharpness of the judgment continues in the parable of the wicked tenants (21:33-43; Sunday 27), for afterwards in verses 43, 45 the chief priests and the Pharisees understand themselves to be the target of the warning that the kingdom of God will be taken away and given to a nation that will produce fruits. Matthew is thinking of the church composed of Jews and Gentiles who believe in Jesus. The parable of the marriage feast (22:1-14; Sunday 28), seemingly adapted from Q, is another instance of the rejection of the leaders. Those invited first by the king are unworthy and do not come; and since they kill the servants sent with the invitation, the king sends his troops and destroys their city. The once independent parable about the man without a wedding garment, which has been added as an ending, deals with a reality that Matthew knows well: Into the church have been brought both bad and good, so that those who have accepted the initial call have to face further judgment. Those Christians who are not worthy will suffer the same fate as those who formerly had the kingdom but were not worthy to keep it (cf. 8:11-12). Thus in none of these three parables is it simply a question of the replacement of Israel by the church or of Jews by Gentiles; the issue for Matthew is the replacement of the unworthy in Judaism (especially the leaders) by a community of Jews and Gentiles who have come to believe in Jesus and have worthily responded to his demands for the kingdom.

There now follows a series of three trap questions: taxes for Caesar proposed by Pharisees and Herodians (Matt 22:15-21; Sunday 29); the resurrection proposed by Sadducees (22:23-33); the great commandment proposed by a Pharisee lawyer (22:34-40; Sunday 30). These are followed by a question proposed by Jesus to the Pharisees about the

---

[20] Famously illogical is the Matthean combination in 21:7 of ass and colt (originally meant as parallel designations of one animal) so that Jesus sat "on them."

Messiah as David's son (22:41-46; not read in the Sunday lectionary). Serving as a bridge to the last great discourse, Jesus' denunciation of the scribes and Pharisees (23:1-36) is an extraordinary Matthean construction. Only 23:1-12 is read in the lectionary (Sunday 31), perhaps because the material is so hostile. Altogether Jesus delivers seven "woes" against their casuistry—woes that function almost as the antitheses of the Beatitudes in chapter 5. Although the seven woes are portrayed as Jesus' critiques of the Jewish leaders of his time, Matthew's readers would probably hear them as critiques of synagogue leaders in their time over a half century later. (And Christians today should hear them as a critique not of Jews but of what generally happens in established religion and thus applicable to behavior in Christianity.) For the Christians of Matthew's church the crucifixion of Jesus would have sharpened the tone of such polemic, and "Amen, I say to you, all these things will come on this generation" (23:36) would have been seen as fulfilled in the capture of Jerusalem and destruction of the Temple in A.D. 70.

The last of the five great discourses, the Eschatological Sermon (24:1–25:46) deals with the endtimes but is phrased in a type of apocalyptic obscurity that mixes the present time of the Gospel readers with future time. None of chapter 24, with its references to false prophets, desolating sacrilege, and flight in the last times, is read on the Ordinary Sundays.[21] Watchfulness is stressed in the uniquely Matthean parable of the ten virgins (25:1-13; Sunday 32). It illustrates well the rule that generally the parables make one point: The uncharitable behavior of the wise virgins in refusing to share their oil with the foolish is not to be imitated, but without that behavior the point of the parable about being ready could not be made. The judgment motif grows stronger in the parable of the talents (25:14-30; Sunday 33), where the message is not one of meriting reward but of dedicated and

---

[21] 24:37-44 constitutes the reading for the First Sunday of Advent in Year A. That the last Sunday of Ordinary Time (Christ the King) and the First Sunday of Advent both have lectionary readings about the return of Christ, the Son of Man, is somehow tied into the idea that we expect the second coming of Christ at the end of time and yet liturgically we also expect a type of second coming at Christmas. If I may be permitted a personal criticism, I think that the use of eschatological readings on the First Sunday of Advent is ill advised; we should conclude the eschatological emphasis with Christ the King and prepare for Christmas by a different type of Sunday readings.

fruitful response by the Christian to God's gift in and through Jesus. The discourse ends with material peculiar to Matthew: the enthroned Son of Man judging the sheep and the goats (25:31-46; Sunday 34 = Christ the King). Since the Son of Man speaks of God as "my Father," this is the Son of God in the apocalyptic context of the judgment of the whole world. The admirable principle that the verdict is based on the treatment of deprived outcasts is the Matthean Jesus' last warning to his followers and to the church, demanding a very different religious standard both from that of those scribes and Pharisees criticized in chapter 23 and from that of a world that pays more attention to the rich and powerful.

* * *

Passages from the rest of Matthew (chaps. 26–28), which constitute the passion, burial, and resurrection narratives, are read in Passiontide (particularly Palm Sunday) of Year A and Eastertime. They have already been discussed in chapters 16–26 above.

Chapter 34

The Gospel According to Mark
(Liturgical Year B)

This is the Gospel that most scholars think was written earliest.[1] In formal courses on the Gospels, besides being studied first, Mark gets more attention as the basic Gospel on which Matthew and Luke drew. The Sunday lectionary, however, reads it in the second or B Year. Since it was practically never read on the Sundays in the pre–Vatican II lectionary, Catholics tend not to be familiar with Mark and often hear it against a background of what they know from Matthew. Care has to be taken to point out Marcan distinctiveness and raw narrative power.

INTRODUCTORY OBSERVATIONS

To familiarize readers/hearers with the Gospel that will be used sequentially beginning on the Third Sunday of Ordinary Time, the following details may be of help. Usually scholars date the writing of this most ancient Gospel to between A.D. 60 and 75, with the most likely date in the range 68–73. By traditional attribution going back to the early second-century bishop Papias, the author was Mark, the follower and "interpreter" of Peter, usually identified as the John Mark of Acts, whose mother had a house in Jerusalem.[2] Some who reject this attribution suggest that the author may have been an otherwise unknown Christian named Mark.

From the contents the author emerges as a Greek-speaker who was probably not an eyewitness of Jesus' ministry, since he makes statements about Palestinian geography that many judge inaccurate. This

---

[1] Is this recognized in the order of the sequential Gospel readings in the weekday Mass lectionary every year: Mark, Matthew, Luke?

[2] He accompanied Barnabas and Paul on the "First Missionary Journey" and may have helped Peter and Paul in Rome in the 60s. The name "Mark," however, was common (e.g., Mark Antony); and we cannot be sure that the Mark and John Mark references of the NT all allude to the same man.

evangelist (whom I shall continue to call "Mark") drew on preshaped traditions about Jesus (oral and probably written)[3] to produce a compact, effective presentation that began with the words "The gospel of Jesus Christ."[4] Independently, Matthew and Luke were to use Mark's Gospel as a basic guide in composing their works, and so Mark must have been considered a good representative of the way Jesus was preached in the larger church. Papias' reference to Mark as the interpreter of Peter may mean that Mark's Gospel was a distillation from and reorganization of a standard type of preaching that was considered apostolic and therefore associated with Peter, the first of the Twelve.

It is very difficult to discern the community that Mark addressed, but internal evidence points to Gentiles who did not know some basic Jewish customs (7:3-4). Mark's tone and emphases suggest a community that had undergone persecution and failure, so that now they needed encouragement. That plus the fact that there are signs of Latin influences on Mark's Greek has led some modern scholars to accept the second-century tradition that Mark was directed to Christians at Rome, for we know that there Christians were persecuted by Nero in A.D. 64–68.[5]

A popular way to trace development in Mark's thought is found in the Gospel outline on page 371. It posits a major dividing point in Mark 8, approximately halfway through the account of Jesus' ministry. There, after having been consistently rejected and misunderstood despite all he has said and done, Jesus starts to proclaim the necessity of the suffering, death, and resurrection of the Son of Man in God's plan. This development, which serves to reveal the christological identity of Jesus, is meant by Mark to teach a lesson. Readers can learn much about Jesus from the traditions of his parables and mighty deeds; but unless that is intimately combined with the picture of his victory through suffering, they cannot understand him or their own vocation as his followers. This outline should help to dispel any

---

[3] Scholars often claim to have reconstructed the pre-Marcan sources with great exactitude. It is very dubious that one can do that, and the reconstructions differ greatly.

[4] Mark uses "gospel" in the sense of "message"; but drawing on his title at a later period, Christians began to speak of written "Gospels."

[5] Other proposals center on regions immediately to the north of Palestine (Syria, the northern Transjordan, the Decapolis).

Christ in the Gospels of the Liturgical Year

Outline of the Gospel according to Mark

1:1–8:26   **Part One: Ministry of Healing and Preaching in Galilee:**
1. Introduction by JBap; an initial day; controversy at Capernaum (1:1–3:6);
2. Jesus chooses the Twelve and trains them as disciples by parables and mighty deeds; misunderstanding among his Nazareth relatives (3:7–6:6);
3. Sending out the Twelve; feeding 5,000; walking on water; controversy; feeding 4,000; misunderstanding (6:7–8:26).

8:27–16:8   **Part Two: Suffering Predicted; Death in Jerusalem; Resurrection:**
1. Three passion predictions; Peter's confession; the transfiguration; Jesus' teaching (8:27–10:52);
2. Ministry in Jerusalem: Entry; Temple actions and encounters; Eschatological Discourse (11:1–13:37);
3. Anointing, Last Supper, passion, crucifixion, burial, empty tomb (14:1–16:8).

(+ 16:9–20)   The long canonical ending (or **Marcan appendix**) describing resurrection appearances added to the Gospel by a later copyist.

notion that because Mark was an early Gospel it is primitive. Rather, Mark has carefully organized the career of Jesus to convey a message.[6]

By the time Mark wrote, Jesus had been preached as the Christ for several decades. To appreciate what this earliest written portrayal contributed to our Christian heritage, one might reflect on what we would know about Jesus if we had just the letters of Paul. We would have a magnificent theology about what God has done in Christ, but Jesus would be left almost without a face. Mark gets the honor of having been the first Christian to have painted that "face" and made it part of the enduring good news.

GUIDANCE TO BEGINNING THE SEQUENTIAL USE
OF MARK IN THE LECTIONARY

On the Third Sunday of Ordinary Time the lectionary begins the consecutive reading of Mark with 1:14. Since so little precedes that verse

---

[6] Organization is a characteristic of Stage Three of Gospel Formation, as we saw in chapter 4 above.

The Gospel According to Mark

in the NT or in the Sunday lectionary of Year B,[7] one does not have the difficulties presented by Matthew and Luke where three and a half chapters precede the beginning of the sequential lectionary reading of the respective Gospel. Yet the very abruptness of Mark needs to be commented on.[8] Christian audiences in general and Sunday audiences in particular, when they hear that Jesus began a public ministry in Galilee, are accustomed to think of a Jesus conceived by the Holy Spirit of the virgin Mary, born in Bethlehem, reared in Nazareth, and prepared for and baptized by JBap in a relatively lengthy scene—none of which is recounted in Mark. In the briefest way Mark has presented the beginning of the gospel of Jesus Christ[9] as the fulfillment of Malachi 3:1 and Isaiah 40:3 about a prophesied messenger (JBap) crying in the wilderness to prepare the way of the Lord. That preparation consists in announcing the one who will baptize with the Holy Spirit, namely, Jesus, who has come from Nazareth and whom a voice from heaven addresses as beloved Son. Then in two verses we are told without any detail that for forty days Jesus was tested by Satan. Presumably Mark's audience knew something more about JBap and about Jesus, but we have no idea whether they knew anything about Jesus' birth or his family (e.g., Joseph is never mentioned by Mark). These differences offer preachers an opportunity to remind Sunday audiences of Gospel differences and of how stories known in one part of the early Christian world may not have been known in other parts.

[7] Only: Mark 1:1-8, the appearance of JBap, read on the Second Sunday of Advent in Year B; Mark 1:7-11, the baptism of Jesus, read on the feast of the Baptism (= First Sunday of Ordinary Time). The very brief Marcan account of the testing/tempting of Jesus (1:12-13 + 1:14-15) is read on the First Sunday of Lent.

[8] Indeed, Marcan brevity presents a liturgical problem, for this shortest Gospel does not provide enough pericopes or segments to cover all the Sundays in Ordinary Time. To meet that problem, in midsummer the lectionary interrupts its reading of Mark at 6:34 (the beginning of the brief first account of the multiplication of the loaves) and substitutes for five Sundays (17th through 21st) the much longer Johannine account of the multiplication—a disputable decision.

[9] Although Mark 1:1 is often treated as a title, the evangelist may have thought of it as a proclamation. The phrase "Son of God," though supported by major manuscripts, may be a copyist's addition. If genuine it provides an inclusion with the identification of Jesus as "Son of God" by the Roman centurion in 15:39 toward the end—the first believing confession of Jesus under that title in the Gospel.

Christ in the Gospels of the Liturgical Year

A worthwhile reflection before beginning the sequential reading of Mark is that, without any angelic announcement of conception, God's voice at the baptism speaking to Jesus of Nazareth, "You are my beloved Son, with you I am well pleased," was enough in Mark's mind for his audience to understand the Gospel story that follows. That voice with its "You are my Son" echoes Psalm 2:7, a psalm used for the coronation of the king of the House of David, and thus points to Jesus as the Messiah. The additional "with you I am well pleased" echoes Isaiah 42:1, which describes the Servant of the Lord as "my chosen one with whom I am pleased," and thus points to Jesus as the Isaian Servant who is to bear the infirmities of many and be led to slaughter for the guilt of all (Isa 53:4-10). Thus the Marcan Jesus who begins his ministry has been revealed to the audience both as royal Messiah and as Suffering Servant. And even a two-verse account of the testing of Jesus by Satan (Mark 1:12-13) was enough for Mark's readers/hearers to be aware from the start that Jesus' proclamation of the kingdom or rule of God, which has now come near (i.e., is making itself felt), will encounter major obstacles.

JESUS BEGINS GALILEE MINISTRY;
CALLS DISCIPLES; AN INITIAL DAY;
CONTROVERSY (1:14–3:6; SUNDAYS 3–9)[10]
The reading on the Third Sunday of Ordinary Time in Year B starts with 1:14, where, after JBap was arrested, Jesus appears in Galilee. The first half of Mark describes a ministry of preaching and powerful deeds (healings, multiplying loaves, calming storms) and teaching in Galilee and its environs. Although Jesus attracts great interest, he struggles with demons, encountering misunderstanding (by his family and, more importantly, by the Twelve, whom he has chosen to be with him) and hostile rejection (by Pharisees and scribes).

Jesus begins by calling four men to be his followers and "fishers" who will catch people (1:16-20), thus presaging that they will have a role in the proclamation of Jesus' message. Indeed, the reactions of these disciples will mark major stages in the Gospel.

---

[10] I remind readers of the suggestion on p. 355, above, as to how one might use the individual sections of my book to accompany the lectionary passages.

The Gospel According to Mark

In describing what appears to be the initial day of Jesus' ministry (1:21-38; Sundays 4–5), Mark familiarizes the readers with the type of things done in proclaiming the kingdom: teaching in the Capernaum synagogue with authority, exorcising an unclean spirit (the continued opposition of Satan), healing Simon's mother-in-law, healing many more diseased and possessed, and finally seeking a place to pray on the following morning only to be importuned by his disciples pressing demands on him. Several factors should be noted. Teaching and an exercise of divine power in healing and driving out demons are united in the proclamation of the kingdom, implying that the coming of God's rule is complex. Those who claim to be God's people must recognize that some of their attitudes stand in the way and they must change their minds; the presence of evil visible in human affliction, suffering, and sin must be contravened; and the demonic must be defeated. Jesus' teaching with authority and power over the demons stems from his being Son of God. Yet Mark never describes Jesus being given such authority and power; he simply has it because of who he is. Paradoxically, the unclean spirit that opposes him recognizes that he is the Holy One of God, while the disciples who follow him do not understand him fully despite his teaching and powerful deeds. In 1:34 Jesus forbids the demons to speak "because they knew him." This is the first instance of what scholars call Mark's "Messianic Secret," whereby Jesus seems to hide his identity as the Son of God until it is made apparent after his death on the cross—the full mystery of his person involves suffering and death.

Jesus' activity and controversies are expanded in 1:39–3:6. Moving through the towns of Galilee, proclaiming the kingdom and healing (e.g., a leper in 1:40-45; Sunday 6), Jesus seeks to avoid an enthusiasm for the wonderful that could give the wrong understanding. His curing sickness is not meant to arouse astonishment but to teach about the way in which God's rule is to destroy all forms of harmful evil, spiritual and physical. At Capernaum, a town on the Lake of Galilee that has now become Jesus' home, Mark centers five incidents (2:1–3:6) where objections are raised by the scribes and the Pharisees and others to his forgiving sins, to his association with sinners, to the failure of his disciples to fast, and to their and his doing what is not lawful on the Sabbath. The first (2:1-12), the third (2:18-22), and the fourth and fifth (2:23–3:6) are read on Sundays 7, 8, and 9. Clearly Jesus is being presented as one who, on the basis of his own higher authority (2:28:

Christ in the Gospels of the Liturgical Year

"the Son of Man is lord even of the Sabbath"), does not fit into the religious expectations of his contemporaries—an attitude that gives rise to a plot on the part of the Pharisees and Herodians to destroy him. The proclamation of God's kingdom is opposed not simply by demons but also by human beings.

JESUS CHOOSES THE TWELVE AND TRAINS THEM AS DISCIPLES BY PARABLES AND MIGHTY DEEDS (3:7–6:6; SUNDAYS 10–14)

Mark closes the previous section and begins this section with a summary (3:7-12) showing that Jesus' ministry was attracting people from an ever-widening region beyond the Galilee of 1:39. Amid this appeal to many, Jesus goes up to the mountain and summons the Twelve (3:13-19), whom he wants to be with him and whom he will send forth (*apostellein*, related to "apostle") to preach. The next chapters show what he does and says when they are with him, presumably to train them for being sent forth (6:7) at the end of this section.

In the sequence 3:20-35 (Sunday 10) we encounter a narrative arrangement that scholars acknowledge as a feature of Marcan style (intercalation or "sandwiching"), where Mark initiates an action that requires time to be completed, interrupts it by another scene filling in the time (the meat between the surrounding pieces of bread), and then resumes the initial action, bringing it to a close. Here the action begins with Jesus' relatives, who do not understand this turn of life where he is not even taking the time to eat (3:20-21) and want to bring him back home. The time it requires to move from Nazareth where they are to Jesus' new "home" at Capernaum is filled in by scribes who come from Jerusalem (3:22-30). The relatives' objection "He is beside himself" is matched by the scribes' "He is possessed by Beelzebul," the one expressing radical misunderstanding and the other antagonistic disbelief. At the end of the intercalation, the mother and brothers of Jesus finally arrive (3:31-35); but now that the proclamation of the kingdom has begun, they have been replaced: "Whoever does the will of God is my brother, and sister, and mother." The intermediary scene with scribes from Jerusalem constitutes one of the Marcan Jesus' clearest statements about Satan, whose kingdom opposes the kingdom of God. With the appearance of Jesus the two kingdoms are locked in struggle. The allegorical parable in 3:27 suggests that Satan is the strong one in possession of his house and goods (this world) and that Jesus is the

The Gospel According to Mark

stronger one who has come to bind him and take his possessions away. The unforgivable blasphemy in Mark 3:28-30 is to attribute Jesus' works to an unclean spirit rather than to the Holy Spirit.

The next subsection (4:1-34) is a collection of parables and parabolic sayings pertinent to the kingdom of God, most of them dealing with the growth of seed. Even though Jesus' ministry is centered at Capernaum on the Sea of Galilee, and the setting of these parables is a boat, it seems that the material of Jesus' parables is taken from the villages and farms of the Nazareth hill-country of his youth. There is no real doubt that historically Jesus phrased his teaching in parables. Because they are polyvalent, the particular point of parables takes on coloration from the context in which they are uttered or placed. Scholars have spent much time reconstructing the original context of the parables in Jesus' lifetime and distinguishing it from the subsequent reinterpretations that took place as the parables were preached in the early Christian decades (both of which pre-Gospel contexts are speculative). Yet the only certain context is the placing of the parables in the extant Gospels—the fact that at times the context differs in Mark, Matthew, and Luke exemplifies the creative use of tradition by the evangelists for their own pedagogical purposes.

In the present Marcan narrative-sequence three seed parables (the sower and the seed, the seed that grows by itself, and the mustard seed) serve as a commentary on what has been happening in Jesus' proclamation of the kingdom (and anticipate the growing incomprehension by the disciples). In the parable of the sower (not read in the lectionary of Year B) the emphasis is on the different kinds of soil. The interpretation supplied in Mark for the Gospel audience, even if not derived from Jesus himself, may be close to the original idea: Only some have accepted the proclamation of the kingdom, and even among them there are failures. Yet the next two seed parables (4:26-32; Sunday 11) stress that the seed has its own power and will ripen in its own time; it is like the mustard seed with a small beginning and a large growth. Those who heard/read Mark were meant to see these parables as explaining failures and disappointments in their own experience of Christianity and as a sign of hope that ultimately there would be tremendous growth and abundant harvest.

Woven into chapter 4 are comments and parabolic sayings about the "purpose" of the parables. Only 4:33-34 is used in the Sunday lectionary (continuing Sunday 11), but a full explanation is necessary.

In particular, 4:11-12, where Jesus says that parables are given to those outside in order that they may not see, understand, or be converted, is an offensive text if one does not understand the biblical approach to divine foresight, where what has in fact resulted is often presented as God's purpose. (Thus, in Exodus 7:3-4 God tells Moses of the divine plan to make Pharaoh obstinate so that he will not listen to Moses—a hindsight description of the fact that Pharaoh resisted.) Mark is really describing what he sees as the negative *result* of Jesus' teaching among his own people, the majority of whom did not understand and were not converted. Like the symbolic visions accorded to Daniel in the OT, the parables constituted a "mystery," the interpretation of which was given by God only to the select (Dan 2:22, 27-28). Others do not understand, and the mystery becomes a source of destruction. Isaiah 6:9-10, which foresaw the prophet's failure to convert Judah, was widely used in the NT to explain the failure of Jesus' followers to convince most Jews;[11] and Mark employs it here (4:12) in comment on the parables. That Jesus' purpose (in the proper sense) was not to obscure is made clear by the sayings about the lamp and the hidden things in 4:21-23 and also by the summary in 4:33-34 that has Jesus speaking the word to them in parables "to the extent they were able to understand it."

Four miraculous actions follow in 4:35–5:43. These serve to remind today's readers that the first-century worldview was very different from our own. Many modern scholars dismiss completely the historicity of the miraculous;[12] others are willing to accept the healings of Jesus, because they can be related to the coming of the kingdom as a manifestation of God's mercy, but reject the historicity of "nature" miracles such as the calming of the storm in Mark 4:35-41 (Sunday 12). However, that distinction finds no support in an OT background where God manifests power over all creation. Just as sickness and affliction reflect the kingdom of evil, so also does a dangerous storm; accordingly Jesus rebukes the wind and the sea in 4:39 just as he does a demon in 1:25. (Lest one think this picture impossibly naive, one should note that when a storm causes death and destruction today,

---

[11] Romans 11:7-8; Acts 28:26-27; John 12:37-40.
[12] Almost half of Mark's account of the public ministry deals with miracles. The evangelist describes them as *dynameis* (= acts of power), not using a Greek word that would call attention to the wondrous, as does English "miracle" (related to Latin *mirari*, "to wonder at").

The Gospel According to Mark

people wonder why God has allowed this; they do not vent their anger on a high/low pressure system.) The victory of Jesus over the storm is seen as the action of the stronger one (3:27), whom even the wind and sea obey.

The struggle of Jesus with the demonic is even more dramatic in the healing of the Gerasene madman (5:1-20), which is not read in the lectionary.[13] The two miracles in 5:21-43 (Sunday 13) are another instance of Marcan intercalation ("sandwiching"): Jesus sets out for Jairus' house in 5:21-24 and arrives to raise Jairus' daughter in 5:35-43, while the time in between is filled in by the healing of the woman with the hemorrhage in 5:25-34. In the story of the woman, notice that power is portrayed as a possession of Jesus that can go out from him without his knowing where it goes. The question "Who has touched my clothes?" with the disciples' sarcastic response and the confession of the woman add to the humanity of the drama. Yet, perhaps unintentionally, they give the impression that Jesus did not know all things—that may be why the much shorter form of the story in Matthew 9:20-22 omits such details. Jesus' declaration "Your faith has saved you" (Mark 5:34; 10:52) shows that Mark has no mechanical understanding of the miraculous power of Jesus. In the Jairus story we hear of the threesome Peter, James, and John chosen to accompany Jesus. They were the first called of the Twelve; and evidence in Paul and Acts suggests they were the most widely known. The "mighty deed" of Jesus is to resuscitate the young girl to ordinary life, but Christian readers may have been meant to see the request of the father "that she may be saved and live" (5:23) and the result that the girl "rose" (5:42) as a foreshadowing of Jesus' gift of eternal life.[14] The scene ends with another instance of Marcan secrecy (5:43).

In 6:1-6 (Sunday 14) Jesus returns to Nazareth, his native place; and this constitutes an inclusion with his dealings with "his own" from

---

[13] One wonders if this miracle, where Jesus drives out the "Legion" of demons and the need for a place to stay leads to their transferral to pigs, was considered too imaginative.

[14] Jesus' raisings from the dead (the daughter of Jairus; the son of the widow of Nain [Luke 7:11-17]; Lazarus) are miraculous resuscitations to ordinary life, similar to those done by the OT prophets Elijah and Elisha (1 Kgs 17:17-24; 2 Kgs 4:32-37). Jesus' resurrection to eternal life is of a higher order, anticipating God's raising of the dead in the last days.

Christ in the Gospels of the Liturgical Year

Nazareth at the beginning of the section (3:21, 31-35). His teaching in the synagogue produces skepticism. The local people remember him as a carpenter and know his family, and so both his religious wisdom and his mighty works have no plausible origin. Jesus acknowledges that a prophet is without honor in his own region, "among his own relatives,"[15] and in his own house. Despite all the parables and the miracles we have seen in the intervening chapters, Jesus' ministry has not produced faith among those who should know him, and his power (which, as we have seen, is related to faith) is ineffective there.

SENDING OUT THE TWELVE; FEEDING 5,000; WALKING ON WATER; CONTROVERSY; FEEDING 4,000; (6:7–8:26; SUNDAYS 15–16, 22–23)

This section begins with sending out the Twelve and ends with their continued misunderstanding (8:21) and has as a major theme Jesus' failed attempt to bring these disciples to satisfactory faith—a failure that will lead to the second part of the Gospel where he proclaims that only by his own suffering and death can that be brought about. In the opening subsection (6:7-33) we encounter once more Marcan intercalation, for the sending out (*apostellein*) of the Twelve is narrated in 6:7-13 (Sunday 15) and their return in 6:30-32 (Sunday 16), with an account of Herod's activity "sandwiched" between in 6:14-29 to occupy the intervening time. The disciples' mission to preach a change of mind, drive out demons, and cure the sick is an extension of Jesus' own mission; and he gives them the power to accomplish this. The austere conditions (no food, money, luggage) would make it clear any results were not effected by human means; and probably Marcan Christians had come to expect such austerity of missionaries. Between the beginning and the end of the mission, in a passage omitted by the lectionary, we are told that King Herod (Antipas) has killed JBap, and now he is worried that Jesus might be JBap come back from the dead.[16] The fate

---

[15] In the context this would seem to refer also to Jesus' mother; both Matthew and Luke omit this phrase from their version of the scene, probably because they knew that Mary had conceived Jesus through the Holy Spirit and could scarcely be included among those who did not honor Jesus.

[16] Apparently Mark 6:17 is not recording precise history: Herodias was the wife not of Philip but of another brother named Herod, and many doubt that a Herodian princess would dance in the manner described. This may well be a popular story—

The Gospel According to Mark

of JBap is a warning of what the fate of Jesus is likely to be—and the fate of those sent to carry on his work.

The lectionary omits the rest of chapter 6 (vv. 34-56), which includes the feeding of the 5,000 and the walking on the water. Rather, it is at this point, as explained in note 8 above, that for five Sundays (17–21) the lectionary reads from John. On Sunday 22 Mark is resumed with selections from 7:1-23, a controversy over ritual purity. Despite all the miracles, what specifically bothers the Pharisees and scribes who come from Jerusalem is that some of Jesus' disciples do not observe ritual purity, a concept that 7:3-4 has to explain to the readers (suggesting strongly that they are not Jews). The controversy leads Jesus to condemn overly narrow interpretations as human tradition that disregards and even frustrates the real thrust of God's commandment for purity of heart. While the basic attitude toward the Law in 7:8, 15 plausibly comes from Jesus, many scholars suggest that the application that has him declare all foods clean (7:19) represents an insight developed within the tradition that Mark espouses. The hard-fought struggles over kosher food attested in Acts and Paul would be difficult to explain if Jesus had settled the issue from the beginning. A sharp contrast to the hostility of the Jewish authorities is supplied by the faith of the Syrophoenician woman (7:24-30; omitted in the lectionary)[17] when Jesus was in the Tyre area. (It is scarcely accidental that Mark places in sequence a controversy over food and the surprising faith of a Gentile who comes spontaneously to Jesus; they were the two major issues that divided early Christians.) If the woman's child is healed at a distance, the next miracle involving the deaf man (7:31-37; Sunday 23) describes an unusual amount of contact between Jesus and the afflicted, including putting his spittle on the tongue and using a transcribed Aramaic formula *Ephphatha*. Mark indicates that the people's enthusiasm about Jesus' power overrides his command to secrecy.

---

further dramatized in art, music, and drama under the heading of Salome's dance of the veils, whereas the biblical account mentions neither Salome nor veils.

[17] Some have been offended by Jesus' response in 7:27, which is not egalitarian since it places the Jews first (the children) and refers to Gentiles as dogs. Such scandal, however, may reflect a failure to accept Jesus as a first-century Jew. Paul too put Jews first (Rom 1:16), and 1 Peter 2:10 echoes the OT thesis that the Gentiles had no status as a people.

Even if in origin the feeding of the 4,000 (8:1-9) may have been a duplicate of the earlier feeding, it has a strong cumulative effect in Mark as another manifestation of Jesus' stupendous power. It is unfortunate that the lectionary omits what follows in 8:11-26, for passages therein dramatize climactically the utter unlikelihood that Jesus will be accepted or understood. In particular the healing of the blind man in stages (8:22-26), peculiar to Mark, serves as a parabolic commentary on the situation of the disciples stemming from all that Jesus has done for them thus far. The man does not regain his sight immediately, for the first action by Jesus gives him only blurry vision. Only when Jesus acts a second time does the man see clearly. The next half of the Gospel will describe what Jesus must do to make the disciples see clearly, namely, suffer, be put to death, and rise.

THREE PASSION PREDICTIONS; PETER'S CONFESSION; THE TRANSFIGURATION; JESUS' TEACHING (8:27–10:52; SUNDAYS 24–30)

Part Two of Mark begins with Peter's confession of Jesus (8:27-30; Sunday 24). Early in Part One of Mark we heard negative judgments about Jesus ("He is beside himself"; "He is possessed by Beelzebul"). Peter's confession comes amid more positive evaluations of him as JBap, Elijah, and one of the prophets. This spokesman of the disciples who has been with Jesus since 1:16 goes even further by proclaiming him as the Messiah, but Jesus responds with the same command to silence with which he modified the demons' identification of him as God's Son (3:11-12). The two titles are correct in themselves, but they have been uttered without including the necessary component of suffering. Jesus now commences to underline that component more clearly with the first of three predictions of his own passion (8:31). Peter rejects this portrait of the suffering Son of Man, and so Jesus categorizes his lack of understanding as worthy of Satan. Not only will Jesus have to suffer, but so too will those who would follow him (8:34-35).

The sequential Sunday lectionary omits the rest of chapter 8 and 9:1-29, but the transfiguration (9:2-10) is read on the Second Sunday of Lent in Year B. It offers another example of the inadequate faith of the disciples. At the beginning of Part One of Mark the identity of Jesus as God's Son was proclaimed during his baptism by a voice from heaven; but the disciples were not present at that time, and thus far in the

The Gospel According to Mark

public ministry no follower of Jesus has made a believing confession of that identity. Now at the beginning of Part Two, as the hitherto hidden glory of Jesus is made visible to three of his disciples, the heavenly voice reidentifies Jesus. The scene echoes the greatest OT theophany, for it takes place on a mountain amidst the presence of Moses and Elijah, who encountered God on Sinai (Horeb). The "after six days" of 9:2 seems to recall Exodus 24:16, where cloud covers Sinai for six days and only on the day after that does God call to Moses. Awkwardly Peter proposes to prolong the experience by building three tabernacles, even as the Tabernacle was built after the Sinai experience (Exod 25–27; 36–38), but in reality he is terrified and does not know what to say (Mark 9:6). The discussion on the way down from the mountain brings up echoes from the passion prediction (namely, that the Son of Man must suffer and will rise from the dead), but now in relation to Elijah. The implicit identification of Elijah as JBap who came before Jesus and was put to death (9:13) may represent the result of early church reflection on how to relate the two great Gospel figures in the light of the OT.

The story of a boy with a demon (9:14-29; omitted by the lectionary) whom Jesus' disciples are unable to expel because of inadequate faith is recounted by Mark at unusual length. The passage in Mark 9:30-48 (Sundays 25–26) contains a mixture of material. It opens with Jesus' second prediction of the passion, which once again the disciples do not understand.[18] In Capernaum Jesus gives his disciples varied instructions pertinent to the kingdom—gathered here as an important last communication before Jesus arrives in Jerusalem to die. In 9:33-35 Jesus warns the Twelve not to seek to be greatest in the kingdom but a servant. The inclusiveness of the kingdom is exemplified in 9:36-41 by Jesus' command to receive a child (i.e., an insignificant person) in his name and his maxim "Whoever is not against us is for us." The protectiveness against scandal (i.e., causing to sin: 9:42-48) would be heard by Mark's readers as pertaining not only to his lifetime but to theirs.

The journey to Judea, instructing the crowds, and a question of the Pharisees are the context for Jesus' teaching on marriage and divorce (10:2-12; Sunday 27). The Pharisees on the basis of Deuteronomy 24:1-4

---

[18] The difficulty in dismissing all these predictions as totally post-Jesus creations is exemplified in 9:31, where many scholars recognize Semitic features and old tradition.

would allow a husband to write out a note divorcing his wife because of "an indecency in her," and rabbis debated whether that indecency had to be something very serious or could be trivial. But Jesus, appealing to Genesis 1:27; 2:24 for the unity created by marriage, would forbid breaking the marriage bond, so that remarriage after a divorce constitutes adultery. (A similar attitude is found among the Jews who produced the Dead Sea Scrolls.) A form of the prohibition is preserved in Matthew (twice), Luke, and 1 Corinthians 7:10-11; and so it is not unlikely that historically there was a controversy in Jesus' life between him and other Jews who held different views about the issue. The difficulty of his position was recognized by early Christians, and the saying soon gathered comments. For instance, Mark 10:12, which extends the statement to a wife divorcing her husband (not a practice envisioned in OT law), is probably an adaptation to the situation of the Gentile hearers of the Gospel, where women could divorce men.[19] Jesus next returns to the issue of those who enter the kingdom (10:13-31). Most think that underlying the children passage in 10:13-16 there is a correction of a wrong attitude that would demand achievement, abilities, behavior, or status on the part of those who are brought to the kingdom, whereas for Jesus the kingdom/rule of God requires only human receptivity, of which the child is a good symbol. This interpretation brings Mark quite close to Paul's notion of justification by faith. But how do adults show or express receptivity? That is the issue behind the section 10:17-30 (Sunday 28), which begins with the question proposed by a rich man. In response Jesus does not depart from the commandments of God enunciated in the OT; but when the man says he has observed them, Jesus lovingly asks him to sell his possessions and give the proceeds to the poor. Is that part of what is necessary to inherit eternal life, or does it apply only to a special discipleship of walking with Jesus? Certainly not all the early Christians

---

[19] Matthew 19:9 has an exceptive phrase ("Whoever divorces his wife *except for immorality* [*porneia*] and marries another commits adultery [verb: *moichasthai*]," that also appeared in Matthew 5:32, but in none of the other three forms of the divorce prohibition (Luke, Mark, 1 Cor). Although *porneia* can cover a wide range of immorality, a likely interpretation is a reference to marriages within what Jews regarded as forbidden degrees of kindred. Matthew would be insisting that Jesus' prohibition of divorce did not apply to such marriages contracted by Gentiles who had come to believe in Christ.

The Gospel According to Mark

sold their possessions; yet 10:24-27 shows that Jesus is demanding what is impossible by human standards but not by God's. Those who make great sacrifices for Jesus' sake will be rewarded both in this age and in the age to come (10:29-31); but the phrase "with persecutions," whether from Jesus or Mark, is an important realistic touch about their fate.

After Jesus' third and most detailed prediction of the passion (10:32-34), James and John raise the issue of the first places in the kingdom (10:35-45; Sunday 29). The challenge by Jesus to imitate him in drinking the cup and being baptized is symbolically a challenge to suffering. (The flight of the disciples at Gethsemane will show that their confident "We can" response is overly optimistic.) Although in the kingdom there are distinguished places prepared (by God), the disciples must learn that the Gentile pattern where kings lord it over people is not to be followed in the kingdom that Jesus proclaims. There service is what makes one great. "The Son of Man did not come to be served but to serve and to give his life as a ransom for many" (10:45) is a fitting summary of the spirit of this kingdom, a spirit anticipated in Isaiah 53:10-12.

The journey toward Jerusalem has a final scene in the Jericho area when Jesus heals the blind Bartimaeus (Mark 10:46-52; Sunday 30). This man who persists in crying out to Jesus for mercy when others tell him to be silent is symbolic of the many who will come to Christ and hear "Your faith has saved you." Mark offers us this scene of gaining sight as a positive element before the somber scenes he is about to describe in Jerusalem.

MINISTRY IN JERUSALEM: ENTRY; TEMPLE ENCOUNTERS; ESCHATOLOGICAL DISCOURSE (11:1–13:37; SUNDAYS 31–33)

The narrative gives the impression that everything described in these chapters takes place on three days (11:1, 12, 20). On the first day Jesus enters Jerusalem (11:1-10), a reading used for the procession with palms on Passion (Palm) Sunday in Year B. Two disciples are sent from Jesus' base of operations on the Mount of Olives, and all is as he foretold. He sits on the colt that they bring back (perhaps an implicit reference to Zech 9:9 about the coming of Jerusalem's king); and he is acclaimed by a hosanna cry of praise, by a verse from Psalm 118:26, and by the crowd's exclamation about the coming of the kingdom of "our father

David." Thus Jesus is being proclaimed as a king who will restore the earthly Davidic realm—an honor but another misunderstanding.

The Sunday lectionary skips over the actions of Jesus (cursing the fig tree, cleansing the Temple precincts) and the parables that are part of the controversies with the Jewish authorities in Jerusalem. By way of an exception to his hostile portrayal of those who interrogate Jesus, Mark describes a sensitive scribe who asks about the greatest commandment (12:28-34; Sunday 31) and wins Jesus' approbation as being not far from the kingdom of God. The opening line of Jesus' response is fascinating; for it cites the Jewish daily prayer, the Shema ("Hear, O Israel . . .") from Deuteronomy 6:4. This means that decades after Christian beginnings Gentiles were still being taught to pray a Jewish prayer as part of the fundamental demand placed by God! The two commandments inculcated by Jesus, combining Deuteronomy 6:5 and Leviticus 19:18, share a stress on love that became what Christians would like to think of as the identifying characteristic of their religion—a characteristic, alas, too often lacking. Jesus' denunciation of the public display of the scribes provides a background for an account of genuine religious behavior, the widow's giving her mite (12:38-44; Sunday 32).

Most of Jesus' activity in Jerusalem thus far has been in the Temple area; and it is after reflecting on the magnificent Temple buildings that, seated on the Mount of Olives, he delivers the Eschatological Discourse (13:1-37)—the last speech of his ministry that looks to the endtimes. The discourse is a collection of dire prophetic warnings (demolition of the Temple buildings; forthcoming persecution of the disciples; need to be watchful) and apocalyptic signs (deceivers, wars, desolating abomination standing where it should not be, phenomena in the sky). Interpretation presents many problems. Assuming that it is sequentially arranged and that Jesus had a detailed knowledge of the future, some have attempted to identify from our point of view what has already happened and what is yet to come. (Literalism particularly distorts the meaning if symbolic elements from OT and intertestamental apocalyptic writings are taken as exact descriptions of expected events.) Even those who appreciate the symbolic nature of apocalyptic and do not take a literalist approach think that in part the Marcan account is colored by what the evangelist knows to have already taken place, for example, persecution in synagogues and before governors and kings. For most readers the "bottom line" from reading

The Gospel According to Mark

through the discourse is that no precise timetable is given: On the one hand Jesus' followers are not to be misled by speculations and claims that the end is at hand; on the other hand they are to remain watchful. One portion of the discourse (13:24-32) is read on Sunday 33, and another (13:33-37) on the First Sunday of Advent in Year B (see note 21, p. 367). Instead of a passage from Mark for Sunday 34 (the feast of Christ the King), the lectionary once more shifts to John (18:33-37)—a section from the passion narrative where Jesus explains his kingship to Pilate.

* * *

Passages from the rest of Mark, which constitute the passion, burial, and resurrection narratives in chapters 14–16, are read in Passiontide (particularly Palm Sunday) of Year B and Eastertime. They have already been discussed in chapters 16–26 above.

Chapter 35

The Gospel According to Luke
(Liturgical Year C)

This is the longest of the four Gospels. Yet it is only half of the great Lucan written work, for Acts was originally joined to it as part of a two-volume tome that in length constitutes over one-quarter of the NT—a magnificent narrative that blends together the story of Jesus and that of the early church. Perhaps more than in any other Gospel the story is intrinsic to the theology; and part of that theology is the way the Gospel story of Jesus prepares for what happens in Acts, especially to Peter, Stephen, and Paul. Luke departs from Mark more than does Matthew and theologically can be said to stand part way between Mark/Matthew and John.

INTRODUCTORY OBSERVATIONS
Precisely because the Gospel is related to Acts, a word is necessary about the authorship and plan of Luke before we begin a reflection on the sequential text of the Gospel, which begins to be read in the third or C Year of the lectionary on the Third Sunday of Ordinary Time with 4:14. This Gospel was probably written about A.D. 85, give or take five to ten years. By traditional attribution the author was Luke, a physician, the fellow worker and traveling companion of Paul. (Less well attested tradition would make him a Syrian from Antioch.) A considerable number of scholars challenge that attribution on the grounds that some of the (inexact) information about Paul in Acts and the theological outlook there cannot be reconciled with authorship by one who traveled with him and knew him well. Yet prestigious scholars of equal rank point out that the companion of Paul implied in the passages of Acts that use "we" was probably not with Paul before 50 or during the years from 51 to 58 and that he wrote almost two decades after Paul's letters (which may not have been known to him). Thus on the basis of Acts, authorship by Luke, companion of Paul, cannot be ruled out.

The Gospel According to Luke

Nor does what one can detect from the contents of the Gospel about the author refute the possibility of authorship by Luke. One can observe that this author (for whom I retain the traditional name "Luke" without prejudicing the identification issue) was an educated Greek-speaker who knew the Jewish Scriptures in that language and who was not an eyewitness of Jesus' ministry. Luke preserves about 65 percent of Mark, which he has taken over in large blocks. Even more than Matthew, Luke eliminates or modifies elements in Mark that he deems insufficiently respectful to Jesus, his family, and companions. He also draws on a collection of the sayings of the Lord (Q) as well as some other available traditions, oral or written.[1] A gifted storyteller with a truly artistic sense of balance, he is the best Greek stylist among the evangelists and has a sense of Greco-Roman culture. He is not precise on Palestinian geography or Jewish family customs, and so probably he was not by birth a Palestinian or a Jew. Yet his book knowledge of Judaism and the Greek OT suggests that he may have been a convert to Judaism before he became a Christian.

From the evidence of the second volume (Acts), the Gospel[2] was addressed to churches affected directly or indirectly by Paul's mission —churches consisting mostly of Gentile Christians (Acts 28:25-28). Serious proposals center on areas in Greece or Syria; but a diagnosis of Luke's intended readers may be more difficult than for any other Gospel. The fact that the Gospel begins in Jerusalem and Acts ends in Rome suggests a sweeping view of the destiny of Christianity, and so Luke would not have been displeased to learn that his Gospel was meaningful to far more than the local churches known to him.

The Prologue (1:1-4)[3] indicates that not apologetics against adversaries but assurance to fellow Christians was Luke's goal: "So that you

---

[1] Q constitutes about 20 percent of the Gospel. Special Lucan sources have supplied the infancy narrative material, hymns (Magnificat, etc.), parables (good Samaritan, prodigal son, Lazarus and the rich man, etc.), information about JBap, Herod Antipas, and other historical figures.

[2] The manuscripts of Luke show a remarkable number of significant differences among themselves, so that some have argued for two editions (especially of Acts) done in different parts of the church.

[3] Resembling the prefaces of Greek histories written to guide the reader, this is one long sentence in a style more formal than that found elsewhere in the Gospel. Among the four evangelists only Luke and John write a few verses explaining reflectively what they think they are about: John at the end (20:30-31), Luke at the beginning.

may realize what certainty you have of the instruction you have received." Luke acknowledges dependence on eyewitness tradition and shows an awareness of other accounts of Jesus but stresses that this account will be orderly. Part of that orderliness is apparent in the way Luke dramatizes his theology in geography and salvation history. One example of geographical theology is that Jesus' whole life was spent in the confines of Judaism, and so the Gospel begins and closes in the Jerusalem Temple (1:8-11; 24:52-53). The church moves from the Jewish world to the Gentile world, and so Acts (1:4; 28:16) begins in Jerusalem and ends in Rome. Another geographical interest (visible in the Gospel outline on an accompanying page) is the prominence given to Jesus' "Journey to Jerusalem," an anticipation of the attention to be paid in Acts to the journeys of Paul. Such traveling is an enduring encouragement to Christians to proclaim Christ to the ends of the earth; and, indeed, in the course of time many great developments in theology have come as the Christian message has had to adapt itself to geographically new and different cultures.

Commentators have traced with many variations the orderly character of Luke's vision of salvation history. One workable proposal is that Luke envisioned three divisions: *Israel* (= a story recounted in the Law and the Prophets, or OT—see Luke 16:16); *Jesus* (= a story recounted in his Gospel, beginning in Luke 3:1); the *Church* (= a story recounted in Acts, beginning in 2:1 and continuing beyond to the ends of the earth until the Son of Man comes). Thus Jesus is the centerpiece binding together Israel and the church—he is the fulfillment of what has been written in the OT Scriptures (4:21); and when he ascends to heaven, the Spirit sent by the Father (Acts 1:4, 8; 2:1-4) makes possible the spread of the church. The time period associated with Jesus may be calculated from the baptism to the ascension on Easter Sunday evening (Luke 24:50-51—see Acts 1:22). Respectively, transitional from the OT to Jesus and from Jesus to the church are two bridges constructed by the evangelist. In Luke 1–2 OT characters representing Israel (Zechariah, Elizabeth, the shepherds, Simeon, Anna) come across the bridge to meet Gospel characters (Mary, Jesus); in Acts 1 the Jesus of the Gospel comes across the bridge to instruct the Twelve and prepare them for the coming Spirit who will establish the church through their preaching and miracles. Thus there is continuity from the beginning of God's plan to the end.

On the Third Sunday of Ordinary Time in Year C the lectionary begins the consecutive reading of Luke with 4:14. Let me introduce that with a few paragraphs calling attention to the evangelist's initial portrayal of Jesus. As with Matthew, so also with Luke: The liturgy separates the infancy narrative (Luke 1–2) from the body of the Gospel and treats it in the last part of Advent and in the Christmas season (with the feast of the Presentation, February 2, included as a prolongation). I have discussed this material in the previous chapters on Advent and Christmas (see also the table at the end of this book), and so I shall not repeat that discussion here. From those initial chapters of Luke readers should keep in mind the strong Jewish tone of the stories about JBap and Jesus. The hymns scattered throughout them (Magnificat, Benedictus, Gloria in Excelsis, Nunc Dimittis), which may be reminiscences of the earliest Christian prayers, are basically mosaics of OT passages. The parents of JBap were of a Jewish priestly family and totally obeyed all the commandments and ordinances of the Lord (1:6). Over and over again Luke reminds us that in all they did the parents of Jesus followed what was prescribed in the Law (2:21, 22-23, 39, 42). If eventually Christian preachers had to turn from Jews to Gentiles (Acts 28:25-28), that is not because Jesus rejected the heritage of Israel.[4]

Luke's account of the public activity of JBap (3:1-20) is relatively long and has been read on the Second and Third Sundays of Advent in this Year C of the lectionary. As might have been anticipated from the attention given to JBap in the infancy narrative, where his annunciation and birth were made parallel to that of Jesus, Luke resoundingly highlights the importance of JBap's public appearance (probably *ca.* A.D. 29) by synchronizing it with the reigns of the emperor, the governors, and the high priests, so that it becomes a world event. With the expression "the word of God came to John the son of Zechariah" (3:2) Luke assimilates JBap's call to that of an OT prophet (Isa 38:4; Jer 1:2; etc.). Quotation of the Isaian prophecy (40:3-5) about the voice crying in the wilderness, which is connected to JBap in all four Gospels, is extended to include "all flesh shall see the salvation of God" as part of Luke's

---

[4] Similarly Acts 2:46; 3:1 show the first followers of Jesus following Jewish Temple prayer practice. See also Acts 24:14, where Paul says, "I worship the God of our ancestors, believing everything commanded by the Law or written in the Prophets."

Christ in the Gospels of the Liturgical Year

Outline of the Gospel According to Luke

1:1-4   **Prologue.**

1:5–2:52   **Beginnings in Jerusalem and Nazareth:** The conception and infancy of JBap and Jesus, plus the boyhood of Jesus.

3:1–4:13   **Preparation for the Public Ministry:** Preaching of JBap, baptism of Jesus, his genealogy, the temptations.

4:14–9:50   **Ministry in Galilee:**
1. Begins at Nazareth; activities at Capernaum; call of disciples (4:14–5:16);
2. Reactions to Jesus: Controversies with the Pharisees; choice of the Twelve and Sermon on the Plain (5:17–6:49);
3. Miracles and parables that illustrate Jesus' power and help to reveal his identity; mission of the Twelve (7:1–9:6);
4. Questions of Jesus' identity: Herod; feeding of the 5,000; Peter's confession; first and second passion predictions; transfiguration (9:7-50).

9:51–19:27   **Journey to Jerusalem:** Divided into three stages by references to continued journey, this contains a high percentage of material proper to Luke:
1. First to second mention of Jerusalem (9:51–13:21);
2. Second to third mention of Jerusalem (13:22–17:10);
3. Last stage of journey till arrival in Jerusalem (17:11–19:27).

19:28–21:38   **Ministry in Jerusalem:** Entry into Jerusalem; activities in the Temple area; Eschatological Discourse (21:4-38).

22:1–23:56   **Last Supper, Passion, Death, and Burial at Jerusalem.**

24:1-53   **Resurrection Appearances in the Jerusalem Area.**

theological concern for the Gentiles. Particularly Lucan is JBap's social teaching in 3:10-14 with its emphasis on sharing goods, justice for the poor, and kind sensitivity. All this is similar to what the Lucan Jesus will emphasize in his ministry, a similarity that explains 3:18, where JBap is said already to be preaching the gospel.

The brief Lucan account of the baptism of Jesus (3:21-22), which was read in the lectionary of Year C on the feast of the Baptism (First Sunday in Ordinary Time), indicates that Jesus was praying at that crucial moment (the Lucan theme of prayer will also mark the end of

The Gospel According to Luke

the ministry: 23:46). In response the Holy Spirit descends in *bodily* form here at the beginning of the Gospel, even as it will come in visible form on the Twelve at Pentecost at the beginning of Acts (2:1-4). Next Luke stops to recount Jesus' genealogy (3:23-38) before Jesus begins his ministry, thus imitating Exodus 6:14-26, which recounts Moses' genealogy after his early beginnings and before he begins his ministry of leading the Israelites from Egypt.[5]

The account of the testing/temptations of Jesus (4:1-13), which the liturgy reads on the First Sunday of Lent in Year C, is introduced by the indication that Jesus was "full of the Spirit," a Lucan emphasis to prepare for the prominent role of the Spirit in Acts (e.g., 6:5; 7:55). The Lucan temptations, like the Matthean, correct a false understanding of Jesus' mission.[6] Particularly noteworthy is that unlike Mark and Matthew, Luke has no angels come to minister to Jesus and specifies that the devil left him till an opportune time. At the beginning of the passion, Luke alone among the Synoptics will be specific about the presence of Satan, the power of darkness (22:3, 31, 53); and on the Mount of Olives when Jesus is tested again, an angel will come to strengthen him (22:43-44), thus connecting the two testings of Jesus.

JESUS BEGINS GALILEE MINISTRY IN NAZARETH; ACTIVITIES AT CAPERNAUM; CALLS DISCIPLES (4:14–5:16; SUNDAYS 3–5)[7]

The lectionary for Year C begins consecutive reading of Luke with 4:14.[8] There, with his sense of theological geography, Luke calls attention to

---

[5] While Matthew's genealogy descended from Abraham to Jesus, Luke's genealogy mounts to Adam (since Jesus will be a savior of all humanity, beyond the physical descent of Israel) and even to God (3:38). Luke's genealogy is never read in the lectionary.

[6] P. 355, above. The most obvious difference between Matthew and Luke is the order of the last two temptations. Was the Q order the same as Luke's, so that Matthew changed it to have the scene end on the mountain, matching the mountain motif of Matthew 5:1; 28:16? Or was the Q order the same as Matthew's, so that Luke changed it to have the scene end at the Jerusalem Temple where the Gospel ends in 24:52-53? Most judge Matthew's order more original.

[7] I remind readers of the suggestion on p. 355, above, as to how one might use the individual sections of my book to accompany the lectionary passages.

[8] Actually on this Sunday the lectionary emphasizes that it is really starting the Gospel according to Luke by beginning with the Lucan Prologue, 1:1-4, and then follows immediately with 4:14. I have commented on the Prologue above.

Christ in the Gospels of the Liturgical Year

Jesus' return to Galilee; he will terminate the Galilean ministry with Jesus' departure toward Jerusalem (9:51). In between Luke places most of the public ministry account that he takes over from Mark, on which he imposes his own order. To explain why Jesus of Nazareth spent most of his ministry in Capernaum, Luke commences with the rejection of Jesus at Nazareth (4:14-30; Sundays 3–4), which is recounted considerably later in Mark 6:1-6 and Matthew 13:54-58. Also, the Nazareth scene is much expanded beyond Mark's "on the Sabbath he began to teach in the synagogue," for Luke supplies the content of the teaching as Jesus comments on the scroll of the prophet Isaiah (the sole Gospel evidence that Jesus could read). The passage (Isa 61:1-2), which reflects the Jubilee-year amnesty for the oppressed, is used to portray Jesus as an anointed prophet and is programmatic of what Jesus' ministry will bring about. (Presumably it would have appealed strongly to those of Luke's addressees among the lower classes—those won over by the preaching of Paul and his disciples described in Acts.) The rejection of Jesus the prophet by those in his own native place echoes Mark; but there is no Lucan suggestion that those rejecting him included his own household or his relatives (cf. Mark 6:4).[9] Jesus' turning to outsiders is justified by prophetic parallels. The fury of the people against Jesus, even to the point of trying to kill him, goes far beyond the Marcan account and serves from the very beginning to prepare readers for his ultimate fate.

Luke recounts activities connected with Capernaum (4:31-44), which now becomes the operational center of Jesus' Galilean ministry. This section is not read on Sundays, but a few remarks about it are useful to understand the picture of Jesus that Luke is developing. The first of twenty-one Lucan miracles (deeds of power) is an exorcism—even though the devil has departed until a more opportune time, Jesus will struggle with many demons. The healing of Simon's mother-in-law (4:38-39) omits the presence of the four fishermen-disciples from Mark's account because in Luke Jesus has not yet called them (see below). Compared to Mark 1:39, which has Jesus going through the synagogues of all Galilee, Luke 4:44 localizes the synagogues in Judea. That may illustrate the vagueness of Luke's ideas of Palestinian geography, since in the next verse (5:1) Jesus is still in Galilee, at the Lake.[10]

---

[9] Anything derogatory to Jesus' mother would conflict with the picture the evangelist painted of her in the infancy narrative.

[10] Or does Luke's Judea simply mean "the country of the Jews"?

The Gospel According to Luke

The miraculous catch of fish and the call of the disciples (Luke 5:1-11; Sunday 5) illustrate ingenious Lucan (re)ordering. The call of the first disciples that Mark had placed before the four Capernaum episodes has been moved after them and, indeed, after a fishing miracle that only Luke among the Synoptics records. That Jesus has healed Simon's mother-in-law and effected a tremendous catch of fish[11] makes more intelligible why Simon and the others followed Jesus so readily as disciples. The call of a Simon who confesses himself an unworthy sinner is a dramatic presentation of vocation and prepares the way for a calling of Paul, who was also unworthy because he had persecuted Christians (Acts 9:1-2; Gal 1:13-15). The theme of leaving "everything" to follow Jesus (Luke 5:11) illustrates Luke's stress on detachment from possessions.

REACTIONS TO JESUS: CONTROVERSIES WITH THE PHARISEES; CHOICE OF THE TWELVE AND PREACHING TO THE MULTITUDE ON THE PLAIN (5:17–6:49; SUNDAYS 6–8)

Drawing on Mark 2:1–3:6, Luke presents a series of five controversies (5:17–6:11), in all of which Pharisees play a role. The controversies involve a paralytic, the call of Levi, fasting, picking grain, and healing on the Sabbath. In them Pharisees criticize many aspects of Jesus' behavior: his claim to be able to forgive sins, his associates, his failure to have his disciples fast, their picking grain, and his own healing on the Sabbath. Even though none of this material is used in the Sunday lectionary, it is worth remembering as background when we read the next subsection, where Luke turns to the favorable reactions to Jesus by recounting the choice of the Twelve (6:12-16)[12] and especially the sermon to the multitude on the plain (6:17-49). That preaching, which is read on Sundays 6–8, is the Lucan parallel to Matthew's Sermon on the Mount (Matt 5–7).[13] Matthew's sermon was directed to the Twelve;

---

[11] Here we encounter Luke's occasional similarity to John, for the fishing miracle occurs in a post-resurrectional setting in John 21:3-11.

[12] The Lucan list of the Twelve Apostles (see also the Eleven in Acts 1:13) seems to stem from a different tradition from that of Mark 3:16-19 and Matthew 10:2-4 (see note 14, p. 358).

[13] Luke's composition from his own material (L), Mark, and Q is only about 30 percent as long as Matthew's.

Christ in the Gospels of the Liturgical Year

but although in Luke the Twelve are with Jesus, he has healed "all" among a great multitude on a plain, and so the sermon is directed to all disciples. Four Lucan beatitudes open the sermon, echoing the program for the ministry read aloud in the Nazareth synagogue. These beatitudes address those who are actually poor, hungry, mournful, and hated "now." The accompanying "woes," perhaps of Lucan creation and resembling the contrasts in the Magnificat, hint at the antagonisms engendered among the addressees by the affluent. The comparable condemnation in James 2:5-7; 5:1-6 might suggest that the reason for the violent dislike was the practice of injustice by the rich. Yet as we shall see in later chapters, at times but not consistently, Luke seems to regard the very possession of wealth (unless distributed to the poor) as corrupting one's relationship to God. Luke's ideal is the community of those believers who give their possessions to the common fund, as he describes in Acts 2:44-45; 4:32-37.

Without the proclamations "You have heard it said . . . but I say to you" that characterize Matthew 5:17-48, Luke 6:27-36 enunciates Jesus' values. Although sometimes these are called "the ethics of the kingdom," that designation is far more appropriate for Matthew, where "kingdom" occurs eight times in the course of the Sermon on the Mount, than for Luke, who mentions "kingdom" only once in the whole sermon (6:20). Thus there is less eschatological tone to the startling demands of the Lucan Jesus for his disciples to love those who hate and abuse them. If, as the author of Luke-Acts would have known, the preaching of Jesus blessing the poor and the hungry attracted many of the slaves and lower class in the Roman world, the challenge to bless those who curse you and pray for those who maltreat you would have been just as difficult for them as the blessing on the poor was for the rich. Many interpreters have commented on the impossibility of running a society in the world known to us on the principle of turning the other cheek or giving your shirt to someone who has robbed you of your coat, but that very impossibility tells us that the kingdom of God has not been realized in our world. So long as there are those like St. Francis of Assisi who try to live out the spirit of the Lucan sermon, the hope that the kingdom envisioned by Jesus can come is not lost. The passage on not judging is an extension of love. We are reminded that the demands are addressed to all who would hear (6:27, 47) and that the demands are not met by those who do not bear good fruit (6:43-45) and simply say "Lord, Lord" (6:46).

The Gospel According to Luke

The Lucan form of the healing of the centurion's servant in 7:1-10
(Sunday 9) has two deputations sent to Jesus rather than having the
official himself come, and has a servant (*doulos*) cured rather than a
boy/son; it may be secondary (compare Matt 8:5-13; John 4:46-54).
The story contrasts a Gentile's faith-response to Jesus with the Jewish
authorities' rejection of him. This is a Gentile who has loved the Jewish
nation and built the synagogue and thus foreshadows Cornelius, the
first Gentile to be converted in Acts (10:1-2). The next miracle, the
raising of the son of the widow of Nain (Luke 7:11-17; Sunday 10), is
uniquely Lucan. This awesome manifestation of power gains Jesus
christological recognition (7:16 echoes the prophet and divine visitation motif of 1:76-78) but also shows his compassionate care for a
mother deprived of her only son.

The material in 7:18-35, which concerns the relation of Jesus to JBap,
is not read in the Sunday lectionary. Actually, as in the other Gospels,
it is crucial for understanding Jesus, since Jesus' reaction to the fate of
JBap shaped his own ministry. Part of his bitterness toward the
Pharisees and the lawyers was rooted in their rejection of JBap, whose
goodness was apparent to all the people, even the tax collectors.

This constitutes background for the beautiful story in Luke 7:36-50
(Sunday 11), which, in the context of a meal at the table of Simon the
Pharisee, involves a penitent sinful woman weeping over and anointing Jesus' feet. It may be composite, since it involves a parable
comparing two debtors. Is the Lucan story the same as that of the
anointing of Jesus' head by a woman at the house of Simon the leper
in Mark 14:3-9 and Matthew 26:6-13, and that of the anointing of
Jesus' feet by Mary, the sister of Martha and Lazarus, in John 12:1-8?[14]
There is also a debate as to whether Luke's sinful woman was forgiven
because she loved much or whether she loved much because she had

---

[14] Many think that two stories, one of a penitent sinner who wept at Jesus' feet
during the ministry and the other of a woman who anointed Jesus' head with
costly perfume, have become confused in the tradition that came down to Luke
and John. Others argue for one basic story. Hagiographic tradition and legend
glued these three stories together and further confused the situation by identifying
Mary, sister of Martha, with Mary Magdalene, whence all the art depicting Mary
Magdalene as a penitent prostitute with her hair loosed.

Christ in the Gospels of the Liturgical Year

already been forgiven. Either meaning or both would fit Luke's stress on God's forgiveness in Christ and a loving response. After the story of this woman Luke describes the Galilean women followers of Jesus (8:1-3) who had been cured of evil spirits and diseases. Three of them are named: Mary Magdalene; Joanna, wife of Chuza, Herod's steward; and Susanna—the first two will reappear at the empty tomb (24:10). Interestingly the other Gospels name Galilean women exclusively in relation to the crucifixion and resurrection, so that only Luke tells us of their past and that they served (*diakonein*) the needs of Jesus and the Twelve out of their means—a picture of devoted women disciples. In part this support anticipates the picture of women in Acts, for example, Lydia at Philippi (16:15).

Rejoining the outline of Mark at its parable chapter (4:1-20), Luke 8:4-15 recounts the parable of the sower and the seed and its explanation, interrupted by the purpose of the parables.[15] There is also a sequence of four miracle stories (8:22-56): calming the storm at sea, healing the Gerasene demoniac, resuscitating Jairus' daughter, and healing the woman with a hemorrhage. Next Luke continues with the sending out of the Twelve (Luke 9:1-6). Having manifested his power, Jesus shares it with the Twelve by giving them authority over demons and sending them to preach the kingdom/gospel and to heal (9:2, 6). Unfortunately none of the material from 8:1 to 9:6 is incorporated in the Sunday lectionary.

QUESTIONS OF JESUS' IDENTITY:
FEEDING OF THE 5,000, PETER'S CONFESSION,
FIRST AND SECOND PASSION PREDICTION,
TRANSFIGURATION (9:7-50; SUNDAY 12)

While the Twelve are away, we are told of Herod's having beheaded JBap (Luke 9:7-9).[16] The important point is the tetrarch's curiosity

---

[15] The hundredfold yield of the seed that fell into good soil is interpreted as those who hear the word, hold it fast in an honest and good heart, and bring forth fruit with patience (8:15). This leads into the arrival of Jesus' mother and brothers (8:19-21). Although drawn from Mark 3:31-35, the import is entirely changed. There is no longer an unfavorable contrast between the natural family and a family of disciples; rather there is only praise of the mother and brothers as hearing the word of God and doing it—they exemplify the good seed and fit the criterion of discipleship.

[16] Luke's omission of the whole Marcan account of Herod's banquet and the dance of Herodias' daughter may reflect a distaste for the sensational.

The Gospel According to Luke

about Jesus (preparing for 13:31 and 23:8). The theme of Jesus' identity is followed out in the subsequent scenes. They begin with the return of the Twelve Apostles and the feeding of the 5,000 (9:11-17, read on the feast of Corpus Christi in Year C), an adapted form of Mark 6:30-44. (For the theology of this multiplication of loaves, see p. 362, above.) Then in what is dubbed by scholars the "Big Omission," Luke skips over Mark 6:45–8:26, thereby leaving out everything from after the feeding of the 5,000 to after the feeding of the 4,000.[17]

Rejoining Mark's outline at Mark 8:27, Luke next presents the three-fold proposal about who Jesus is and Peter's confession (9:18-20), introduced by the typical Lucan note that Jesus was praying. In the sequence Peter's "the Messiah of God" is Luke's way of answering Herod's "Who is this?" ten verses earlier. This confession is greeted by Jesus' first passion prediction (9:21-22), but there is in Luke (unlike Mark/Matt) no misunderstanding by Peter and no chastisement of him. The combined 9:18-24 is read on Sunday 12; after that, however, the sequential lectionary skips Jesus' teaching about the cross (to be taken up "daily") in 9:23-27; the miracle story of the boy with a demon (9:37-43a), where typically Luke suppresses most of the Marcan emphasis on the incapacity of the disciples to heal this child; and the second prediction of the passion and the dispute about greatness (9:43b-50)—once more softening the picture of the disciples. The one passage from this whole area of Luke that makes its way into the Sunday lectionary (on the Second Sunday of Lent in Year C) is the transfiguration (9:28-36), set in the context of Jesus praying. The Lucan account describes glory as present already in Jesus' earthly career (9:32—an outlook present in John's Gospel also); yet it also affirms the suffering aspect of the Son of Man, for Jesus talks to Moses and Elijah about his "exodus," that is, his departure to God through death in Jerusalem. Both glory and suffering are affirmed by God's voice that identifies Jesus as Son and Chosen One (Suffering Servant).

* * *

[17] Presumably the Lucan evangelist saw these as doublets and decided to report only one; but the differences from the Marcan account of the 5,000 and the presence of another variant in John 6:1-15 may mean that Luke combined two accounts in the one multiplication of the loaves he reports.

Christ in the Gospels of the Liturgical Year

At this point Luke begins his long account of the journey to Jerusalem (9:51–19:27), which really constitutes the second half of the Gospel account of Jesus' public ministry. In 9:51 the evangelist introduces it by a subpreface (somewhat comparable to 3:1-2) to mark off major change. The time is coming for Jesus to be taken up (to heaven), and so he sets his face for Jerusalem, where he is to die. Luke is portraying a Jesus who knows his destiny and accepts it from God. The long journey is (an artificial) framework, as Luke leaves the Marcan outline for almost all this second half of the Gospel and inserts large blocks from Q and from his own sources. The choice of a journey as a framework is probably dictated by a desire to create a parallel to Paul's journeying in Acts. This section of the Gospel is most characteristically Lucan and supplies proportionately a high percentage of Sunday readings. The material may be divided into three subsections according to the points in 13:22 and 17:11, where Luke reminds us of the framework of the journey.

FIRST TO SECOND MENTION OF JERUSALEM
(9:51–13:21; SUNDAYS 13–20)
We have seen some parallels between the Gospels of Luke and John, but now we perceive that they are also far apart. Among the Gospels only Luke has the hostile encounter with a Samaritan village (9:51-56; Sunday 13), which is diametrically the opposite of the warm reception given Jesus by the Samaritans in John 4:39-42. Very Lucan is Jesus' refusal of the vengeance upon the Samaritans proposed by James and John. The dialogue with three would-be followers (9:57-62) highlights the absolute demand imposed by the kingdom. We saw a sending of the Twelve in Mark 6:7-13, Matthew 10:5-42 (woven into the Mission Discourse), and Luke 9:1-6. Only Luke has a second mission, the sending of the seventy-two (10:1-12; Sunday 14). The doubling may be designed to prepare for Acts, where the Twelve function prominently at the beginning of the mission only to have the initiative pass to others, like Paul, Barnabas, and Silas. The need for a second sending in the Gospel (10:2) is explained by the size of the harvest. Does the designated "seventy-two" echo for Luke the LXX numbering of the nations in Genesis 10:2-31 and thus prognosticate the ultimate extent of the harvest? Joy at the subjection of the demons marks the Lucan return of the seventy-two (10:17-20)—compare the unemotional return of the Twelve in 9:10. Jesus sums up their mission (and perhaps the mission

The Gospel According to Luke

of the church as Luke has known it) in terms of the fall of Satan.[18] Why the disciples should rejoice because their names are written in heaven (Luke 10:20) is explained by what follows (not read in the Sunday lectionary). Jesus thanks the Father for revelation (10:21-22), a passage that has Johannine parallels. That the disciples have been chosen by the Son to receive the revelation is shown in the blessing of 10:23-24, a macarism that acknowledges what they have seen.

The reading for Sunday 15 begins with the lawyer's question about eternal life and Jesus' response about the love of God and neighbor (10:25-28). Although the lawyer is posing a test, Jesus likes his answer; and that leads into further probing by the lawyer and the parable of the good Samaritan (10:29-37), which is peculiar to Luke. Since the commandment to love leads to (eternal) life, the lawyer seeks casuistically to know to whom the commandment applies; but he is told that one can define only the subject of love, not the object. The Samaritan is a subject whose range of love is unlimited, perhaps preparing for Acts 8 with its positive picture of the reaction of Samaritans to the gospel. The story of Martha and Mary (10:38-42; Sunday 16) is another instance where material peculiar to Luke has Johannine parallels (John 11:1-44; 12:1-8). Yet there are also major differences: The brother, Lazarus, is absent from Luke; and the family's home at Bethany in John is two miles from Jerusalem, not a village on the way from Galilee and Samaria to Jerusalem, as in Luke. The import of the Lucan story is that heeding the word of Jesus is the only important thing—a lesson harmonious with the earlier answer about the love of God and neighbor as the basic observance necessary for eternal life. It demonstrates that what is required is not complicated.

Similarly uncomplicated is the instruction given to the inquiring disciple about the Lord's Prayer (11:1-4; Sunday 17)—a shorter and in some ways older wording than that preserved in Matthew (p. 357, above) but also less eschatological. The encouragement to pray is continued by the uniquely Lucan parable of the insistent friend (11:5-8), a story redolent of Palestinian local color, for it envisions the whole family crowded into a single-room house. Q material on insistence in asking (11:9-13) is added to make the point. The most important variant

---

[18] The authority over serpents and scorpions given to them in 10:19 is similar to that in the post-resurrectional mission in the Appendix or Long Ending attached to Mark's Gospel (16:17-18).

from Matthew 7:7-11 is the promise in Luke 11:13 to those who ask: Matthew has good things given by the heavenly Father; Luke has the Holy Spirit given, as verified in Acts.

The Sunday lectionary omits all the material from 11:14 to 12:12, a good deal of which describes controversies (and in the Gospel sequence prepares readers for the struggle to take place at Jerusalem in the passion).[19] One omission is a particular loss: the peculiarly Lucan beatitude cried out by the woman in the crowd (11:27-28). The interchange involves two blessings with priority being given to obedience to God's word—this priority has been anticipated in the two blessings of 1:42-45. Sunday 18 resumes sequential reading with the pericope on greed and the parable of the rich barn builder (12:13-21), which is distinctively Lucan. The hope to divide an inheritance equally or to enlarge a growing business, understandable in itself, runs against the contention that a consuming interest in material possessions is not reconcilable with interest in God. Ideally Christians are asked to live by the maxim, "One's life does not depend on what one possesses" (12:15; see Acts 2:44; 4:34). The fate of the barn builder reflects the expectation of an individual judgment taking place before the general judgment at the end of the world.

The reading for Sunday 19 (12:32-48) begins with the instruction, "Sell your possessions and give alms" (12:33), but then Luke shifts the topic to the necessity of faithful watchfulness. In the midst of Q material (that Matt 24:43-51 has incorporated into the Eschatological Sermon) Luke 12:41 is an insert: a question by Peter as to whether this teaching is "for us or for all," which is never specifically answered. However, since the next saying involves a steward who takes good care of the household, one may judge that there is a greater obligation on the apostles and on Christian leaders. The threat of punishment for the servant who does not watch in 12:46 is qualified by the Lucan addendum in 12:47-48 distinguishing between the punishment of those who had knowledge and those who did not. (In narrating the hostile treatment of Jesus in the passion, Luke will be the most attentive of all the Gospels to distinguish between the leaders and the people.) That distinction leads into a frightening description of the diverse results of

---

[19] The assurance that "the Holy Spirit will teach you what you ought to say" when facing hostile synagogue and secular authorities (Luke 12:11-12) takes on added significance in stories that illustrate the trials of Christians in Acts.

The Gospel According to Luke

Jesus' ministry (12:49-53; Sunday 20). In eschatological language Jesus speaks of the fire he is to bring on the earth and the baptism of being tested that is part of his destiny. Division, not peace, will be the result; the prediction in Luke 2:34 that Jesus was set for the fall and rise of many in Israel is now made more precise in terms of how families will be split. Since other statements esteem peace (2:14; 19:38) and unified families (role of JBap in 1:17), the results of Jesus' ministry are ambivalent, with a thrust in both directions. Evidently much of this will happen soon, for Jesus expresses ire at people's inability to read the signs of the present time (12:54-56).

In 13:1-9 (read in Year C on the Third Sunday of Lent) Luke offers examples of destruction to inculcate repentance. We have no other knowledge of Galileans who were killed by Pilate while offering sacrifice (at Jerusalem) or of the fall of a tower in Siloam (a pool in Jerusalem), although some have thought that the former incident explains the enmity between Herod, the tetrarch of Galilee, and Pilate, which Luke reports in 23:12. The parable of the fig tree (13:6-9) offers one more chance for the tree's bearing fruit before being cut down. Many have wondered if it is not a benevolent Lucan form of the cursing of the fig tree in Mark 11:12-14, 20-23 and Matthew 21:18-21 and thus a miracle that has become a parable. The lectionary omits 13:10-21, the healing of a crippled woman and the twin parables of the mustard seed and the leaven.

SECOND TO THIRD MENTION OF JERUSALEM (13:22–17:10; SUNDAYS 21–27)

As Jesus moves on to Jerusalem and passes through cities and towns (13:22-30; Sunday 21), a tone of pessimism appears. Evidently not many are listening, and so the question arises whether only a few are to be saved. Jesus' answer underlines the unpredictability of response: Some of those invited last will be first, and the first will be last. The lectionary omits a key passage (13:31-33) for understanding Luke's sequence, since the Pharisees' report of Herod's homicidal hostility offers the explanation for Jesus' going on to Jerusalem. The reader is probably meant both to think that the Pharisees are telling the truth and to distrust their motives, since they may have been trying to get Jesus off the scene by urging him to save his life through departure from Galilee. Paradoxically, Jesus knows that going to Jerusalem will lead to his death. (Herod will reappear during the Roman trial when

Christ in the Gospels of the Liturgical Year

Pilate turns Jesus over to him for judgment.) Jesus' thoughts about his destiny lead into the plaintive apostrophe to Jerusalem (13:34-35): As a prophet Jesus will die there, but the city will be punished for what it does to prophets.

The next three episodes (14:1-24) are set in the home of a prominent Pharisee: the Sabbath cure of a man with dropsy, two instructions about conduct at dinner, and the parable of the great banquet. The middle one, read on Sunday 22, offers an interesting contrast. Sitting in a lower place so that eventually, to everyone's admiration, one may be brought higher is both good manners and self-serving. But inviting to a banquet beggars and the infirm and not inviting one's friends and relatives represents the upside-down eschatological values of the kingdom. Thus this teaching, peculiar to Luke, combines worldly and unworldly wisdom for those who live in a world where God's kingdom is coming near but has not fully come. Afterwards, without mentioning Jesus' departure from the Pharisee's home, Luke has Jesus talking to the accompanying multitude about the cost of discipleship (14:25-35; Sunday 23). Peculiarly Lucan are the prudential parables worthy of an OT Wisdom teacher about the need to calculate the cost before starting a house or beginning a war. This message is very different from the more prophetic stance of not worrying about the needs of this life, inculcated earlier in 12:22-34.

The whole next chapter consists of three parables: lost sheep, lost coin, lost (prodigal) son (15:1-32; Sunday 24; also Fourth Sunday of Lent in Year C). Matthew 18:12-14 works the lost sheep parable into the Sermon on the Church addressed to the disciples; Luke addresses it (and his own other two parables) to the Pharisees and scribes who object to Jesus' keeping company with sinners. The references to joy in heaven show that the parables give a lesson in God's loving mercy and dramatize the value of those whom others despise as lost. In the first two Luke has a man and woman respectively as dramatis personae (shepherd, housekeeper). The lost or prodigal son stresses that the elder brother should not be jealous of the father's benevolent treatment of the sinful younger brother, and that fits the context of correcting the Pharisees' attitude toward sinners. Beyond that, the point made in the middle of the parable at 15:20 is important for understanding the concept of Christian love. The portrayal of the father running to the younger son and kissing him before he can give the prepared speech of repentance could serve as an illustration of

The Gospel According to Luke

Romans 5:8: "God's love for us is shown in that, while we were yet sinners, Christ died for us," and 1 John 4:10: "In this is love, not that we loved God but that God loved us."

Many have found difficulty with the uniquely Lucan parable of the unjust steward (16:1-13; Sunday 25) because it seems to commend to the disciples a shady business practice; but what is praised is the prudent energetic initiative of the steward, not his dishonesty. Diverse sayings dealing with wealth have been attached to the parable, but it is debated at which verse they begin: 8b, 9, or 10. Overall they serve Luke's theological tenet that abundant money corrupts and that the right way to use it is to give it away to the poor and thus make friends who can help in heaven. The next lectionary reading (16:19-31; Sunday 26), the uniquely Lucan parable of the rich man and Lazarus,[20] also concerns the damning effects of wealth. The different fates after death are not based on the rich man having lived a life of vice and Lazarus having been very virtuous; they are based on the rich man having had a comfortable and well-fed life, while Lazarus was hungry and miserable (16:25). This attack on the Pharisees' love for money (which would also serve as a warning for Christians, e.g., Acts 5:1-11) is made sharper by a second point, made at the end of the parable. If they do not listen to Moses and the prophets, they will not listen to someone come back from the dead. To Luke's readers/hearers this would appear prophetic, for Acts will show that people did not listen even after Jesus came back from the dead.

The topic changes as Jesus addresses to his disciples four unrelated warnings on behavior (17:1-10). Cautioning against scandalizing others, they stress forgiving fellow disciples, the power of faith, and the distinction between great achievement and duty. The last two on faith and duty are read on Sunday 27. The warning about doing one's duty, which is peculiarly Lucan, is an interesting challenge: The disciples who have followed Jesus might get the idea that they had done something great, but they are to tell themselves that they are unprofitable servants who have done only what they were supposed to do.

---

[20] This is another similarity between Luke and John: Only they mention a Lazarus, and the theme of resurrection from the dead is connected with him in both Gospels.

This begins with the uniquely Lucan cleansing of the ten lepers, including the thankful Samaritan (17:11-19; Sunday 28). Jesus has been traveling toward Jerusalem since 9:51, and in 9:52 his messengers enter a Samaritan village. That at this point in the story he is still passing between Samaria and Galilee tells us that the journey is an artificial framework (and also that Luke may not have had a clear idea of Palestinian geography). Yet the framework explains why there is a Samaritan among the lepers, indeed, the sole leper to show gratitude and thus to receive salvation. His reaction anticipates the glad reception of the good news about Jesus by Samaritans in Acts 8:1-25. The lectionary skips the eschatological teaching in 17:20-37 and picks up again with the uniquely Lucan parable of the unjust judge (18:1-8; Sunday 29), designed to encourage the disciples after the warnings of future judgment. If continued petitioning persuades a totally amoral judge, how much more will their persistent, confident prayer be heard by God, who vindicates the chosen ones. The theme of prayer leads into the Lucan parable of the Pharisee and the publican (or tax collector: 18:9-14; Sunday 30). Beyond exhibiting God's mercy to sinners, the story raises the issue of the rejection of the Pharisee, who is not justified. The Pharisee is not a hypocrite, for although a bit boastful, he has lived faithful to God's commandments as he understood them. Is the problem that although he thanks God, he has not shown any need of God or of grace or forgiveness? Or does the Lucan Jesus come close to Pauline thought that observing commanded works does not justify by itself?

The rest of the material in chapter 18 (15-43), including the third prediction of the passion,[21] is omitted in the Sunday lectionary, which resumes with the colorful scene, set in Jericho and peculiar to Luke, involving Zacchaeus (19:1-10; Sunday 31). Beyond Jesus' kindness to a tax collector deemed a sinner, the story illustrates Luke's attitude toward wealth: Zacchaeus is a rich man, but salvation can come to his house because he gives half his goods to the poor.[22] The parable of the

---

[21] Luke 18:31-34 hews close to Mark 10:33-34 even to the point of predicting that the Gentiles will spit upon and scourge the Son of Man—something that never happens in the Lucan passion narrative!

[22] In 18:22-23 Jesus will ask a very wealthy would-be follower to give away *all* that he has to the poor. Is the spirit of sacrifice rather than the percentage the important issue?

The Gospel According to Luke

pounds (19:11-27), seemingly the Lucan variant of the Matthean parable of the talents (25:14-30), is not read, even though it has incorporated the distinctive story of a nobleman who goes to a far country to receive a kingship: His citizens hated him and sent an embassy to try to prevent his being appointed king, only to have him come back as king and slay them. This omission is unfortunate, for Luke means the story to prepare his readers for the rejection of Jesus in Jerusalem, his crucifixion as King of the Jews, his return in resurrection, and the ultimate destruction of Jerusalem.

ENTRY INTO JERUSALEM; ACTIVITIES IN THE TEMPLE AREA; ESCHATOLOGICAL DISCOURSE (19:28–21:38; SUNDAYS 32–33)

At the end of his long journey that began in 9:51 Jesus arrives at Jerusalem where his "exodus" or departure to God will take place. He will stay overnight at Bethphage and Bethany in the near environs of Jerusalem, but most of his activity there will be centered in the Temple area, and at the end he will deliver an eschatological discourse.

The royal entry into Jerusalem (19:28-40), read as part of the procession with palms on Passion (Palm) Sunday in Year C, stays close to the Marcan account (11:1-10) but changes the theme from the bystanders' enthusiasm for the arrival of the kingdom to the *disciples'* praise of Jesus as king (see John 12:13). In Luke 7:18-19 the disciples of JBap posed to Jesus their master's question, "Are you the one to come?" Now the disciples of Jesus confirm that he is. Luke includes a refrain about peace and glory that resembles the Gloria in Excelsis (2:14). The lectionary skips the whole section in 19:41–20:26, which involves predictions of the destruction of Jerusalem,[23] the cleansing of the Temple, and the warning parable about the vineyard. There Luke describes how the chief priests and the scribes seek to destroy Jesus for this teaching but are frustrated by his popularity among "all the people"—a preparation for the benevolent Lucan picture of the people in the passion narrative.

---

[23] Scholars debate whether the description in 19:43 is so precise that Luke must have written or at least rephrased it after the historical destruction by the Romans. Also in place of Mark's abomination of desolation, Luke 21:20 speaks of Jerusalem surrounded by armies (from a knowledge of what happened in A.D. 70?).

The lectionary picks up again with 20:27-38 (Sunday 32) with the hostile question posed by the Sadducees about the resurrection, a passage that not only highlights Jesus' stance about resurrection in general but also prepares us for his own resurrection. Once again the lectionary passes over more of the Jerusalem disputes and teaching (20:39–21:4), so that when it resumes (21:5-19; Sunday 33) we are in the Eschatological Discourse. As in Mark/Matthew, admiration of the Temple buildings elicits from Jesus a prediction of the destruction of the Temple (21:5-6); and that leads into a discourse on the last things— a speech particularly complicated in Luke by the fact that Jesus has already exhorted to eschatological vigilance in 12:35-48 and given eschatological teaching in 17:20-37. Unlike Mark/Matthew, Luke situates the discourse in the Temple as a continuation of his daily teaching there (19:47; 20:1; 21:38); and there is more interest in what happens to Jerusalem, for some scholars would maintain that 21:8-24 refers to the fate of Jerusalem, while 21:25-36[24] refers to the fate of the world when the Son of Man comes. These points are worth noting: 21:12 speaks of persecution for the sake of Jesus' "name" (see Acts 3:6,16; 4:10; etc.); 21:13-15 promises that a wisdom that cannot be contradicted will be given when it is time to bear testimony (see 7:35; 11:49; Acts 6:3,10); 21:18 supplies extra confidence to Jesus' followers, for not a hair of their head will perish (see 12:7). The reading for Sunday 34 (feast of Christ the King) is taken from the Lucan passion narrative (23:35-43), as Jesus on the cross speaks to the "good thief"—see the next paragraph.

* * *

Passages from the rest of Luke, which constitute the passion, burial, and resurrection narratives in chapters 22–24, are read in Passiontide (particularly Palm Sunday) of Year C and Eastertime. They have already been discussed in chapters 16–26 above.

---

[24] Passages from this (21:25-28, 34-36) are read on the First Sunday of Advent in Year C. See note 21, p. 367.

Chapter 36

The Gospel According to John
(Latter Part of Lent; Post-Easter Season)

While all four evangelists had a theological goal, in a special way the
author of this Gospel has been known as John "the theologian";[1] and
many regard this as *the* theological masterpiece among the Gospels.
Yet it has no liturgical year of its own in the lectionary. The fact that
the principal consecutive reading starts in the middle of Lent every
year means that a special effort has to be made to call attention to the
uniqueness of this Gospel and why it has this unusual treatment in the
lectionary. The following observations are made with that in mind.

INTRODUCTORY OBSERVATIONS
The Fourth and last of the canonical Gospels was written in the period
A.D. 80–110. More precisely, many think that the Gospel was composed
in two stages and date the writing of the body of the Gospel by the
evangelist to the 90s and the addition of further material by a final
editor or redactor *ca.* 100–110 (about the same time as the Third Epistle
of John). Second-century tradition identified the evangelist as John the
disciple, who reclined on Jesus' bosom at the Last Supper—and this
John was understood to be the son of Zebedee, one of the Twelve, who
wrote the Gospel in his old age as an improvement to supplement the
other Gospels. There are many internal reasons, however, to doubt
that the evangelist was an eyewitness apostle (apostles are never mentioned!), and certainly this Gospel is no mere supplement.[2] Although I

---

[1] From the ancient Greek designation of him as *ho theologos*, traditionally rendered
in English as John "the divine," a usage stemming from that generous time when
theologians were known as divines.
[2] In fact, although it begins with JBap and ends with the passion/resurrection,
with the exception of the multiplication of the loaves and walking on the water,
John and the Synoptic Gospels have very different content for both the public
ministry of Jesus and the Last Supper.

shall continue to use the traditional designation (as I did for the other Gospels) by referring to the evangelist as "John," most commentators, Protestant and Catholic, do not think John son of Zebedee wrote the Gospel. Many think that the evangelist read the Synoptic Gospels or at least Mark, but a somewhat larger group thinks the Fourth Gospel reflects tradition independent of but similar to that preserved in Mark.

The compositional history is complicated by the Gospel's references (direct or indirect) in the Last Supper, passion, and resurrection accounts to a "disciple whom Jesus loved," a figure who is somehow involved in the composition (19:35; 21:24). He is never named; but besides the ancient thesis that he was John son of Zebedee, there are many modern theories about his identity. Probably the quest is misplaced energy, for his effectiveness as a model disciple is enhanced by the anonymity with which the Gospel surrounds him. Indeed, if we learned his name, we might be none the wiser; for he may not have been named in the rest of the NT.

Reading this very different Gospel is helped if we understand its origins. The following workable hypothesis, which with variations has considerable following, does justice to many factors visible in the final Gospel. In Stage One of Gospel Formation (chap. 4, above) there was a disciple of Jesus, perhaps from the Jerusalem area, who had a different background from the other disciples who became known as the Twelve Apostles. His memories of the ministry and his interpretation of them had a different cast and history from those associated with preaching by the Twelve (Stage Two of Gospel Formation—their preaching became the common heritage in the larger church and was eventually digested by Mark). The Christian community in which this disciple lived and whose thought about Jesus he shaped made other converts of a different background, for example, Samaritans (see 4:39-42; 8:48). Their presence, plus the very "high" christological articulation of the faith of the Johannine Christians (John is the only Gospel to call Jesus "God"), antagonized Jewish synagogue leaders, who thought the Johannine Christians no longer believed in one God but two. (Their hostile charges about making Jesus equal to God are reflected in 5:18; 10:33; 19:7.) Hearings, trials, and debates shaped the Johannine tradition and explain the Gospel's strong emphasis on testimony, witness, and listing of arguments (see 5:31-47). Eventually the Johannine Christians were thrown out of the local synagogues (9:22, 34; 12:42; 16:2), with the effect that (even though many of them were of Jewish birth) they turned extremely hostile to "the Jews." They became all the more insistent that the correct evaluation of Jesus as divine decided one's relation to God—even to the point of becoming corrective of others who claimed to follow Jesus (6:60-66; 12:42-43). More than likely the disciple lived through many of these developments and served as guide and encouragement, especially when the Johannine Christians were orphaned by the synagogues. That made him the model disciple for the community, the one who embodied what the love of Jesus meant. In short, to the community he was par excellence "the disciple whom Jesus loved," the Beloved Disciple.

All this (reconstructed) community history preceded the writing of the Fourth Gospel (thus before Stage Three of Gospel Formation); and although the evangelist would have been influenced by it, he was not writing about the past or trying to persuade or refute adversaries. Probably a disciple of the Beloved Disciple,[3] the evangelist reorganized the tradition he received[4] so that those who follow Jesus might have the kind of faith that would give them eternal life, namely, *the faith that Jesus was God's only Son possessing God's own life and had come into the world from above that people might be given that life (and thus be begotten by God) and become God's children.* To this reorganization the evangelist brought noteworthy dramatic skill, so that the Gospel's lengthy narratives, like those of the Samaritan woman (John 4), the man born blind (John 9), and Lazarus (John 11), became highly effective vehicles of encounters leading to faith. Apparently, after the basic Gospel was completed, a redactor made additions (chap. 21; perhaps 1:1-18), a process that took place early enough so that no text of the Gospel has been preserved without these "additions."[5] Although the Johannine

---

[3] Plausibly there was a number of Johannine writing disciples, that is, a "school" or following influenced by the Beloved Disciple; see 21:24: "We know that his testimony is true"—the testimony of the Beloved Disciple who bears witness to these things. The school could have included the evangelist, the redactor or final editor of the Gospel, and the author(s) of the epistles.

[4] Some think the tradition consisted of sources (collection of "signs"; collection of discourses; passion narrative) that the evangelist combined; others think of a process of several editions in which combinations had already begun. In either case there is little to support the radical thesis that much of the material the evangelist included came from alien sources and had little to do with Jesus as he actually was.

[5] The story of the woman caught in adultery (7:53–8:11) is not part of the redaction. Found only in some manuscripts, it was probably an old story about Jesus

tradition was shaped in the area of Palestine, the actual writing of the body of the Gospel probably took place elsewhere (traditionally and plausibly in the Ephesus area, but some opt for Syria).

GUIDANCE TO BEGINNING THE SEQUENTIAL USE OF JOHN IN THE LECTIONARY
On page 413 I give a brief outline of the Gospel that calls attention to the main themes of its theology as worked out in the flow of the narrative. There is no Sunday liturgical year of John, and the lectionary usage every year is somewhat nomadic:[6] incipiently at Christmastime, partly in Lent, and partly in the Eastertime. Consequently readers need to keep an eye on the Gospel's outline to get some sense of how the liturgical selection relates to the evangelist's intent. One can debate the wisdom of the framers of the lectionary: Would introducing a fourth year into the Sunday cycle give greater attention to John and enable it to be read on its own terms? Or is the use of John every year a way of demonstrating that it is different from the particular Synoptic Gospel being read that year and that its exalted message needs to be heard always if we want a larger Gospel picture of Jesus? In one way John is timeless: Its eloquent statements about light, love, faith, and judgment can be effective by themselves without historical context. In another way John is timely, formulated in the context of a community's spiritual growth and reactions to its own era. For example, on the Fourth Sunday of the Easter period in each year of the triennial cycle, a different paragraph from John 10 (which portrays the Good Shepherd) is read, thus preserving an ancient tradition of a Good Shepherd Sunday from the pre–Vatican II liturgy. The picture of Jesus as the Good Shepherd who knows his sheep by name, loves them, and lays down his life for them is timeless. Yet the polemic against others who are thieves and bandits and hired hands who run away leaving the sheep to be scattered, while it is adaptable, probably was aimed by

---

added later to the Gospel by a copyist in an area where the church was overcoming its reluctance to forgive adultery. Gradually it found its way into manuscript copies, particularly in the West, and was accepted as canonical Scripture.

[6] One of God's graces in this more ecumenical period is that several different churches use the same Sunday lectionary. A very perceptive discussion by a Lutheran scholar (on which I draw freely) is applicable to both the Lutheran and Roman Catholic Lectionaries: C. R. Koester, "The Fourth Gospel in a Three-Year Lectionary," *Word & World* 10 (no. 1, 1990): 21–26.

The Gospel According to John

the evangelist at specific late-first-century targets in the synagogues and other Christian groups. These targets are detectable when the chapter is read in its Gospel sequence.[7] To do justice to all the potentialities of such Gospel readings one needs to reflect not only on the pastoral concern of Christ for his sheep but also on the ways that his concern is helped and hindered by human pastoral care and church structure.

By way of another example, Jesus' magnificent Last Discourse (13:31–17:26) was spoken in the Gospel sequence on the night before he died; but readings from it appear in the lectionary on the Sundays and weekdays after Easter and before Pentecost.[8] Jesus spoke words like "I shall not leave you orphans: I am coming back to you; in just a little while the world will not see me any more, but you will see me because I have life and you will have life" (14:18-19). At the Last Supper their primary reference was to Jesus' return after his death, but in the liturgy they are shifted to an indefinite future coming. One should not ask which perspective is true, for his words have both a timely and a timeless aspect. It is not accidental that the evangelist has been portrayed as an eagle who by climbing on high can see what is to come before it arrives.

STYLISTIC FEATURES

John is a Gospel where style and theology are intimately wedded; and whether reading it or explaining it to others, one should be conscious of the features explained below.

1. *Poetic format.* In a few sections of John many scholars recognize a formal poetic style, even marked by strophes, for example, the Prologue and perhaps John 17. But the issue we need to consider is much wider: a uniquely solemn pattern, often dubbed semipoetic, in the Johannine discourses. The characteristic feature of this poetry would not be parallelism of lines (as in the OT) or rhyme, but rhythm, that is, lines of approximately the same length, each constituting a clause. Whether or not one agrees that the discourses should be printed in poetic format (as many Bibles do), the fact that Jesus speaks more solemnly in John than in the Synoptics is obvious. One explanation

---

[7] For example, the Pharisees who refused to see, criticized in the immediately preceding 9:40-41.

[8] As the table at the end of this volume indicates, this material is treated in chapters 27–32.

Christ in the Gospels of the Liturgical Year

Outline of the Gospel according to John

1:1-18   **Prologue:** An introduction to and summary of the career of the incarnate Word.

1:19–12:50   **Part One: The Book of Signs:** The Word reveals himself to the world and to his own, but they do not accept him:

1. Initial days of the revelation of Jesus to his disciples under different titles (1:19–2:11);

2. First to second Cana miracle; themes of replacement and of reactions to Jesus (chaps. 2–4);

3. OT feasts and their replacement; themes of life and light (chaps. 5–10): Sabbath—Jesus, the new Moses, replaces the Sabbath ordinance to rest (John 5); Passover (6); Tabernacles (7:1–10:21); Dedication (10:22-42);

4. The raising of Lazarus and its aftermath; the coming of the hour (chaps. 11–12).

13:1–20:31   **Part Two: The Book of Glory:** To those who accept him, the Word shows his glory by returning to the Father in death, resurrection, and ascension. Fully glorified, he communicates the Spirit of life:

1. The Last Supper and Jesus' Last Discourse (chaps. 13–17);

2. Jesus' passion and death (chaps. 18–19);

3. The resurrection: four scenes in Jerusalem (chap. 20); Gospel Conclusion (20:30-31): statement of purpose for this writing.

21:1-25   **Epilogue:** Galilean resurrection appearances; second conclusion.

draws on the OT: There divine speech (by God through the prophets or by personified divine Wisdom) is poetic, signaling a difference from more prosaic human communication. The Johannine Jesus comes from God, and therefore it is appropriate that his words be more solemn and sacral.

2. *Misunderstanding.* Although he comes from above and speaks of what is "true" or "real" (i.e., heavenly reality), the Word-become-flesh must use language from below to convey his message. To deal with this anomaly, he frequently employs figurative language or metaphors to describe himself or to present his message.[9] In an ensuing dialogue

---

[9] In a sense the Johannine figures or metaphors (16:29) are equivalent to the Synoptic parables, for in John the reality represented by the Synoptic kingdom of

The Gospel According to John

the questioner will misunderstand the figure or metaphor and take only a material meaning. This allows Jesus to explain his thought more thoroughly and thereby to unfold his doctrine. Stemming from the Johannine theology of the incarnation, such misunderstanding has become a studied literary technique. Jesus is a stranger from above who will inevitably be misunderstood by humans from below. He speaks of heavenly realities using the language of this world, but people will think he is speaking of worldly things (which for them are the only realities).[10]

3. *Twofold meanings.* Sometimes playing into misunderstanding, sometimes simply showing the multifaceted aspect of revelation, often a double meaning can be found in a dialogue involving Jesus. (1) There are plays on various meanings of a given word that Jesus uses, meanings based on either Hebrew or Greek; sometimes the dialogue partner may take one meaning, while Jesus intends the other.[11] (2) In the Fourth Gospel the author frequently intends the reader to see several layers of meaning in the same narrative or in the same metaphor. This is understandable if we think back to the circumstances in which the Gospel was composed, involving several time levels: There is a meaning appropriate to the historical context in the public ministry of Jesus; yet there may be a second meaning reflecting the situation of the believing Christian community. For example, the prediction of Jesus that the Temple sanctuary would be destroyed and replaced in 2:19-22 is reinterpreted to refer to the crucifixion and resurrection of Jesus' body. The Bread of Life Discourse seems to refer primarily to divine revelation and wisdom in 6:35-51a and to the eucharist in 6:51b-58. As many as three different meanings may have been intended in the imagery of the Lamb of God (1:29, 36: apocalyptic Lamb, paschal Lamb, and Suffering Servant who went to slaughter like a lamb).

4. *Irony.* A particular combination of twofold meaning and misunderstanding is found when the opponents of Jesus make statements about him that are derogatory, sarcastic, incredulous, or at least inadequate in

---

heaven stands among people in the person of Jesus. In the Synoptics the parables are frequently misunderstood, just as the metaphors are in John.

[10] See John 2:19-21; 3:3-4; 4:10-11; 6:26-27; 8:33-35; 11:11-13.

[11] For example, various terms in 3:3, 8 (birth/begetting; again/from above; wind/Spirit); "lifted up" in 3:14; 8:28; 12:34 (crucifixion and ascension in return to God); "living water" in 4:10 (flowing water and life-giving water); "die for" in 11:50-52 (instead or on behalf of).

Christ in the Gospels of the Liturgical Year

the sense that they intend. However, by way of irony these statements are often true or more meaningful in a sense that the speakers do not realize but that the reader is supposed to recognize. For instance, when the Samaritan woman asks sarcastically, "Surely, you don't pretend to be greater than our ancestor Jacob who gave us this well?" (4:12), Jesus does not answer or need to—readers/hearers know that he is greater. When the Galilean Jews who know Jesus' father and mother pose an absurdity, "How can he claim to have come down from heaven?" (6:42), Jesus does not need to answer—readers/hearers know that the parentage that truly matters is his Father in heaven, about which these scoffers are ignorant.[12]

5. *Inclusions and transitions.* The careful structure of the Gospel is indicated by certain techniques. "Inclusion" means that John mentions a detail (or makes an allusion) at the end of a section that matches a similar detail at the beginning of the section. This is a way of packaging sections by tying together the beginning and the end. A large inclusion is illustrated by 1:1 ("The Word was God") and 20:28 ("My Lord and my God").[13] By way of transition from one subdivision of the Gospel to the next, the evangelist likes to use a "swing" ("hinge") motif or section—one that concludes what has gone before and introduces what follows. For example, the Cana miracle terminates the call of the disciples in John 1, fulfilling the promise in 1:50 that the disciple who was called would see far greater things, but also opens the next subdivision of 2:1–4:54, which runs from the first Cana miracle to the second. The second Cana miracle concludes that subdivision but by stressing Jesus' power to give life (4:50) prepares for the next subdivision (5:1–10:42), where Jesus' authority over life will be challenged. Since the liturgy does not follow sequentially through John, an effort will be necessary to highlight what the evangelist intended.

6. *Parentheses or footnotes.* Frequently John supplies parenthetical notes, explaining the meaning of Semitic terms or names (e.g., "Messiah," "Cephas," "Siloam," "Thomas" in 1:41, 42; 9:7; 11:16), offering background for developments in the narrative and for geographical features[14] and even supplying theological perspectives (e.g., clarifying references from a later standpoint in 2:21-22; 7:39; 11:51-52; 12:16, 33; or protecting Jesus' divinity in 6:6, 64). Historically, some of these may

---

[12] See also 3:2; 7:35; 9:40-41; 11:50.

[13] See 1:19 with 1:28; 1:28 with 10:40; 2:11 with 4:54; 9:2-3 with 9:41; 11:4 with 11:40.

[14] For example, 2:9; 3:24; 4:8; 6:71; 9:14, 22-23; 11:5, 13.

The Gospel According to John

reflect a situation where a tradition transmitted at first in one context (Palestinian or Jewish) is now being proclaimed in another context (Diaspora or Gentile). As footnotes, they are difficult to read in public; but in the liturgy they offer a marvelous opportunity to reflect on how much pedagogy had to go into the proclamation of the Christian message, since terms known to one group or generation were not known to another group or generation.

I have explained these stylistic features because without attention to them those reading or preaching on John will miss a very important part of the Gospel's communication.

REFLECTIONS ON THE PROLOGUE AND INITIAL PASSAGES FROM THE BOOK OF SIGNS (1:1–2:12)
Let me remind readers once more that large portions of John have been treated in previous chapters (table at the end of this volume). Accordingly I concentrate here on specific passages not discussed in those chapters.

THE PROLOGUE (1:1-18). While Mark is content to begin his Gospel with the heavenly declaration at the baptism that Jesus is God's be-loved Son, Matthew and Luke start their Good News with an angelic proclamation of Jesus' divine identity at his conception. John reaches back even before creation to identify Jesus as the Word who was God. The church uses this at the third Mass of Christmas and on the last weekday Mass of the Christmas octave in order to bring out the fullest meaning of what that feast reveals. There is no higher understanding of Jesus in the NT than John 1:1, "The Word was God"; and the evan-gelist will remind us of this by way of inclusion at the end of the Gospel when Thomas confesses Jesus as "My Lord and my God" (20:28).

Serving as a preface to the Gospel, the Prologue is really a hymn that encapsulates the Johannine view of Christ and anticipates what we shall be told in narrative form in the Gospel. A divine being (God's Word [1:1, 14], who is also the light [1:5, 9] and God's only Son [1:14, 18]) comes into the world and becomes flesh. Although rejected by his own, he empowers all who do accept him to become God's children, so that they share in God's fullness—a gift reflecting God's enduring love[15] that outdoes the loving gift of the Law through Moses. One

---

[15] The "grace" and "truth" of 1:14 probably reproduce the famous OT pairing of *ḥesed*, that is, God's *kindness* (mercy) in choosing Israel independently of any merit

background of this poetic description of the descent of the Word into the world and the eventual return of the Son to the Father's side (1:18) lies in the OT picture of personified Wisdom (especially Sirach 24 and Wisdom 9), who was with God in the beginning at the creation of the world and came to dwell with human beings when the Law was revealed to Moses. In agreement with the tradition that JBap's ministry was related to the beginning of Jesus' ministry, the Prologue is interrupted twice, viz., to mention JBap just before the light comes into the world (1:6-8—JBap is not the light but bears witness to the light) and to record JBap's testimony after the Word becomes flesh (1:15—Jesus existed before JBap).

OPENING DAYS OF THE REVELATION OF JESUS UNDER DIFFERENT TITLES: JBAP AND THE FIRST DISCIPLES (1:19-51). On January 2–5, the days before Epiphany, the lectionary reads from this section of John, which unfolds the mystery of Jesus in a pattern of separate days (1:29, 35, 43); part of it is read on the Second Ordinary Sunday (1:29-34 in A Year; 1:35-42 in B). John illustrates a gradual recognition of who Jesus is through testimony by JBap and through confession of their understanding of Jesus by the first disciples. *On the first day* (1:19-28) JBap explains his own role totally in relation to Jesus. JBap becomes briefer and briefer in rejecting titles for himself and voluble only in predicting the coming of one of whom he is unworthy. JBap thus anticipates 3:30: "He must increase while I must decrease." It is noteworthy that a legal atmosphere colors the Johannine narrative from its first page, for JBap is interrogated by "the Jews,"[16] and he testifies and does not deny. As I explained above, this suggests that some of the Johannine tradition was shaped in a forensic context, probably in a synagogue where Christians were put on trial for their beliefs about Jesus. When read in the liturgy it reminds us of our duty to bear witness to Jesus, sometimes in a hostile context, sometimes in an indifferent one. *On the next day* (1:29-34) JBap explains Jesus' role. As befits "one sent by God" (1:6), JBap has special knowledge of Jesus and perceptively recognizes Jesus as the Lamb of God, as one who existed beforehand, and as God's

---

on Israel's part, and ʾĕmet, God's enduring *fidelity* to the covenant with Israel that embodies this kindness.

[16] The evangelist may well be a Jew by birth; yet as pp. 409–10 and 420 explain, in general he uses this expression with a hostile tone for those of Jewish birth who distrust or reject Jesus and/or his followers.

chosen one (or Son—disputed reading of 1:34). But now JBap must begin his assigned task of revealing Jesus to others who will be Jesus' first disciples.

On the next day (1:35-42) Jesus is followed by Andrew and another disciple of JBap.[17] Andrew hails Jesus as teacher and Messiah and brings his brother Simon to Jesus. Anticipating Simon's role as a disciple (see 6:67-69), Jesus gives him a new identity as "Cephas," using the transliterated Aramaic word for "rock," which equals the Greek name for Peter (cf. Mark 3:16; Matt 16:18). Already this initial scene tells us much about discipleship. Jesus poses an initial question in John 1:38, "What are you looking for?" and follows in 1:39 by "Come and see." Yet it is only when those invited remain with him that they become believers. All that is still true of those who would be disciples today. *On the next day* (1:43-51) Jesus finds Philip, who in turn finds Nathanael; and Jesus is identified as the one described in the Mosaic Law and the Prophets as the Son of God and the King of Israel. (Notice the pattern of discipleship: Those initially called go out to proclaim Jesus to others with a christological perception deepened through that very action.) In Mark (15:39) only after Jesus dies does a human being recognize him as "Son of God," and in Matthew (16:16) this is a climactic confession by Peter in the middle of the ministry. In John such confessional titles proclaimed by the disciples at the very beginning, although true, are somewhat elementary; for they do not fully express the divinity of Jesus, the Word who existed before the world began.[18] Thus Jesus promises a vision of "far greater things" and speaks of himself as the Son of Man upon whom the angels ascend and descend. For the other Gospels the sight of the Son of Man accompanied by the angels will come only at the end of time; for John that occurs during the ministry because the Son of Man has already come down from heaven. The church is wise liturgically to use John's account of the first days of Jesus shortly after Christmas; it is telling believers that no matter how much they may know about the Christ

---

[17] Is he the one who by the second part of the Gospel will have become the disciple whom Jesus loved?

[18] The oldest tradition is that the Fourth Gospel was written to improve on the other Gospels. That is too simple, but in terms of christological insight John certainly goes beyond the tradition common to the Synoptics. After all, it claims to stem from a disciple who was closer to Jesus than anyone else.

who has come into the world, if they remain his committed disciples, they have much more to understand.

The First Cana Miracle (2:1-12). The "far greater things" promised by Jesus begin to occur in Cana on the third day after the call of the disciples. The church uses this reading on the Second Sunday of Ordinary Time in Year C. In this it is continuing an old liturgical practice of three epiphanies or manifestations of Jesus: On the feast of the Epiphany a star reveals Jesus to the Gentiles; on the next Sunday (First of Ordinary Time), which is the feast of the Baptism, a heavenly voice reveals him; now on this following Sunday Jesus reveals himself. In what John calls a sign Jesus replaces the water prescribed for Jewish purifications by wine so good that the headwaiter wonders why the best has been kept until last. This wine represents the revelation and wisdom that Jesus brings from God (Prov 9:4-5; Sir 24:21[20]), fulfilling the OT promises of abundance of wine in the messianic days (Amos 9:13-14; Gen 49:10-11). And so through it Jesus has manifested his glory, and his disciples believe in him. An intertwined motif involves the mother of Jesus, whose family-style request on behalf of the newly married ("They have no wine") is rebuffed by Jesus on the grounds that his hour had not yet come. Yet the mother's persistence that honors Jesus' terms ("Do whatever he tells you") leads him to grant her original request.[19] She will reappear at the foot of the cross (John 19:25-27), where her incorporation into discipleship will be completed as she becomes the mother of the Beloved Disciple.

REFLECTIONS ON PASSAGES FROM THE REST OF THE BOOK OF SIGNS (2:13–12:50)

This constitutes most of Part One of the Gospel. Yet now the liturgical use of John departs from a sequential treatment to a topical one, and the topics differ in ways from those that the evangelist planned—see Outline of Part One, page 413. (This would be a very appropriate moment for readers to look at a sequential commentary on John, for example, my brief paperback done for Liturgical Press, *The Gospel and Epistles of John: A Concise Commentary*.) Let me discuss three major motifs visible in the liturgical readings from John's account of the

---

[19] Similarly in the second Cana sign the royal official's persistence wins his request after a rebuff (John 4:47-50; cf. Mark 7:26-29).

remainder of the public ministry—with Lent as the principal setting for the first two.[20]

1. INCREASING CONFLICTS ABOUT JESUS' IDENTITY, LEADING TO PLOTS TO KILL HIM. These constitute the major part of the weekday lectionary for the last weeks of Lent, as visible in the table at the end of the book; they prepare readers for Jesus' death on Good Friday. In his lifetime Jesus certainly had conflicts with Pharisees, Jerusalem Jewish authorities, and the parts of the Jerusalem populace that sided with authorities.[21] Nevertheless, the Gospel represents a situation that goes beyond Jesus' lifetime, and "the Jews" include Jewish authorities but cannot be confined to them. The expulsion of Johannine Christians from the synagogue led to a feeling of alienation whereby, even though they may have been of Jewish parentage, Johannine Christians no longer were considered or considered themselves as Jews. For them "the Jews" were those people who opposed and even persecuted them (16:2) and were the heirs of those who had opposed Jesus. This usage of "the Jews" is entirely religious and has nothing to do with racial, economic, or social prejudice. It is irresponsible in my judgment to deny that such antagonism existed or to seek to disguise its presence in translations of John;[22] nevertheless, *those who read, interpret, or preach on John in our time must take extreme care to prevent the correct, literal translation from being used against Jewish people in our time.* The historical situation must be explained, and one must insist that the Bible does not always give us examples to be imitated[23] but at times examples to be learned from painfully.

2. DRAMATIC STORIES OF FAITH RESPONSES. For many centuries, dating back to the ancient Jerusalem liturgy, the church has singled out stories from John to be read with special solemnity during Lent. In our

[20] This public ministry ends in 12:50, but a few passages from the Last Supper (13:1-15, 21-33, 36-38) are read in Holy Week as the conclusion of Lent.

[21] Attempts to remove all references to "Jews" or to translate them simply as "the authorities" falsify the historical situation; this was a time when Jews fought other Jews bitterly over such issues as Temple worship, calendar, and interpretations of the Law, to the point of putting one another to death.

[22] The Johannine Jesus at times speaks as a non-Jew (or, at least, not as one of *those* "Jews"): "written in your Law" (10:34); "in their Law" (15:25); "as I said to the Jews" (13:33).

[23] Compare the many OT examples of Israel's rejoicing at the slaughter of other peoples who occupied Palestine.

era three of them—the most sacred *narratives* in the Gospel accounts of Jesus' public ministry—appear on the Third, Fourth, and Fifth Sundays of Lent in the A Year (with special provisions made for the B and C years, so that there may never be a Lent in which they are not proclaimed). They are the Samaritan woman at the well (John 4), the healing of the man born blind (John 9), and the raising of Lazarus (John 11). During the Lenten season from the earliest days people were being prepared for baptism, and John's stories fitted beautifully into the process of Christian initiation. In time, the three narratives were read at specific stages in the Lenten preparation of catechumens for baptism on Holy Saturday.[24]

The woman at the well: Coming to faith and living water. This first story (John 4:1-42) illustrates how difficult it is to come to Jesus in faith because of the various obstacles that stand in the way. If I were freely composing a story of conversion, I might imagine a central character eager to receive God. John is more realistic: Many people have a chip on their shoulder in regard to God because they feel beaten down by the inequalities in life. The woman smarts from the Jewish dislike for Samaritans, especially for Samaritan women. And that is her first obstacle to dealing with Jesus. "How can you, a Jew," she comments sarcastically, "ask me, a Samaritan woman, for a drink?" Jesus does not answer her objection; he is not going to change instantly a whole world of injustice. Yet he can offer something that will enable the woman to put injustice in perspective, namely, living water. He means water that gives life; she misunderstands it as flowing, bubbling water, contemptuously asking him if he thinks he is greater than Jacob, who provided a well. (Is not "No thanks—I already have all I need" our first reaction when someone tries to interest us in something new religiously?)

Ironically, as John expects the reader to recognize, Jesus is greater than Jacob; but again Jesus refuses to be sidetracked from his main goal, and so he explains that he is speaking of the water that springs up to eternal life, a water that will permanently end thirst. With masterful touch John shows her attracted on a level of the convenience of not having to come to the well every day for water. (People are not

---

[24] The material pertaining to these three stories is taken from a *Catholic Update*, reused as chapter 4 in my *Reading the Gospels with the Church* (Cincinnati, St. Anthony Messenger Press, 1996). That press has graciously allowed me to draw on it here.

The Gospel According to John

so different today when they are attracted to the message of those media evangelists who promote a religion that makes life more comfortable.) To move the woman to a higher level, Jesus shifts the focus to her husband. Her reply is a half-truth, but Jesus shows that he is aware of her five husbands and of her live-in who is not her husband. Today also, a far-from-perfect past is not an uncommon obstacle to conversion. To be brought to faith people must acknowledge where they stand, but they can take hope from the fact that Jesus persists even though he knows the woman's state. He does not say to the woman, "Come back after you straighten out your life," for the grace that he offers is meant to help her to change.

Confronted with Jesus' surprising knowledge of her situation, the woman seeks to take advantage of the fact that he is obviously a religious figure. Her question about whether to worship in the Jerusalem Temple or on Mount Gerizim is a typical ploy designed to distract. When is the last time she worried about such theological differences? Even today when we encounter someone who probes our lives, we are often adept at bringing up as a distraction some old religious chestnut so as to avoid making a decision. Once more Jesus refuses to be sidetracked. Although salvation is from the Jews, a time is coming and is now here when such a cultic issue is irrelevant: Cult at both sites will be replaced by worship in Spirit and truth. Nimbly the woman tries one more ploy by shifting any decision to the distant future when the Messiah comes, but Jesus will not let her escape. His "I am he" confronts her with a current demand for faith.

What follows, enacted dramatically on two stages, reveals even more about faith. In center stage we observe that the disciples who have now been with Jesus for some time understand his heavenly symbolism no better than the woman who encountered him for the first time. When he speaks of the food that he already has to eat, they wonder if someone has brought him a sandwich! Jesus has to explain: "My food is to do the will of the One who sent me . . ." (John 4:34). On side stage, we find that the woman is still not fully convinced, since she poses to the villagers the question "Could this be the Messiah?" The villagers come and encounter Jesus for themselves, so that their faith is not simply dependent on her account but on personal contact. We are left to surmise that by being instrumental in bringing others to believe the woman's own faith came to completion. And at last she drank of the water of life.

Christ in the Gospels of the Liturgical Year

The man born blind: Faith grows amidst trials. If the story of the Samaritan woman has illustrated an initial coming to faith, this next carefully crafted narrative (9:1-41) shows that often first enlightenment does not result in adequate faith. Sometimes faith comes only through difficult testing and even suffering. St. Augustine recognized that this man born blind stands for the human race. And the initial dialogue where Jesus proclaims, "I am the light of the world" alerts us to the fact that more than physical sight is involved. The basic story of the man's healing is simple. Jesus approaches the blind man, anoints his eyes with mud mixed with saliva, and tells him to wash in the Pool of Siloam. The man does so and comes back seeing.

Beyond this, however, the early Christian community who first heard John's account probably picked out elements of their own conversion and baptism in the blind man's story. They might recognize something familiar, for example, in the blind man's coming to see the light by being "anointed." Anointing became a part of baptism very early; and "enlightenment" was a term for baptismal conversion, as we see in Hebrews 6:4; 10:32 and in the second-century writer Justin. John hints further that the water has a special link with Christ, since he tells us that "Siloam," the name of the pool, means "the one sent," a frequent description of Jesus. No wonder that in early catacomb art the healing of the blind man was a symbol of baptism!

Besides recognizing a baptismal theme in this story, readers of John would also be taught that a series of testings may be necessary before sight really comes. Only gradually and through suffering does the man born blind come to full faith and enlightenment. There are at least four steps in his progress, each involving an encounter: (1) At first, when queried by the onlookers, the man born blind knows only that "the man they call Jesus" healed him (9:11). (2) Then, brought before the Pharisees and pressed with theological questions, he advances to the conclusion that Jesus is "a prophet" (9:17). (3) Next, after being threatened with expulsion from the synagogue, he recognizes that Jesus is a man "from God" (9:33). (4) Finally, having been expelled, he encounters Jesus himself, who has sought him out and now asks point-blank, "Do you believe in the Son of Man?" It is then at last that the man says, "I do believe" (9:38: perhaps the baptismal confession required in the Johannine church).

How many of us who have a traditional faith stemming from our baptism come to believe in our hearts only when difficult decisions test our faith in God and Christ? It is then we understand what it means to say, "I do believe." Yet within John's story it is not only from the man born blind that we learn about faith. His being healed produces a division (Greek *krisis*, whence English "crisis") among those who interrogate him. In the Johannine view an encounter with Jesus or his work forces people to decide and align themselves on one side or the other. Particularly interesting is the division caused among the Pharisees (9:13-17). John presents favorably those Pharisees who decide that Jesus cannot be sinful because he does such signs (healings), but we should also seek to understand the other Pharisees who decide that Jesus is not from God because he does not keep the Sabbath. Their thinking probably went along these lines: God commanded that the Sabbath be kept holy; our ancestors decided that kneading clay was menial work that violated the Sabbath; Jesus kneaded clay on the Sabbath, and so he violated God's commandment. Might not faithful Christians today judge along similar lines if someone violated what they had been taught as a traditional interpretation of God's will? (And might they not be offended if their decisions were greeted with the sarcasm with which the man born blind reacted to the Jewish authorities' decision about Jesus?) The difficulty with such reasoning is the failure to recognize that all human interpretations of God's will are historically conditioned—those we regard as definitive tradition are *true*, but *in regard to the issues that were in mind when they were formulated*. Hebrew slaves in Egypt had to work with clay to make bricks for the pharaoh, and so kneading clay would justly be classified as servile work forbidden on the Sabbath. But those who made that classification scarcely thought of kneading a scrap of clay to open a blind man's eyes. Jesus is the type of figure who raises new religious issues and inevitably causes offense to those who attempt to solve those issues quickly on the basis of previous situations. Recognition of that should facilitate important insights. It was not necessarily out of malice that many genuinely religious people of Jesus' time (who were Jews because of where they lived) rejected him. If Jesus came back today, he would be equally offensive to religious people of our time, including Christians. We should be careful about religious judgments that apply, without nuance, past decisions to *new* situations.

Finally, we can learn about faith from the parents of the blind man. John contrasts the man born blind, who step-by-step was brought to sight physically and spiritually, with the opposing religious authorities, who could see physically but gradually became blind spiritually (9:40-41). Yet the evangelist is also interested in those who refuse to commit themselves one way or the other. The parents know the truth about their son, but they refuse to say anything about what Jesus has done for him lest they be thrown out of the synagogue. Today there are those who decide for Jesus at a great cost to themselves and those who for various reasons do not believe in him. Perhaps an even larger group would be those who have been baptized and nominally accept Jesus but are not willing to confess him if it costs anything. In John's view that is as serious as to deny him.

The raising of Lazarus: Faith tested by death. As we come to the final narrative (John 11:1-44), we should take note of the different staging techniques in the three stories. The Samaritan woman remained close to Jesus for much of the drama at the well and entered into a fairly long dialogue with him. The man born blind said nothing to Jesus at the beginning, was not in contact with him through most of the scene, and exchanged words with Jesus only at the end in a moment of piercing light when he confessed Jesus. Lazarus never says a word to Jesus (or anyone else) and appears only in the last verses. In each story we are dealing with a different stage of faith. The Samaritan woman illustrated an initial coming to faith; the man born blind illustrated an incipient faith that acquired depth only after testing; the Lazarus story illustrates *the deepening of faith that comes from facing death.* John tells the Lazarus story in such a way that we are led to a more profound understanding of death even as the disciples and Martha and Mary had to intensify their understanding. Like his sisters, Martha and Mary, Lazarus was loved by Jesus; and so when he dies, the disciples are troubled by Jesus' seeming indifference. They misunderstand when he speaks of Lazarus' sleep. As with blindness in John 9 (of which we are reminded in 11:37), life and death are used to teach about earthly and heavenly realities.

Martha, who is the chief dialogue partner in the drama, already believes that Jesus is the Messiah, the Son of God, and that her brother, Lazarus, will participate in the resurrection on the last day. Yet hers is an incomplete faith, for she wishes that her brother had never died and hesitates when Jesus orders Lazarus' tomb opened. Jesus can and does bring Lazarus back to earthly life, but that is not his purpose in having come to this world from above. (A man brought back from the grave is not necessarily better off or closer to God than those who have not yet died.) Jesus comes *to give life that cannot be touched by death*, so that those who believe in him will never die (11:26). True faith has to include a belief in Jesus as the source of unending life. Such immortality, however, cannot come in Jesus' public ministry; it awaits Jesus' own resurrection. Consequently, we encounter more unexplained symbolism in the Lazarus narrative than was present in the stories of the Samaritan woman and the man born blind. We are never told, for instance, that Martha and Mary came to understand fully Jesus' words, "I am the life." In another instance we hear that Jesus shuddered, seemingly with anger, when he saw Mary and her Jewish friends weeping. But the evangelist does not clarify why Jesus reacts in this way at what seems like well-intentioned grief (11:33, 38). Nor does John supply an interpretation of why Lazarus emerges from the tomb tied hand and foot with burial bands and his face wrapped in a cloth (11:44). Only when we read the account of Jesus' tomb in 20:6-7 does that symbolism become clear. Jesus rises to eternal life, never to die again; therefore he leaves behind in the tomb his burial wrappings and the piece that covered his head, for which he has no need. Lazarus was brought back to life enveloped in burial clothes because he was going to die again.

Thus, although the raising of Lazarus is a tremendous miracle bringing to culmination Jesus' ministry, it is still a sign. The life to which Lazarus is raised is natural life; it is meant to symbolize eternal life, the kind of life that only God possesses and that Jesus as God's Son makes possible. How does this fit into Lenten reflections on faith? Even after the struggles of initial faith (the Samaritan woman) and a faith made mature through testing (the man born blind), facing death often constitutes a unique challenge to belief. Whether the death of a loved one or one's own death, it is the moment where one realizes that all depends on God. No human support goes with one to the grave; credit cards, health insurance, retirement programs, and human companionship stop at the tomb. One enters alone. If there is no God, there is nothing; if Christ has not conquered death, there is no future. The brutality of that realization causes trembling even among those who have spent their lives professing Christ, and it is not unusual for people to confess that doubts have come into their minds as they face death. Paul cries out that death is the last enemy to be overcome (1 Cor 15:26), an insight that John captures by placing the Lazarus story at the end of Jesus' public ministry. From it we learn that no matter how fervently catechumens or already baptized Christians make or renew a baptismal profession in Lent, they may still face a last moment when their faith will be tested. For so many of us it will be precisely at that moment, when we are confronted with the visible reality of the grave, that we need to hear and embrace the bold message that Jesus proclaims in John's Gospel: "I am the life." Despite all human appearances, "Everyone who believes in me shall never die at all." We begin Lent with the reminder that we will return to dust. We end at Easter with the proclamation of new life.

3. BAPTISMAL AND EUCHARISTIC MOTIFS. In a previous section in this volume, *A Once and Coming Spirit at Pentecost*, I discussed the Nicodemus dialogue in John 3:1-21 and the multiplication of the loaves/Bread of Life discourse in John 6:1-69 as they are used in the weekday readings of the post-Easter weeks. The baptismal gift of life and the eucharistic nourishment of that life flow from the resurrection, whence the placement.

Passages from the rest of the Gospel of John (the Book of Glory, plus the Epilogue [13:1–21:25]) are read in the liturgy of Good Friday and of the Eastertime. They have already been discussed in chapters 16–26 above.

The Gospel According to John

Overview of the Use of the Gospels and Acts in the Sunday and Seasonal Mass Lectionary

Liturgical Season	Matthew (chapters)	Mark (chapters)	Luke (chapters)	John (chapters)	Acts (chapters)	Where Treated in This Book
Last Week in Advent	1		1			Chap. 5–10
Christmas and Octave (Epiphany; Presentation)	2		2	3rd Christmas Mass (and Dec. 31) Prologue: 1:1-18 Jan. 2: 1:19-28		Chap. 11–15 for Matt and Luke Chap. 36 for John
Baptism (= 1st Ordinary Sunday)	3:13-17	1:7-11	3:15-16, 21-22			Chap. 33–35
Second Ordinary Sunday				1:29-42; 2:1-12*		Chap. 33–36
Ordinary Sundays before Lent (beginning with 3rd Sunday)†	YEAR A first part of 4–25, beginning with 4:12	YEAR B first part of 1–13, beginning with 1:14	YEAR C first part of 4–21, beginning with 4:14			Chap. 33–35
Last Weeks of Lent (Weekdays and Sundays)‡				2:13–12:33		Chap. 36
Passion (Palm) Sunday	26–27	14–15	22–23			Chap. 16–21
Good Friday				18–19		Chap. 20–21
Easter Sunday and Octave	28	16	24	20–21		Chap. 22–26
2nd-7th Weeks of Easter Season (Weekdays and Sundays)				3; 6; and 10; Last Discourse: 13:31–17:26	1–28	Chap. 27–32
Pentecost Sunday				20:19-23	2:1-11	Chap. 27–32
Ordinary Sundays after Pentecost	YEAR A later parts of 3–25	YEAR B later parts of 1–13 (interrupted for five Sundays by John 6)	YEAR C later parts of 3–21	(See under Mark, Year B)		Chap. 33–35

* John 1:19-51 is read on January 2–5, a fluctuating period depending on the date of the 1st Ordinary Sunday on which the Baptism of Jesus is celebrated.
† See explanation in Part 2, chapter 4 of this book.
‡ John is read in Lent on the 3rd and 4th Sundays (A, B years) and 5th (A, B, C). John is read on Lenten weekdays from Monday of the 4th week to Tuesday of Holy Week (from 4:43 to 13:38).

Scripture Citations Index

Old Testament

Genesis
1:2	88
15:8	72
16:7-12	88n5
21:6	72
35:19-21	117–18
37:11	120
45:5	65

Exodus
2:1-10	65
4:17	108
7:3-4	377
12:10	190
12:22	189
19	276

Leviticus
17–18	334
22:1-8	122

Numbers
22–24	48, 108
23:7	108
24:7, 17	108

Deuteronomy
13:1-3	147
21:6-9	171
21:22-23	173
22:20-27	62
23:2(1)	312
28:1, 4	91

Joshua
2	56

Judges
3:9	79

1 Samuel
1–2	122
1:3, 17	73
1:11	92
1:24-28	49
1:25	124–25
2:1-2	81, 92
2:1-10	73
2:7-8	93
2:10	85
2:20	125
2:21	76
2:21, 26	137

2 Samuel
7	84, 89
7:12-13	64
7:24-26	55
15:30-31	166
17:23	169

1 Kings
1:48	82

2 Kings
4:42-44	300

Job
19:25	327

Psalms			Hosea	
2:7	104, 228, 373		2:25	254
22	162, 172		10:8	180
22:8-9	161, 172			
22:19	161, 188		Joel	
31:5-6	181		2:10-11	162
42:6	166		4:16	162
69:22	161, 172			
87:6	115		Amos	
106:10	188		8:9	162
111:9	79			
			Micah	
Wisdom			5:1(2)	117
15:11	251			
			Zechariah	
Sirach			14:4ff.	166
50:20	236			
			Malachi	
Isaiah			3:1	73, 372
1:3	116			
6:3	119			
7:14	66–68			
40:3	372		**New Testament**	
41:10	220			
42:1	228, 373		Matthew	
50:6	159		1:1	48, 59
52:15	160		1:1-17	50–58
53:10-12	384		1:18	59–60
54:1-4	180		1:18-19	61
55:8	54		1:18-25	59–69
66:12-13	126		1:18–2:23	209n2
			1:20-21	66
Ezekiel			1:21	127
3:1-3	16		2:1-23	107–11
14:17	128		2:2	127
37:9	251		2:20	63
47:10	259		4:1-11	355
			4:15	216
Daniel			5:1–7:29	356–58
7:9	209		5:32	34
7:14	218		6:1-18	357
9:24	74		8:1–9:38	357
10:6	209		10:1-42	358–59

Christ in the Gospels of the Liturgical Year

11:1–12:50	359–61	13:34-37	157
12:1-8	64	14:8	199
13:1-52	360–61	14:26-52	155–57
13:52	67	14:53-72	157–59
13:53–18:35	361–65	14:65	147
16:16-17	46	15:1-20	159–61
19:1–25:46	365–68	15:21-47	161–64
19:9	34	16:1-8	198–203
22:41-46	60	16:8	202–04
24:37-44	367n21	16:9-20	203–07
26:30-56	166–68		
26:57–27:10	168–70	*Luke*	
27:1	147	1–2	71–72
27:11-31	170–71	1:1-4	388–89
27:32-66	172–74	1:5-7	124
27:62-66	209–11	1:5-25, 57-66, 80	70–85
28:1-10	211–15	1:18	72
28:11-15	215–16	1:26-56	86–94
28:13-15	243	1:28, 30, 31	88
28:16-20	216–20	1:36-37	91
28:20	66	1:54-55	94
		1:57-58	75
Mark		1:67-79	77–85
1:1	372	1:68-69	79
1:16-20	373	1:76-77	82
1:21-38	374	2:1-21	112–20
1:39–3:6	374–75	2:10-11	94
3:7-19	375	2:11, 34-35	47
3:20-35	375–76	2:22-40	121–30
3:21	87	2:41-52	131–42
3:21, 31	139	3:16	88
3:31-35	87, 129, 189	3:21ff	46, 391–92
4:1-34	376–77	4:1-13	392
4:35–5:43	377–78	4:14–5:16	392–94
5:1-20	378	4:22	138
6:1-6	378–79	4:31-44	393
6:7–8:26	379–81	4:36	138
8:22-26	200	5:1-11	257, 394
8:27-30	381	5:17–6:49	394–95
9:14-48	382	5:34-35	322
10:32-34	384	7:1–9:6	396–97
10:46-52	384	7:18-35	396
11:1–13:37	384–86	7:27-28	74

7:36-50	396–97	1:19-51	417–19
8:13	119	2:3-4	139
8:14-15	397	2:13–12:50	419–27
8:15	120, 141	3	297–99
8:19-21	141	4:1-42	421–22
8:19-23	129	4:37-38	259
9:7-50	397–98	6	299–302
9:51	222	6:51	34
9:51–13:21	399–402	6:51b-58	260
10:38-42	400	7:38-39	190
11:1-4	400–01	7:53–8:11	410n5
11:27	91	9:1-41	423–25
11:28	91	9:35-38	282n9
12:32-48	401–02	10	263, 313–15
12:51-53	129n16	10:14	247
13:1-9	402	10:17-18	193
13:22–17:10	402–04	11:1-44	425–27
16:16	74	12	313–15
17:11–19:27	405–07	12:44-50	315
18:19-24	149	13–16	325–29
19:38	77	13:1	139
19:47	138	13:1-15	17
22:39-53	176–78	14:12	206
22:43-44	177n3	16:13-15	328
22:54-71	178	17	343–44
23:1-25	179	17:19-20	259
23:26-56	179–82	18:1-12	183–84
23:34	177n3	18:3, 12	149
23:42	181n5	18:13-27	184–85
24:1-12	223–25	18:28–19:16a	185–88
24:10	225	19:25-27	128
24:12	225, 244	19:16b-42	188–91
24:24	244	19:37	146
24:13-35	226–31	20:1-9	17
24:33	230	20:1-10	242–45
24:36-53	231–36	20:11-18	246–48
24:37-40	250n12	20:19-23	249–52
24:41-42	232	20:24-29	252–54
		20:29	257
John		21	255–56, 343–44
1:1-18	85, 416–18	21:1-8	256–58
1:8	84	21:9-14	259–60

Christ in the Gospels of the Liturgical Year

21:15-17	314
21:15-19	260–65
21:20-24	265–66

Acts
1–2	71
1:1-12	236–41
1:8	309
1:14	129–30
1:18-19	169
2:14-41	275–77
2:14-36	277–79
2:36-41	279–83
2:42-47	284–89
2:32, 36	104, 118, 145
2:38	234
2:43-47	80
3:1-26	291–93
5:30-31	145
5:31	118
6:1-6	304-07
6:7–7:60	307–09
8:1-40	309–12
8:26-40	311
9:1-30	312–13
9:31-43	313
10:39-40	145
11:3	309
11:19–12:25	320–22
13:1–14:28	322–25
13:33	104
14:8-11	324
14:23	324
14:26-27	325
15:1-29	331–34
15:30-39	334–35
15:40–21:14	335–40
16:9-10	336
16:11-40	336–37
17:1-9	337
19:1-18	338
19:11-17	339

19:21	339
21:15–28:31	341–43
23:6-9	296–97
28:21	342n10
28:25-28	388
28:28	128

Romans
1:3	326
1:3-4	46, 90
4:25	150
5:8	54
10:14-15	19
11:11-12	293

1 Corinthians
7:10-11, 12-14	35, 383
11:23-26	17, 289
11:24	34
12:28	263
15:3-5	235
15:5	231
15:5ff	214, 246
15:50	233

2 Corinthians
| 11:24 | 323 |

Galatians
1	333
1:12, 16	46
2	331–32
2:11ff.	334
2:14	335

1 Thessalonians
| 2:14-15 | 148n2, 187, 293 |

Hebrews
| 5:7-8 | 151, 167 |

Scripture Citations Index

1 Peter			*3 John*	
5:1-4	340		9	263
1 John			*Revelation*	
4:1	263		1:10	253
2:27	263		10:9-10	16

Select Topical Index

anamnēsis, 289
Anawim ("Poor Ones"), 80, 92
Annunciation to Joseph, 59–69
Annunciation to Mary, 86–95
Antiochus Epiphanes, 128, 169
anti-Semitism, 150, 420
apocalyptic, 173
apostellein, 250, 375, 379
Aquiba, Rabbi, 109
Augustine, Saint, 423
Augustus (Caesar), 114–15, 137
   pax Augustae, 115

Babylonian Talmud, 148, 171
   Sanhedrin 4:5, 171; 43a, 148
Balaam, 111
Baldovin, John F., 14
baptism, 280–82
Barnabas, 295
Barrabas, 160n2, 170, 295, 322–23
Beloved Disciple, 185, 188–90, 193,
   243–44, 248, 258, 265–66, 344,
   409–10
ben Kosibah, Simon (Bar Cochbah),
   109
Benedict XVI, 10–11
Benedictus, 77–85, 288
Bonneau, Normand, 13n1
"breaking of the bread," 229–30, 231,
   288–89, 302

Calvin, John, 52
Canticles of Luke, 77–82
Catechism, 14

Christology, 113, 133
   I AM, 184, 193
   Jesus' self-knowledge, 140
   Preexistence, 133, 183
   Son of God, 158, 163, 170, 187, 282
   son of Man, 158–59, 282, 309
Cleopas, 227–28
Constitution on Divine Revelation
   (Dei Verbum), 9, 12–14, 114n3,
   122n2, 150n3
Constitution on Sacred Liturgy,
   13–14
Cornelius, 316–17
Council of Trent, 198n5

David, King, 54–55
diakonein, 305n4, 397
Didache [10:7], 323
Dead Sea Scrolls, 80, 89, 126n13, 229,
   285, 289, 383

Emmanuel, 60, 65–66, 68, 110, 220
Epistle of Barnabas [15:9], 253n18
Essenes, 67, 216
eucharist, 230, 260, 289, 302

formula citations (Matthew), 356n12
"Fulfilled in Your Hearing," 18

Gamaliel, 296–97, 303
Gloria, 118–19
Good Shepherd, 247, 259n8, 263–64,
   343–44
Gospel of Peter, 179, 213, 216

Hellenists, 307–12
Herod (Herodian kings), 179, 303, 320, 322
historical critical method, 9–11
Holy Spirit, 251

Infancy Gospel of Thomas, 132, 135, 136n5, 138n12
"Instruction on the Historical Truth of the Gospels," 8, 30–39, 99–101, 147, 192n1
intercalation, 375
"Interpretation of the Bible in the Church," 11n10, 38
irony, 414–15

James the Greater, 320n8
James the brother of Lord, 303
"the Jews," 187, 216, 420
Joseph of Arimathea, 173, 181, 190–91
Josephus, Flavius, 65, 134–35, 307n6
  Antiquities of the Jews, 2.9.3, 65; 4 [#348], 135
  Life, 2 [#9], 134
Judas, 169–70, 183
Justin Martyr, 13, 207
  1 Apol 67, 13; Apol 1.45, 207

Kiefer, Ralph, 13
koinōnia, 285–88, 302, 305, 318, 320, 329
krisis, 252, 424

Lazarus, 425–27
"lifting up of the son of Man," 151
Luther, Martin, 52

Magnificat, 81, 92–94
maranatha, 288, 357
Marialis Cultus, 95
Mary (model disciple), 120, 129–30

Mary Magdalene, 164, 204, 211, 224–25, 243, 246–48
Messianic Secret, 374
metanoia, 234, 279–80, 292
Midrash, 102
Migdal Eder ("Tower of the Flock), 117–18
Mishnah, 148, 171
Mount of Olives, 166, 235, 240

Nero, 370
Nunc Dimittis, 125–30

Paraclete, 327–29
passion predictions, 151, 155
Passover, 275n1
Paul, conversion, 312–13
Paul VI, 95
peace, 249–50
Pentecost, 275–76
Pharisees, 165, 171, 210, 296–97
Philo, 276
Pilate, 153, 292
Pliny, 92
Pontifical Biblical Commission, 31n2, 36n5, 38
porneia, 35
prayer, 287, 391–92
Protevangelium of James, 62n4
Psalms of Solomon [8:15], 240n34

Quirinius, 114, 123

Redaction criticism, 9–10
Rahner, Karl, 18

Sabbath, 289
Sadducees, 165, 171
Samaria, 310–11
Sanhedrin, 148–49, 157, 159, 168–69, 178, 293–94, 296–97, 341–42
Sermon on the Mount, 352, 356–58

Shemoneh Esreh (Eighteen Benedictions), 79, 187
shepherds, 117
Sibylline Oracles, [III, 316], 128
Simon Peter, 225, 243, 262, 264–66, 321, 344, 418
Stephen, 308–10
Suffering Servant, 158, 159, 228, 373, 398, 414
Sulpicians, 3n1

Teacher of Righteousness, 229
teaching, 290

Thomas the Twin, 252–54, 257
Twelve, the, 305–6, 320–21

universalism, 126

veil of the Temple, 162–63

"The Way," 285n3
Winter, Paul, 148

Yahweh (YHWH), 292

Zwingli, Ulrich, 52–58

Select Topical Index